D0290319

Inquiries into
the Fundamentals
of Aesthetics

The MIT Press
Cambridge, Massachusetts,
and London, England

Inquiries into
the Fundamentals
of Aesthetics

Stefan Morawski

This book was set in Alphatype Futura light,
by University Graphics, Inc.,
printed on Finch Title 93,
and bound in G.S.B. S/535/317
by The Colonial Press, Inc.
in the United States of America.

Library of Congress Cataloging in Publication Data

Morawski, Stefan.
    Inquiries into the fundamentals of aesthetics.

    Includes bibliographical references.
    1. Aesthetics. I. Title.
BH39.M618   111.8'5   74-6123
ISBN 0-262-13096-3

To Lee Baxandall

Contents

Foreword

Before assuming these phenomena are [sun] spots, which would suit us, let us first set about proving that they are not — fried fish. We crawl by inches. What we find today we will wipe from the blackboard tomorrow. And if we find anything which would suit us, that thing we will eye with particular distrust. In fact, we will approach this observing of the sun with the implacable determination to prove that the earth stands still, and only if hopelessly defeated in this pious undertaking can we allow ourselves to wonder if we may not have been right all the time; the earth revolves.

Bertolt Brecht, *Galileo*

This passage from Brecht* is a vigorous expression of the genuinely scientific spirit — especially as it is presented in the work of Karl Popper — and, in fact, of the spirit of inquiry in general. That spirit, I suppose, is never easy to sustain, unless one has the passion of Galileo (or of Brecht's Galileo, who is not the same). In our time, as in his, domestic pressures are powerful, whether in the form of threats or of apparently countervailing obligations, while the modern barriers between nations and regions also make genuine intellectual cooperation difficult on an international scale. The spirit of inquiry is far from dead, however; and, indeed, it seems to me very much alive in the work of Stefan Morawski — one of the

most fertile and probing marxist aestheticians at work today.

It is not my function in contributing this Foreword to offer fuller explanations of Morawski's theses — he is perfectly capable of speaking for himself — or to make objections before the reader has had the opportunity to hear what he has to say. But I welcome the opportunity to express my sense of the general significance of these essays and to offer some comments that I hope will help that significance to become plain.

Philosophers, critics, artists, and others in the United States who are concerned with the arts and who are in one way or another engaged in thinking about the problems of aesthetics have had all too little chance to learn about the work that is being done, and has recently been done, by marxist aestheticians writing in languages unfamiliar to them. A few of the chapters in this volume have previously appeared in English, but the others reveal to us, for the first time, the range of problems that have been the concern of Stefan Morawski, and the zest and erudition with which he has dealt with them.

This volume represents only a part, but a substantial part, of Morawski's work in aesthetics. Though written at different times (during the years 1961–67), its essays form a coherent whole

* I am grateful to Lee Baxandall for calling it to my attention.

because of their pervasive marxist methodology. Moreover, they deal with the most fundamental problems of aesthetics. The first part of the book is concerned with basic axiological categories, the second with the chief aesthetic values (here Morawski omits a detailed study of the value of form, to which he attaches great significance, but which he sets aside for separate discussion because of the complications alluded to in Note 6 to "What is a Work of Art?"), the third with issues concerning the genesis and function of artistic values.

Although it is, in the final analysis, the expression of his own philosophical individuality, Morawski's aesthetic method reflects several converging influences. Not only is he a profound student of marxism, well acquainted with the various strands within that broad movement of ideas, but in his hands marxism is a living system that reaches out to new problems and new solutions. Although he shares the same basic orientation as such other original marxist thinkers as Lukács, Fischer, and Lefebvre, he has carried several lines of philosophic thought a good way beyond them. He is the heir of the strong tradition of Polish analytical philosophy, and has assimilated the important ideas of that seminal phenomenological aesthetician, Roman Ingarden, whose influence has reached far beyond the borders of his native Poland. Morawski has read widely and thoughtfully in the work of Russian, American, British, French, Italian, and German aestheticians, and he has a rich experience of classical and contemporary works of art, most notably painting, literature, and film. It is not surprising, then, that he has a habit of singling out central and fundamental problems to tackle, or that he typically sees them in a broad philosophical and cultural perspective.

The key to Morawski's complex but coherent theory of art is his consistent vigilant historicist orientation. . . . we must constantly direct a selective and value-alert attitude towards the fluctuations in culture which aims to valuate and revaluate the *constant and recurrent* elements of value, without ever assuming that a matter of axiology is settled for all time.

Though he is the first to admit that his historical method is as much a program for future inquiry as a set of verified conclusions, his aim is a vindication of this standpoint, a demonstration that it offers the soundest hope for establishing aesthetics on a solid foundation. This viewpoint necessitates investigation of the genesis of art in human culture, examination of its functions in human life, and discovery of the aspects and elements of art objects which remain constant throughout their long history. The aim is to provide an empirical basis for objectively defensible judgments of works of art, for a pluralistic openness to the values of the arts, including most especially their cognitive values, and for a clearer understanding of the artist's social role which will help make it possible to liberate his creative powers and end his alienation along with that of his society.

One of the most widely debated issues in American and British aesthetics during recent decades has been that concerning the definability of "art," or of "work of art." Morawski's way of tackling this issue is characteristic of his thinking in the range of artistic experience and knowledge that he brings to it, in his determination to take due account of both the internal aspects of the work of art and its social relationships, and in his judicious conclusion: a provisional definition framed so as not to be closed to future artistic developments.

Morawski's aim is to "develop an idea of art which can hold its ground despite the current crisis" of practice and definition in the visual arts, poetry, music, the dance, theater, and film. He is opposed both to traditional attempts to identify a single necessary and sufficient condition of art and to the neo-Wittgensteinian view that the concept of art includes no necessary conditions but is a "family resemblance" concept.

Moreover, he does not concede that the definition need be either arbitrary or relative. Instead — and this may possibly be the most original of his hypotheses — he develops a set of four criteria that together constitute a definiendum for "work of art." His argument for them is historical: they are based on "historically traced invariants" among objects that have been considered, despite all their differences, as works of art. The criteria offered and carefully defended are:

1. being a "structure of qualities" that are either sensuously presented or semantically designated;

2. having a "relative autonomy of structure";

3. being an artifact, at least in a broad sense; and

4. being an "individual expression."

All are present to some degree, Morawski holds, in any object with a claim to consideration as a work of art, but the last two are "weak" conditions, in that they are sometimes present only in a low degree and may be hard to discern. Morawski wants to keep his concept of art open and flexible to accommodate the avant-garde, yet determinate enough to be useful.

One consequence drawn from the definition will perhaps occasion some surprise, because the transition is rather swift. "On the basis of the definition of art proposed here, I think we may justifiably conclude that art provides, as many have assumed, *a special mode of cognition of reality.*" Even if we grant that every work of art is, in some broad sense, an expression of the artist's state of mind, some aestheticians will argue that the link with the "reality" outside that mind may in some works be a tenuous one. Morawski would presumably reply that the artist cannot help but reflect social forces and physical conditions, however indirectly and even distortedly, in his work. Yet here, again, he is anxious to avoid any one-sided and oversimplified view. His concept of art allows for the mediation of truth about reality by the artist's mind; he rejects the too simple concept of mimetic art that he finds in some marxist aestheticians. At the same time, he conceives of the expressive content of art, not as something that can be detached and dealt with by itself, but as tied to form, as living in the form. And it is this that enables him to make out a cogent case for the importance of artistic experimentation and artistic freedom.

Each artist has a way of discovering the world, of giving it proportion, form, and color; he judges, stimulates, and obliges us to think and rethink about certain aspects of things, whether it be by recalling them to us or by making us discover them; he charms us by his language and composition. Therein lies the essence of the moral function of art. This function can only come from crea-

tive freedom. ["The Vicissitudes of Socialist Realism"]

Another feature of Morawski's aesthetic theory that may puzzle American aestheticians is his identification, or collapsing, of the questions "What is art?" and "What is good art?" Many contemporary aestheticians have worked hard to establish and clarify such a distinction, and they would relinquish it reluctantly, if at all. To define "art," Morawski holds, is to propose a theory of "artistic value." Of course, it has often been noted that the word "art" can be used in a laudatory way, as a kind of nonce-normative term, and it has also been argued that many so-called definitions of art are concealed judgments about what is more noteworthy or desirable in works of art. However, Morawski means something more. He wishes to separate two kinds of normative judgment in aesthetics and criticism: what he calls "valuation" and "evaluation." To valuate an object artistically is to report the presence in it of "artistic values," which are those properties that confer upon the object the status of a work of art and at the same time give it worth *as* art. To evaluate, on the other hand, is to grade, in a broad sense; we evaluate X when we say it is a better work of art (or a better painting, say) than Y, or that it ranks among the masterpieces.

This distinction is an interesting one,

and its importance is emphasized by Morawski. Some aestheticians who would agree that every work of art has some degree of artistic worth would nevertheless hold that to say a work of art is a *good* work of art is necessarily to make at least a very broad comparative judgment—it is better than average, or better than most—and, hence, to evaluate it. It is indeed difficult to separate the two procedures. Even in Morawski's system they are conceptually tied, since evaluations are built up by summing valuations (see "The Criteria of Aesthetic Evaluation"), although he holds that there are also further criteria, beyond the presence and intensity of artistic values, that are legitimately taken into account in making an estimate of the comparative value of two works of art. Among these further criteria are novelty and originality, which he designates as "artistic." (His discussion casts much light on these interesting concepts.) Others he designates as "non-artistic," including social and political aspects of the work.

Every genuine work of art has by definition its residual (artistic) values— its constituent properties, expressive qualities, mimetic features. To make this point of view fully understandable and to defend it adequately would, of course, require a general theory of value. Unfortunately, Morawski's theory of value—which he has developed in

other essays, as yet untranslated—is only touched on here. He holds that there are "value facts," distinct from "facts *sensu stricto*"; they are established in "acts of appreciation," in which objective data and subjective elements come together. They are no less empirical than other facts, but they are "more dependent on individual attitudes, on *hic et nunc* cultural contexts." That is why the search for a sound definition of "work of art"—i.e., for a definition that can hold up through the process of artistic change and development—must be based on historical evidence of comparatively permanent types of appreciation.

In "The Criteria of Aesthetic Valuation," Morawski maps the location of his own position for us by presenting a general survey or typology of theories of artistic value. I find myself very much in sympathy with the lines of criticism that he directs against the theories he rejects. I must admit that I don't subscribe to all of his objections, and I would want to raise an occasional question. For example, I don't think that "those who fall back on an analysis of aesthetic experience as the sole basis of artistic value" really undermine their theory by admitting there are objective traits that give rise to aesthetic experience; I think Morawski does not do full justice to the account of value in terms of "potentiality" or "capacity." But I cite these points of disagreement not at all out of disrespect for Morawski's argument but to suggest the kind of continuing dialogue that I, for one, would want to carry on with him—a dialogue that is, in fact, the best tribute that a reader can pay these essays.

The importance of taking an historical perspective towards the problem of defining "artistic value" is a theme that runs through this essay and the equally thoughtful essay "The Objectivity of Aesthetic Judgment." Here he suggests that we must study the genesis of art and its emergence from an entanglement with other cultural concerns into a specialized form of activity with its own distinctive function. We must understand the factors that are at work in its history, both those that affect its development from the outside (such as political and technological forces) and those that are at work internally (such as stylistic imperatives). We must look for the "constants" or "invariants" in the appreciation of art to discover what is central to the artistic enterprise and distinctively valuable in it. Furthermore:

A necessary condition for being able to say anything at all about the objectivity of aesthetic judgments [by which I understand Morawski to mean, to ascribe objectivity to aesthetic judgments] is the existence of certain natural, social, and cultural regularities which combine to fix some biologically and culturally sta-

ble ways of selecting aesthetic objects as peculiarly coherent structures and of producing objects called works of art.

I don't think I agree completely with this last statement, and I believe that many further questions could be raised about the complex logical relationships between historical and sociological study, definition, and valuation. It seems to me clear, however, that Morawski's plea here is a valid one, and that it is properly addressed to contemporary aestheticians. The kind of knowledge he has in mind is certainly connected with the adoption of particular concepts of art and theories of artistic value, and it is a kind of knowledge in which we have been notably lacking.

The problems raised by the activity of defending evaluations involve further distinctions that Morawski discusses in an interesting way—e.g., between novelty and originality, between content criteria and form criteria, and (a distinction he evidently regards as of central importance) between "mimetic" and "realistic," or representational, works of art. Whereas mimetic art reproduces (in a changed form) the external features of things, realistic art captures their "typical moments" or "essential aspects of reality" (see the wide-ranging and deeply thought out essay "Mimesis and Realism"). Morawski is careful to disclaim any commitment to ontological essences — the essential is "historically concrete and variable." Indeed, one of his aims is to work out and defend a very broad concept of realism under which, for example, a short story by Kafka or a motion picture by Fellini can find a place and a high artistic justification. He is rightly skeptical of attempts to get at the cognitive status of literature through the concept of being "true to human nature," because it seems to him a profound historical truth that what is distinctively human is at all times a function of social relationships, which are always in the process of being changed. But that does not prevent certain widely varied literary works from seizing upon and illuminating important features of a particular phase of the historical process, and becoming (as in authentic socialist realism) an "affirmation of a particular reality by means of an attitude critical of everything apathetic and inert in it, everything lagging behind the ideals of that society."

The justification of art for the marxist, as for the Deweyan instrumentalist, must, in the last analysis, lie in its contribution to human welfare. In his essay "Major and Marginal Functions of Art in a Context of Alienation," Morawski makes interesting use of three classical myths to crystallize his view of the principal functions: art as a means by which man is restored to harmony with his environment; art as a means by which moral conscience and the sense of social obligations are quickened in human beings; and art as a means of victory over degrading and destructive forces. This is a very high conception of art; but Morawski gives his thesis weight and content by a most interesting analysis, and telling examples, of the three ways in which art can be false to itself by failing to fulfill these functions. The aesthetic alienation that he describes so convincingly — whether due to art's taking into itself "the mystification and myths it has not engendered," or to its having to waste its substance in resisting these encroachments, or to its being driven into a false aestheticism in which the artist becomes the eternal outsider, who washes his hands of his society — is something that all thoughtful students of the arts are aware of. Morawski's own thinking has confirmed his belief that this alienation can probably be fully and permanently avoided only in the kind of socialist society envisioned by Marx and later marxists. For Morawski, this must be a libertarian socialism; he believes that the arts can only fulfill their functions if they are allowed freedom to develop in accordance with their own natures and the creative insights of artists. To those who desire a nonsocialist society, or a less completely socialist one, or who seek another road to socialism, his argument poses a serious — and very valuable — challenge. After all, one stands little chance of getting at the truth if one cannot, like Brecht's Galileo, accord full weight to all the evidence that can be adduced for those views one is at first most disinclined to accept.

Monroe C. Beardsley
Temple University

Preface

Most of the essays in this volume were written in the period from 1961 to 1967 and have been extensively revised for the present edition. My chief aim during those years was to come to grips with the axiology of aesthetics from the marxist standpoint. At the time, this was a virtually untouched region of inquiry. Only a few authors in this philosophical tradition had tentatively scouted its possibilities, the most ambitious and comprehensive of such endeavors being the late works of Georg Lukács.

Part 1 of this volume turns directly to the problems of marxist axiological-aesthetic foundations. (I should stress that I, along with other similarly minded scholars, work with a particular kind of marxism, and it has become evident that no monopolistic, dogma-oriented interpretation can do justice to the wealth of the marxist heritage.) The next two parts relate intimately to the analysis in the opening part: Part 2 discusses some principal artistic categories with the emphasis provided by the special interests as well as competences of the marxist viewpoint; and Part 3 focuses on the functional aspects of valuation and evaluation.

Although it is not an all-embracing study in the traditional sense of an aesthetic "system," the volume does proceed systematically (in the *historicist* sense) with the material that is taken up. The issues of the genesis, structure, and function of artistic (aesthetic) values, and of the criteria corresponding to their determination, form the framework of my general methodological strategy and guide my procedure in the particular instances.

I have not included here my essay surveying the subject matter and the method of aesthetics, but I do wish to mention briefly its suggested perspective. I there assert my deliberated meta-aesthetic position that aesthetics as a philosophical discipline is primarily concerned with peculiar *valuational qualities;* it is for this reason that I am opposed to any scientifically oriented prescriptions for research (i.e., opposed to the aim or hope of establishing measurable, quantitative aesthetic data). I do not, however, reject the application of empirical methods (biophysiological, psychological, sociological, semiotical, etc.) to inquiry in this field. The crux of the problem concerns how to unite these particular procedures with the general and pervasive philosophical methodology which, whether consciously or perhaps unwittingly, any given investigator-scholar will put into operation. My contention is this: the marxist historicist methodology offers the advantage of these particular procedures while, at the same time, it provides the deepest insights into the dialectical interrelations between the

relatively autonomous aesthetic field
and its sociocultural setting.

A final word needs to be added
about the present situation of art and
aesthetics. I am fully aware that the
traditional categories which I have tried
to use in an up-to-date way are in need
of reconsideration. This is a point I
make several times in the course of
discussing the constituent artistic values
and the chief criteria of evaluation.
What, for instance, is now to be made
of the broad and persevering antiart
movement? I think that what is needed
is a thorough study of the civilizational
tremors of the postindustrial era and a
rethinking (in a marxist perspective, I
would urge) of the interaction of creativity and traditionally defined art
(which may now be an historically receding phenomenon). My current work
is addressed, in part, to this matter.

The present book would not have
appeared without the friendship and
help of Lee Baxandall, who, while giving the proper shape and nuance to the
essays in this version, offered me his
time, energy, and suggestions. M. C.
Beardsley read the whole of the text
and gave his criticisms; for this I am
most obliged, and I shall be pleased if
the book can now stand the test of his
critical mind.

Part I

Basic Axiological Problems

Chapter 1

The Criteria
of Aesthetic Valuation

I must begin with a warning: I can within the space of a single chapter neither explain completely what I mean by "aesthetic value," nor expound satisfactorily the philosophical underpinnings of my views in this area.[1] Rather, the scope of this chapter will be deliberately modest. I shall first define a typology of the various competing axiological standpoints—that is, the value-oriented principles—that have been applied where aesthetic problems have been disputed, showing how these standpoints mutually "criticize" one another. I shall then briefly sketch my own conclusions in this area where marxist research has so far been scarce, arriving at what I hope to show to be some generally sharable principles of aesthetic value.

The Place of Axiology in Aesthetic Theory

The problem I have taken as my starting point, aesthetic value, is not in the least arbitrarily chosen. On the contrary, it has been the chief if not the exclusive attraction for aestheticians since early in this century. I may direct the reader to three widely used anthologies of aesthetic thought published in the United States.[2] Two of them—one edited by Eliseo Vivas and Murray Krieger, and the other by Morris Weitz—start off with a consideration of what is "essential" to art, as art. The third, edited by Melvin Rader, moves to the axiological problem less directly; its opening two sections deal with the creative process and the structure of artistic composition. Nonetheless, implicit in Rader's organizational strategy is the exploration of various efforts *to define art*, and this is confirmed by the opening paragraphs of his Introduction which deal with this topic explicitly. In Europe, Raymond Bayer's important treatise confirms my choice in this matter.[3] Then too, Lalo and Souriau in France, Pareyson and Morpurgo-Tagliabue in Italy, all agree that preliminary to the settling of any other issues, aesthetics must deal with this question of value. Guido Morpurgo-Tagliabue, the author of the sole recent work synthesizing the tendencies in contemporary aesthetics, emphasizes this point: "Through the entire tradition of aesthetic doctrines, the axiological datum is present. Far from being novel, it emerges with the earliest thought on the nature of beauty and art. We need only to separate it from certain encrustations, from the ontological-cosmological attitudes that distort it."[4]

The problem for initial discussion, then, may be phrased thus: What is artistic value? I use the word "artistic" rather than "aesthetic" to emphasize my view that

An early version of this chapter appeared in Polish in *Kultura i Spoleczenstwo*, 1962, no. 4. A revised version appeared in Russian in *Philosophical Studies* (Tartu State University), vol. X (1966). An English version followed in *The Journal of Aesthetic Education*, vol. V, no. 1 (1971).

value composed by artists, artistic value, is the specific type and primary model
for all aesthetic value. In other words, the value treated here is objective-subjective.
"Artistic" refers to the objective, "aesthetic" to the subjective aspect of the same
methodological area. In this view, not only can art draw on and embody nature,
it is in fact the chief model for responsiveness by which on the whole we project
aesthetic evaluations onto nature. We also derive from art the model in light of
which, and given certain contexts, we designate some events or objects in everyday
life as "aesthetic" objects.

Yet some of my readers may still object if we do not start by considering the
facts of either aesthetic creativity or aesthetic reception (experience) as the means
for gaining an orientation to artistic value. Indeed, it is impossible to neglect entirely
the claims that aesthetic experience may make as the yardstick for developing our
axiological criteria, since one of the foremost orientations for establishing aesthetic
value has pegged its very legitimacy to the assertion that the experience of art
provides a mandate as to which objects shall be valued as works of art. (I shall
explore this standpoint in due course.) I must, however, reject the claim that aesthetic creativity sets the standards for basing our axiological criteria. (That creativity
is susceptible to an axiological approach is, of course, not to be disputed, but that
is not the question here.) I will give three reasons for deciding not to base my orientation to aesthetic value on the creative act:

1. The traits of creative activity, when philosophically analyzed, seem uniform,
even where the processes and results of artistic creation are the most diverse. This
conclusion is supported by many studies.[5] Admittedly, some scholars have found
reasons to describe a differentiation in the creative processes of art; Monroe
Beardsley, for example, has boldly and adeptly described a variety of "normal"
patterns of artistic creation.[6] Nonetheless, we are left to ponder why the range
of objectified results of creativity proliferates beyond any "normative" range of
patterns for artistic creativity.

2. The creative act is one of exteriorization, which produces an objectified result;
and while we may grant that the inner experience of the artist will be of crucial
interest to the psychologist, what interests the aesthetic axiologist is the product
of that creative process. (Benedetto Croce's aesthetics has lost much of its interest
for later aestheticians precisely because he placed his whole emphasis on the interior processes.) It might be retorted that if we do exclude the interior aspect of
artistic activity, we shall have no way to discuss the "gestures" whose tradition
goes back to dada and Marcel Duchamp, since the acts of "antiart" relate far more

to psychological attitudes than they do to objectified art objects. Here I disagree. The principal aim of dada is to suffuse ordinary life with art and to imbue ordinary objects with its attractions, rather than allowing our notions of art to be confined to the scarce "works of art" owned by a privileged few. Given this interpretation, John Cage or Marcel Duchamp should not be seen as the creators of new and astonishing para-artistic "gestures" — which, in turn, an art-starved and art-worshipping public may isolate and venerate — but as *provocateurs* whose aim has been to generate a heightened aesthetic alertness among the public and to direct this attitude onto socially perceptible data.

3. If we ask how indeed we are to describe the creative process, we find that generally this task leads us at last to study its exteriorization, that is, the art object itself (this is also true of the process-oriented, one-time events called happenings). Patently, this must be the procedure for objects made long ago and for whose "mysterious" creative process we have no other data but the result itself.

In this respect, the analysis of aesthetic experience has to proceed differently, since the "reception" of an art object consists of innumerable actual experiences of it. The reception has a composite character and an immediacy which can be interrogated as a recurrently present and an integral phenomenon — assuming, of course, a substantial correspondence of the present experience to the inherent qualities of the object evoking it. (It may be added that probing the aesthetic experience should, in fact, yield some evidence concerning the nature of the artist's activity. That is, the ideal recipient of an art object would recapitulate much of the experience of the artist in fashioning the work. A mediocre response to the same object would distort in part the artist's aim and attitude.)

Given these reflections, if they are deemed acceptable by the reader, it will then be necessary to approach the problem of aesthetic axiology in terms of objectified aesthetic value. The problem, "What is artistic value?" may accordingly be reformulated into "What is the work of art?" We shall then face two orders of difficulty, as many specialists remind us. There are, first, terminological difficulties in approaching the art object which is our subject matter, and, second, difficulties that emerge in precisely defining the particular object that occupies our attention (which is also to say that our method of inquiry has to be clarified).

Gunnar Myrdal has stressed in his highly useful study *Value in Social Theory* (1958) that an explicit orientation on the question of value is necessary in scientific work as well as in the humanities; and the experience I and colleagues of long standing have had of the genesis and function of scientific inquiry convinces me of the truth of Myrdal's view. Ernest Nagel has also argued in *The Structure of Science* (1961) that the humanities are in no way exceptional in this respect; that the natural scientists must face up to this same problem, this "logical crux," to use Myrdal's phrase. But Myrdal, while greatly illuminating the axiological character of scientific statements, goes too far; and I must agree with Nagel that if the more extreme versions of these arguments were correct then scientific statements would be meaningless beyond the social contexts of their origin (which of course do have their specific axiological coloration).

However, given these variations among the contexts and the objects with which we must deal in valuations, it is right to speak of "facts in a strict sense" (the data about which we may make statements), and to demarcate from these another category that we may call "value facts" (the data about which we can only offer our judgments). Value facts will always be dependent on the individual's approach and on his temporal and cultural context; his judgments will be derived from objective qualities, but from objective qualities that are always a little equivocal. This is not to suggest that only the long-sanctioned idea of *adequatio rei et intellectus* properly assures the objectivity of one's approach to the external world. On the contrary, it is a mistake to believe that value facts are immune to any means of verification and, accordingly, should be barred from our inquiries. Value facts are more than idiosyncratic and are not merely personal, although their intersubjectivity possesses a character that is different from the truth or the falsity of atomic propositions.

In tracing this demarcation, some authors follow the Anglo-American tradition of Josiah Royce, Charles Stevenson, and Ludwig Wittgenstein and assume a total dichotomy between evaluation and description, with the corollary that art (unlike science) can only provide a sensual-emotional selective approach to the world. Other aestheticians—for example, Beardsley, Rader, or Thomas Munro—would hesitate to divorce value from description; but they provide no clear constructive solution.[7] A demarcation of this approximate kind has to be made, but just how it is to be made is a key problem for methodology. An axiological aesthetics that has not settled this issue is hampered from the start.

Aesthetics must first clarify its approach to aesthetic value as such, and then, subsequently, it can concern itself with the hierarchies among these values and objects. This separation of tasks was well understood by both David Hume and Hippolyte Taine. If the reader can agree to this separation too, then we shall be nearer to resolving whether, in discerning the irreducible characteristics of art (i.e., of artistic value), we at the same time do *describe* art (i.e., make statements about artistic values and not mere sensual-emotional utterances about art). To my mind, we do indeed describe art, notwithstanding that the intent of the description is different from that undertaken in a scientific approach to physical or biological data. In the latter case, certain neutral objects and events are described, while in the former case the data are values, that is, a distinct sort of phenomena that is constituted by our very intervention. In other words, an act of pure cognition does not involve such subjective elements as emotion and will so far as the definition of the character of a given fact is concerned, while every act which we may term "appreciative" does depend on the melding of certain given objective data with precisely this kind of subjective participation for the constitution of the particular value fact. (The importance of the analysis of value facts for philosophy proper will be apparent. As an integral aspect of the history of the species, and of course of humanity's changing cultures, value facts provide a basis for the recurrence of some types of judgments among aestheticians over the course of many centuries. This is to say that the value judgment is both *assertive* and *normative*, and that the axiological norms of aesthetics may thus be founded adequately on a set of qualities that have been accepted repeatedly in various cultural frameworks and in different times.)

This much considered, how shall we proceed to artistic valuation with the aim of achieving an "objective" description of value? We should first be scrupulous about our intentions: we will demarcate facts *sensu stricto* from those value facts which are bound up with our emotions and will. Then, we will take pains to seek verifications of our valuational criteria through placing them in the broadest axiological context. In other words, we seek to achieve *intersubjective* descriptions of the valuational norms. This is a complicated and tricky endeavor, but the "logical crux" is that neither these values nor the criteria of our valuation can be clarified until we have fully understood how we derive the criteria. The norms which justify our choice of value facts must be supported on a foundation which is not totally personal, and which is not absolutely (neutrally) objective, but which is, rather, *sociohistorical.*

Our century has seen the abandonment of the nineteenth century's efforts to describe the fundamental status of art by referring it to physiological (biological) equivalents. We may be sure this is due to the rise of cultural-anthropological understanding. Experiments are carried out today in the name of the old assumption; but their advocates, who are cybernetically oriented, prefer to regard their hypotheses as being of a propaedeutic character. Meanwhile, the specialized sciences carry forward the work of defining artistic values in the ways the species has established them in its cultural development. The gestaltists, for example, are concerned with certain properties that they consider peculiar both to the psychophysiological structure of the species and to the character of the material world. Some of their studies argue persuasively that the human artistic (aesthetic) sense has evolved through a process which embraces an enormous range of internal and external factors that comprise the sociocultural environment wherein *homo faber* has made his way from the beginning.[8]

There are five points with regard to the subject matter and method of aesthetic valuation which I think should be emphasized here:

1. We must take care to separate the task of *defining* artistic value from the task of *scaling* or *grading* the various achievements of artistic value in specific works of art (i.e., judging what makes the superior and inferior work of art). Some aestheticians frame this issue as the distinction between constituent qualities (art's goodness) and the relative heightening of these qualities "as constituted" (i.e., art's greatness). This distinction is advanced by C.I. Lewis, Karl Aschenbrenner, and, especially, Stephen Pepper.[9] I do not accept the whole of their axiological systems, but I agree with these writers on the necessity of disentangling this pair of problems. I believe that, terminologically, this can be done the more easily if we apply the term "valuating" to the problem of artistic values — that is, to the discovery of the common distinguishing traits for a class of objects called works of art. The term "evaluating" should then be restricted to the determination of a scale, rank, or hierarchy for such objects, employing explicit criteria to determine whether work X surpasses work Y. A question arises here which will be properly discussed in the chapter on "The Criteria of Aesthetic Evaluation": When we have valuated, have we not already determined the criteria of evaluation? Moreover, with a finding that artistic value pertains to an object, do we not already claim a *degree* of that value?[10]

2. In common with every other branch of knowledge, the task of aesthetics is descriptive and explanatory. However, the data described and clarified by aesthetics (as an axiological discipline) are object-entrenched valuational qualities and the values pertinent to them. By aesthetic "values" I refer to such artistic categories as (a) form; (b) expression; (c) mimesis; (d) the construction-function-form syndrome in the applied arts, and so on. By "valuational qualities" I refer to (corresponding

to the values named above): (a) balance based on relations of dissonance or consonance; the variation of one theme or many themes of parallel significance; (b) delicacy or crudity; harshness or suavity; (c) illusion or authenticity as the aim in handling the material; novelty or familiarity; broad and deep scope or superficiality; (d) a constructive format and its particular functional dynamism; sleekness or homeliness; ease or discomfort. The valuational qualities, which are concretely manifest, have been analyzed often and in great specificity as providing the basis and the proof of designated value categories; it is thus inappropriate to think of factual description as a mode of knowledge inaccessible to aesthetics. The valuation of art, far from asserting a subjectivist or otherwise arbitrary normativism, is concerned with the terra firma of facts.

3. "Good" and "bad" are terms which may be used by aesthetics to denote the conclusions of valuation—but not in a noncomparative, isolated fashion. The aim of valuation should be to present art's fundamental values as distilled from the broadest range of human experience.

4. In attributing "artistic value" to an object, we make a distinction between works of art and nonart. Assuming that the term "artistically valuable" means that we have found an (aesthetic) "good," we may then use the term "bad" to describe objects whose value as art objects we find questionable due to specific *deficiencies* of their structure. However, it often occurs that such defects are not so glaring as to disqualify such objects as art objects; they are simply "bad" or deficient works of art.[11] I prefer not to use the term "disvalue" to name the negative pole of the axiological spectrum. Why not? Because an "ugly" art object would still be an "artistically valuable" object (not a "disvaluable" one) regardless of our complaints about specific aspects. As for "ugliness," it is a term with a minus attached to it, but it should nonetheless be kept quite separate from the idea of disvalue. In practice, "ugliness" can be used to mean either: (a) the opposite of "beautiful," where "beautiful" is taken to mean not the essential quality of art per se but rather a particular formal ideal (see the discussion on this point in Chapter 2); or (b) the condition of being devoid of value, as in cases where, due to artistic incompetence, the object fails to rouse aesthetic emotions and the anticipated goodness is absent. In the former case, ugliness is achieved with artistic values even if its interest is of a different order than the differing (and taste-ordering) category of "the beautiful"; in the latter case, the essential aesthetic values are lacking (but there's still no question of "disvalue").

5. Anyone asking "What is the work of art?" or, more generally, "What is art?" no matter how circumspectly must eventually face the challenges and rebukes of Ludwig Wittgenstein. In his *Philosophical Investigations* (1930), para. 77, we read: "Anything—and nothing—is right. And this is the position you are in if you look for definitions corresponding to our concepts in esthetics and ethics." Briefly, we can agree that the definition of art must not be artificially, too rigorously, or confiningly imposed. But I shall not wholly abide by Wittgenstein, mainly because the premises of my findings are chiefly historic rather than linguistic; and I shall agree with Melvin Rader that Wittgenstein's watchword "Beware of definition" would be better phrased: "Seek definition, but distrust it."[12]

In the remainder of this chapter, I want to work through a classification of the various theories of artistic value, relying on definitions of art supplied by the authors themselves. (As Stolnitz has said:[13] "Each of the major theories of art . . . told us what to 'look for' in the work of art. Each thereby established criteria for judging art.") I will then use this classification as the basis for my own theoretical construct, on the assumption that a lucid choice of philosophical (or scientific) method is indispensable to value interpretation.

In scrutinizing the chief solutions to the problem of value, the order will be:

1. psychological *subjectivism;*
2. ontological *objectivism;*
3. the *sociological* point of view, with a consideration of its tendencies to both the subjectivist and objectivist poles;
4. a close look at *relationism* that will permit us to work out a constructive position grounded in marxism's historical method.

The classificatory assumptions adopted here are common in present-day scholarship. The novelty will consist in the articulation of some distinctive sociological solutions and in the discovery of some significant shadings of implication in extreme subjectivism (psychologism) and extreme objectivism (ontologism). Similar mappings have been published by Beardsley, Stolnitz, Heyl, and others; but still there are many nuances to my interpretation that I believe might be of interest. Readers who are, however, not interested in the itinerary may find its results, and my own positive proposal, described at the beginning of the section on "The Conceptual Framework of Aesthetic Criteria."

That is the plan, in a nutshell, for the next segment of this chapter. All my descriptions of the axiological positions will stress the *criteria* by which artistic (aesthetic) valuations are made; this is because I have found that, in order to develop a fundamental orientation to the constituent elements of art, it is necessary to marshal and analyze the chief "justifying" (philosophical) "reasons" for one's conclusions.

Subjectivist Criteria

Although still favored by many representatives of the semantic school, the subjectivist point of view has not stood up to the test of critical analysis. Let us consider the arguments presented by psychologists on its behalf, starting with Polish representatives. The extreme version of subjectivism has been argued by J. Segal and W. Witwicki, and a moderate version by Stanislaw Ossowski (before 1934) and Mieczyslaw Wallis.[14] The extreme wing held that aesthetics cannot become a science or even a philosophy, since—in their view—aesthetic values are strictly a matter of individual experience and are impossible to verify. Witwicki speaks of the chance character of art: Each individual develops aesthetic preferences according to the needs of the moment; and the "beauty" of an object depends on whether and how it pleases someone at some moment. We can speak of this as a drastically relativizing psychologism.

By what criteria do its representatives term some experiences "aesthetic" and some objects "works of art"? There is no objective standard—only the capricious and never centered emotion or will is in play. At best, this orientation can be regarded as justification for the platitude de gustibus non disputandum, "there is no accounting for tastes." But since on this interpretation even the "reasoned" taste cannot claim to be more than the private (perhaps mad) idiosyncrasy of an individual, the relativist psychologist must appear ridiculous when he declares for our instruction, having put on his "theoretical" cap, what is possible and permissible in aesthetics.

Suppose he tells us that aesthetic pleasure (putting it more generally, aesthetic satisfaction) is, at least potentially, a generally human attribute. Here he would begin to found a theory for aesthetic experience. Yet he would at the same time be departing from his drastic relativism. He would be introducing a hedonistic conception (still, however, acknowledging the individual differences), or perhaps an emotionalistic conception, or a combination of the two, as a theoretical basis for describing the fundamentals of aesthetic experience.

Hedonism and emotionalism have so often been criticized that I shall not dwell on them, but only recall to the reader that these conceptions seek ultimate justification in some peculiarity of the aesthetic pleasure (or emotion). But merely to assert such peculiarity and stop will not do; something specific needs to be said about its character (to speak of mingling impressions, feelings, and images is not enough to constitute a distinctive character). Certainly, a specific condition evoked in the appreciator seems to be the logical next step in the argumentation.

Here Segal's work is pertinent. In 1908–10, another Polish aesthetician, Michal Sobeski, pressed Segal with the contention that an objective basis for experience may be ascertained from the study of forms. Segal's response was that each art object has its own particular beauty which is confirmed by a given individual in the course of a given experience—and there is no way to verify the accuracy of (provide criteria for) his perception, since the particular beauty is subjective, that is, it is only determinable by perception. Segal adduced two supporting arguments: (1) there can be no "objective" criteria of beauty, since if there were we would be able to locate these necessary and sufficient traits in every object called beautiful; and (2) such necessary and sufficient traits do obtain in aesthetic experience (he had in mind the Kantian theory of contemplation). Segal didn't substantiate this latter argument and it contradicts his notion of a beauty which can be only privately grasped. The former argument is also unsubstantiated, but in its course Segal makes several concessions to the objectivist position. He concedes that, in the act of aesthetic contemplation, certain objects may more nearly correspond to one's mood than do others; and he adds (without acknowledging its implications) that ugliness occurs as an absence of certain technical criteria, compositional elements, and so forth.

This Kantian notion of contemplation to which Segal resorts is a good example of what must happen to one's arguments if one pursues the devious roads with their arbitrary dead ends which branch out from the notion of a generally human aesthetic experience as the value-orienting standpoint. Kant had furnished his position with at least two major conceptions: disinterestedness and semblance (virtuality). He also stated the premise (basic to his orientation) that the human mind is endowed with certain predispositions of attitude that lead to certain kinds of experience. His controlling category was disinterestedness (it would in later aesthetic history be supplanted by the equivalent ideas of detachment and isolation). To this tradition one has to address the question: Detachment (or isolation) from what? The followers of Kant have proposed three possible answers:

1. Disinterestedness with respect to all other life experiences. This answer is highly vulnerable, for we cannot help mingling our immediate apprehensions of an object with the patterns and other memories drawn from our previous contact

with art objects—and with the impressions of our nonart experiences too. The viewer of representational art especially is sure to associate his sensations with a fund of recollections that have their source beyond art. John Dewey and his followers have so thoroughly demolished the idea that art can be detached from our previous experience that I need say no more on the question.

2. Disinterestedness with respect to the past and future. The "immediacy of the moment" is emphasized by this answer; and here the unexamined implications of the whole notion stand out more clearly. We see that, both here and in the preceding answer, the sense of disinterestedness would emerge no less strongly during the intense experience of a highway crash, a thrilling scientific argument, or the act of sex. Evidently, aesthetic contemplation must somehow be distinguished from the other varieties of engrossed detachment. How shall this be done? Must we not relate the characteristics of this aesthetic mood to the characteristics of the kind of object that implicitly invites (evokes) the peculiarities of aesthetic contemplation? Post-Kantians have sometimes sought to combine versions (1) and (2) of disinterestedness; they see the experience of art as "immediacy" combined with a detachment which means not so much nonreferral as apracticality. However, cannot an identical description be given of engrossing religious or philosophical contemplation? We can use the idea of an "apractical attitude" but we must supplement this conception.

3. Disinterestedness with respect to any possible materiality ("realness") and, in consequence, an emphasis on the virtuality (semblance) of the aesthetic object. This third answer is helpful in discussing representational works of art. It is clearly inappropriate, however, with regard to such avant-garde objects as earthworks and happenings, as well as art that is wedded to technology.

Reviewing the Kantian idea of contemplation, we can conclude that it does not satisfactorily come to grips with aesthetic experience. It is in some respects too limited, ignoring aspects that we know to be integral to aesthetic appreciation, and it is in others too loose, applying to nonaesthetic states of mind which should not fit in. One advantage we get from looking into the Kantian theory of contemplation, we may add, is a greater confidence in the likelihood of the aesthetic (artistic) object providing the proper starting point for our analysis of uniquely artistic values.

My reader may now remonstrate with me: "You have made your job of persuasion too easy. The contemplation theory is, after all, not the sole orientation that supports the primacy claims of (a universally valid) aesthetic experience in the defining of aesthetic value. Even though it is true that some do not find the contemplation theory superseded, still you might have taken on a more formidable opponent." Well, I must make this answer: *very many* specialists still have not found the contemplation theory to provide less than they desire by way of an analysis of aesthetic experience. Edward Bullough in his well-known essay revives it in his notion of "psychical distance"; and numerous authors lean implicitly on this orientation. I cannot consider here all of the alternative theories of aesthetic experience, but perhaps some key examples may be cited, drawn from the three anthologies mentioned earlier.

The notions of aesthetic experience cluster into three theoretical categories: empathy, wish fulfillment, and illusionism. Each category suffers, as did contemplation theory, from being at once too limited and too loose. A therapy-oriented *wish fulfillment* theory was presented early in the century by Freud and Jung. However, both declared that this psychic process did not exclusively base itself on aesthetic experiences (although art was considered important to wish fulfillment). Moreover, Freud and Jung pointed to a specific content within artistic objects which, they said, was necessary to actualize the repressed libidinal energy of the person experiencing the art. *Empathy theory* is useful for reminding us of the expressive "tertiary qualities": those qualities that we project into objective data and then read back out of them. But it is enough for us to state this point concerning the theory's degree of relevancy to see how basically the premises of original *Einfühlungstheorie* have been narrowed. (For further discussion see chapter 5, "Expression.") *Illusion theory*, strictly interpreted, relates to the figurines in wax museums and stresses their likeness to the real prototypes. More laxly, the theory speaks to a stylized representationalism. It has the fault that it depends on a single kind of art; and mimesis is ever increasingly under attack as the kind of art that should be centrally considered in the analysis of artistic value. We see then that in each of these alternatives to contemplation theory it is a certain kind of object which proves evocative of a certain category of response or experience; hence, it is impossible to accept claims by these orientations to have superseded contemplation theory or to have obviated the necessity of analyzing the aesthetic object.

I was led into examining the contemplation theory of aesthetic experience with its Post-Kantian improvements and also its competition due to Jakub Segal's reliance on its mode of defending the valuational primacy of the "appreciative" moment. Returning now to Polish subjectivism, we can continue to trace how the claims of the art object's traits have gained a progressive recognition.

When he began his career, Mieczyslaw Wallis adopted an orientation not dissimilar to that of Segal or Witwicki—seeing the aesthetic object as eclipsed by the aesthetic experience, which was purportedly the sole legitimate subject matter for aesthetic valuational analysis. As his investigations matured, though, Wallis was to destroy the basis for his early views. In his essay on "Aesthetic Propositions" (1932), Wallis urged a distinction between personal and impersonal propositions. The latter would be grounded, he thought, on the specifics of perception: these criteria would include an absence of defects in the sensory organs, a strong impressionableness, a definite background, the ability to grasp the artist's intentions, and a normal psychic condition. What Wallis did not elucidate were the circumstances under which an aesthetic background is built up or the capacity to comprehend art is acquired. Wallis gave no fuller definition of the aspects of aesthetic experience. If we note his insistence that the experiencing person must effectively be a perfect observer (responsive to all the demands made by the art object) for the "impersonal propositions of aesthetic experience" to be validated, and also his remark that to account for differences in aesthetic values we must take account of historicocultural changes, then we will be left with the firm conviction that Wallis's contextual psychological orientation is inadequate.

A later Wallis study with a psychological thrust, "Aesthetic Values, Gentle and Harsh" (1949), holds that aesthetic value is built up by experience; but in this discussion it appears that changes of artistic values, and even the fading of whole artistic eras, occur as the result of the coterminous needs of artists and their audiences. This is an added historical-evolutionary thesis, even though it is connected to the thesis arguing for a common psychic structure; for it emerges that Wallis despairs of explaining on strictly psychological grounds how it may happen that "gentle" or harmonious aesthetic values are preferred in one period while in another period "harsh" or disharmonious values are more liked. He notes the effect of describable traits in objects in evoking these disparate values (for example, the small or tiny is called beautiful and the gigantic is called sublime), and also, of course, the effect of formally evocative traits. He also notes the impact on art appreciation of the objective (economic, religious, and national) facts in the evolution of society and culture.

Stanislaw Ossowski, in the first edition of his *Foundations of Aesthetics* (1933), adopted the contemplation theory in its improved "immediacy" version. The next year he started to turn away from this psychological bias; and he carried the investigatory trail much further.[15] From the start he had rather doubted that aesthetic experience could be understood as an isolate, unassociated with other types of experience; thus, a definition which reduced it to a unique mode of perception had to be mistaken. Next, Ossowski doubted that a human subject could discover a necessary and sufficient objective attribute, or set of attributes, and his essay on "Subjectivism in Aesthetics" regarded aesthetic values as both ontologically and epistemologically unverifiable. From here, however, he went on to argue, in the second edition of *The Foundations of Aesthetics*, for an intersubjective verification (founded on the social and historical recurrence of certain values), a view he advanced as early as 1936 in the article "The Sociology of Art," published in the journal *Preglad Socjologiczny*. Ossowski now saw the orientation of Witwicki as "aesthetic nihilism."

A similar curve of retreat from extreme psychologism is evident elsewhere. We can, for instance, see the centrality of a subjectivist interpretation of artistic value in C. J. Ducasse, *Art, The Critics, and You* (1944), or E. Bullough, *Aesthetics* (1957, essays dating from 1907–20). While Ducasse had argued in *The Philosophy of Art* (1929) for a universal principle of "objectified feelings" (i.e., communicative and expressive emotions commensurate with the given object), fifteen years later he had become a psychological relativist. *Art, The Critics, and You* is astonishing in its "dogmatic liberalism"—that is to say, every singular, momentary experience is acknowledged and extended respect as fixing an artistic value, and there is consequently no standard for adequate aesthetic experience. Bullough's "psychic distance" theory is more reasonable, since it advances facts that others may not ignore; we shall have to agree with him that too much distraction by life's concerns (or, on the other hand, an excessive interiorization of the art object) is disturbing to the aesthetic reception. That is, if our personal interests cause the social references of the art object to become the compelling attraction, then a certain necessary "distance" is lost; while if social references wholly elude us, then the "distance" is excessive and an inherent resonance of the work of art is lost. The question I raise with Bullough, however, concerns *which objects* will command our aesthetic attention and generate the requisite distance. He didn't ignore this problem, but he leaned to a moderate subjectivism. He did, however, evince the same hesitation about proposing a subjectivism as we previously found in statements by Wallis and Ossowski, and these reservations help to show why subjectivism is untenable.

I might also mention here the psychologized version of Croce which we find in the writings of R. G. Collingwood. Here Croce's philosophical premises—which see the lyrical intuition couched in an all-pervasive Spirit—are cast out as irrelevant to Collingwood's expressionist idea, which sees aesthetic experience as an intuitive empirical response to a sincere lyricism. Again, though, discussable benchmarks are lacking.

Members of the semantic-linguistic school have disparaged the position of Croce as "essentialist"; curiously, however, their own orientation is inclined towards subjectivism. I do not want to bring up the difficulties with the irreducible semantic-linguistic approach here, but will reserve the inquiry for an occasion when the philosophical foundation can be more fruitfully probed. I can, nonetheless, note some of the developmental positions. An early figure is I. A. Richards, who differentiated emotive from referential language quite sharply, and who discussed poetry as emotive (again, however, with no benchmarks). In the spirit of Richards, the so-called *Wienerkreis*, "Vienna circle," held that value judgments could be neither "true" nor "false," but functioned rather to present a norm persuasively or imperatively and were a kind of metaphysical utterance.

Alfred Ayer leaned towards subjectivism too. Even though he said he couldn't share an axiological position which assumed that value judgment merely "asserts" the presence of a given emotion, this did not keep him from assuming (with the Vienna circle) that value judgment is "nonprepositional" in character. Ayer sought to keep a distinction between the two positions but this proved untenable. Anyway, hadn't Ayer noted that value judgments may function as the empirical statements of individual or collective tastes? Adding (this is crucial) that these tastes are anchored by psychology and sociology, we may conclude that, according to Ayer's position (and Collingwood's too), the status of so-called lyrical/emotional value can be constituted only by referring it to emotional "givens" of the human subjects.

Aesthetics was not much influenced by the early Austrian and British linguistic-semantic philosophers (although I. A. Richards had an effect). The chief impact came after the Second World War when the primary text was Wittgenstein's *Philosophical Investigations*, paragraphs 65 to 77. Wittgenstein proposed the elimination of rigorous definitions in favor of "open" concepts with indefinite borders; these should only be used to indicate, for example, that such-and-such objects at a given moment, and owing to some degree of family resemblance among themselves, can be termed works of art. This family resemblance is not derived from common traits of phenomena but from relationships among phenomena of a given class. Wittgenstein stressed that the outer limits of a class are blurred (*verschwommen*) because these relationships among phenomena are different in each specific case investigated.

Charles L. Stevenson, for instance, following Wittgenstein, holds that a class of poetical works can only be indicated with an ostensive definition (by means of "look and see").[16] This orientation has been used —unjustifiably —to deduce that artistic values are a matter of subjective choice. On this interpretation, to cite a poetical work as a value (that is, as an aesthetic phenomenon) is to propose a personal and quite arbitrary recognition of certain traits of an object as being artistically valuable. The reader may find this leaning of postwar linguistic philosophy best illustrated in the collection of articles entitled *Aesthetics and Language* (Oxford, 1954). Arnold Isenberg and Margaret Macdonald there argue that aesthetic values emerge from the eye of the beholder.[17] There is, they hold, no way to ascertain the objective correctness of an aesthetic judgment; all judgments of this order are only efforts at persuasion, easily refuted. However, American aestheticians of several orientations have vigorously opposed this deduction from linguistic philosophy,[18] and I think it must be clearly said that, taking the evidence as a whole, it is unfair to consider linguistic philosophy a subjectivist orientation to aesthetic axiology. Nor should we neglect Wittgenstein's own warnings against psychologism. We may most plausibly view his proposal that we "look and see" what he describes as "the dawning of an aspect," in terms of an equivocal blending of relationism with sociologism. (I shall come back later to analyzing why I view Wittgenstein's orientation to aesthetic values in this light.)[19]

There is yet another reason why linguistic philosophy should not be thought fundamentally subjectivist: even its followers most prone to give it this reading have been compelled to temper their views (e.g., Morris Weitz). They guard themselves, and we cannot call them outright subjectivists. Nonetheless, Wittgenstein's premise of "open concepts" does encourage some followers in the direction of psychologism, and particularly in matters of aesthetic valuation and evaluation.

Looking over these instances, the subjectivist approach seems innocent of the means to defend itself. Every theory which seeks to derive its axiology from aesthetic experience alone emerges as deficient. Each such orientation is at once too loose and too limited, as already noted. Also, there are many of these theories, and they are mutually incompatible, each ruling out the next one. The empathy school leaves no place for the illusionist approach; illusionists have no use for *Einfühlungstheorie*; both of these approaches cancel out the "pure" contemplation school, and so on.

We may add that, while not doing full justice to the diverse aspects of art experience, these approaches likewise smuggle in this or that concession to objective
properties which give rise to this or that aesthetic attitude. Another example may
well be cited in this context: Aram Torossian's *Guide to Aesthetics* (Palo Alto,
1937), which is in effect a *summa* of twentieth-century subjectivist arguments that
it is experience alone which decides what objects will be considered aesthetic; by
the time Torossian is done, however, it emerges that some patterns possess objectively verifiable expressive qualities which decide artistic value.

I would not want to conclude this section without explicitly stating my high regard for the many ongoing studies of aesthetic experience considered as an integral
component of the creation of aesthetic value. My criticisms are directed only at
the futility of the one-sided orientation which believes in aesthetic experience as
the alpha and omega of the aesthetic realm. To be precise, I cannot share the ultra-
skeptical subjectivism of, say, J. O. Urmson's "What Makes a Situation Aesthetic?"[20] which sees the aesthetic experience as mere hypostasis—to me, more seems
involved than just attention to a certain object in particular circumstances, for there
is evidence, which I find convincing, that so-called aesthetic objects have shared
traits and that the evoked responses are correspondingly similar. I should say here,
in connection with Urmson's interest in attention, that we must not confuse the
aesthetic attitude with aesthetic experience. The problem of *attitude* involves such
concepts as disinterestedness, detachment, distance, and attention—and in aesthetic research the aesthetic attitude is relevant to the experience but is not identical
with it. I shall offer a tentative synthetic analysis of aesthetic attitude and experience before the end of the chapter. Here, it will be sufficient to state that I get more
help from Bullough's idea that some objects generate more aesthetic distance than
do others, than I get from Ducasse or Segal or the empathy school.

Most useful, I discover, is the gestaltist theory of a process of formation of aesthetic patterns, which find their reference in definite psychophysiological dispositions of the human species. Gestaltism seeks to discover the laws which govern
the entire, integral aesthetic transaction (its subjective and objective components);
in approaching this goal, it pushes across the threshold of a strictly psychological
theory. The same can be said, in another manner, of the treatment of aesthetic
experience by Roman Ingarden. His *Studies in Aesthetics* (in Polish; Warsaw, 1957–
58) regard the development and the rhythm of aesthetic experience—its core processual qualities and qualitative patterns *(Gestaltqualitäten)*—as intimately related

to the aesthetic object; Ingarden speaks of experience as constituted in relation to
a primary intentional object (a literary text, a painted surface). Again, aesthetic
experience has its objective, functional value correlative.

Objectivist Criteria

Objectivism, the antipode of subjectivism, may also be called the ontological position. Among its defenders are phenomenologists (including Mikel Dufrenne), so-
called formalists, neoexistentialists (including Louis Lavelle; cf. his *Traité des valeurs*
[Paris, 1951]), and some aestheticians of empirical tendencies (such as Theodore
Greene). In Poland, the chief representatives are Ingarden and Jerzy Galecki. On
what do the objectivists found aesthetic value? The answers are several:

1. on qualities (objects) that are held to pertain to some kind of special reality
whose a priori laws may be discovered through intuition;

2. on certain empirical properties which are not, however, considered subject
to social and historical variation; or

3. on an attitude of *Sollen* ("ought"), which is not based on a justifying ontological statement. (It might be called a "deontological" attitude.) Included here are
George E. Moore's "antinaturalistic fallacy," and Robert Hartman's *The Structure
of Value* (1967), which sees the valuable as emergent from an object that perfectly
fulfills the definition conferred on it. Objectivism has many nuances within these
chief categories; I cannot mention all of them, but we may examine some characteristic tendencies. [21]

Although Ingarden stated that he had not gotten beyond the initial steps of his
theory of value, we find an ambitious argumentation, suggesting why values "are
not relative" but have objective character, in several of his important texts. [22] He
said in 1948: "Values have their existence as particular qualifications of certain
objects which are distinguished by their harmoniousness and excellent structuralization. . . . They are not accessible to everyone but only to persons able to attain
to quite special and rarely met criteria as respects their particular perceptive dispositions." [23] Ingarden went on to cope with specific difficulties, such as the supposedly unambiguous relationships among the aesthetically neutral qualities (e.g.,
the material), the aesthetically significant qualities (e.g., symmetry, elegance, originality), and the criteria of positive or negative value (e.g., beauty or ugliness). His
fundamental position remained unaltered throughout his studies: he argued, on the
one hand, that artistic values (i.e., creative techniques) produce the objective character of the aesthetic values whose polyphonic patterns will determine the proper

response and appreciation, and, on the other hand, that an intuition not given to everyone reveals in the aesthetic object this *Wertqualität* which abides there independently of incidental experience and of the evaluative judgment.[24]

A similarly complex and developed argumentation has been attempted by some formalists (e.g., Clive Bell and Stanislaw Ignacy Witkiewicz). Most formalists, however, have been content with asserting little more than that a truly artistic practice has infallibly aesthetic results — that is, that the creation of formal values is an elemental fact, an indelible and permanent act of communication. Accordingly, a satisfactory personal criterion of artistic values is assumed to emerge as one gains experience in applying the senses and reason; a purely subjective intuition is ruled out since it is assumed that the senses and reason will be educated intersubjectively.

Wilhelm Worringer, in his *Abstraktion und Einfühlung* (1908), assumed an objectivity derived from an innate human drive to create patterns that are geometrical (nonorganic). Others have hesitated to propose such a "genetic" thesis. Instead, they link artistic values to the so-called permanent properties which they either dub "empirically obvious" or interpret as ontologically absolute.

Adherents of the nongenetic, absolutist orientation include Theodore Greene and C. E. M. Joad. Greene believes that the objectivity of aesthetic value corresponds to the experience of the amateur no less than to that of the connoisseur ("empirically obvious"); he goes on to argue that even a partially "subjectivist" solution cannot establish more than the inclinations of *X* or *Y*.[25] Joad provides a more consistent and full version of objectivist theory. In *Matter, Life and Value* (London, 1929), he shows that the subjectivist theory fails due to a faulty theory of cognition; he likewise brings out the circularity of the argument that the art experts are conceded to know artistic values merely because laymen who are playgoers, art buyers, etc., do not have the confidence to assert their conflicting tastes (this assumes that only those who are not experts are expert enough to judge). Joad holds that aesthetic value cannot be an entirely relative matter, even granting that only individuals can find and valuate it — it has independent existence and (here Joad takes a flying leap into the camp of Plato) is ontologically absolute.[26] This, however, leaves us at another arbitrary blank wall with an expert telling us what his thinking has revealed must be behind it, and in this respect Joad's position does resemble that of the phenomenologists who cite an emotional intuition as the source of their certainty that art's value consists of special (objective) qualities that are specifically patterned (this is the view of Max Scheler and Jerzy Gałecki).

In contrast, the deontological view offers a no less arbitrary objectivist orientation; its position likewise depends on the projected attribution of objective value rather than on an analysis of how such value comes to be located in historically situated objects; it is, as Hartman concedes, a modern metaphysical version of objectivism. Let us, then, draw up a balance sheet of the objectivist orientation to aesthetic value, leaving aside the paradoxes of deontologism.

Those who affirm the objectivist axiological solution argue that:

1. Certain objective properties do exist and they provide the sole basis for artistic values.
2. These properties evoke the distinctively aesthetic experience.
3. They alone provide the basis of the aesthetic judgment.

Beyond these common tenets, the objectivists diverge. The most extreme dogmatic position says that the fixed set of objective properties (which for them are generally nonempirical) defy verification, but that contemplation reveals their ontological absoluteness and transcendant constancy. (Here is Plato's notion of a Hyperborean beauty, and Schelling's "absolute beauty" which is revealed when subject and object achieve identity.) Phenomenologists point to a number of aesthetic values and insist that these are given to our encounter by direct experience, which will produce an intuitive recognition; they thus appeal to evidence that is more-than-empirical. The advocates of the nonempirical, absolutist standpoint usually are of monist persuasion, a framework that can be shared, and also readily argued within, by those authors oriented towards empiricism. The empiricists, however, regard aesthetic value as an immutable, sensuous given (or, at least, one graspable by reason), a given pertaining to a specific property or set of properties. If we assume such properties, there can be no problem of the undefinability of value; the mode of being is empirical (examples of definitions that correspond to this position on aesthetic value are the idea of "unity in diversity," or of perfection, as articulated by Leibniz, Wolff, or Baumgarten).[27]

A statement of empirical objectivism that is cleansed of any remnant of an imputed hypostatized ordering principle in the cosmos is George Birkhoff's *Aesthetic Measure* (Cambridge, Mass., 1933), which argues for a constant objective beauty such as corresponds to a mathematical formula of ancient Pythagorean inspiration. Birkhoff's formula is $M = o/c$ (where M is the degree of aesthetic value, o the degree of order, and c the degree of complexity in a given system of properties). The most aesthetically valuable works are those possessing maximum order with minimum complexity (which is not to insist on minimal elements). Birkhoff found the formula no less workable for the lyric aspect of poetry than for polygonal forms, but the limits of the approach are suggested when the author himself sees it as being most rewarding for dealing with metrical or spatial composition (poetry or abstract form). A more recent mathematical formulation of objective empiricism is Gunsenhäuser's principle $M = R/H$ (where R is the subjective redundancy and H the statistical information on Claude E. Shannon's model).[28] A similar scientizing of the idea of "aesthetic measure" through a mathematical presentation can be found in the work of Max Bense.

There are, of course, less dogmatic empirical objectivists who do not think that objective properties are all marshaled in a single, immutable canon of value. They see instead a number of modes of aesthetic measure; they speak of symmetry, proportion, harmony, and other indicia. These varying modes correspond to various aspects of the given relationships of part to part and of the parts to the whole. Invariably, however, the character of the relationships proves integral and objective. This sort of moderate objectivism was stated by Dürer and Diderot, for instance (the latter in "Le Beau" [1751] especially, and also in his later writings). Moderate objectivism is also the term we may use for any notion of form conforming to a permanent, uniform pattern; this would be the case even where a single, rigorous prescription of form (e.g., Hogarth's S-line) is abandoned for multiple patternings of an objective form, and even where the idea of variants on a single, permanent form gives way to a relative latitude of permitted forms, since the latitude always turns out to be restricted in principle. Thus, Edmund Burke defined two distinct categories, the beautiful and the sublime; and when writers of the later eighteenth century ventured to add a third distinct category, the picturesque, the range of form was still not greatly diversified.

This leads us to inquire about the *least* dogmatic objectivists. They are the empiricists who see a variety of differing systems of properties. Their pluralism emerged on behalf of an objectivist orientation only in the twentieth century. Although latitudinarian, these authorities allow that the diversity of systems may overlap in the scope of a single object. Some of these pluralists (Ruby Meager and Helen Knight in England, and Monroe Beardsley in the United States) also take pains to note that art objects never are totally unique; that, while the relationships within art objects are impermanent, the relationships of the parts to the whole may often be repeated and it is on this basis that the aesthetic judgment is gradually shaped.[29] One pluralist who does not make this stipulation is William E. Kennick. He finds the artistic values in every art object to be freshly anchored; those of any given art object are quite distinct from those of any other.[30]

Reviewing the objectivist criteria of aesthetic valuation, we note first that those tendencies that are the least empirical are likewise the least rewarding. Certainly, it is arbitrary and not helpful (unless no other solution is to be found) to claim that objective properties simply exist and that they defy verification. No less arbitrary is the choice to ignore the evidence of contrasting broad styles and epochs in the history of artistic values. The most extreme objectivism may turn its back on specific definition, preferring to regard Beauty as a mystery that surpasseth reasoning and to which none but a select few are prepared to obtain access. We may in turn point out, however, that this dogmatic, metaphysical apriorism, this refusal to define data and approach, brings extreme objectivism very close to extreme subjectivism.

What if the objectivist grounds an absolute principle in empirical forms? Today we look back at Burke or Hogarth as rather quaint aestheticians; the idea of encompassing the facts evident in art objects by means of a single (or two- or three-fold) narrow principle of the aesthetic seems anachronistic. Gustav Fechner gave us another instance of this futility when he worked out an "experimental" aesthetics to "confirm" a postulated principle of ideal harmony in any given system of properties. Such experiments are no more authentically open to the influence of raw data than was the mathematical scheme of Birkhoff. Recently, the experimental curiosity of objectivists has been far more open and cautious. Those I have termed the moderate objectivists now lean towards a multidimensional system of relationships, all having parity for aesthetics. Yet to them we must answer: Since you admit that a *single* canon of aesthetic value may be manifested in *different* systems, is it not logical to forego the presumption of a single canon and to continue with probing the particular systems?

This brings us to those objectivists who carry this suggestion to the particularist zenith of finding no repetitions of values among works of art, and uniqueness in every instance. We cannot deny that the multiplicity of raw data have here been faced up to, but we may well ask whether there are not some recurrences of valuational qualities that have been neglected. The excessively particularizing tendency, as seen in Kennick, seems about to step back across the antipodal threshold to a position scarcely distinguishable from subjectivism; for, if it is true that objective qualities cannot be reduced to a single canon, the next step would seem to be not simply to declare everything in sight a unique value, but instead to study under what circumstances and for whom certain particular qualities become the different constituents of aesthetic value. It is a logical and beckoning matter for inquiry, whose answer will shift us away from objectivism.

Relationist Criteria

We now turn to a preliminary inquiry into relationism as it differs from and criticizes objectivism. Heyl, Beardsley, and Stolnitz have rightly declared that aesthetic value is always value *for someone*.[31] It is, simply put, relational; or, in another terminology, it is instrumental.

So far so good, for the premises of relationism. However, with this orientation also, we cannot countenance the "pure" approach, no matter how clearly it surpasses the subjectivist and the objectivist standpoints. Stolnitz, an aesthetician who is close to relationism himself, brought this out in a critique of C. I. Lewis, the prominent American specialist in aesthetic valuation.[32] Lewis sought to cope with the status of the objectified aesthetic value by using the notion of the "potential" of art objects. In employing this conceptual tool, however, he largely lost sight of the actual values, their circumstances, and those who related to them. The shifting context of art objects and their reception does require an explanation such as pure relationism for the most part overlooks, for an abstract "potential" is not the way to get out of the problem of the here-and-now as it differs from the many, diverse thens-and-theres. In point of fact, Lewis uses an underdeveloped version of relationism that scarcely goes beyond emphasizing the interdependency of object and subject. This bare relationship should lead us to investigate criteria for the conditions within which the instrumentality is aesthetically achieved; that is, to the question: Under what circumstances does a correspondence (i.e., an adequate relation between subject and object) appear?

Up through the eighteenth century, the circumstances which resulted in this correspondence were generally attributed to the dispositions of the deity, an explanation I have elsewhere termed "aesthetic divinism." Yet even then, some interest was paid to the psychophysiological question (by Edmund Burke, for instance). As theoretical hypotheses became increasingly well-founded on the historical human reality and were explored with empirical tests and analyses, however, the metaphysical approach to relationism lost plausibility.

A *sociological* paradigm of relationism emerged in the nineteenth century; it viewed the adequate relation of object and subject as oriented by shared predilections and norms which were, in turn, delimited by space and time. We may note that the instrumentalists agree with this conception. They attempt to solve the question of adequacy, however, without coming down clearly on the side either of sociologism or of relationism. Their premise is that the X (aesthetic object) and Y (aesthetic experience) establish one another. To explain this mechanism of mutual feedback they posit some kind of *faculté maîtresse* (to use Taine's durable phrase). But it is left uncertain whether the aesthetic object functions as the means engendering certain collective psychosocial ends, or the object functions merely instrumentally to arouse these (collectively unanimous) responses. To put it otherwise, instrumentalists wish to stand with the relationist orientation without winnowing carefully the arguments they accept from a pure sociologism. The result is that their instrumentalist position remains highly ambivalent.

If it is true, however, that the dispositions of the deity, and also the delimited sociocultural norms, fail to clarify satisfactorily the problem of the instrumental correspondence of the object to the subject, where else may we turn with our empirical investigation? We are left to investigate the *natural* conditions of human artistic creation and reception. The relationist orientation must look, accordingly, to the competing approaches of psychology within a biophysiological context. This is what Burke naively proposed; today, sophisticated science aims to lend specific data and interpretation to a purely logical relationist notion of the "potential" agreement between what is valuable and the valuing agent.

Gestaltism is, I believe, the empirical approach that best explores the specific basis of relational adequacy. There is by no means a homogeneity within the gestaltist school. Some representatives, such as Ehrenfels and Wertheimer, emphasize the psychophysiological characteristics of the human subject that lead to the perception of phenomena in the form of patterns. Others, and here I mean Köhler, Koffka, and Rudolf Arnheim, who is the leading aesthetician of gestaltism, stress that these pattern-creating propensities of the human subject mesh with some pattern-forming characteristics of the perceived phenomena. Thus, Koffka sees aesthetic value emerging from a dynamic interaction of stimulus and reaction.[33]

What is suggested here is that, beyond the objective existence of color, form, and their combinations, there also exist the "physiognomical properties" of these elements with their patterns—such properties as joy or sadness, for example. These are termed "tertiary qualities" since they are generated by the conjuncture of subjective receptivity and objective data.

Beyond that finding, Arnheim has written in "Gestalt Psychology and Artistic Form" that the principle of pattern (also termed the principle of similarity) is only a corollary to a more general law which holds that phenomena tend to gravitate towards the simplest available coherent patterns.[34] The human organism is connected with the form of the world outside it through isomorphic relationships, and both are controlled by the principle of economy, which states that, in man and the world alike, there is a complex fecundity coupled with a propensity towards preservation, towards pattern, and towards compactness. Arnheim's argument does not halt here; using this framework, he goes on to try to differentiate the characteristics of the strictly artistic patterns. He may speak of the balance and simplicity of the art object; or, drawing on Koffka's concept of the "physiognomy" of an object, he may cite the expressiveness of the various elements of a pattern or of the pattern as a whole. Expression is inherently symbolic, explains Arnheim, since all apprehended patterns must pass through the capabilities of the mental (brain) structure; that is, they must conform to the mode of "visual thinking" by which human perception has to process the outer reality and render its patterns meaningful. By "symbolism," Arnheim thus indicates not only the so-called content of art, but, especially, the structure of art objects as a whole.

We may summarize then: the fundamental gestaltist principle (gravitation to a balance which requires simplicity and economy) seems to have clear application to such phenomena in the nonhuman world as crystals, and in the arts to the rondo (music), the haiku or limerick (poetry), declamatory couplets (the stage), etc. We might logically expect such art objects to be considered the highest forms; yet neither Koffka nor Arnheim wishes to go this far, and they both seek instead for supplementary principles. Thus, gestaltism's aesthetic conception is incomplete at best —and some would consider the basic notion of gestalt too vaguely formulated and the isomorphic hypothesis unsupportable.

There is no doubt that the gestaltist theses require more refinement. But, despite these charges, the orientation as a whole is in no way disproven. As early as 1920, Wolfgang Köhler could compare the principle of structure with the second law of thermodynamics. L. L. Whyte has more recently remarked on the astonishing similarity between physical and biochemical processes and those that transpire within the cortex:[35] in both types of processes a pattern-formation occurs, the chief point of distinction being that the processes within the brain include a conscious selection and synthesis of the most diverse material. According to Whyte, the aesthetic meaningfulness of the cerebral functions is derived from a controlled, formative plasticity, from the structuring of interconnected patterns of volatile elements.

We may or may not accept the hypothesis that innate dispositions towards patterning exist. However, if the correspondence of the objective and subjective aspects of the aesthetic field is to be accepted, we must bear in mind the finding of recent perception theory that an experience of a given object is never merely pristine and entirely imminent. The patterning transaction, that is to say, amounts to more than a passive perception of an object (stimulus) by a mind (response) here and now. Gestaltists do say that the response is active and selective, but they do not effectively acknowledge the influence of our store of past experiences. We do have expectations when faced with contexts of perception similar or dissimilar to those of the past. Gestaltism, stating that we visually categorize the world after having patterned it, neglects this intermingling of cerebral with sensory factors. Indeed, we perceive by a filtering process which largely selects what we know from our past. I do not speak here, of course, of the more nebulous and indeterminate subject matter of perception, but rather of perceived sociocultural patternings.

If this interpretation is tenable, then we should say that human history (the psychosociological context) has some bearing on each perceived pattern. Even the way in which we conduct aesthetic valuation cannot be regarded as an exception; all the more so, if we find a theoretical basis for the patterning of value in the character of human perception (which, of course, relationists do). This is one more reason why the aspect of relationism in the gestaltist conception does not relieve us of the need to face gestaltism's difficulties and pitfalls.

In what way does a specifically aesthetic pattern differ from other kinds of pattern? Does every process of pattern-formation have its aesthetic aspect, or is pattern-formation perhaps centrally aesthetic in character? With regard to the first question, we must decide whether gestaltism's definition of aesthetic pattern depends on its related notion of the "tertiary qualities" (i.e., on a "physiognomic" or "symbolic" expressiveness). Whatever our answer may be, we shall still have to deal with the issues implicit in the second question.

There are other difficulties. Arnheim has largely failed to concern himself with this problem: In what sociohistorical context are the given patterns perceived as aesthetic values, and how is this dimension of pattern-response to be interpreted? For instance, his essay "The Perceptual Analysis of a Symbol of Interaction" (Confinia Psychiatrica, 1960) discusses the ancient Chinese symbols for yin (earth) and yang (heaven) within a framework of Taoist philosophy which, though superbly employed from a psychological standpoint, is yet one-sided since he gives insufficient attention to the cultural context. This is perhaps the greatest difficulty for the gestaltist contribution to relationism. Its exploration of human nature is simply inadequate as the sole frame of reference; relationism must also be concerned with the sociohistorical situation. At times, Arnheim has done so quite impressively. His study of Picasso's *Guernica*[36] is an instance, for here he sees the formative artistic process and the final "fixing" of the expressive-symbolic whole in close connection with "the condition of the world" and the political commitment of the painter. B. C. Heyl has also developed in this direction, although unevenly;[37] his tendency is to instrumentalism and he aims his shafts chiefly at the sociological approach — very intelligently — in the task of disproving the latter's sufficiency when used by itself.

Of the positions examined to this point, the relational standpoint will seem the most solidly justified. Especially is this so if we move, as we now shall, to establish relationism in a thoroughly historicist framework.

To this end, we shall want to proceed now with an eye on the writings of Herbert Read, Maud Bodkin, and Northrop Frye, with special attention given to Walter Abell's *The Collective Dream in Art* (Cambridge, Mass., 1957). I must warn, though, that the "historicism" of these writers is frequently of Jungian inspiration. Consider Read's essay "The Dynamics of Art" (in *Eranos-Jahrbuch*, 1952). In discussing engrams and the gestaltist notion of pattern, Read seeks for a dynamic framework solely in "archetypes" and the functions of myth. The conclusion to be drawn is that those aesthetic patternings and themes which enjoy more than a brief reception are pervasive of all of human culture and all of human history — and that this ubiquity has a primarily psychological explanation. Consider how Read applies this seemingly historical approach. In the name of a "universal human nature," he offers a purely naturalistic interpretation of relationism; in this sense, Read treats the "archetypal myths" that he finds through history as fundamentally empirical and suprahistorical. As a consequence, social history becomes little more than a vast screen onto which are projected the so-called inherent myths of mankind. I must object. This is a pulling inside out of the correct procedure for studying social history. The objective data of history are precisely the fundamental data we should use to develop a relational description of the various myths, archetypes, *topoi*, etc.

Sociological Criteria
In developing a sociological understanding of aesthetic value, we must start by distinguishing between two sociological approaches. One is totally *relativist* and

is tantamount to psychologism; the other is the ally of relationism and furnishes the premise of a truly *historicist* perspective.

Underlying the concept of sociological relativism — instrumentalism, Beardsley calls it, following Dewey — are these notions: that different social groups will decide on aesthetic matters differently, and that, even if a great many agree on certain values, other social groups or strata will surely disagree; that, in different periods, different traits of objects will be deemed aesthetically valuable; and that collective tastes rather than individual tastes are worthy of exploration. In the phrase of Juan Flo: "An aesthetic object is an act of cultural faith."[38]

This position is most precisely articulated by George Boas. In *A Primer for Critics* (1937) and *Wingless Pegasus* (1950), he argues that the emergence, spread, and survival of any given set of values is due to the mystifications of "experts," snobbery, and the inertia of habit. Propaganda and prestige may entrench them; yet aesthetic values are so insubstantial that they may be regarded as merely instrumental, having only limited significance for some persons at some time.[39] Only an unjustifiable "metaphysics" could attach a "terminal" (objective) meaning to aesthetic values. (Boas adduces as evidence the ups and downs of the *Mona Lisa*, *Hamlet*, and Bach's music in aesthetic evaluations through the years.)

We must be grateful to sociological relativism for marshaling the facts of a precipitously variable social reception even in the case of objects now widely admired as the highest art. We must not underestimate this shifting response factor; yet we must also be critical of Boas' account of social reception. After all, not all responses to art objects are of an equally aesthetic character. Often such objects are appreciated or condemned on grounds which are negligent or at times completely omissive of aesthetic qualities. From the sociological standpoint, such responses (which may be moral, political, or religious) have their place. Especially is this so when the social context itself considers political or religious values to outrank other kinds of value. Nonetheless, is anything conclusive said regarding aesthetic valuation when relativism brings up the empirical data to prove that transient or irrelevant responses may affect the approval or disapproval of certain aesthetic objects? Surely not; and if through the signs of fickle regard for an object we are given even mild cause to suspect the presence of aesthetic values, the sociological plea of *de gustibus non disputandum* is overruled in favor of our obligation to search for these values.

If we were not prepared to do this, how would we ever be able to understand the universally accepted distinction between high art and mass-media or "popular" art? It doesn't matter in discussing this distinction whether one despises the very idea of mass media (mistakenly, I will add) and condescends to folk or popular art objects. (Another clear distinction has to be made here: at present the "arts" of the mass media are frequently little more than solidly crafted entertainment, often merely pastimes, while artistic values are integrally present, if perhaps in a second-ary capacity, in most of folk or popular art. The mass media as presently consti-tuted should not be confused with popular art creation.) The point I wish to make is that if the sociological argument is unreservedly pursued we should have to place commercially sponsored entertainment, the so-called folk and popular arts, and the "fine arts" on an equal plane, for all that concerns a sociological standpoint is that there be interest and appreciation.

Yet, perhaps this is not fair. Boas and the other relativists may not want us to take their criteria literally and apply them unstintingly and exclusively. Their aim may be more limited and strategic — it happens often enough — namely, to seize and compel the reader's attention to this or that neglected matter. If this is the case, we should note that the relativists do persuade us that the works of da Vinci or Shakespeare or Bach were long neglected by virtually everyone (just as were their own contributions to aesthetic theory and criticism, we may add), and that, even in a single time and place, different social groupings do often respond in irrecon-cilable ways. Relativism fails, however, to make any larger case. To do so, it must become what we described above as the particularist version of objectivism, ac-cording to which the various and possibly irreconcilable aspects of an art object may each be justified objectively. In moving to this position, however, sociologism is brought quickly to dealing with the issue of why and for whom an object exists as art. (This problem was explained in my concluding remarks on the excessive particularization of objective values: if to declare everything in sight an objective value is to approach subjectivism, then one begins to try to pattern the acts of ap-preciation and their recurrences, and to see what coherences and sociohistorical norms begin to emerge).

Perhaps the more stubborn relativists won't make this step at all; perhaps they will insist that contemporary opinion alone decides what is or is not art. This stand forces us back into the instrumentalist limbo; or it could, if we let it. We need not let it, though, since there are arguments which lift our viewpoint above the in-strumentalist pitfalls. These are some of the matters of evidence which should interest anyone seeking to orient a valuational effort:

1. Why have certain aesthetically valued aspects or properties of objects been similarly valued in quite different circumstances and times?

2. Is it permissible to fragmentize an art object, even atomize it, seeing it as a jumble or grab bag of discrete and often conflicting aesthetic presences which may be valued by anyone differently from anyone else and also differently on various occasions?

To the charge of atomizing the whole of an object, relativism may respond that this is indeed a reasonable position on the way objects are received either by individuals or by groups. In the first case (the summing of individual assertions of values), relativism falls into the trap of subjectivism; in the second case (the response of temporally and spatially confined groups) relativism simply repeats its central, perennially weak thesis. Thus, when an unqualified sociologism is pressed to defend its standpoint, it has to fall back — on particularist objectivism, on psychologism, or on relationism.

Perhaps it will seem unlikely, but Ludwig Wittgenstein appears to stand substantially, if not wholly, within the relativist perimeters as here considered. To some extent I have had to translate or convert Wittgenstein's vocabulary and philosophical premises, so as to make them concordant with my procedures here. However, this is not a step without precedent, for it has already been said among his interpreters that Wittgenstein's late philosophy is anthropocentric. His lectures and conversations on aesthetics of 1938 make evident that his thought had two tendencies:[40] a relationist one, and an instrumentalist (or, more broadly stated, ethnocentric) one. His peculiar kind of relativism is predominant when he is talking of the expressive traits of art, which we have to endeavor to absorb and figure out in the same way we puzzle over a person's facial expression. He declares that the whole of a poem or a painting is taken in through a "looking-at" and that we should persist in the experiencing act to learn what response the art object properly evokes (i.e., Do we respond approvingly or reject it?).

The basis of this directly apprehending response is scarcely describable according to Wittgenstein, and to attempt an account of his suggested approach would lie beyond the scope of this chapter. I might mention that his approach was of a piece with his antiscience campaign, waged starting with the Tractatus. It will suffice also to note that he differentiated the whole-and-immediate apprehension of aesthetic objects from the "pointing-to" employed in the analysis of nonaesthetic phenomena, and he also mentioned the stock of associations which any recipient brings to the act of directly apprehending an art object.

Now to his instrumentalist tendency. Wittgenstein declared against any idea of the beautiful because it would imply a permanent and objective set of criteria of the beautiful. It is true Wittgenstein stopped short of recognizing the (as he termed it) "Aha!" response—a momentary and private satisfaction—as being appropriate to art. He argued that proper (right) aesthetic judgments will offer justifications by pointing to certain reasons, that is, to qualities that exist in the work of art.

But what did he mean when he declared that such reasons were "occasional"? Wittgenstein argued that a primitive tribesman or a visitor from Mars would have other uses for objects than we do; that is, an environment or the total culture of a given period is decisive for our axiological-aesthetic motivations. Other fragmentary thoughts—concerning the rules which prevail for both musical composition and the tailor's trade—also seem to allude to environmental norms. One fragment mentions works of art which, like the Beethoven symphonies or the Gothic cathedrals, transcend the appreciation evoked according to the "rules" of an era and derive their stylistic character instead from the personality of the creator. Here, we may understand great individual style in two senses, either as a value which actually surpasses the paradigms (games) of an epoch, or as a value which, although contained within the contemporary framework, still is personally realized (Wittgenstein can also speak of individual style as representing that of the epoch, and vice versa).

How do Wittgenstein's two tendencies, as documented in the notes of his lectures and conversations, find confirmation elsewhere? Moore's exegesis of Wittgenstein's 1930–33 lectures brings out their relationist character. Wittgenstein held that the beautiful can not be equated with the merely agreeable, nor is it an objective constant. He said that, in order to assess a composition by Brahms for its values, we must first hear it in many performances; then, by comparisons, we can determine the work's properties. If relationism is pervasive in the 1930–33 period, we may guess that it was, in fact, the very groundwork for the ethnocentric, relativist tendency which emerged in his work afterwards, for both lead in the same direction—our concrete situation and the given linguistic practice determine our aesthetic responses or apprehensions on the basis of a holistic, intuitive grasp of the artistic (para-artistic) object.

In his preparations for the *Philosophical Investigations*, contained in the *Blue* and *Brown Books* (1933–35), appeared the motif of the expressiveness of art. Once again, the particularity of the given object is stressed; and the insight one has into it is said to be verifiable by comparison and sampling. In these texts, Wittgenstein makes no mention of the rules, paradigms, and formulas of an era. He does, however, discuss language games and the results they imply for communication (*Brown Book*), with an emphasis on the dependency of language on its cultural setting. It is possible that Moore, in discussing the earlier phase of Wittgenstein's thought, was silent about sociological, ethnocentric matters because his own interest (as was true of J. Casey later) chiefly ran to the question of "motives" versus "causes." Certainly, Wittgenstein was fascinated with this latter question, both in general and as it applied to art. He did say that Freud's causal, depth-psychology approach to dreams, jokes, and anxieties, while it aspired to science, in reality propagated a new myth. This conclusion interests us because Wittgenstein regarded psycho-analysis as he did aesthetics, as a body of knowledge relevant to motivations and reasons (thus justifying our "looking-at" procedures) but in no way touching on "causes." This is such a complex matter that I cannot even briefly get into it here. Yet I shall not refrain from observing that Wittgenstein's position is not as clear-cut as may appear. He insisted on disengaging motives (which we may know) from causes (which we may only conjecture); and although, he said, we do try to understand both, we can justify only the motives, no matter how intently we pursue the causes. We cannot reject his distinction of motives and causes; but then he took the added step of demanding that we drop causal inquiries from our aesthetic research. He made this demand frequently and explicitly — nonetheless, he was brought to concede the possibility of linking the (available) reasons and the causal nexus (in the *Brown Book*, Harper Torchbook edition [New York, 1960], p. 58), particularly if the chain of reasons was pursued backwards tenaciously ad infinitum (*Blue Book*). Wittgenstein held out no hope of his personal success in this quest. Yet in the *Philosophical Investigations* (para. 198) he did, in point of fact, link training and custom with a causal nexus. Thus, it appears — also in regard to his ideas about conforming to rules and accepting the influence of the cultural environment (motives which he traces to training and teaching) — that the aesthetic valuational operation does not exclude causal explanation. However, I cannot systematically pursue this problem here, and must leave Wittgenstein's thought on the matter without a satisfactory resolution.

In sum, Wittgenstein does employ the arguments of relationism (in an obscure version) and of instrumentalism (which his students would refer to as his linguistic

naturalism). Neither tendency will necessarily reach back so as to refer to a conjectured underlying "cause" for aesthetic valuation. The general relationist's logic
is clear: he will describe *objective* qualities as the "reasons" which justify his statement; the cautious instrumentalist, however, will describe only such "motives" as
are *shared* by the social group to which he belongs (he will, nonetheless, usually
go on to cite causes for his sociological preferences and aesthetic norms).

That, briefly, is Wittgenstein's connection with the sociological position on aesthetic value. The orientation of his followers is rather different. A teacher should
not be held responsible for everything done in his name or under the influence of
his ideas, of course. (Anyone who has read *Under the Net* by Iris Murdoch will
see, in the description of the relationship between Hugo, the character standing
for Wittgenstein, and his disciple Jake, a glimpse of the bizarre way in which a
philosopher's legacy can be taken over and altered.) To my mind, it is completely
symptomatic that Wittgenstein's tendency to relationism has been minimized or
overlooked. The relationist tendency is quite unmistakable in the *Philosophical
Investigations* (i.e., the treatment of looking-at an artistic whole; also, the interrelations between similar cases), in *Zettel* (157: the soulful expression of musical
composition); and in the lectures of 1933–35 and 1938. Yet what has been done
by Anglo-American aesthetics with Wittgenstein's legacy? The relationist aspect
has dropped out of sight. What remains is emphasized in one of two ways: as instrumentalism (a valid but overstressed aspect of the legacy); or as subjectivism
(and this, as discussed earlier in the essay, is invalid and interpolated).

The influence exercised by Wittgenstein and particularly by his school is enormous, and I want to take the time to examine this heritage with some care. Followers of Wittgenstein in aesthetics have concentrated their attention on the concept of art. They say that any definition of art which finds necessary and sufficient
criteria of an aesthetic object undoubtedly makes an "essentialist" claim. This
argument has been presented by Paul Ziff in the United States since 1953, the
year of William Elton's edition of *Aesthetics and Language* in England. Morris
Weitz, in a widely studied essay of 1956, "The Role of Theory in Aesthetics," further drained the ambition of philosophers to arrive at a satisfactory definition of
art. More recently, a range of positions has emerged within the Wittgensteinian
sphere of influence; and the concept of aesthetic value has been disputed, for
example, by Maurice Mandelbaum, Erich Kahler, Mary Mothersill, Monroe Beardsley, and George Dickie in the United States, and by Ruby Meager in England.

Let me stay a moment with Weitz. The position of his early essay may be summarized with two complementary propositions: first, instead of speaking of art's common properties, as did traditional aesthetics, we should speak only of "strands of similarities"; and second, the criteria and reasons we cite in determining the properties of art are continuously altering. He concludes that one can only operate with an "open concept" of art. Now, I think I needn't dwell again on the error of thinking "open concepts" are important *only* when discussing aesthetic problems — the working concepts of every science must be modifiable and emendable, and the generalizations must be adjusted in a dynamic context which draws on the entire world of ideas.

Weitz is rather ambiguous in discussing the "strands of similarity" which make up a family of works of art. Writing of Wittgenstein's notion of art as a game, he suggests that art may only be defined arbitrarily and gratuitously in the narrow boundaries of a moment of history, by an operation of "looking-at" and pointing out chosen aspects. This is a psychological relativist position, and Weitz only expands it slightly when he speaks of the collective "looking-at" performed by certain groups, such as the artists and critics who then propound a new "ism." Elsewhere — while discussing the nature of tragedy, and just in passing — Weitz states that the concept of art is based on common properties and that the aesthetic conception of these properties is shared among persons in a cultural milieu. This is a sociological relativist position in the ethnocentric version.

Now, a definition of art could be called (to use Max Black's term) a "reported" definition if we were applying the sociological relativist approach; while from a psychological relativist standpoint the definition would be "programmatic" at best. Weitz commands a cool logic and an intention to resist all intrusions of "essentialist" ungainliness in defending his psychological relativist tendency; but still his position is vulnerable to all the objections to a subjectivist orientation that we have previously noted. The dismissal of any common properties of art objects remains arbitrary; and we are likely to associate Weitz's claims with those of the neopositivists that values are only a projection of emotional states.

I should emphasize again that Wittgenstein is not responsible for such conclusions, although he is often held to be the fount of them. In the *Philosophical Investigations* Wittgenstein modified his own previous rigorism with respect to being and language, laid down in *Tractatus*. Indeed, in the later phase of his philosophy he saw the world as so multitudinous and diverse that language might be suited to it only when flexible and *verschwommen*. Whereas in *Tractatus* he had looked for ontological unconditional necessities on the premise that the limits of the world were to define the limits of language (and vice versa, for the logical discourse sets the boundaries of any significant confirmation or denial), in *Philosophical Investigations* the limits of our language (culture) are seen in any given circumstances to define the limits of the world. No longer is factual discourse opposed by him to strictly logical discourse: philosophy, like art and religion, cannot be more than descriptive; it must abandon the futilities of theorizing.

I leave aside here the picture theory and the account of unsayable things in the parts of *Tractatus* that indubitably point towards Wittgenstein's later solutions. There still remains in *Tractatus* a demarcation between the sayable and the nonsensical for which no appropriate verbal expression can be found. In the *Philosophical Investigations* these difficulties are surmounted. However, the preference for *verschwommen* language is not to be regarded as a tolerance of gratuitous or merely slack definitions. And as I have tried to show, there is not room in Wittgenstein's proposal of "looking-at" patterns of expression (which in his view tend to correspond to everyday human responsiveness) for psychologism. In sum, then, the "family resemblance" notion of Wittgenstein does not support Weitz's axiological subjectivism, but Weitz does correctly find support in Wittgenstein for his instrumentalist tendency.

These same two tendencies of the school of Wittgenstein appear in Paul Ziff's essay "The Task of Defining a Work of Art" (1953) and in Frank Sibley's "Aesthetic Concepts" (1959), both presented in *Philosophical Review*. Ziff was more tentative than Weitz. He still conceded a continuity in the aesthetic tradition, and he simply pointed to the continual shiftings in the idea of art. He stressed, more firmly than Weitz, the "reasonableness" of definitions within their social context. We could agree with Ziff to discard the terms "true" and "false" as applied to definitions of art if we could also reach agreement with him and others that these terms should consequently be permitted only a logical sense, as with reference to "atomic" propositions. This step would, however, leave us with no ready means to cope with the conceded continuity in the idea of art. Because Ziff's position is much more sociologically oriented than that of Weitz, however, we are encouraged by this instrumentalist argument to seek an overview which passes beyond the particular sociocultural setting and to fix some generalized and historically founded affinities of aesthetic value. Ziff's formulations in no way appear to deter us from asserting, for example, that Poussin's *The Rape of the Sabine Women* has evoked an identical or strikingly similar aesthetic response among various social groups in different periods. Can we not reasonably conclude this?

Presumably, we may also stipulate that this response is due not to the painting's genre, nor to the galleries where it has hung, nor to the artist's skill and reputation considered apart from the painting, nor to the subject matter (many properly ignored paintings on this theme exist) — rather, the response is particularly due to a complex formal structure, the merits of which successive generations of viewers from highly diverse backgrounds have perceived as yielding a distinctive value. If this much is so, we have to ask why and how this property of the painting should stand out as the work's *necessary and sufficient condition* as an art object. It is through such self-questionings that instrumentalism is able to move towards application of its competence to generalized and historically founded problems and thus to participation in a more than strictly relativist stand.

Sibley's essay stresses the liabilities of the aesthetic concept which result from its being rule-conditioned and rule-governed; in his opinion, no artistic entity could possess a set of properties which might yield definite and constant criteria of aesthetic value. I will save my full response to this argument until I have proposed valuational criteria. Here I wish only to indicate how Sibley appeals to instrumental arguments: On the one hand, he relates our concepts of art to the dynamic non-aesthetic context of our life habits, changing vocabulary, and the like — inculcated by a "causal" training and teaching, I may note with reference to the earlier discussion of Wittgenstein's notion of "cause" — and, on the other hand, he relates the concept of art to a common human potential (i.e., a natural sensibility), and here again (as in Wittgenstein's lectures) there is an important relationist tendency alongside the instrumentalism.

To conclude with the legacy of Wittgenstein and the sociological orientation, I want to return once again to Weitz, this time to his *Hamlet and the Philosophy of Literary Criticism* (1964). At first we see him making magisterial use of the instrumentalist interpretation of critical history, as he demonstrates how representative critics of Shakespeare in various periods have applied "reasons" for their judgments which were paradigmatic for the periods. Weitz proposes a sharply demarcated phasing of the critical procedures he has acknowledged as feasible: description, explanation, and evaluation. However, he goes further and argues here and there in his second part against Charles Stevenson that a critical interpretation can be explanatory and that an evaluative approach need not provide only imperative, normative utterances. I do not believe that his proposal of a sharp phasing corresponds to the most productive critical practice. Doesn't explanation usually begin to develop in the full tide of description? Aren't evaluations perhaps most solidly established if they organically emerge in the course of the explanatory operation? And don't the three distinguishable operations merge together into a tightknit interpretation?

I cannot here make an appropriate analysis of Weitz's illuminating inquiry into the structure of *Hamlet* and the phases of its critical reception, but I shall state what I learned from following his interpretive studies: I learned—and this departs from Weitz's own deductions—that the valuational "reasons" that critics supply to their readers are most useful and persuasive when the critics have founded their essays on these problematic matters:

1. the historical context of the art object;
2. the multisided and multilayered structural pattern of the art object (i.e., the recognition of a multiplicity of valuational qualities together with their selective apprehension);
3. the historical record of valuational approaches to the work;
4. the aesthetic concepts, understood in their continuity and mutability.

Weitz's interpretive readings of Shakespeare criticism, as I say, contributed to this statement of fundamental critical guideposts, but Weitz does not embrace these conclusions. What are his conclusions? He would agree that some descriptions are supported by the art object and that some are not. He would agree that descriptions are validated to varying degrees by the art object, and that the same holds for the validation of explanations and even of evaluative utterances. Weitz thus feels justified on the basis of the text per se in turning down the interpretations of Knight, Fergusson, and Jones as the least plausible *Hamlet* valuations among those that he considers. The interpretations of different aspects by Bradley, Wilson, Spencer, Stoll, and Campbell are, in the same way, judged to be legitimate. Weitz believes critics must at a minimum test their interpretive "reasons" on: Hamlet's feigned madness (its degree is another issue); Hamlet's passion and melancholy *(taedium vitae)*; Hamlet's intellect (which rather than retreating spurs the hero's actions forward to his own destruction). Additionally, in the Elizabethan context, critics should have no doubts about orienting themselves to the adulterous character of Gertrude and the hypocritical character of Claudius. The inner core of the Hamlet mystery may be highly difficult to describe (let alone explain and satisfactorily evaluate); but we reasonably expect a critic to interpret: the drama's metaphysics (to be or not to be); its aesthetic context of genre expectations (the revenge tragedy); and the historical confrontation that is represented (a truth-seeking individual hemmed in by a conventional world of opportune lies). The descrip-

tions and explanations of the Hamlet-Ophelia and the Claudius-Gertrude relationships may be expected to vary within rather wide and legitimate limits; but precisely
the ambiguity (the *vagueness*) of these structural points makes for a significant
dimension of the play. The interpretive criteria brought to *Hamlet* have been numerous and diverse to be sure (certainly, the work has been denigrated as well as
praised without reserve); but I should say that no critic who pays attention to the
structure of his chosen art object could fail to interpret certain properties as values
positively possessed by *Hamlet*. These would include: its profound truthfulness
to many aspects of living (within the historical moment; also in the sense of striving
towards a universal human ethos); its impressive display of diverse and mercurial
passions; and its arresting imaginative power, in the sense of a richly individual
and yet coherently developed imagery. On a foundation of these properties, one
may evaluate *Hamlet* as obviously a good art object.

Why do I use "goodness" rather than Weitz's "greatness"? At this point we
are still attempting to define the concept of aesthetic valuation, that is, the fundamentals of value in art. Thus a "scaling" term ("greatness") is not appropriate.
One can say only that there is a value, and consequently, since in my estimation
any value fact is positive, there is some goodness realized here. This kind of fundamental, plain, or indisputable value is discerned by explanatory interpretation,
which is, in turn, predicated on a descriptive interpretation with respect to such
data as, for example, what the text says sentence by sentence, and also (and primarily) the structural pattern of the art object in its historical situation. As I have
suggested, even the descriptive phase involves a degree of explanation: the data
must be both discerned and interrelated in their capacity as value facts.

I should again stress here that, in presenting the common traits in the centuries-
long criticism of *Hamlet*, I am using Weitz's analysis but drawing my own theoretical conclusions, which are not his. It may be that his are different because I
am concerned for aspects of the valuational operation which he either does not
find significant or considers misleading. This is to say that there are philosophical
differences between us, and philosophy is the ultimate clarifying or obfuscating
choice. What I find especially remarkable is Weitz's destructive summation of his
own constructive findings. The apparent reason for this is that Weitz seeks to
stress his points of divergence from earlier *Hamlet* scholars rather than his agree-
ments; moreover, he fears entrapment by a "real definition" of the meaningful
structure of this play. He thus postulates an absolute schism between the critic's

evaluative operation and the discovery of values which would obviously claim the recognition of *any* scholar of *Hamlet* at any time and which, accordingly, would remain unaffected by variations in critical norms.

Weitz sees just two options. Either a single and definitive interpretation would have to be enforced on all critics in all eras; or we must concede that no single set of properties can supply the common frame of subject matter for all critics in all eras. Given this choice, naturally Weitz preferred the second course. He was likewise unwilling to admit any latitude of ambiguity to some central properties of *Hamlet*, such as might be considered integral to the "goodness" of this masterpiece. I must say that I find Weitz's skepticism bracing in many respects, but it seems to disable this very competent and precise scholar at the transition point which might take him beyond instrumentalism.

I do not think Weitz has the weight of argument on his side. Instead, I see a preconceived bias against evidence that indicates the existence of recurrent and constant phenomena. His bias is not unlike that which we found in the work of George Boas. Weitz can make impressive use of logic; and he asserts his position only after a sustained confrontation with a classical dramatic touchstone of artistic valuation and with some of the best criticism that the play has inspired. And yet, he and Boas are close on several points. They do not allow fundamental aesthetic valuation to go a step beyond a statement of one's justifying reasons (i.e., beyond pointing to some qualities that have caught one's attention). The valuation operation is held to be legitimate only for the one occasion and in the given circumstances: the temporal scope is limited, and only a delimited social sampling is "reported."

I oppose these terminal restrictions placed on the use of the interpretive findings because in my philosophy the dynamics of the value alterations themselves may be interpreted, and the variables taken into consideration, without resorting to "essentialist" arguments. This is not my diagnosis alone: the reader may think of Pitirim Sorokin's studies in cultural dynamics or of Clyde Kluckhohn's comparative approach to the values within a single society and between various societies, just to mention two examples. Indeed, it seems most logical that the *permanency* of the flux in valuations should become the fundamental orienting subject matter into which *any* axiology might inquire.

Some leading theorists of value dynamics in the United States, such as Melvin Herskovits, are of the opinion that there are, in the last instance, no value invariables. They give as one reason the cultural (environmental) conditioning which extends even to our perceptual faculties. Their opponents use arguments which equally compel our attention. I find myself in agreement, for instance, with Nicholas Rescher's fine chapter on the dynamic changes in value assessment and value scales, where he writes: "Few things are immutable in human affairs, and man's values reflect this (itself abiding) circumstance. But there are, fortunately, at least some fundamental stabilities in the human condition, and it is preeminently these that are reflected in our adaptively well-established value-systems."[41] Rescher has ethical values primarily in mind; but among the kinds of values whose status is less rather than more vulnerable to the revolutionary transformations in social history, the aesthetic values should, I think, be included. Rescher uses a method to study value and locate its stability in the human condition which is not my own. Interesting, however, is the affinity of approach. It is more important that a transition beyond a strict sociologism be achieved than that the theories be identical. Meanwhile, even in its most illuminating version, which is ethnocentrism, the sociological orientation is most fruitfully regarded as a steppingstone to further investigations.

Possibly my reader will disagree, and will not want to "advance" beyond the findings of the ethnocentric interpretation. All I ask is that my own historicist orientation not be condemned in advance, before the reader has had a chance to consider the evidence and arguments. Even if my presentation is judged a failure, the process of inquiry should be illuminating. And even failures are a kind of positive result in the sense that a new, negated hypothesis has been added to one's store of knowledge.

What precisely is to be our subject of inquiry? It is whether aesthetic values may occur which last longer than a single period and are found in several geographical locations. As I hope to make clear, this line of approach is implicit in the Marxian methodology. Nonetheless, marxism was seemingly not so understood by George Plekhanov, the founder of Russian marxism, nor does the evidence suggest that it was so understood by Paul Lafargue or Franz Mehring, prominent, marxist writers on literary and other problems in the period of the Second International who, together with Plekhanov, introduced and propagated the principles of a sociological relativism during the classical period of formation of the marxist interpretation of phenomena. Taking leave of the relativist version of the sociological orientation, then, we can say that it has been advanced by nonmarxists and marxists alike.

Towards an Historicist Orientation

Building then on the ethnocentric-relativist version of the sociological orientation,
I now consider the sociological orientation's second version. Our investigation of
historicist sociologism must be thorough and careful. It will lead us to examine
culture in its process of development, for evidence makes it clear that the process
of development began in late primitive times when aesthetic values developed
an independence from practical and magical relationships. Since that crucial period,
despite the changes in the systems of social organization, the constancy of some
properties of art objects seems to be confirmed.

I realize that this viewpoint as an orientation for valuation is not widespread
in the United States or in Western Europe. Neither is it unknown. Arthur Child, for
instance, has asserted a kind of objectivity of artistic values, and he has justified
this objectivity in terms less of human psychology than of sociohistorical development.[42] He argues that while individuals differ in their interpretations of values
due to social (extra-aesthetic) causes, yet the variations are secondary as compared with the objectivity of the values preserved and confirmed in the history of
culture.

Child does not clearly identify the historically invariant values; he does not
sketch their genesis; and he does not ask why some endure, and how they differ
from those that turn out to be evanescent. Yet his work does distinctly shift the
discussion onto an historical basis; as does that of Giovanni Salinas.[43] Their essays
point the way to the possibility of superseding an exacerbated relativism. To those
authors—Chambers, Boas, Kellett, etc.—who describe only the continually shifting
fashions of art, its "whirligig of taste," the stabilities of history are but a ghostly
background against which "taste" is the manifest proof of the contemporary values
in society and culture. The determination of taste is frequently ascribed to ideological (class) and ultimately to social considerations, with mediations provided by
religion, politics, morality, philosophy, etc. Undeniably, these fluctuations of value
are present and they often may seem the most prominent evidence. Nonetheless,
the strands of continuity within the cultural and historical fabric should not be
denied prior to investigation of their possible occurrence.

How should such an investigation be organized? I should first remark that it
will be concerned not only with the evidence of continuity in history but also with
the basis for values in nature (i.e., the predispositions founded on human biology).
One other preliminary remark seems called for: When I speak of the continuity,
recurrence, or permanence of artistic properties, I refer to those relatively objective

traits that have been valued more or less from the time of their creation as aesthetic values. This is *not* tantamount to "the test of time" concept put forward by some relativists who feel that the judgment of today's generation may be regarded as ultimate. André Malraux implies such an "acquisitions standard" for *le musée imaginaire;* but to let today's opinion prevail in every case against all the past evidence is to allow subjectivism to enter through the back door of the museum, thrusting a sociological credential into its hands. Emil Utitz has already confronted this partial idea of enduring values and proved that the claim *non omnis moriar* has to be confirmed with persuasive evidence of an excellence of formal structure, which he termed the *Gestaltungsweise.*[44]

There are a number of pitfalls awaiting the search for recurrent values of art in history. These can, however, be made explicit and anticipated. We should, for example, guard against presuming that once an aesthetic value has been created, it will remain in effect through all history and everywhere. An objectivist *and* sociological standpoint, such as historicism builds on, could not make that assumption; we must remain skeptical of the absolute permanence of any value. Another possible and related misunderstanding is the assumption that the coherent body of artistic values must include all of the heterogeneous, multitudinous, and loosely itemized attractions of art that the relativists bring up. This is only to point out that the objectivist *and* sociological orientation can easily slip into its negation: either an antirelationist dogmatism or a "panaestheticism" which undermines aesthetics when it ignores the distinctions between aesthetic phenomena and other cultural phenomena that are properly termed political, moral, religious, utilitarian, etc.

How are we to avoid these pitfalls? There is but one way, which is to maintain a vigilant historicist orientation. In other words, we must constantly direct a selective and value-alert attitude towards the fluctuations in culture which aims to valuate and revaluate the *constant and recurrent* elements of value, without ever assuming that a matter of axiology is settled for all time.

Given this general orientation, a suitable organizing principle of procedure is presented by the Marxian methodology in its attempts to pursue a consistent historicism (of course, not all the history-oriented relationists are marxists). This procedural approach emphasizes the problem of genesis. I have not mentioned "genesis" as a focus of methodology before, but it necessarily must occupy a key position in the philosophical framework proposed here. Why? My hope is to explain why and how some aesthetic values enjoy survival despite the continuous changes in social conditions and individual preferences. If I am to do this, I must try to reconstruct the process by which these values come into being, and I should interpret their most remote history against a setting of the fluctuations in culture. The marxist conception offers a solution to the task. Marx stated the premise thus: "The *senses* of the social man are *other* senses than those of the nonsocial man. Only through the objectively unfolded richness of man's essential being is the richness of subjective *human* sensibility (a musical ear, an eye for beauty of form — in short, *senses* capable of human gratifications, senses confirming themselves as essential powers of *man*) either cultivated or brought into being."[45] This premise — a preliminary to Marx's later investigations, and presented in his *German Ideology* as well as the *1844 Manuscripts* — holds that the genus *homo sapiens* had predispositions to aesthetic perception, but that these were formed only in a humanizing (i.e., social) context.

If this is so, how precisely do the biological predisposition and the social human environment interconnect? Plekhanov in his *Letters Without Address* (1900) speculates about those animal and primitive human "drives" that condition the human creative activity and perception that eventually comes to be called aesthetic. Among such "drives" or "instincts" Plekhanov mentions: sexual attraction, an imitative impulse, and a responsiveness to antithesis, to symmetry, to rhythm, and to animistic phenomena. Another marxist work which, under the influence of Darwin, goes further in deriving the human sense of beauty from documented animal behavior is Karl Kautsky's *Materialist Conception of History* (1927, the summary of his life's work). Christopher Caudwell, a later marxist, argues in his essay on "Beauty" (1938) that the artistic process emerges from instinct and is molded by the process of labor in a social environment.[46] In *The Necessity of Art* (1957), Ernst Fischer presents a not dissimilar theory: there are, he says, preaesthetic elements in nature (among his examples are the structures of crystals and of living organisms). Meanwhile, the aestheticians in the Soviet Union have debated a natural as opposed to a social emergence of aesthetic value for many years.[47] In view of these marxists' arguments on behalf of a presocial, naturalistic explanation for the genesis of aesthetic behavior, how can anyone agree with the critics of marxism who say that the marxist interpretation is strictly oriented to sociological relativism?

To come to grips properly with the problem of the genesis of aesthetic values, I want to give full consideration to Marx's orientation. This will be best achieved if, instead of restricting myself to his explicitly artistic and aesthetic texts, I turn to his writings which approach the basic historical problems so as to suggest methodological solutions. The aim, again, is to reconstruct the origin of what I have termed aesthetic value.

The historical and logical procedures of inquiry used by Marx in *Capital* supply a useful model for the present investigations. Here, Marx applies a scrupulous method which, while ranging from the primitive elements of barter to the complex formations of finance capital, nonetheless traces minute transformations. Marx uses a logic that is, according to Engels, at bottom "no other than that selfsame historical method, only freed from historical form and from hindering accidents."[48] This logical method yields a precise presentation of the historical processes, as well as their artifacts, because Marx first seeks to define the newly emergent structure, so as to illuminate the "essential" elements and relationships that in later historical development will be elaborated and crystallized.

According to Marx's model of historical genesis, the initial elements of a structure are certain to be modified; many adjunct and supplementary traits will be taken on; in some cases the initial elements may be submerged from view. Conversely, even if the process of transformation is untidy, yet it occurs without unaccountable ruptures; the changes in the once emergent elements are explicable, and are due to their increasing influence, to the feedback-response to this developing role, and to the overall maturation of the phenomenon and its context. The Marxian notion of the *peculiarity* (the specific status) of the object of inquiry considered at any given moment is predicated on this conception of the genesis of particular structures.[49]

There have been many reservations expressed towards this historicist methodology. At least since Dilthey, readers have been asked to reject the genetic "determinist" analysis (concerned with strictly extra-aesthetic phenomena) in favor of an "intrinsic" structural analysis (concerned strictly with the character of the object). Who has made this demand? Among others, there are the followers of the *Lebensphilosophie*, the phenomenologists and the existentialists whom they influenced, the structural linguists (Ferdinand de Saussure through the Prague circle to Roman Jakobson), and the anthropological structuralists (Claude Lévi-Strauss and his school).

Without question, the general method of the several structuralist lines of descent differs from that of Marx; not only in that they have another understanding of the idea of a structure, but also and primarily in that Marx didn't conceive of the problem of genetic analysis or of structural analysis in terms of an either-or exclusivity. Rather, he experienced the need of *both* approaches and he interrelated them intricately; he believed he could not expect to interpret the basic traits of phenomena accurately apart from understanding their process of emergence.

Marx considered that no structure appears with complete fortuity. It arises as a component of some process; and we can assume that the defining traits of the phenomenon were formed in the context of the many other phenomena with which it was integrated and which helped to shape it. For example, the modern human species is more fully understood because the genealogy and characteristics of the ancestors of humankind have been researched, back as far as (it now seems) the dryopithecine ape.

We know how wildly philosophers could miss the mark of anthropological knowledge when they merely conjectured about the essential traits of "man," his "humors," god-given qualities, etc. The last two centuries have provided a much more complicated and more accurate picture of human genesis. One of the more fascinating aspects of genetic interpretation is the opportunity that it gives to observe the interplay of natural and cultural forces, and a good example of this is the animal and civilizational components of the emergence of aesthetic value.

We should correctly expect easier going when the object of inquiry is this more specific problem of aesthetic value. What we need to learn is how and to what extent the traits of the "aesthetic object" and the "aesthetic experience" can be clarified by discerning these phenomena historically and, above all, as newly emergent phenomena still closely integrated with other heterogeneous phenomena. An example of a subject for inquiry is the emergence of the relative autonomy of aesthetic objects (more on this later) in the era when the autonomous trait was still scarcely to be perceived and was perhaps even resisted as unwelcome for some purposes. Some of my readers may object that an intentional project of this sort — to seek the first beginnings of roughly known if not conjectured characteristics — is certain to find just what it hopes to find; moreover, the objective and historical method is time-consuming, uncertain, and demanding of immense knowledge, compared, for example, with the phenomenological intuitive grasping of an object's essence with no preconceptions. To this I shall answer: To fail to see an object in its context and its process of development, where its components may become functionally known, is a sure way to obtain arbitrary apprehension and understanding of the object.

Admittedly, we will not get far in using the genetic approach and the objective orientation to historicist contexts if we seek fixed, forever-settled determinants, which are the mandate for dogmatic interpretation of present-day structures. Instead we must have an eye for the continuous give-and-take between structures and their contexts. An ahistorical determinism has nothing in common with the method of Marx. In brief: (1) Any given *structure* should be examined for its genetic process of formation so as to illuminate its character and function. (2) The *historical process* should be examined as it impinges on the object of special inquiry. In their further development, the internal and the external fields cooperate, and their interaction provides the fundamental qualities of the *X* to be studied.

The Conceptual Framework of Aesthetic Criteria
I have sketched a typology of the various principal solutions to the problem of artistic value. It will help if we draw a balance sheet of what we have ascertained to this point.

1. This is not the first such typology, whether formulated or implied. However, none of those I am familiar with have attempted to distinguish among the variants within the major types of value criteria. In contrast, what have we determined?

a. Subjectivism has at least these variants: extreme or "nihilistic" subjectivism; a moderate version; and a subjectivism which inclines to acknowledge a universal foundation for the aesthetic experience and thus borders on a psychologically oriented relationism.

b. Ontological objectivism has at least three variants: a metaphysical version, postulating a special or privileged order of existence for aesthetic value, the properties of which may or may not be definable; a deontological objectivism, which holds that values are attributed by persons to the traits of objects which in some way coincide with personal, metaphysical claims upon such objects (the *Sollen* — "ought to be so" — syndrome); and an empirical objectivism, which recognizes one single permanent quality of beauty or (in the pluralist case) a variety of such permanent qualities.

c. Relationism has two principal versions: logical, schematic relationism, which builds on the abstract idea of "potentiality"; and empirical relationism (e.g., gestaltism).

d. Sociological relativism has two principal variants: the extreme particularist version, which recognizes only different, circumstantial collective tastes or predilections, which occur here and there in given historical contexts; and an instrumentalist tendency of sociological relativism, descriptive of more permanent properties which are termed beautiful in a given short-term tradition and social grouping. (This last tendency lends assistance to relationist analysis.)

e. Sociological objectivism likewise has two possible versions: panaesthetic sociological objectivism; and a sociohistorical objectivism.

The reader may wonder why I take the trouble to discriminate within the major axiological categories. I do this, not to be pedantic, but to find why it is that unreconciled differences should remain where, for all intents and purposes, two scholars appear ready to agree on common fundamentals of axiology. There is also another reason. We can glimpse with some certainty now that there is a perpetual equivocation within every one of the axiological orientations: between the Scylla of subjectivism and the Charybdis of ontological objectivism.

2. We further notice from studying the typology that just a single one of the five major axiological categories is devoid of the least smidgeon of verification from everyday experience. This is the ontological (and the "deontological") end of the objectivist spectrum, which holds that aesthetic value is a priori an absolute property. A "nub of rationality" can be conceded even to this speculative orientation; and it is retrieved from metaphysics by the ethnocentric and relationist approaches.

3. Experience with its empirical access to data would seem to lend greatest credence to two orientations in the typology: psychologism and sociological relativism. The "nub of rationality" in psychologism is that values always are given to the individual; yet, to make this empirical truth the alpha and omega of one's axiology is to be sure to arrive at a dead end. Of sociological relativism much the same can be said, but on a broader basis; by drawing on empirical data, the historical mutability of values is shown; when this use of data is also applied to the problems of aesthetic objects, instrumentalism emerges, and the possibility of relationism appears on the horizon.

4. Of the axiological paradigms I have identified, that which offers the greatest scope for the substantial analysis of aesthetic value (succumbing to neither Scylla nor Charybdis) is relationism; but relationism still awaits the fullest available development of its empirical foundations. It, too, must have its "nub of rationality" supplemented — here, by the analysis of historical considerations which affect the relationship between subject and object.

5. The typology counsels us, on balance, to orient our further inquiry both objectively and historically (relying on the relationist paradigm, as I have noted). In other

words, this should be our deduction when we observe how the alternative major conceptions of value—psychologism, absolute objectivism, sociologism—all choose silence after having stated very elementary facts. What I propose must, in contrast, serve to deepen the analysis of valuation and evaluation. A relationism which looks to objectivity and historicism can encompass and elucidate value both as it mutates and as its traits recur in widely different times and places.

6. Where did this typology come from? Two of its major orientations (indeed its "cornerstones") go back to the start of aesthetic thought, for objectivism was the outlook of the Pythagoreans and subjectivism was the profession of the Sophists. Relationism emerged with Basil the Great and the scholastics and formed a bridge to the work of Thomas Aquinas. A universalist approach to aesthetic experience was apparent in Philodemos, long before Hume and Kant. Psychological relativism is stated by the thirteenth-century Polish philosopher Vitelius, but it can also be attributed to the remarks of Socrates on functional value. Sociological relativism can be located in the ideas of Giordano Bruno and, especially, the architectural thinker Claude Perrault. Historicism was, ironically if you will, the last of these orientations to emerge historically. Its founders were Vico and Herder.[50]

7. It might help to elucidate the typology if I demonstrate how its major conceptions interrelate in terms of the dynamics and contradictions of the valuational activity—in particular from the standpoint of the object of analysis (see figure 1). My own choice of valuational field is, of course, historicist relationism—and perhaps figure 2 will clarify its approach to the object of valuation.

Now, all these major conceptions make the claim that they should be accepted as the foundation for valuating art. Each wishes to provide our criteria, but they are not all equally concerned to provide justifications to sway our judgment and clinch their claim. How is orientation X or Y to justify its criteria for calling a given object artistically valuable? Let me take the case of subjectivism, which, especially in its extreme version, disdains to provide self-justifications. Even if it does explain—aesthetic value is "a liking which lasts for the given moment" might be the words—still, no appeal to objective verification is made; we are simply presented with a claim.

It may seem odd, but the objectivist axiology in its metaphysical (ontological) version similarly omits to refer to anything objective which can be tested. Metaphysical objectivism relies on intuition as its proof: the sole reason advanced is the state-

ment by the valuator that he has privileged or divine access to the faculty of perceiving the aesthetic values in their metacontext. The extreme objectivists are willing to divide the audience of art into the blind and those blessed with vision; rather
like the idea of *civitas diaboli* and *civitas Dei* in Augustine.

No matter that the request for reasons is turned aside by the extreme positions of
both subjectivism and objectivism. No matter that we cannot "refute" the meta-
statements offered. There are still *criteria implied* by these positions with which we
may argue. What do we mean by criteria? How do we know which criteria are
adequate? Usually we indicate standards, that is, some sort of justification with

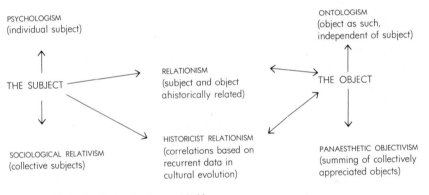

Figure 1.   The Major Modes of Valuational Fields.

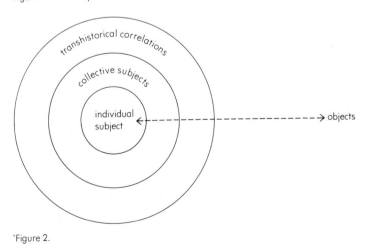

'Figure 2.

which we hope to make our statements appear plausible rather than merely sound unanswerable. If we are asked for our criteria, and we have these standards, we should then be able (optimally) to point to properties or traits (i.e., characteristics) of an object that will yield persuasive evidence in support of our statement or judgment. Whether this evidence should be considered as constant, or as contextual (or even circumstantial)—this is precisely the moot question. The etymology of the word "criteria" counsels us to seek to distinguish truth from untruth, value from unvalue.

In this quest for certainty, our justifications will primarily be centered on empirical standards or indices as the means to win arguments. At least, this strategy has worked rather well for the proof or disproof of cognitive statements; but will it aid us to verify the problems of value? I think the appeal to empirical evidence is less efficacious in valuational problems, but then it is not as conclusive with respect to epistemology in general as is often thought. The reader may know Désiré Mercier's older but often cited *Critériologie générale ou la théorie générale de la certitude*, which demonstrates the plethora of disparate epistemological criteria on which philosophers rely. There is not to this day final and conclusive agreement on the rules of certainty with regard to evidence or even on the means for distinguishing an "adequate" knowledge from rank error. What do the philosophical dictionaries advise? That a criterion involves — truth-value. Well and good. Yet just here is where the problems explode into philosophy and the different orientations cease to be able to persuade one another.

Wittgenstein, famed as the epistemological paladin of recent philosophy, fought against error and inexactitude on the field of criteria. What was his view of the difficulties? First, that while we must seek the "best possible" evidence, we must be prepared to make do with other grades. However, merely suggestive or symptomatic data cannot provide evidence, since no trustworthy basis exists for inferring from such phenomena of experience a statement or judgment about them. Second and worse, the problem seemed to Wittgenstein to lie not so much in the selection of evidence which can be verified as in the question of whether criteria can be framed as definitions or whether the training (practice) which prepares a person to apprehend (accede to) the criteria must be emphasized. There were many varieties of usage of criteria which disturbed Wittgenstein. The notion, for example, that a sensuously given sign finds its criterion when it is correlated to the thing signified, seemed to him a quite vacuous idea of criterion.

Another token of the prevailing distress is *Meaning and Knowledge: Systematic*

Readings in Epistemology, a popular textbook edited by Ernest Nagel and R. B. Brandt (New York, 1965). The authors included in this anthology are able to agree on one issue only: the purely formal stipulation that a distinction must be maintained between the criterion and the defining operation. This failure to achieve a common ground on any step but the most elementary is common in epistemology. The criteria invoked to separate truth from error are almost ludicrously numerous and disparate. The more serious and pressing, then, is our need resolutely to solve this problem of criteria for our present inquiry.

These are, then, some prominent appeals to reasons; valuational criteria might be claimed to correspond to: a privileged special universe of data not accessible to all; everyone's total experience; the logical rigor of the argument; the pragmatic results it can produce; intuition, possibly mystical; the guidelines imparted by some authority who (or which) is acknowledged; what we consider and proclaim to be, quite simply, self-evident.

In our effort to compare and select among the criteria lucidly, a proposal by C. G. Hempel seems to me apt.[51] He says that criteria are truly useful — in other words, clarifying and explanatory — when they afford a general conceptual framework within which we may restate a particular *explicandum* and proceed to systematize its substance theoretically. If we can agree to this, as I do, then we must declare that the so-called traits of evidence — or as others call them, the justifying characteristics — do not self-evidently establish the status of what we believe we know. Once this assumption is made, however, it may cast us adrift in the ocean of evidence which now is considered semiopaque, and there may seem no saving raft of conceptual structure which can be more than a deceptive and humiliating mirage.

In other words, we all want an unassailable rocklike foundation for our statements about evidence. Where shall we find it, and how shall we find it? Aren't we caught in a vicious circle where we justify all of our observational statements with an appeal to data evidence, and try to validate our selections among sense impressions, perceptions, and so on, with an appeal to the very criteria which, in turn, require some unassailable reasons in evidence before we are able to rely on them? Let us assume that we seriously do want solid knowledge and not mere protocol statements. Our epistemic procedure must then have cognitive premises which are of a broader than epistemological reach and character. What can comprise such premises? They will be determined by a philosophical conception of *homo sapiens,* history, and nature.

In indicating the necessity of a conceptual foundation, I have had to be almost impossibly brief; but, as I said at the outset of the chapter, it is also almost impossible to delineate the fundamentals of my philosophy in a book deeply involved with aesthetic questions. To serve up my philosophical *carte du jour* in a slapdash short-order fashion would do violence to both it and the alimentation of my reader. Still, I do hope to have indicated the uncertainty about the certainty principle which is the lot of general criteriology today. The situation in my specific field, aesthetics, is even less resolved. Here too, a choice of epistemological criteria will at last induce the valuator to make axiological (philosophical) assumptions. The reader may shake his head and wonder how, if epistemology itself is so fraught with criteriological issues, it will be possible to come to grips with the ultimate criteria of aesthetic value. One solution might be to clarify the typology of the major solutions to aesthetic valuation, as I have done, and then let the problems drop without attempting to determine the bedrock axiological criteria through a debate which might possibly prove futile. However, this obstacle of sorting through the conflicting and complementary criteria of the typology does not seem to be one that can or will long stand.

This difficulty is not exceptional in its stubbornness; indeed, everywhere, facts and values appear to be in a mutual and dependent tension. The intersubjectivity of valuational criteria must thus be understood in light of the intersubjectivity of scientific investigations, and the families of values and their possible hierarchies must be considered. On every hand the axiological quandary just cannot be escaped; and it often is the "missing link" in an otherwise interesting argument. For example, in Peter Caws's *Science and the Theory of Value* (1967), the author observes the problem of facts that do not dovetail with values, and of values that go beyond any set of facts; but he does not resolve the question. Or consider Risieri Frondizi's *What Is Value?* (1971): the author expostulates on the various distances at which values may stand from the "terra firma" of facts; he sees a range going from subject-dependent, socially variable values, which are the sort he ascribes to gastronomical, political, and legal phenomena, all the way over to an objectively given, universally human version of morality; and he can thus be puzzled and misled by the function of values because he lacks an understanding of the necessity of a bedrock conceptual axiology.

The applied axiology of a field such as aesthetics is immobilized without such fundamental underlying decisions. By commencing with a typological analysis of the extant applied criteria, we have at least a dense, extensive, and ample idea of the resources of aesthetic criteriology, while a theorist who starts with only his own

perceptions and formulations would work from an impoverished model of valuational possibilities.

Having started, however, we cannot evade Frank Sibley's insistence, in his previously mentioned essay "Aesthetic Concepts," that it will prove impossible to formulate aesthetic criteria which are definite and constant—rule-conditioned and rule-
governed—with which to approach any given set of properties. Let me restate
Sibley's argument. Suppose we attempt to take account of *all* the distinctive and
various properties of all the innumerable objects which are called art; would we
then, on the basis of the sum, be able to define the criteria of aesthetic (artistic)
value? It should be clear that Sibley's enumerative approach, with its instrumentalist assumptions, would lead to no definite or constant standards. However, I think
he frames the problem wrongly. The empirically given data as such seem to me the
only relevant evidence in just two matters—when we want to know: (1) the medium (material) of an art object; and (2) the technical skill of the artist (how well he
chisels, modulates tonality, lays on paint, controls his movement, etc.). These aspects are by no means unimportant to the creative process and to the attainment of
the art object; nor are they partitioned as by a Chinese wall from the value-imbued
aspects of the art objects. Yet I will insist that the matter of the medium and of the
technique (these sole questions settled strictly by the empirical facts) concern pre-
artistic (or para-artistic) values.

In attempting to valuate art, we are concerned with the wholes rather than the
particular elements; and even if one single quality should constitute the whole of
the value (I will admit the possibility), still its value could not be verified by its perceptually grasped traits, since then we would have the vicious circle where the
single quality (the X) is deemed an artistic value, and the supporting evidence (criterion of value) is none other than just this quality being investigated.

By citing an atypical, one-element pattern, do I cheat in treating the problem of
empirical evidence as the possible criterion? Consider a more complicated, more
representative case: a valuable whole which is a complex of elements A, B, C, etc.
Here, we cannot simply reduce the whole to the *sum* of the perceptually grasped
A, B, C, etc., but we do perceive a *pattern* of the whole, and it may be asked why
we cannot seek our axiological supporting evidence in this configuration of the A,
B, C, etc. This is to argue that we should be able to prove artistic criteria by reference to the elements of consonance, thematic variation, and dominance of a motif
in a pattern—or, perhaps, it will be by reference to the elements of dissonance,

pounding repetition, or kaleidoscopic richness. In any case, the reason we do not
do this is because we are then immediately back within the vicious circle. Precisely
the elements of the composition are denoted as the value itself; how then can we
use them as the axiological criteria? It's a bit like the Molière character saying that
opium opiumates. In other words (and coming back again to Sibley): Isn't it a matter
of also looking for the axiological regularities as such, which provide the criteria
and ultimately also our axiological-aesthetic orientation, rather than looking solely
at the properties as such, which are governed or conditioned by regularities? Moreover — assuming my typology bears on the question — the regularities ("rules") are
not infinite; indeed, the "rules" may be subsumed in some fundamental procedures.
I should add that the point I am making is pertinent to each of the five major orientations to value — to psychologism no less than to ontological objectivism, relationism, sociological relativism, or historicism — because each of these standpoints
does discriminate between the data considered and criteria, and because each
axiological paradigm operates by subordinating the specifically cited reasons to
the axiological-aesthetic principles which it applies.

   Every statement or judgment of value, then, is conditioned by an axiological
thesis which has its support in a philosophical framework of statements or judgments. These are the contexts within which the ultimate criteria of aesthetic valuation operate:
1. characteristics of the aesthetic experience;
2. characteristics of the aesthetic object;
3. interrelational aspects of the aesthetic subject and object;
4. characteristics of the socioaesthetic setting (collective opinions of the object); and
5. characteristics of the aesthetic subject and object which historically are observed
   to have recurrence.
Certainly, this perspective differs from the reliance on empirical proof of value within the valuated object in the tautological fashion, evasive of the necessary axiological explications, which we noted in Sibley.

   In proposing this criteriological table, I have left aside the actual, empirical, observed (or implied) characteristics of the objects of an aesthetic valuation. To specify
these characteristics is the job of applied criteriology (having, of course, previously
used the data to establish the ultimate axiological and philosophical framework).
In this sense, we consciously "commit an error" in persistently speaking of certain
particular objects and experiences as though obviously or fundamentally "aesthetic." No set of qualities has such a priori, absolute existence. To impute such

characteristics it is first necessary to have an axiological orientation such as is here
delineated.

The valuational search for "rules" demands and calls such criteria into explicit
being; while the formulated criteria lend clarity and a focused procedure to the
valuator's undertaking. However distinctive and however varied, aesthetic values
and valuational qualities must be regarded as criterion-conditioned; and behind
the aesthetic criteria stand, of course, the ultimate axiological-philosophical
orientations.

When Sibley speaks, then, of rule-governed conceptions (by which term he
indicates such valuational qualities as harmony, disharmony, charm, melancholy,
representation, or deformation, which the valuator describes in the *given* work
of art), we can best take these as *specific reasons* offered to justify and particularize an axiological orientation already adopted, whether deliberately or un-
knowingly. Such reasons can at times be haphazard, but most often they particularize and evince one or another fundamental orientation. Of course, here the
ultimate criteria are more or less veiled behind the subcriteria (the specific valuational qualities which are cited), but a definite axiological context and the conditioning individual and sociohistorical variables may and must be described.

It is almost habitual for critics within a specific field of the arts to use the
subcriteria which are handy and prominent rather than applying the criteria for all
aesthetic value. Moreover, these subcriteria for a special field are often mistaken
for aesthetic fundamentals.

Ultimate criteria may also be lost from sight if the function of an art object (most
often, its reception) is accepted as a (sub)criterion which exhausts the interest of
the given observer. Often the functional subcriterion that is applied is political,
moral, or religious; such subcriteria may be, and readily are, admitted as surro-
gates into aesthetic valuation (for more on this matter, see chapter 3, "The Criteria
of Aesthetic Evaluation"). I should add that it is impossible to cope with these surrogate criteria merely by pitting *other* (aesthetic) *subcriteria* against them. What is
needed is a basic clarification of the valuational question through a confrontation with fundamental principles. And since the ultimate criteria are veiled behind
the subcriteria, they must be brought forward by analysis. Seeking to present the
necessary and sufficient (rule-governed) properties which will justify us in calling
object X a work of art and the state of mind of Y an aesthetic experience, we are
forced to more and more fundamental criteria, until, at length, we arrive at an irreducible axiological-aesthetic position oriented by definite, implicit, or manifest

philosophical premises. The typology of such positions is a useful aid, for it enables us to select among the five major orientations with a knowledge of past experience and the alternatives provided by aestheticians — hopefully, offering a means to eliminate needless confusions and pitfalls.

On this basis, the historicist orientation affords, in my view, the sturdiest axiological-aesthetic solution and hence the best means of verification of aesthetic values. Earlier I sought to prove the superiority of this orientation; now I wish to move into a further description and articulation of its premises. Let me first go back briefly to a remark I made earlier about Wittgenstein, where I stated that his distinction between motivation and the causal nexus was helpful. Why is this so? When I respond to an art object, my response clearly is *motivated* by it, but the *causation* of the response is not necessarily comprised in my responding. Although I can give *reasons* for having the response, *explanation* ought to be considered another matter. I can supply supporting evidence with regard to certain proper-ties — of my state of mind, of an object, or of both in context — while not stating any causes and effects. However, the causation problem ought to be faced squarely when we analyze matters back to ultimate aesthetic criteria. For example, if a subjectivist says he calls X valuable, and the reason he gives is that he likes it, we should be able to press him further. We will want to get him to add that he sees no causes worth mentioning and that the sole motivation which he will admit is that of preference (liking) for the value. We would similarly want the relationist to try to explain *why* a correlation emerges between object and subject (this motiva-tional field, he says, is crucial to his orientation); and the sociological relativist will be asked for the *why* of his substantiating reasons. In this connection, C. G. Hempel has recently given an instructive analysis proving the possibility of passing from understanding (empathy) to explanation of the disposition of a given indi-vidual.[52] In terms of my argument, precisely the historicist orientation seems able to give the fullest explanation of its discerned specific reasons (motivations). In other words, the historicist can give the strongest available *reasons for his reasons:* he will develop a relationist position, broadened and qualified with historical understanding, with the resultant causal explanation *deepened* through investigation of the *genesis* of artistic value and of aesthetic experience. (For a central application of the relationist and historicist explanation of artistic value, see chapter 2, "What Is a Work of Art?" while in the next section I shall consider the problems and uses of genetic inquiries.) Briefly, the relational-historicist position studies the accumulated knowledge of ethnocentric (and also transcul-

tural) aesthetic transactions, from the origins to the present, so as to locate in these
processes the ultimate foundation of aesthetic valuation. Let me reiterate that the
kind of historicism that I present here should be distinguished on the one side
from the *Historismus* (of Meinecke and others) popular following World War I,
which leads to sheer relativism; and on the other side from a quasi-theological
(teleological) treatment of the historical process, which invests history with
eternally fixed solutions (i.e., an immutable axiological status). My contention is
that one must search for temporal aesthetic paradigms and for invariants, always
recalling that no invariant may be pronounced valid beyond the historical data
available to the present moment.

I perhaps need scarcely add that a relational-historicist will not introduce the
whole scope of causal explanation into the specific valuation of every given X.
Neither do we expect such an apparatus of theory from the average amateur of art
or from a journalist-critic. Nonetheless, persons concerned with having an explanation for their judgments should take care that the immediate reasons given for
describing an art object are consciously regarded as criteria that point back to an
ultimate axiological-philosophical choice which, in turn, entails a methodological
procedure. Not every one of the major axiological orientations encourages us to
inquire into the causes which lie behind the values that motivate persons (values
that, on the other hand, are finally situated in social history and/or in nature); but
in my opinion the most enlightening of the axiological standpoints do precisely
this.[53]

The Origins of Aesthetic (Artistic) Value

It follows from the foregoing outline of the theoretical framework for valuational
activity that we should investigate the *origins* of aesthetic (or more precisely, artistic) value, to see whether the best research and thought on this matter backs up
and contributes to the historicist approach on valuation. It is, however, a complex
question; and the following pages will be, at most, a suggestive introduction.

Stimulating marxist discussions of the genesis of artistic value have come
recently from Ernst Fischer and, especially, Georg Lukács.[54] In the course of
describing my approach, I want to distinguish it from theirs.

Fischer, although well worth reading on this question, nonetheless does not
really consider the emergence of art insofar as this is a problem of its *differentiation* from certain preconditions (among them labor, rhythm, magic, sexual symbols).
While dating art from the introduction of the division of labor, he fails to deal

with the *process* of its origination. This is to say that he omits to locate among the
preconditions their germinal protoartistic qualities which eventually will be
transformed into the primary traits of that new formation of social consciousness
which is art. Also, Fischer omits to provide a tentative definition of art in his
second chapter where it would be needed to move discussion forward, and this
indeed stems from methodological irresolution whether to be concerned solely
with the external context of art, or instead to attempt a geneticostructural approach, which would describe a defined artistic pattern that materializes as part of
a sociocultural process in which labor and magic are closely integrated. Nor does
Fischer adequately deal with the questions of magic and production, both central
to the process, and this leaves him unprepared to say which of the two (or both
equally?) was dominant in developing the earliest vague yet unmistakable traits
of art. Nevertheless, his interpretation does bring out the fact that labor and
magic do not merely "prepare for" the emergence of art but are the activities
from which aesthetic value emerges.

Lukács' leaves us in no such uncertainty as to methodological premises and intentions. He moves with deliberation to study the genetic process of art from the
outside and inside, treating it as a complex, dialectical whole. He tends to describe
magic as the dominant precondition and magical symbolism as the germinal origin
for artistic mimesis. However, Lukács' undeviating insistence that mimesis does
provide the operative core of the artistic phenomenon bars him from a full appreciation of certain aspects of art which are persuasively indicated by Fischer —
and which may be summarily described as formal structure, emergent from a
rhythm and a symmetry that, in turn, acquire values due to the historical human
experience of models in nature and, above all, in work. To claim that Lukács ignores such aspects would simply be untrue; but he does underestimate them in
his estimate of the emergent traits of art.

In the remarks that follow, I shall note where I differ with these recent, important
marxist texts. (Let me add that it would be irrelevant to take up the issue with
some earlier marxists, such as Plekhanov or Kautsky, whose thought on the
origins of artistic value was influenced by nonmarxist sources.) The reader should
bear in mind the overarching unity of methodologies which, despite differences,
characterizes the marxist approaches presented here.

As against the positions of Fischer and Lukács — and, by extention, myself —
it might be rejoined that scholarship has for decades recognized the centrality of
labor and magic to the birth of art; therefore, what is so "marxist" about our

thesis? With some reservations, I accept the premise of this argument. But its conclusion seems incorrect, and here is why:

1. If I consider the views most widely acknowledged on the origin of art, it emerges that most are quite one-sided. These four hypotheses are the commonest: (a) *Labor* is called the primary determining factor (Karl Bücher through Franz Boas and his followers). (b) *Magic* is termed the key determining factor (James Frazer's *The Golden Bough* through Leonard Adam's *Primitive Art* and the ideas of today's ethnologists who hold that primordial myth shapes art). (c) *Play* is termed the key to the birth of artistic and aesthetic experience (Karl Groos through Johan Huizinga's *homo ludens* to contemporary studies of leisure as the foundation for human fulfillment). (d) *Sexuality* is termed the primary determinant (Freud and his school). These are predominant approaches to the question, although, undoubtedly, many attempts are made to combine approaches.

2. Even when combinations of the approaches are tried, these are decisively different from what marxists offer as a procedure. Take two telling instances: (a) Claude Lévi-Strauss includes both primitive myth and technical skills *(bricolage)* in his interpretation. However, his methodology does not pay attention to the genesis (in the strict sense of this term) of phenomena at the birth of art; he is not interested in the *process* whereby structures emerge. (b) Herbert Read sees the primordial evolution of art occurring in two stages: the first vitalistic and the second constructive. In the vitalistic phase, symbolic magic combines with eidetic imagery to produce the work of art; in the constructive phase (the neolithic period), the labor element predominates. It should be evident from these two examples that even where a pair or more of factors are included, methodology remains the ultimate question.

Because a positing of relevant factors is so distinct from the development of a suitable methodology, Georg Lukács found, when he came to ask the marxist procedural question (How, and in what way, do antecedent factors shape works of art and also enter into them as specific traits in early sociocultural evolution?), that not a single nonmarxist scholar had directly posed the operative problem.

Marxism thus has its own method on this question, and despite the fact that nonmarxists may employ some of these elements too, the following expectations seem its most salient conceptions: (a) historically, artistic activity comes before aesthetic experience (aesthetic experience being understood as the apt appreciation of an art object); and (b) art's structural traits are shaped by antecedent genetic stimuli. Both of these matters need further explanation.

I interpret any social phenomenon in two dimensions that are best thought of as intermeshed but distinct: one idiogenetic and the other allogenetic. The idiogenetic dimension (from the Greek *idios*, "one's own") includes the totality of *inner* elements of a developing phenomenon, and the allogenetic (from the Greek *allos*, "other") includes the totality of *outside* elements effective on a given process. We may say that the allogenetic analysis looks at the *primary patterns* inasmuch as they produce a *new* pattern. Primary patterns, in my view, include the biosphere of human activity as much as the natural and manmade environment.

I have already suggested the two fields of primary patterns that have chief importance in the allogenetic analysis of emergent artistic value: magic and work. The artistic (new) pattern in its process of formation is studied by the idiogenetic approach, which finds such elements as rhythm or mimesis operative in integrating a new, original whole.

From the integral standpoint of the historical processes, we can say that primary patterns are the precondition of, and lend substance to, such semi-autonomous, particular structures as primordial art objects through a process of interiorization that draws on the productive and magical activities. In the structure of the new class of objects, the primary patterns now participate in the transformed aspect of formal characteristics and iconic symbols. In other words, allogenesis and idiogenesis are coterminous processes which together result in the structuring of an art object. *Homo faber* works (but magical strategems are among his trusted modes of production); *homo ludens* plays (and yet this playing occurs in a context of labor or as a necessary preliminary to labor); and these are one and the same person. Play as leisure is the later-emerging activity of necessarily productive humanity. But as the activities of civilization increase and ramify, and as communicative and practical targets and know-how increase, so too do the autotelic activities grow, directed into ever more varied structures.[55]

This two-sided methodology now leads us to restate the process of the genesis of artistic value, for we wish to describe both the external conditions and the internal process in a methodologically adequate fashion. Let us first make some further assumptions explicit. We can only approximately guess as to when the species *homo sapiens* began to show some aesthetic promise, on the basis of a developing physical and mental aptitude for generating this and other kinds of distance between the species and other modes of nature. Scholars in several different fields have estimated that the first evidence of "art," so-called, could have occurred in the upper paleolithic period, no nearer than 40,000 years to

The Origins of Aesthetic
(Artistic) Value

our era. We must, however, be cautious, for it is certain that our present attitudes distort the data. The primitive tribesmen who produced the objects which we admire quite evidently had no aim and thus no awareness of making art.

If we now consider our methodological resources, and we weigh this dilemma of the discrepancy between what the cavedwellers thought to produce and what they indeed produced, we realize that what is to be studied is the *gradual* historical evolution of a specifically and acknowledgedly artistic field. The sociocultural context in which this process took place was magical/productive, or productive/ magical if you will. Tools were increasingly improved, enabling the worker to pass from rudimentary useful labor to the incorporation of more refined patterns and structures. The work was always touched by some element of magic, for the totemic (zoomorphic) mode of consciousness of that era was ubiquitous; but the animistic perceptions and beliefs, rites and symbolism were deeply practical in aim. They were, in fact, inseparable from the social praxis of the day, since magic was *opus operandum inoperans* (in Mauss's apt phrase). These primary polarities have a dialectical cohesion that admits tensions, ambivalences, and oppositions. We can thus delineate, in the extrinsic sphere, the development of means of produc- tion—from flake and core tools, through efficient scrapers, adzes, wedges, cutters, and the like, continuing to pottery and basketry, and spinning and weaving at the dawn of the neolithic era—and, at the same time, a development of signs and ritual initiation in the magical sphere—from the rude steatopygic symbols for sexuality, apotropeic tattoos, the wondrous pictograms found in the caves of Altamira and Lascaux, Le Roc de Sers, Marsoulas, and Les Combarelles, to finally the earliest religious ceremonies.

It should be borne in mind that, according to the newest findings of Louis Leakey, *homo habilis* is two million years old and the available data allow us to state that the history of human tool-making reaches back at least a half-million years, to the early and middle Pleistocene age. There is no parallel evidence of magical rituals from this same early era. Yet the absence of data is not con- clusive proof that *homo sapiens* then lacked the capability to produce symbols. In any case, the empirical data testify beyond any doubt to a primordial tool- making disposition of humanity, spurred by the harsh necessities of the fight for survival.

As concerns what we know today of the beginnings of art, the evidence appears to point to a time much, much later than the origin of human civilization. In my view, the same two factors which a number of anthropologists have found requisite for the rise of civilization—tool-making plus magic and ritual—are indispensable for the emergence of art. As I cannot provide here a detailed survey of the background to art's origin, I might refer the reader to Gordon Childe's books for the changing condition of the productive capacities of the species, and to the French scholar Henri Wallon for the history of the emergence of intelligence, which meant the transition from magical to realistic thought. A number of standard works describe the early evidences of art; the theoretical ineptitude of most of these studies may be disregarded, although some authors, such as Leroi-Gourhan, offer a stimulating insight into the primitive world view. Especially worth mentioning on the specifics of early art is Max Raphael's *Prehistoric Cave Paintings* (Princeton, 1945); some of its theses may now appear dubious but the text as a whole is unsurpassed due to its philosophical-historical approach to the problem of form-content relationship in Dordogne art.

I should like to venture some hypotheses to be followed up, on the strength of information in the above and related studies and in the light of our foregoing clarifications:

1. It does seem fair to postulate that artistic sensibility developed at an earlier era than did aesthetic sensibility. Members of the species "did" art before they "appreciated" art. Given the primordial conditions, with production and magic pressed into the service of immediate needs, millions of years would have been consumed in the refinement of productive and magical activity before "art" might conceivably have been institutionalized (the idea of the artist) and an aesthetic experience and attitude could emerge.

2. Through this timespan which the contemporary mind can scarcely encompass, and at a creeping pace scarcely to be recognized by today's harried slave of technology, the artistic activity did slowly evolve; and it remained imbued with both magical symbolism and utilitarian functions. The external stimuli were modestly absorbed and "internalized" within the product itself: rhythm and symmetry were emulated, and sexual and cosmic symbols provided the vocabulary for iconic, sensuously given communication. Increasing craft skills lent themselves to more finely articulated and coherent wholes. The quality of art objects which we today call form then emerged primarily around attributes such as rhythm, symmetry, and proportion, as a part of directly productive endeavors— although magical rites were also imbued with rhythmic cadences. Conversely, the birth of mimesis was primarily tied up with magical symbolism—although such symbolism also appears in many artifacts crafted by primitive man. Accordingly,

the two main aspects contributing to art's genesis cannot be sharply demarcated as stemming from quite opposite phenomena at the start of civilization.

3. When did art which we would consider *consummate* become possible? I would conjecture: only as these more and more sophisticated "wholes" also took on another trait, that of *autotelicism* (from the Greek *autos*, "self" and *telos*, "end" or "completion"). Very gradually, these objects came to be fashioned with the avowed intention of evoking a special kind of response, one that came near to that of the maker of the object or the doer of the performance. The transition to autotelicism should not be placed earlier than the peak of the neolithic era. This new acknowledgment of the intrinsic qualities of the "wholes" went together with a decay of the earlier integrity of the magical/productive context. The reason for this breakup of the seemingly eternal verities of animism was the increase of the results and control obtained by labor. The more effectively the species worked, the less did magic obsess the mind. The dialectics of the development of our species hung chiefly on the unity or disunity of this dualism. The neolithic era saw a revolution in technics and material production — very much surpassing the sweep and impact of the industrial revolution of our eighteenth century. The parallel upswing of the autotelic interest and tolerance was marked by the emergent dominance of geometrical design. The magical, symbolic meanings continued alongside, or else allusively veiled within the geometrical forms, as affirmations of prior symbolic representations; but the primary aim was now the artisans' and users' delight with the internally regulated order of ornaments on baskets, blankets, pots, etc. The role of magic was eventually taken over by religion, which made its own claims on art; but I need only note here that the composition of the religious object is such that its potential for autotelicism is not effaced.

4. A spur to autotelicism, as suggested, was the gradual relinquishment by magic of its pervasive capacity to imbue every element of reality with a fetishistic function oriented to the fantastic understanding and/or mastery of life conditions. This was due not only to geometric stylization but also to the change in representation, which remained the practice of primitive humanity; representation became increasingly autotelic as it grew more deliberately and ably *mimetic*. The pictograms on the cave walls, where their function had to be more occult than meant for delight, still performed symbolic functions — but the prototypes for these ideograms (the stags and buffalo and hunters out in the real world) were more "naturally" presented, while the totemistic and fantastic functions receded.

Mimesis began to establish a new semiotic code (*Aeschylus in Athens* and later studies by George Thomson explore the transition).

5. To find increasingly realistic traits does not justify a description of "naturalism." This error is still frequently committed in handbooks on prehistoric times, but I want to stress very strongly that depiction in the paleolithic era was not a detailed rendering of that world, and we can derive from it no "report" on the external conditions of the tribesmen at the dawn of mankind. Mimesis remained very close to a magical realism. Man still confronted nature and the animal was still the principal mediation in the Altamira or Lascaux frescos, the bison with a turned head from Mas d'Azil, and the hunting scenes from Hoggar. We are here offered a synthetic grasp of the existence of our primordial human species: the powerfully graphic portraits of bison, rhinoceros, horses, lions, and so on, were elements of a paleolithic vision founded on the zoomorphic principle. Its main aspects were slaying and copulation (procreation), both reflective of the effort to survive and the need to contest vigorously and resourcefully with nature (the servitude/mastery syndrome).

The above examples are evidence of mimesis as a process occurring at once *within* the magical world and *against* it. Mimesis gradually became liberated from the primacy of magical patterns, and, when we compare the work of the barbaric era with the savage antecedents, we see that representation has become *imitatio*. It might be rejoined that the subsequent neolithic era does not permit the above conclusion, because its essential characteristics involved geometrical design, and representation was stopped in its evolution to appear only later and in a new guise. Can it then be termed the selfsame mimesis in evolution? I think the only sensible reply is as follows: The *essential* features of the neolithic era did not eliminate the mimetic impulses and the practice that corresponded to them. It would be arbitrary to hold that between, say, 5,000 and 2,500 years ago, the time of Homer, all representationalism disappeared from primitive arts. Clearly, art for the home gained a priority in this era due to developed technical-material conditions which encouraged the species to ever more refined shaping of objects for everyday practical use. Yet let us note that while at this time artistic form became an *enhanced quality* of the created wholes (and was, let me add, a continuation of the painted cave compositions that date from the Magdalenian era), so did the equally primitive African culture, for example, continue and deepen the mimetic trend (sites in Rhodesia provide the positive evidence).

We may conjecture a similar process in the syncretic expression of dance, song, and poetry. George Thomson's *Marxism and Poetry* (1946) sketches the transition from recitation to written poems, from inspiration and trance to composition, from anonymous utterance by and for the whole community to individual utterance. This passage is parallel to a transition from hypnotic, magical symbolism to epic narration about the world.

6. If these hypotheses on the origin of art are accepted, we can conclude that, although the primitive creator's intention will never be discovered, we are nonetheless justified in describing as "art" these structured qualities probably meant only as communication. Retrospectively and looking from "above" on this millennia-long process of groping for form and mimesis united with one another in expressive, relatively autonomous wholes, we can see first the *protoaesthetic constituents*, which become increasingly conspicuous and cogent, and next (by the midpaleolithic era) some *initial artistic structures*. I believe my hypotheses are not merely a reading of aesthetic criteria into a primeval context to impose an historically and axiologically alien frame of reference on an object of study having uncomprehended circumstances, purposes, genesis, and function. Aware of that danger, we do and must begin with the scrutiny of specific structures ascribed to particular eras through scientific testing procedures. It seems certain that art was not a priori given to mankind, nor did it emerge suddenly. Rather, art slowly became art as known in recorded history. The sets of qualities apparent in artifacts from the Auvignac period date the evolution of the art phenomenon from earlier than the first intentional, self-conscious art activities known to us. If we admit works from ancient Egypt and Greece as art, the traits we admire in them are revealed *in nuclei* in paleolithic beginnings. Marx has it that human anatomy is the investigator's clue to the anatomy of apes, accepting that while the ape is not a *homo sapiens* both species are simians (primates). An analogous comprehension of the sculpture of Lespugue through study of the work of Myron or Praxiteles is also reasonable.

How does the foregoing analysis stand up in the light of recent empirical research by paleolithic scholars? A number of doubts have been introduced on matters that had once seemed settled. For instance, it is asked whether the cave sites of drawings really were sacred for magical purposes — the patterning of footprints within and without the caves, and some evidence of children in the presumedly ritual precincts, lend evidence to the doubters. Why were so few mammoths and reindeer depicted, since they were a chief aim of the hunts, if the drawings had the magical function of enabling the kills? Nor is the fact of frequent overpainting, or superimposition of the presumably esoteric images, ignored by the questioners. Indeed, how do we know the drawings were made before hunts? Could they not have been made afterwards, perhaps long after the event? In view of such issues raised by recent anthropological discussion, I would like to note that some matters seem yet well beyond dispute even among the prehistorians and ethnologists—and reasonably so, if one cautiously reconstructs the integral structure of primitive society, its material basis, and the evidence of the activity of *homo sapiens* in that era.

On what matters does something like unanimity seem to prevail among experts in this field?

1. An "art for form's sake" interpretation gets no support from the experts who explain this initial period.

2. The mind of the aboriginal, it is agreed, seems to be characteristically attracted by the goal of an extension of his powers into the environment through magical attitudes and the making of tools, which increasingly achieve the dual result of placing *homo sapiens* in control of eventualities while lending the species a certain distance on the flux of experience.

3. The principal role of animals in the iconography leads all scholars to conclude that the sympathetic magic of the hunters was a chief spur to artistic activity as such.

4. Agreement prevails as to the *general* totemic significance of primitive art; the only difficulty seems to be to elucidate the concrete circumstances, the reasons, and the aims of the given totemic context.

5. Sexual (mythological) motifs are everywhere understood—especially since Leroi-Gourhan's investigations—as the energizing element in primitive symbolic magic.

Now, it is just because there is substantive agreement on these fundamental matters that I dare to argue that the contemporary empirical data do support the philosophical-historical interpretation I propose here. I will also insist that my analysis, while corresponding to the best available evidence, also goes further than the findings of particular research. I urge this because only a philosophically founded and coherent theory can raise and encompass the final problems of art's origin. Whether or not it is the marxist interpretation which emerges triumphant among other competing philosophies in offering the fundamental context is, however, a meta-aesthetic issue which I shall not attempt to argue here.

Given this short statement of basic considerations and hypotheses for interpreting the origins of art and with it the genesis of aesthetic value, I can now elaborate on certain points. First, we may tentatively define the art object in its nascent structure; we may say that it composes a relatively separated and self-coherent whole produced by acculturated and learned skills, that it has some formal qualities (such as rhythm, symmetry, proportion) in a harmonious arrangement, and that also it has eidetically given symbolic meanings which a perceiver can relate to the real world. I do not think I need to add this to the tentative definition, but I shall say it anyway: these "wholes" were the expression of attitudes pervasive to the given primitive society. Only much later did idiosyncrasy—that is, a heightened individual expression—begin to occur among the makers of these objects. I should again emphasize that the saturation of art objects with the implicit aims of magic and labor did not cease for more millennia than we can comprehend. Indeed, the degree of independence achieved by artistic value throughout history has been entirely in a context of the dialectical development of magic and production, considered in their unity. Not until the nineteenth century of our era was there ever—in all history, so far as I am aware—the overt declaration of a break from the subordination of artistic value to utility value or fetish value.

What about the character of aesthetic *experience* in the primitive eras? I have suggested that the emergence of this sensibility depended on the progress of art—the disposition to aesthetic response developed as a feedback or responsiveness among craft workers who became creative in acting on the nuances they noticed in the items they made for productive and occult use. It was surely the case that aesthetic awareness could become explicit, highly articulated, and farflung only when the artists had an institutional recognition conferred on their skills and talents. On the one hand, it is true that *all* aesthetic experience is "object-embedded." On the other hand, the apt response is realized only where the perceiver has gained sufficient separateness from nature (here, see Marx's *1844 Manuscripts* on the difference between the animal and the humanized senses) and where a tradition of experience with the protoartistic dimension has accustomed the sensibility. At the initial stage, the protoaesthetic sensibility scarcely glimpsed any motive to grow disencumbered of its pervasive utilitarian and magical (later religious) conditionings and responses. Nonetheless, the protoaesthetic capacity developed and spread, and its autotelic character in turn gained recognition. (I cannot stress too strongly that these events occurred inconspicuously and took longer than we can comprehend.)

This relative autonomy of aesthetic experience took a position parallel and complementary to that of artistic structure, though less noticed perhaps. However, when the individual subject in early history would interiorize his perception of an artistic whole and savor ecstasy from the intensity of his equilibrium, his wish would be to know this experience more vividly and definitely. At this point, I would introduce the idea of *psychic homeostasis*—a synthesis of all faculties of spirit or mind, suspended for the purpose of contemplating the "rival world" presented by art. This homeostatic equilibrium has the most proximate correlation with the "playful" quality of creative activity. For a long time, the playfulness of the art activity was obscured or denied by the scarcity-and-utility mentality of historically primitive contexts. Then, long after play was acknowledged to pertain to the artists' manipulation of materials, techniques, and symbols, the centrality of this same play quality in aesthetic sensibility was widely unacknowledged.

These propositions relate not only to the historicist philosophical orientation of marxism; they are also relevant to some of the generalizations reached by Monroe Beardsley. The traits of unity, complexity, and intensity, argues Beardsley, may be accepted as characteristic of both art objects and the aesthetic experience. I find that these traits correspond to my concept of a coherent whole comprising a "rival" world that is separate from the real world and pervaded with a richness of cohesively patterned qualities, or sets of qualities, which are immediately given and symbolically meaningful. It is, moreover, illuminating to bring out two points on which Beardsley's conception differs from mine. First, an ahistorical method is used to arrive at the conclusions: Beardsley appears to want to describe some principles of invariable artistic value, this despite the instrumentalism of his *Aesthetics*, which has an ethnocentric amplitude that spans the European tradition. Second, Beardsley discovers value in aesthetic objects only when they evoke (arouse) aesthetic experiences, and the value (goodness or greatness) of the experiences is decisive for him. My own view is that aesthetic experiences are attendant on and thus subordinate to the primordial artistic activity. Looking at this issue historically, there seems no good reason to presume the cavedwellers to have experienced contemplation of a peculiar kind, since (however some among them may have excelled) the whole community partook of producing primeval art objects—and since art and artists were not yet designated as such, we may be certain, not even implicitly. Later, when the complex aesthetic field was established in the civilizational context, it could more or less readily command attention and receptiveness. Yet, no matter how relatively autonomous in more than one sense the aesthetic experience may become, it acquires this status only in dependence on and in feedback with the art object. Even so, although Beardsley and I have differences, I am struck by the affinity of our findings in the face of the disparity of our premises.

A further interesting fact is the healthy result brought about at the insistent prodding of aestheticians who see no way to establish a definition of aesthetic value or of aesthetic experience. Those of us who continue to seek definition have been helped and encouraged in refining our methods and statements by the negativism of critics who insist on pointing to everything problematic or in need of further study. Indeed, the arguments of the antidefinitionists have done a great deal to persuade me that, everything considered, the historicist position provides the most cautious and sound basis for examining properties in the aesthetic field.

More than the above I really cannot attempt here with regard to presenting the genetic interpretation and its tentative findings. However, it may be worthwhile briefly to confront the geneticostructural approach advanced by marxists with another and different structuralism that is much admired today in Europe and also in the United States. The structuralists have done much to spread an understanding of the art object as an autotelic whole. They are usually careful to speak of the entity they analyze as comprising strictly the synchronic aspect of the art object, which cannot be comprehended without adding the diachronic analysis. "History," they say, is implicit in every pattern, and they add that each "historical process" gives rise to the formation of such patterns. We find these statements in Jacobson, Lévi-Strauss, and in their structuralist forefathers (e.g., Mukarovsky from the early 1930s), and, nonetheless, there is considerable difficulty in taking such formulations as an aid to improving a methodology. The problem lies in the failure of structuralists to confront real history. They do not become involved with the genesis of structures or the explanation of cause-and-effect results and meanings. However, it is just such conditionality which most needs analysis.

Let me state the problem more generally. In considering the relations between art and reality, can we confine our attention to just the semiotic-functional dependencies? If we think we can, then do we accept that such an unarguably determinant dimension with regard to the particular art object as is provided by the broadly understood traditions of culture may thus be subsumed? If so, then what about the specific causal effect of other social phenomena in relation to this category? I think the answer must be no on both accounts. In many respects, the entity as it is studied by the structuralists will remain inexplicable. Their method considers an already given structure subject to modification that, however, does not go beyond the limits of semiotic change.

The marxist rejects this conception; and must instead ask how the given structure emerges from the nonartistic field. This geneticostructural inquiry must, of course, start with the structure (whole) which is given, that is, with the result of an historical process which has to be reconstructed and scrutinized. The *later* phenomenon is something of a guide to explain and understand the *earlier*, and perhaps even the *original* from which it stems. We are thus compeled to inquire how, through the long history of art, internal and external factors have cooperated to this end. In brief, what we look for is the process of the origin and then the evolution of a phenomenon. What we consider is a process of continual tension, reaction, and compensation, with the archaic and the plainly conventional, the invigoratingly new and the challengingly "avant-garde," all in constant flux with prior patterns, which are, thus, being continually upset. The process is conditioned and precipitated chiefly by extra-artistic phenomena, on a foundation of the extant background of artistic resources, and is, of course, most immediately influenced by the present artistic context.

Every social pattern — and so each artistic pattern — is subject to this rule of causality, and explication should seek not to ignore or pass it over lightly. For an example of causal processes we might consider the tensions and conflicts of the ideologies (distinctly inflected structures of thinking) which have their referential basis in the class structure and conflicts of society. When we consider the relations of art and reality in this dimension, perhaps we note the clash and tension between what the particular artist creatively "asserts" in his work (through the moral of a story, direct declamation, choice of genre or subject matter, etc.), and a socially classdominant or even pervasive idea of what social relations, or art itself, should be thought to be. This sort of discontinuity, the novelty characterizing structures of art enhanced and inflected by an aura which is causal, can be conceptualized in terms of a disparity between the *psychogenesis* and the *sociogenesis* of an entity.

If we had to rely only on a structuralist methodology for our approach to the "diachronic" processes, then we might do no better than to go back to Juriy Tinyanov and Boris Eichenbaum. They had a splendid grasp of the *idiogenetic* problem. However, a marxist is not satisfied with the idiogenetic causal explanation alone. Idiogenetic development remains incomprehensible in the absence of an account of the *allogenetic* dimension which interacts with it. Just this methodological step was taken by the Czech theorist of literature Jan Mukazhovski in the late 1930s.

It is not enough to scrutinize phenomena for conjunctures — that is, for mere convergences of elements in a longer and more durable flux of elements and prop-erties. These occur often, and are obvious. What is more significant is the possi-bility of certain invariant combinations.[56] The geneticostructuralist interpretation may most securely verify such invariants (constants), if they are traceable, precisely because of its incessant concern for the patterns of development within the frame-work of the history of culture from its dawn up to our time. Our attention ultimately goes then to these aesthetic constants which we look for whether we are delving into the origins of art in various places, or are concerned with our own time of in-ternationally-knowing restlessness with art. Of course, we do not expect an abso-lute identity of characteristics when aesthetic objects or experiences from such geo-graphically or temporally incongruous contexts are compared. There cannot be a strictly commensurate identity of cross-cultural patterns. But if we look for at least a remarkable similarity among some kinds of traits, shall we be disappointed?

I have no wish to anticipate here the circumstantial analysis applied in the next chapter, but some observations can be made in a framework of the geneticostruc-tural method that would be badly compromised if it could be proven that the art of today shatters traditions of artistic value which were agreed upon over thou-sands of years. After all, is it not true that *mimesis* is no longer a central aspect of art, that *craftsmanship* (a contribution of skill or technique) and even an *artifact* (a material accomplishment, or "object") seem no longer essential? However, if we then look into earlier aesthetic history, could we not find grounds for seeing these tendencies as actually reverting to some archaic, and even protoartistic prac-tices of art? For, indeed, some members of the avant-garde are devoted to a *para-technological* approach, while another grouping seeks to stir ancient emotions through *pararitual*. Such tendencies, moreover, diminish individuality in art.

In response, some scholars have forecast the death of art itself. This obituary seems wrongly conceived; and yet, there likely is *an end to plausibility for certain definitional ideas* of the traits of art. Some long-accepted assertions may vanish, such as that concerning art's individualism; but will there not remain — beyond all the haphazard convergences and the ruptures of pattern — some fundamental valu-ational traits, not as an absolute identity, but instead manifested variously in a continuum? Here I would especially cite the ongoing, recurrent evidence of a di-rectly given perception of a "rival," relatively autonomous "world," which has heightened, peculiar properties that some person's ideation has organized.

A comparable conclusion seems warranted if we examine aesthetic experience through the ages. The avant-garde's accomplishments seem to de-emphasize the aesthetic experience of a free play of psychic energies; and the homeostatic harmony of a receptive spirit which acquires balance appears unsought. Intended, or at least principally achieved instead, is a state of unease or of being off-balance and riddled by tension; this psychic response is closer to the gambler's fevered, apprehensive anxiety than it is to the relaxed almost equestrian control that once was attributed to *homo ludens*. What else do we notice as characteristic of the experience of avant-garde art? Doesn't the experience of some of this art depend on *protoartistic phenomena* which are reminiscent of earliest culture? Phenomena which, accordingly, immerse us, in part, in the practical (technical) or symbolic (cognitive) activities which also cradled the aesthetic traits proper at art's origin? Suppose the neolithic person had somehow set down the protoaesthetic experience in a description comprehensible to us. Wouldn't we presumably interpret it as responsive to a basically practical activity which, however "graced by" decorative or expressive "touches," was yet an extensively contingent mode of experience? Nonetheless, although contemporary aesthetic experience departs from what art was said to evoke a century ago, and although at points it also seems to approach the task-oriented description we ascribe to the origin of aesthetic reception, there still seem to be invariables. What does remain, when long-term but inessential notions of fundamental aesthetic response have been stripped away?

1. The experience is still evoked by an aesthetic object.
2. It may still be felt to "trigger" a homeostatic balance of our psyche.
3. Due to direct stimulation by a "rival" object-world, an exhilarating play of mental energies may be initiated (even if cursorily, and even if peppered with annoyances and a preoccupation with contingencies).

From this analysis, I provisionally conclude that the genetic interpretation substantially contributes to our criteriology of aesthetic value, that is, to our discernment that some properties of objects and of experiences are constants and others are variables. True, I do expect to find some constants, and I may be especially keen for data that point this direction. In this respect, I place a good deal of confidence, philosophically, in the witty dictum of Marx (in his *Grundrisse*) that, as to method, the human anatomy is the best clue to the anatomy of the ape. Undoubtedly, no one can entirely rid himself of the preconceptions that stem from his contemporary and personal viewpoint. Yet it does seem possible to make effective use of the contemporary "clues" to any category of antecedents. In thus approaching the preparations for contemporary aesthetic value and experience, I use historical researches which start from the origins of civilization and come up to the present in considering the aesthetic artifacts and the recorded opinions of artists and audiences. Here, I have only been able to make the most abbreviated application of this means of inquiry, chiefly confining myself to a hypothesis concerning the origins of aesthetic activity. This same methodological approach has to be applied to, and checked against, the evidence of constants and variances in subsequent periods. The problems increase; the approach must be more complexly fashioned as the materials available to aesthetic valuation accumulate. However, the axiological conclusions will also begin to firm up and a pattern of reciprocal elucidation and checking will appear. The causal knitting which the genetic interpretation looks for helps to minimize error. If the historical inquiry described had complete success, we should be able to valuate with axiological accuracy even the most recent and avant-garde tendencies of artistic activity. I am skeptical that this degree of historical and valuational mastery can be achieved. Still, my belief is that it must be sought. But it should be pursued cautiously, no matter what temptations encourage a rush for certainty.

Of particular help for the axiology of art would be a rigorous and exhaustive project to study its autotelicism (i.e., the relative and always tenuous autonomy of art), as we experience it in contrast to the actual world that art "rivals." A scholar might want to couple to this study an analysis of the recurrent temptation which artists feel to erect an "ivory tower" in rejection of the claims made by the world (which provides the nourishment for all art) on its wards. Obviously, such studies cannot be pursued without touching on the problem of general (i.e., social) and particular (i.e., aesthetic) alienation and disalienation.

Another task which the geneticostructural method must tackle is centered on what Beardsley has termed "regional qualities," in other words, those elements or sets of elements which are to be found only at certain places and times, but which do nevertheless constitute value. That certain qualities occur prominently only to disappear or suffer neglect and contempt (they are, of course, fused with more durable values) is an effect which arises at sociohistorical conjunctures. We can, for instance, understand the successes even of so-called formalism, or of the utilitarian tendency, as being due to the temporal predominance of "regional" qualities. In sum, if, due to the time and the place, the role of any favored artistic qualities becomes disproportionate, then we can speak (borrowing a term from Thomas

Kuhn's study of the structure of scientific revolutions) of the prevalence of *aesthetic paradigms*, as opposed to what I have termed the *aesthetic invariables* or constants.

Synthesis: Towards the Valuation of Today's Art

I want to conclude with some comments concerning the valuation of the contemporary state of the arts. Naturally, my viewpoint is that of sociohistorical relationism, its axiology being the only one which takes effective account of the prior history of human culture, including especially the tendency of the aesthetic object to become set off from adjacent life phenomena. Lacking such fundamentals, a valuational orientation would be hard put to discriminate the fundamental from the ephemeral properties of art objects.

Can art be defined in terms of a single property? Such definitions have been tried by many scholars. Others, however, whose approaches go back to Dugald Stuart and Hippolyte Taine, explicitly settle for nothing simpler than a set or complex of properties; and it is in this trend that I too find the most stimulating efforts and the most promising opportunities. As Morris Weitz has shown, the single-trait approach to valuating art has always drawn a blank.[57] The single criteria proposed by formalism, voluntarism, emotionalism, intellectualism, and intuitionism were all proven inadequate or mistaken. We could also add to his list: sensualism (the criterion of art as a given in sensuous-concrete form); operationalism (the criterion of art which includes everything manmade); and axiologism (the criterion of art which includes every sensuously apprehended value — the iconic interpretation). Yet, and regrettably (as I tried to bring out while discussing Wittgenstein's reception in the United States), the proposal regarding criteria which Weitz in turn makes (his *pars construens*) is oddly feeble. More adequate is the position of DeWitt Parker in his study, "The Nature of Art."[58] No single property but a complex of characteristics is definitional, Parker argues. He names three properties which he thinks outstanding: reliance on the imagination to provide satisfaction; social significance; and an inner harmony of the work. Still more convincing is the proposition of Beardsley, cited earlier.[59]

What have the Soviet marxist authors considered to be the basis of valuation? Many of their texts display an inherited encumbrance of stereotyped utterances (e.g., "art is thinking in images") which have little usefulness when one tries to solve the core difficulties. Other formulations are completely wrong: such as the as-

sertion that realism is the specific constituent property of all art. Among recent
assessments, there has been some favor for the criterion of "poetic pathos" (a term
also used by Belinsky), a property understood as synonymous with "the ideologi-
cal-emotional-sensuous content" of a work of art.[60] This axiological preference is
stated by Moisei Kagan and also by Leonid Stolovich, whose work *The Object of
Aesthetics* develops criticisms of competing interpretations of art and so carefully
argues its author's own approach as to have drawn much attention.[61] In its own
way, however, the solution attempted by Kagan and Stolovich seems as one-sided
as those surveyed by Weitz.

A complete and acute assessment of the contemporary state of the arts requires,
among other measures, an account of all of the possibly relevant phenomena, that
is, an account of the work accepted as being significant by most artists and scholars. The theories of the Soviet scholars are hampered because their conception of
what may and may not be art is too arbitrary and discriminatory. In comparison,
the historicist viewpoint gives the advantage of allowing a comparison of novel
trends with all of the contemporary, broadly recognized achievments in art that
working artists closely consult in orienting their new aesthetic strategies, as well
as with masterpieces and lesser works of a more distant past that provide indices
of certain substantial principles of regularities which have so far endured. The next
chapter, "What Is A Work of Art?" seeks to provide a definition adequate to contemporary artistic praxis. Four distinct criteria are there suggested; and the one that
nowadays seems still predominant and decisive relates to a coherent field created
by the art object, achieved with the special characteristics of the art structure.[62]

Again, no one of the conditions for artistic status that I single out is sufficient in
itself. The art object presents a coherent, relatively *self-sufficient* whole; it is composed of a compact expressive harmony of *formal qualities* and of eidetically given
symbolic meanings; it is an *artifact* that is the product of skills which must be acquired and disciplined; and it is the work of a *given individual* whose objectified
traits pervade it to greater or less degree. These aspects function in the aggregate,
they are an *ensemble* of complementary value-laden properties.

Every work of art is a sign referring to reality, if only in the sense that it is a
symptom (token) of the real: it is genetically and functionally related to reality.
And yet the sign is simultaneously "transparent" and "opaque." Charles Morris'
article "Esthetics and the Theory of Signs" (1939), elucidates this point. Its "'trans-
parency" relates the art object to the external world; its "opacity" is a function

of the object's integral structure of perceptual qualities, which together with their attributes (ideas, representation, expression) create the relatively autonomous value. The subjective criteria so often applied to determining whether an object is art are activated by the "opacity" dimension of the work, so to speak. In other words, there is a sheer pleasure in gazing on the harmonious sensuous elements (*quod visum placet*); and there is a kind of playful recreation in this giving of attention, an articulation of the "surplus energy," which art furnishes beyond any moral or practical or cognitive functions.

Originality is not an attribute of every art object. However, every work will be (as I have mentioned) representative of a given artistic individuality, and the magnitude of this aspect is determinable in each specific case. How is the individuality measured? Each work of art carries on open dialogue with both its tradition and the gamut of artistic practices current at the moment; and there is, to some extent, a modification, as well as perpetuation, of these available values, properties, and materials. Following the suggestion of S. K. Shaumian, the Soviet linguist, we might say that art objects are "phenotypes" within the context of "genotypes": that is, every artist has a dependency, dialectical in character, on his historical situation and the traditions inherent to his vocation. I would add that the phenotype has some possibility of shattering an accepted genotype (which occurs in cases of great artistic originality). The functioning of the genotype is central to the historical processes; and one function of originality is to prepare the way for a new genotype.

In the next chapter I will offer a tentative definition of artistic value which needs further factual verification, just as does the handling of the genesis of artistic value presented in this chapter. To say this is to advertise that the accumulation of facts may point to different conclusions. The chief problem in verification, I should add, has to do with the differences among the major ethnocultural traditions. Is it reasonable to expect that the same constants would recur in the Indian, the Chinese, and the European heritages of art and aesthetic experience? This question must be studied without equivocations. A collective approach is needed, for surely only the coordination found in a research institute entirely devoted to this question, and drawing not only on aestheticians and art historians but on anthropologists as well, can hope to provide a conclusive answer.

The methodological strategy which I propose does require just such resources for its full implementation. I should also add that the usefulness of the present hypothesis will not be lessened if its tentative conclusions are finally disproved. However, on the evidence available (see, for example, the Fall 1965 issue of the *Journal of Aesthetics and Art Criticism*), it appears that the recurrence of basic properties will prove transcultural. Why? Such concepts as harmony, rhythm, symmetry, mimesis, expression, catharsis, and *homo ludens* occur again and again in the cultures of East and West.

Finally, I must emphasize that it is inherent to the principles of my methodology that the values of art as we define them carry no prescriptive force for the future of art. We can make no blueprint of what is to come. We can only study the present, very unsettled situation from the standpoint of what have been the constants, and inquire of recent developments, which seem to annihilate form and take the shape of life itself, whether they in fact destroy everything in the aesthetic tradition. Happenings seem careless of artistic structure, but do they depart entirely from aesthetic patterning? In this light, it would seem an error should anyone want to dismiss the present analysis "because there have been later artistic developments" (which in their turn, of course, will be challenged and eclipsed).

In any case, Umberto Eco's fascinating *Opera aperta; forma e indeterminazione nelle poetiche contemporanee* (Milan, 1962) offers persuasive argument that the "open" artistic structure—Eco sometimes calls it the "work of art in action"— will continue to assert an internalized coherence and specificity in the familiar matrix of our everyday world. Indeterminacy and ambiguity are the most ancient telltale traits of works of art; and, thus, what we see at present, Eco holds, is simply a modification in the expected role of the artist, the perceiver, and the result which relates and unifies them.

This standard triadic schema has grown elastic or fluid, much more dynamic. The process of *theatricalization* of the fine arts and music shifts the attention to *creativity itself*, downgrading the created product; the *act of expressing* reduces the lasting result of the expression to secondary importance. Even literature has become involved to a point, though it is resistant to this trend of theatricalization. There is, for example, Julio Cortazar's *Rayuela* (1963), a stochastic playing of the artist's thoughts in such way as to entangle the reader in the search for the meaning of his existence and, also, the meaning of what is termed the domain of art. Perhaps the future of art will demand a modification (i.e., extension) of the concept of structure (pattern). A work of art's internal structure might lose some of its significance; instead, there would predominate the structure of a *scene* that comprehends the artist, the public, and their mutual achievement. Beyond this we must not anticipate. We should bear in mind, as respects the lacunae in the prognosis, that no *rebus instantibus* definition of art could say more. It appears, to my way of thinking, that aesthetics may profit from the example of Hegel's "Owl of Minerva," which never ventures forth until dusk. Aesthetics should follow artistic developments and not attempt to precede them.

Notes

1. Unfortunately, my essays on the nature of value facts (a question which is only briefly touched upon in this chapter) have not yet been translated into English. They have been published in Polish in *Studia Filozoficzne* (no. 4, 1967; no. 1., 1968).

2. M. Rader, ed., *A Modern Book of Esthetics*, 3rd ed. (New York, 1960); E. Vivas and M. Krieger, eds., *The Problems of Aesthetics* (New York, 1953); M. Weitz, ed., *Problems in Aesthetics* (New York, 1959).

3. R. Bayer, *Traité d'esthetique* (Paris, 1956), pp. 234, 238–239.

4. G. Morpurgo-Tagliabue, *L'Esthetique contemporaine* (Milan, 1960), p. 612.

5. See, for example, B. Ghiselin, ed., *The Creative Process* (Berkeley and Los Angeles, 1954).

6. M. C. Beardsley and H. M. Schueller, eds., *Aesthetic Inquiry: Essays on Art Criticism and the Philosophy of Art* (Encino, Calif., 1967), pp. 171–187.

7. N. Rescher presents a conception which is similar to mine on many points in his *Introduction to Value Theory* (Englewood Cliffs, N.J., 1969). For to ask whether values are well or ill founded, and to proceed to abolish the supposedly insuperable fact/value dichotomy and to admit perfectly objective standards, means to accept the peculiar factuality of values. I cannot describe here the detailed differences that separate Rescher's approach from my own. Let me only state that his formula for value (p. 9) — it is oriented to rationalized action entrenched in a positive attitude having concern for some beneficial state of affairs — does excellently fit economic or ethical behavior, but I doubt whether it encompasses, say, the aesthetic or purely cognitive values. For this reason, I prefer to understand values as a set of qualities (or a single quality) characterizing a given object, event, or action, dependent on sustaining agents, which should be viewed in sociohistorical short-term and long-term contexts, and entailing some specific, beneficial kind of experience, both in those individuals who initiate the constituting of this set of qualities (or single quality) and in those who respond to it. This tentative formulation also comprises aesthetic (artistic) values, in which case "action" applies only to the creative process and to one's contact with aesthetic objects, while the beneficial aim is "optimum success in conveying the artistic message to the world" and "achieving the peculiar satisfaction we term aesthetic." The aesthetic (artistic) value may be demarcated from others which are also intrinsic by the fact that it functions in several dimensions: it is sustained by natural, biophysiological values as it releases in the recipient a kind of equilibrium (homeostasis); it is primarily of a social and spiritual character, but can contribute as well to material and sociopolitical well-being. Note too that all of these dimensions provide data for the factual aspects of value analysis.

8. See, for example, K. Koffka, "Problems in the Psychology of Art," in *Art:A Bryn Mawr Symposium* (Byrn Mawr, 1940), pp. 209–220; R. Arnheim, *Art and Visual Perception* (Berkeley, 1954); and L. L. Whyte, ed., *Aspects of Form* (London, 1951), where the physicist, the neurophysicist, the biochemist, the botanist, etc., pool their understanding of aesthetics.

9. C. I. Lewis, *An Analysis of Knowledge and Valuation* (LaSalle, Ill., 1947), chs. 14 and 15; K. Aschenbrenner, "Aesthetic Theory—Conflict and Conciliation," *Journal*

of *Aesthetics and Art Criticism*, vol. 18, no. 1 (September 1959); S. Pepper, *The Sources of Value*, (Berkeley, 1958), ch. 13.

10. Rescher, *Value Theory*, also emphasizes the need for a philosophical delineation between neutral and value-laden objects and the importance of first determining value and only then ranking it. He speaks of these two operations as "valuation" and "evaluation" (pp. 65–66) — but he then proceeds unaccountably to use the term "evaluation" in another context to describe the fundamental axiological task: the defining of the valuable as such and prior to ranking. Rescher and I also agree in conceiving of a scale of value along which the differing degrees may be posted; this is what I have called, in my 1962 essay upon which this chapter is based, the "fundamental axiological-aesthetic continuum," which corresponds, I believe, to Rescher's ordinal value-scale.

11. Rescher, *Value Theory*, pp. 64–65, discusses such matters in terms of "worth."

12. Rader, *Modern Book of Esthetics*, p. xviii. See also F. C. Sparshott, *The Structure of Aesthetics* (Toronto, 1963), ch. 5 and the conclusion of ch. 17.

13. J. Stolnitz, *Aesthetics and Philosophy of Art Criticism* (Boston, 1960), pp. 371–372. Sparshott proves this point from the meta-aesthetic point of view in his *Structure of Aesthetics*, chs. 1 and 2. In the course of treating the various aesthetic theories which bear on the basic aesthetic problems, Sparshott succeeds in showing that philosophical commitment and axiological decisions are involved in the discussion of the meaning and validity of a concept of art, of the nature and kinds of aesthetic experience, and of judgment. For this reason, he justly calls aesthetics a philosophy of man.

14. J. Segal, "The Psychological Character of the Fundamental Problems of Aesthetics," *Przeglad Filozoficzny* (no. 8, 1911), 369–429; W. Witwicki, "A Letter on Aesthetics," ibid. (nos. 1–2, 1949), 25–35; S. Ossowski, *The Foundations of Aesthetics* (Warsaw, 1933), and "Subjectivism in Aesthetics," in *Ksiega pamiatkowa ku czci T. Kotarbinskiego* (Warsaw, 1934); M. Wallis, *Aesthetic Propositions* (Warsaw, 1932), and *Aesthetic Values: Gentle and Harsh* (Lodz, 1949); all works in Polish. I should stress that I do not attempt to cope here with the entirety of the views represented by these writers. I have restricted myself to what is predominant in the works mentioned and which, moreover, is relevant to my attempted typological scheme. In justice to the above-cited scholars, I must state that, for instance, M. Wallis, in his contribution "Verité et validité des propositions esthétiques" to the *Travaux du IX Congrès International de Philosophie* (XII: Paris, 1937), said that the aesthetic experience proper actualizes all of the aesthetic potentialities of the perceived object.

15. See note 14, above. For my own review of the third edition of this work, see "An Introduction to the Labyrinth of Aesthetics," *Studia Filozoficzne* (no. 5, 1959).

16. C. L. Stevenson, "Interpretation and Evaluation in Aesthetics," in M. Black, ed., *Philosophical Analysis* (Ithaca, N.Y., 1950); and "What is a Poem?" *Philosophical Review*, vol. 66, no. 3 (July 1957), pp. 329–362. A similar position is developed by Weitz in two essays: "Criticism without Evaluation," *Philosophical Review*, vol. 61, no. 1 (January 1952), pp. 59-65; and "Reasons in Criticism," *Journal of Aesthetics and Art Criticism*, vol. 20, no. 4 (Summer 1962), pp. 429–437.

17. M. MacDonald writes: "So to affirm that a work of art is good or bad is to commend or condemn, not to describe it" (p. 129). A. Isenberg says: "The truth of *R* never adds the slightest weight to *V* because *R* does not designate any quality the perception of which might induce us to assent to *V*" (p. 139). By "*R*" Isenberg means reason — the basis for value judgment — and by "*V*" he means the verdict, the judgment itself. There is left only the eye of the beholder, "whose praise or censure" in fact decides *N* (the norm), which comes to be asserted as a general statement that whatever possesses such and such qualities is *pro tanto* good.

18. B. C. Heyl, *New Bearings in Esthetics and Art Criticism* (New Haven, 1943), part 2, sec. 2; M. C. Beardsley, *Aesthetics: Problems in the Philosophy of Criticism* (New York, 1958), sec. 27; Stolnitz, *Aesthetics and Philosophy of Art Criticism*, pp. 409–419; D. Walsh, "Critical Reasons," *Philosophical Review*, vol. 69, no. 3 (July 1969), pp. 386–393. Since this chapter was initially written, the representatives of the linguistic trend in aesthetics have altered their views in some respects: see C. Barrett, ed., *Collected Papers on Aesthetics* (Oxford, 1965); and M. Mandelbaum, "Family Resemblances and Generalizations Concerning the Arts," *American Philosophical Quarterly* II(1965), pp. 219–228.

19. See also the interpretation given in J. Casey, *The Language of Criticism* (London, 1966), chs. 1 and 2. Casey draws on comments of G. Moore (*Philosophical Papers*, X) in respect to Wittgenstein's lectures of 1930–33.

20. This article can be found in J. Margolis, ed., *Philosophy Looks at the Arts* (New York, 1962).

21. Stolnitz, *Aesthetics and Philosophy of Art Criticism*, pp. 390–419, offers an interesting analysis of this conception. He sees in it two principal tendencies — one denying the possibility of a definition of values, the other admitting this possibility. Common to both approaches is the notion that if two persons make contradictory judgments about one and the same value, just one of them can be right: the one having "good taste."

22. See "On the Relativity of Values," *Przeglad Filozoficzny*, vol. 44, nos. 1–3 (1948), in Polish; "La valeur esthétique et le problème de son fondement objectif," paper delivered to the Third International Congress of Aesthetics, Venice, 1956; and "Bemerkungen zum Problem des ästhetischen Werturteils," paper delivered to the International Congress of Philosophy, Padua, 1958.

23. Ingarden, "On the Relativity of Values," pp. 92–93. I simplify here to the extent that I have left aside the problem of those artistic values which, according to Ingarden, are relative in their status of aesthetic values but also, qua intentional, have objective existence. Since this chapter appeared in its initial form, Ingarden has published a collection of all his axiological essays on questions of aesthetics, *Experience, Artwork, Value* (in Polish; Cracow, 1966). My critique of this book appeared in *Estetika* (Prague), 1970, no. 1.

24. Many complexities of interpretation in the phenomenological conception have been neglected here; however — and Ingarden stresses this moment particularly — the aesthetic object comes into existence as a product of intentional attitude, aesthetic experience in turn being unthinkable without the object having taken form. In

this sense, employing Ingarden's own interpretation, we might define his position as
relationist.

Complications of a similar nature are
raised by his latest statement: that *Wertur-
teilen* (i.e., verbalized aesthetic judgments)
do not necessarily articulate objective standards. This indeterminate conclusion precludes the possibility of obtaining axiological certitude here.

All the same, the objectivist version which
emerges from the pronouncements of Ingarden himself would appear to be more
correct. Why? First, because, with reference
to the latter point, he insisted on the objective character of the *aesthetische Bewer-
tung* (i.e., appraisal) which is the mediator
between the aesthetic experience and the
verbalized judgment. Second, though the
former point entails a complicated nexus
and would indeed require a detailed analysis of Ingarden's system, we can simply
repeat after Ingarden that the aesthetic
experience is founded on the artistic-tech-
nical "skeleton" (the primary intentional
object) and that the aesthetic object, which
is the terminal, absolute value regardless
of the different possible concretizations,
must necessarily comprise some kind of
reconstruction of the underlying valuational
qualities inherent in the schematic structure that we call the work of art. I am using
Ingarden's terminology here, and I should
add that in his view "objectivity" has diverse meanings depending both on one's
philosophy and on the kind of data under
study. According to the phenomenological
standpoint, those aesthetic values which
are of heterogeneous (i.e., dependent on
cognitive processes), secondary intentional
character (intrinsic both to the experience
and to the concretized object), are no less

objectively given than is the primary intentional dimension.

25. T. M. Greene, *The Arts and the Art of
Criticism*, 3rd ed. (Princeton, N.J., 1952)
pp. 4–5. In this same work, the author,
letting himself in for inconsistency, terms
artistic values a "tertiary quality," that is,
he justifies their objectivity by saying they
are dictated by certain inner mechanisms
as well as by the intrinsic properties of the
works of art. Such an understanding approaches gestaltism in the relationist variant
(the structures of the subject corresponding
to the structures of the object). See the article
in which the notion of tertiary quality is
thoroughly analyzed: C. C. Pratt, "Aesthetics," *Annual Review of Psychology*
(1961), pp. 71–92.

26. He calls such values subsistent objects,
in order to compare them with concepts
which are neither physical nor psychic
objects. For Joad on aesthetic value, see
Vivas and Krieger, *Problems of Aesthetics*,
pp. 474–479.

27. We should not omit to mention that
behind these formulations is located the
notion of deity, the Great Architect who
shapes and orders the world supernally.
Nonetheless, we have to deal here with
empirical attitudes, since the deity is understood in the guise of a most competent
watchmaker who has set everything going;
the frame of reference is the empirically
given mechanisms which, it is assumed, will
be comprehensible to everyone's reason.

28. See R. Gunsenhäuser and H. Kreuzer,
eds., *Mathematik und Dichtung* (Munich,
1965), pp. 295–311.

29. See M. C. Beardsley, "On the Generality
of Critical Reasons," *Journal of Philosophy*,
vol. 59, no. 18 (August 1962), pp. 477–
486.

30. W. E. Kennick, "Does Traditional Aesthetics Rest on a Mistake?" *Mind*, vol. 62 (1958), pp. 317–334.

31. Heyl, *New Bearings in Esthetics*, pp. 125–145; Beardsley, *Aesthetics*, pp. 530–543; Stolnitz, *Aesthetics and Philosophy of Art Criticism*, pp. 419–437.

32. Lewis, *An Analysis of Knowledge and Valuation*, chs. 12–15. I should add that, despite his general relationist outlook, Lewis wavers continually in his conclusions; now toward psychologism (the contemplative state, acquiescence to what is immediate in the mind, as a basis of value) and now toward objectivism (value as a property inherent in the object). The weakness of Lewis' position lies in his relationism being purely a logical proposition. Hence, he is given over to monotonous reiteration of an unvaried motif.

33. Koffka, "Problems in the Psychology of Art."

34. In Whyte, *Aspects of Form* pp. 196–208. The premises and conclusions of this kind of approach were set out by Arnheim in *Art and Visual Perception*. The same ideas are developed in his recent *Visual Thinking* (Berkeley, 1969). Notably again, nothing said there with regard to the intelligence of sensory responsiveness — shape patterns as a kind of abstraction, structuring as the recognition of generic traits, and the grasping of relationships within a whole — provides a key to the strategy for distinguishing aesthetic wholes. I set aside here the problem broached by Arnheim in chapters 2 and 3, where he seems to hold that authentic thinking is always and primarily visual. This biased, untrue thesis could not in any case be helpful in elucidating the complex response to pure and impure verbal media (literature, theater).

35. L. L. Whyte, "A Scientific View of the 'Creative Energy' of Man," in M. Philipson, ed., *Aesthetics Today* (New York, 1961), pp. 349–374.

36. R. Arnheim, *Picasso's Guernica: The Genesis of a Painting* (Berkeley, 1962).

37. See Heyl, *New Bearings*, pp. 141–144.

38. Atti del III. Congresso Internazionale di Estetica, Torino, 1957, p. 177.

39. Instrumentality means something different here from what it means to the relationists. The latter describe only the relation between a particular individual and a given object. What Boas indicated is the functional, changing relations between a particular social group in a given situation and a given class of objects, which, owing to considerations of one kind or another, are determined to be works of art. Heyl, Beardsley, and Stolnitz have, in some of their recent statements, clearly inclined to this interpretation, thus proving that no firm line demarcates relationism from sociological relativism. This kind of sociological standpoint is defended by Teddy Brunius, the Swedish aesthetician, when he speaks of the ethnocentric foundation of aesthetic value. (See his essay "The Uses of Works of Art," in Beardsley and Schueller, *Aesthetic Inquiry*, pp. 12–25.)

40. These lectures were reconstructed from students' notes and were issued only in 1967 in C. Barrett, ed., *Wittgenstein: Lectures and Conversations on Aesthetics, Psychology, and Religious Belief* (Berkeley, 1967).

41. Rescher, *Value Theory*, p. 118.

42. A. Child, "The Socio-Historical Relativity of Aesthetic Value," *Philosophical Review*, vol. 53, no. 1 (January 1944), pp. 1–22.

43. G. Salinas, "Storicita del giudicio estetico" [The historicity of aesthetic judgment], *Rivista di Estetica* (May–August 1960), pp. 213–221.

44. E. Utitz, *Grundlagungen der allgemeinen Kunstwissenschaft*, vol. 2 (Stuttgart, 1920), p. 292.

45. K. Marx, *Economic and Philosophical Manuscripts of 1844*, 2nd ed. (Moscow, 1961), p. 108. The pertinent texts are now presented in K. Marx and F. Engels, *On Literature and Art*, ed. L. Baxandall and S. Morawski (St. Louis, 1973).

46. "Our own proposition about beauty is this: whenever the affective elements in socially known things show social ordering, there we have beauty, there alone we have beauty." And: "Art, then, conditions the instincts to the environment and in doing so changes the instincts." Christopher Caudwell, *Studies and Further Studies in a Dying Culture* (New York, 1958), Part II, pp. 106, 112.

47. For rejections of a basis in nature, see V. Vanslov, *Problems of the Beautiful* (Moscow, 1957), and L. N. Stolovich, *The Aesthetic in Reality and in Art* (Moscow, 1959). Both works are in Russian; their positions are criticized (in English) by Victor Romanenko, in S. Mozhnyagin, ed., *Problems of Modern Aesthetics* (Moscow, 1969), pp. 121–157. Ivan Astakhov likewise defends a natural foundation, ibid., pp. 158–186. I might add here that Stolovich expresses an undue severity toward Dmitryeva's remarks recognizing "the elementary principles of beauty" in nature itself. Dmitryeva does not assert, as did Todor Pavlov, the existence in nature of preaesthetic and presocial elements. Rather, she simply puts forward an hypothesis analogous to that of the gestaltists. It may well be that Dmitryeva is perfectly correct. She is not unaware that natural properties are activated aesthetically only in a social environment. When Marx, in *A Contribution to the Critique of Political Economy* (Chicago, 1904), pp. 20, 211, wrote of a diamond on the breast of a harlot and, particularly, of the natural splendor of gold and silver, probably he had in mind such elementary protoaesthetic traits. I have set forth and analyzed the discussions by Soviet aestheticians regarding the genesis of artistic value, in the second chapter of my book *Between Tradition and a Vision of the Future* (in Polish; Warsaw, 1964).

48. K. Marx and F. Engels, *Collected Works*, vol. 13 (Moscow), p. 497.

49. See the interesting treatment of this matter by E. V. Ilyenkov, *The Dialectics of the Abstract and the Concrete in Marx's 'Capital* (in Russian; Moscow, 1960).

50. See the survey study by Wladyslaw Tatarkiewicz, "Objectivity and Subjectivity in the History of Aesthetics," *Philosophy and Phenomenological Research* (December 1963). It must be added that Tatarkiewicz leaves the historicist approach out of his account. Moreover, in light of arguments I have set forth here, his terminology seems vulnerable. He does not distinguish relativism from objectivism and he ignores any meeting ground of subjectivism with relativism. It may also be worthwhile to add to my own succinct account, above, that not only did relationism emerge from a context of objectivist-oriented medieval aesthetics, it also arose from the subjectivist trend in the eighteenth century; Hutcheson, Burke, and Kames, for example explained the correspondence of subjective and objective components as due to divine intervention. Attentive exegesis of Hume's "Standard of Taste" and Kant's *Kritik der Urteilskraft* will locate a relationist strand in the arguments. The third phase of this approach — in the shape of instrumentalism (i.e., the correspondence of a given set of values and given collective aesthetic opinions in a definite limited context) — came with socio-historical analysis as practiced from Mme. de Stael through the *doctrinaires* to Hippolyte Taine.

51. See C. G. Hempel, "Problems and Changes in the Empiricist Criterion of Meaning," in Nagel and Brandt, *Meaning and Knowledge*, pp. 17–27.

52. See C. G. Hempel, "Formen und Grenzen des wissenschaftlichen Verstehens," *Conceptus*, vol. 6, nos. 1–3 (Innsbruck, 1972), pp. 5–18.

53. I would like to express my thanks to Professor C. G. Hempel for his critical reading of this section and for encouraging me to keep my position.

54. E. Fischer, *The Necessity of Art* (New York, 1964), chs. 2 and 4; G. Lukács, *Die Eigenart des Aesthetischen* (Neuwied, 1963).

55. Marx, in the *1844 Manuscripts*, posed the question of the genesis of aesthetic value, or to use his own phrase, how primitive man made the transition from a magic-utilitarian attitude to a "mineralogical sense." To put it differently: How did socio-historical processes liberate a human artistic-aesthetic activity? Did they release natural powers? Marxism does not seem to deny *a limine* the contributions of gestaltism. Rather, it is able to assimilate and develop them, for it recognizes that early man — before he could create the first cave drawing, before he could tentatively pantomime the social performances he observed, before he could find aesthetic significances in color — had to go through a considerable development (preparation for a free practical and intellectual activity, the hands' mastery of numerous skills, the ability of people to understand one another with the aid of

language, the mastery of the mind over reality). In other words, if he thinks the gestaltists correct in saying that man is endowed with an innate propensity for "pregnant" structures, yet the marxist will want to return the investigation to the domain of culture (history) to test historically the biophysiopsychological hypothesis about a visual "thinking" in patterns.

Marxism affords a sophisticated and illuminating theory of labor considered as a process of "the humanization of nature" and, at the same time, the humanization of man. The conditions we have mentioned function only in a concrete social setting — which it is necessary to study thoroughly. When Marx wrote, in *A Contribution to the Critique of Political Economy*, that "the sensation of color is, generally speaking, the most popular form of aesthetic sense," he appeared to treat color as a natural aesthetic property. However, it is also Marx who cautions that this aesthetic function of color (i.e., gold and silver) is linked with a specific form of wealth. This problem is not elaborated or resolved by Marx. In any case, it appears to me that Marx's idea of beauty as one of "measure" (in German, *Mass*) accords with the gestaltist concept of "structure," and also with the "rhythm" of the inner and outer world of man as studied in the splendid essay by R. Bayer, "L'essence du rythme," in *Revue d'Esthétique*, vol. 6 (1953), pp. 277–290.

56. This problem was taken up by F. Braudel on a different philosophical basis; see "Histoire et science sociale: La longue durée," *Annales*, no. 4 (1958). His distinction of the history of "circumstances" (i.e., chronological history) from a "histoire de longue durée," is strongly analogous to my own distinction of sociological relativism from the historicist position proper.

57. M. Weitz, "The Role of Theory in Aesthetics," *Journal of Aesthetics and Art Criticism*, vol. 15, no. 1 (September 1956). Incidentally, this scholar held, in his *Philosophy of the Arts* (1950), a position much more restrained in its critical aspects and, as I see it, much more fruitful in its concluding deductions.

58. D. H. Parker, "The Nature of Art," *Revue internationale de philosophie*, no. 4 (1939), pp. 684–702. D. W. Gotshalk in his *Art and the Social Order* (Chicago, 1947) advances a similar conception, which centers upon the second of the properties here listed. Art is multivalent; yet it is vital to lend assistance to what is the basic value among the others (the term "multivalent" was introduced by the well-known American anthropologist Franz Boas). Gotshalk's trend of analysis approximates my own to some extent.

59. M. C. Beardsley, "The Definition of the Arts," *Journal of Aesthetics and Art Criticism*, 1961, no. 4.

60. See M. S. Kagan, "On Ways of Studying the Peculiarity of Art," *Problems of Aesthetics* (1960), pp. 46–84, an essay especially interesting for its polemical demarcations. Related articles by this author in English can be found in *Current Digest of the Soviet Press* (November 18, 1959), and *Soviet Studies in Philosophy* (Summer 1968). Kagan carries forward the position stated by A. Burov in his book (in Russian), *The Aesthetic Essence of Art* (1956 — excerpt in *Soviet Literature*, 1957, no. 3, in English), according to which art, appealing to all of of our psychic capacities, may be characterized as the synthetic embodiment of human life.

61. Thus Stolovich: "Man's aesthetic relation to reality is an integral, sensual — i.e., iconic, emotional and ideological relation, which psychically affirms man's place in reality." "Art — or the artistic — is a synthesis of the objective and subjective aspects of the aesthetic relation of man to reality." L. N. Stolovich, *The Object of Aesthetics* (in Russian; Moscow, 1961), pp. 69, 73.

In his book *The Aesthetic in Reality and in Art* (in Russian; Moscow, 1959) Stolovich offers another definition of the aesthetic. He speaks of "the dialectical unity of the material form with the sociohuman content" (p. 70). But such a definition leads to a peculiar "panaestheticism," that is, the admission of all phenomena which in some sense express the domination of man over nature (e.g., the gesture of a man who has gone up a high hill, or a diagram by a learned biologist), as aesthetic phenomena. Stolovich advances a number of important remarks regarding form as a characteristic trait or artistic value (pp. 51, 155–158); however, he also skews these remarks, as time and again he mixes up the genesis of the values in the labor process (whereof he writes sagely) and their significance within the structure of the work of art.

62. Dorothy Walsh justly termed art an alternative reality, as distinguished from possessing either the physical or the schematic (ideal) mode of existence ("The Cognitive Content of Art," *Philosophical Review*, vol. 52, no. 5 [September 1943], pp. 433–451). Many authors note this characteristic moment of art. Especially productive, in the scientific sense, is the view of Roman Jakobson who speaks of a poetic fragment as a specifically organized linguistic expression which "violates" the colloquial usage of

Chapter 2

What Is
a Work of Art?

The idea of art is at present undergoing a crisis. The definitions being offered are almost ludicrously numerous and diverse, while some writers express doubts about the possibility of any definition at all. I feel that any attempt to conceptualize art which hopes to prove persuasive must adopt a strategy which encompasses the uncounted variations among works of art, and does not exclude any field of artistic activity or any facet of cultural history. No easy task! Yet nothing less than this seems useful. How should we make a start? Our initial assumptions should not be overly simple, for we would then find ourselves hemmed in by them later on. The differences among the various arts should be examined carefully so that we shall not be tempted to isolate a single field of art as the universally valid aesthetic model. Various arts should be repeatedly consulted, and we should seek especially to determine what might be the common substratum (if not precisely bedrock) on which the arts gain their purchase and find their elaboration. By "substratum" I wish to indicate the long duration of specific historical situations, characterized by conflicts of many kinds which precipitate various attitudes, including philosophical and aesthetic orientations. Integral to the historical situations are specific sociopolitical and socioeconomic processes which often induce entire transformations of the precedent ideas about human beings and their world. While acknowledging and even emphasizing such great variations and transformations in and among the historical situations, we will also ask whether it is possible to locate some recurrent sociocultural data. Understood in this way, the substratum—and also the possible long-enduring definition of art which has to find its foothold there—must prove problematic in the extreme.

How indeed shall we conceive the origin and constitution of a possibly permanent phenomenon which we call art and which we consider by means of diverse aesthetic categories? The awareness of the problematic character of conceptualization has rapidly increased since the turn into the twentieth century. Nearly every long-preserved world view has been cast in doubt by recent scientific and technological discoveries as well as political events of a revolutionary character (starting with the October Revolution). Given these transformations in the domain of thought as a whole, it is not surprising that the previous idea of art has not held. The principle that art is constituted primarily by an imitation of reality, an idea which the European tradition had accepted since the Renaissance, has been over-

Written in Polish in 1964, this chapter was published in *Zeitschrift für Aesthetik und allgemeine Kunstwissenschaft*, vol. 14, no. 2 (1969). Its first appearance in English was in L. Baxandall, ed., *Radical Perspectives in the Arts* (Baltimore, 1972).

thrown by antimimetism. It is indispensable that we grasp this and other shifts in judgments concerning art in all of their *developmental character* and *concreteness*. Only then can attempts at definition be adequately verified.

Recent Developments

We may begin with the shift to a preponderantly antimimetic orientation towards the basic notion of art. It is symptomatic of such changes that in this instance diverse and indeed mutually antagonistic movements in the art world contributed to the end result. The decorative surfaces of the nabis and Matisse and the new use of space of Cézanne and the cubists undermined the *construzione legittima* of Alberti and Leonardo. Painters could now superimpose simultaneous views, thus adding a time dimension. The break with the impressionist-pointillist method of patterning small flecks of color, culminating in a form-and-color whole, was almost as great. Whether more or less mimetic, the "rival world" approximating our normal world was banished. Yet the ingenious new worlds of painterly imagination generally retained references to reality and they were in no sense divested of all objectivity or spaciousness. (The work of Léger and Picasso testify to this.)

The break with the precedent idea was carried further by those who sought to evoke reflex responses with coloristic systems and who were obsessed with the symphonic expressive impact of hues (Kandinsky, Delaunay, Larionov, Goncharova). The ultimate possibilities of an abstract art were deduced by Malevich, Mondrian, and Strzemiński. And what of the dadaists and the constructivists? Their immediate tradition was not fauvism or Delaunay's Orphism, but cubism —especially the synthetic forms. The pursuit of unprecedented optical inputs was abandoned, in favor of provocative "exact" duplicates of fragments of reality (Ernst's collages) or engineering feats (Tatlin, Rodchenko, El Lissitsky). While the analytical cubists and the Orphists invented means to present a uniquely fashioned object in painting, the dadaists and constructivists championed the painfully non–art objects of everyday as the basis of their aesthetics. But in any case *mimesis was excluded*, and the traditional, sharp distinction between art and the actual world was abandoned. Brancusi's sculpture *Bird in Space* was treated as an ordinary piece of metal by New York customs officials. This is as indicative of the modern status of mimetism as the dadaist protest in Duchamp's urinal, entitled *Fountain*, or Picabia's inkpot, *The Holy Madonna*.

Dada was an eruption that helped to destroy the prior distinction between art and nonart by attacking the concept of mimesis and also by exalting the idea of *ugliness.* An end was put to the absolute primacy of the beautiful (in its earlier sense, oriented to Greek and Renaissance models). The naturalists had earlier brought the ugly into art, but the dadaists, along with the surrealists, were the first to attack directly the "isolated" and "harmonious" character of art which some believed could free us from the necessity of understanding our moral and political responses to it. For the naturalists, ugliness had been similar to the sublime and the tragic; above all, it was a protest against the beautiful and its claim to exclusivity. The dadaists and surrealists also preferred the ugly in the name of life. They took a new look at the social order, and their imaginations respected neither dogma nor boundary.

The dadaist attitude was revived with the spectacles concocted by Yves Klein in Paris. When Klein's model climbed into a tub of blue paint and then impressed her "pose" on a white canvas, more than a moral scandal was involved. This was a destructive aesthetic gesture from an artist who evoked illusionism in art the better to debunk it. Robert Rauschenberg's *The Bed* (1962) consists of the artist's own blanket and pillow which he has sprayed with color. Here is at once a furtherance of the dadaist protest against aestheticism and a mockery of a civilization in which possessions are everything. Not dissimilarly, Wladislaw Hasior, a Pole, exalts banality by using rubbish as his basic material, which he proceeds to ornament with plebeian motifs from folklore. Ugliness is here given a symbolic sense owing to the tradition to which the artist relates and which he at the same time deconsecrates.

A parallel should be seen between protests against such principles as the imitation of given reality or the rule of the beauty of antiquity, and the challenging of the aesthetic principle of generally understood, real, and logical necessities. In accordance with prevailing thought, nineteenth-century writing employed an omniscient narrator whom the reader could equate with the author himself, whose implicitly accepted task was to describe and finally explain the settled facts of human existence. In painting and sculpture, the meaning of the images could similarly be deduced from an internalized order. When such art lost its religious organizing principle, trust was still placed in philosophy or in science, or in both.

The twentieth century has seen this confidence in order and necessity undermined. The arts have become a field for independent philosophical exploration, and the idols of earlier times have given way to His Highness, Accident.

A clear-cut distinction must be made here. On one side we place the subjective manifestations, the visions that we associate with the stream of consciousness or the unconscious. On the other side we locate the efforts, prominent in the fifties and sixties, to consider experience itself as a kind of lottery. (Sometimes an actual machine was used to approximate the demise of any human sense of necessity in events.) Inspiration is a precious notion for those involved in the former approach; the idea runs through Bergson's *élan vital*, Freud's method of free association, and Breton's "inner model" and "automatic writing." In the visual arts, the tendency evolves from fauvism and expressionism through surrealism to, more recently, action painting.

Those who see experience as a lottery are indebted to information theory and are fascinated by antientropic systems of given elements and the unexpected emergence of new combinations of these elements. This sense of liberty to conceive new dispositions of material elements is seen in such recent experiments as op art and all of the plastic-luministic-kinetic efforts to achieve unprecedented arrangements in desanctified spaces. In his novel *Joker*, the Polish writer Kazimierz Brandys portrays the convulsions of contemporary civilization and the uncertainty of everything which might have continued to provide a basis for the generalizations of the aesthetician. He says of the artist's response to the confusion in the world that the task of the writer is to give embodiment to an "invisible" world, by which he means the writer's own constructs. The application to visual arts is immediate, where "invisible" may be taken to certify the inclusion of any or all physical or psychical phenomena in a work, whether these elements are eruptions from the artist's ego or unconscious or the result even of "chance" games played with the material according to stochastical laws alone.

These often elaborate forays in the name of accident or liberty against constant and comprehensible regularity started in the first decades of our century, at the same time that another tendency was crystallizing. Moholy-Nagy tried, his wife says, to execute an art object by issuing directions over the telephone, his aim being to *avoid all individual intervention* in the evolving work. By denying direct contact he hoped to get a cool and precise structure that could readily be duplicated. His aim was a depersonalized, purely intellectual beauty (if that term is still applicable in this context). This was a confirmation, from the artist's viewpoint, of the thrust of *artisan* and now of *machine products* into the domain of art. This trend probably began with William Morris and triumphed with Gropius; aesthetics has not since been able to deny it. Some basic precepts had accordingly to be revised—for example, the thesis, advanced by eighteenth century aestheticians and carried on by Benedetto Croce, that *original expression* is the chief precondition for a work of art. To be sure, that thesis is still defended by existentialists and Catholic personalists, but in the 1930s it had already been sharply disputed by Walter Benjamin and Lewis Mumford, who in their discussions of art in the era of machine reproduction, asked: What credence indeed can be given to the requirement of original expression when machines turn out aesthetically pleasing products without limit? This argument was reinforced by the findings of art historians and ethnologists who studied primitive and Oriental art as well as that of the Middle Ages and found that in many eras entrenched example and canonic rule were essential (and sometimes more important than the artist's individual expression).

Two more aesthetic antiprinciples can thus be added to those formulated earlier (antimimetism, pursuit of ugliness and a raw reality, and emphasis on accidentality). The first concerns *serial production* as against individual creation. (In some artistic manifestos, such as the Bauhaus and the Proletcult, the denial of individual creation is a result of the call for artistic collectivism.) The second concerns *machine production* as against handwork. The latter phenomenon derives from an appreciation of serial and mass products as aesthetically valuable creations. And because of recent scientific and technological advances, the emphasis has shifted further: now the focus is not so much on the impersonal product as on the *productive forces*. Do-it-yourself equipment is able to produce an object which the maker can and does describe as a work of art.

The latest developments seem to be continuing this shift. Minimal art—with its zealously antiexpressionist tendency, now closely oriented to architecture—can be reckoned an elaboration of the engineering-constructivist idea. Conceptual art has gone further than either the depersonalized technological art of constructivism or the destructive gestures of dada, and its critical stance is accordingly the most extreme. Conceptual artists assume that their product is primarily and rightly an *inquiry into* the troubled status of art, and that they should undertake their work in a manner similar to that of the critic. Dadaists sought to dissolve art into the life flux; conceptualists have the same aim, but they turn their backs even on the art market and the public. Their particular frame of reference is precisely the predominant *problematic* outlook of our time.

I do not wish to bring forward every piece of evidence encouraging a new view of the visual arts. It is enough to show that *the boundaries between the artistic and the nonartistic have been blurred*. In poetry, a similar development has occurred which is due to the incessant claims of various prose-oriented schools. The time-honored image, which palpably asserted its reference to an object, has been

replaced by a grid system of imaginative representations and concepts intended
to create an atmosphere at once emotional and intellectual. Another development
is the poetry of rebellion, which makes use of blunt idiom so that nothing will inhibit communication—a lyricism breaking away from the forms of melodic prosody
and the rhythms of balanced strophes. In both of these literary tendencies, the
old boundary stakes have become unfixed. Contemporary literary works are rather
like rhymed reportage, vivid philosophical essays, or prose statements in which
unusual care is taken to compose the word order.

   Many artistic manifestos have been issued to buttress such tendencies, and there
is no need to discuss all of them here. I shall mention just two movements, futurism
(in Russia) and imagism (in England), which sharply questioned the sense and value
of artistic fiction. Admittedly, there are differences of theory and practice, but we
should not overlook the kinship of Osip Brik, Vladimir Mayakovsky, and Viktor
Shklovsky with T. E. Hulme and T. S. Eliot. They share the concept that poetry provides, among other things, an equivalent to social and philosophical attitudes.
These attitudes are expressed not through description but through *signs*. Instead
of traditional rhyme and stanzaic construction, these poets demand *inner rhythm;*
instead of eidetic metaphor impressing itself on the reader with little impairment,
they demand an abstract metaphor operating on the imaginative faculty and emotions in a conceptual framework. The Polish avant-garde groupings *Zwrotnica*
(Switch Station) and *Linia* can also be placed here.

   What does this mean for representation in writing? Employing a minimum of
words to evoke a maximum of associations, eschewing the rhythmic-melodic heritage and the "banal" images of ordinary speech, placing a premium on poetic
craft, constructing determinate structures, and pursuing expressive means that
lead off and away from the material world, favoring elliptical turns of phrase and
compound effects—these are the features of an antimimetic poetics. What happens
is that poetic and prosaic language are no longer polarized, lyrical and narrative
communications are diminished, and the listener is urged to an *intellectualized* response. There is no doubt that this poetics has a determinate relation to the historical moment: it speaks for culture and against nature, for cognitive intellectual
effort and against intuition, for a vision of the future and against the inadequacies
of the present.

   Modern poetry, like painting, has appropriated the ugly to its aims. Although
the distasteful fascinations in Eliot's "Prufrock" are not identical to the ugly as
handled by the Polish poets Stanislaw Grochowiak and Miron Bialoszewski, there

is a common acceptance of reality and a desire to name it without euphemism, in its ordinary and often displeasing defectiveness. Again as in painting, accident has been firmly established in modern poetry. The catastrophic underlying attitude has erupted far more pervasively than in visual art because the verbal medium has much more capacity to express it. But poetry has *not* lent itself to machine manufacture, although some parasurreal texts have been thus accomplished. Collectivistic tendencies can be found, however, especially in the first decade of Soviet writing.

Problems with the Old Aesthetics

The foregoing examples were drawn from the visual arts and literature, but the trend is also discernible in every other field of aesthetic activity — it seems to dominate our period. What is it that ultimately has happened to art in the twentieth century that leads us to speak of the crisis in the idea of art and that hampers our search for an adequate definition of the aesthetic object? The problem is both historical and theoretical, and to avoid artificially separating the two aspects, we should construct a model — a patterning of the evidence — which corresponds as fully as possible to the artistic phenomena and aesthetic ideas which are crosspollinating in our time.

I think the most useful framework for the model that we shall find is the patterning of aesthetic ideas in the first decade of the twentieth century. At that time the capitalist system, whose sociopolitical stability had been highly plausible through the entire industrial revolution, was deteriorating. The revelatory thought of Marx, Freud, Einstein, Nietzsche, and Bergson was making rapid gains, while the established philosophical, religious, moral, and aesthetic ideas were losing credence.

What were the traditional aesthetic principles which were under attack?

1. *A definite hierarchy of values exists, reflecting a settled order in the world.* The artist must only find his own means to express the known truth. By these means, which are sensuous and imaginative, the artist confirms and gives homage to his own place in this order — the place, that is, reserved for Beauty.

2. *All true art ultimately relies on mimesis.* The kinds of representation may be different, but every artist (including the architect and the composer) somehow conveys his own attitude towards the social and psychosocial phenomena that he renders for an audience. Artists, in their own ways, intensify and condense our sense of being in the world, which includes feelings as well as observations. (On the relation between expression and mimesis, see chapter 5.) Although other aes-

thetic categories were distinguished and respected, mimesis was nonetheless acknowledged to have primary significance.

3. *The artist commands a special talent which he has developed and disciplined over the years into skill or virtuosity (techne).* His position is institutionalized — recognized by an academy, granted advanced schooling, etc. His technique demarcates the artist from the ordinary person with a merely amateur interest in art.

4. *Art manifests an outstanding individuality.* The more we study and experience the emanations of the artist, the more we partake of his genius from afar. The artist is a kind of sacred person or prophetic spokesman.

5. *The domain of art consists of three interdependent yet distinct factors: the artist, the work of art, and the audience.* The role of the last is to respond, as fully as possible, to the experience of the artist as it has been embodied in and transmitted by the work of art, which is the most important element of the triad. *Ars longa, vita brevis;* all of the values of the preceding four points are preserved in this mediating object, the guarantor of the author's immortality.

What has become of these principles, acknowledged by all only fifty or sixty years ago? Artists no longer defer to a fixed body of knowledge and truth, and much of the old religion and morality has vanished. The twentieth-century artist is on his own (even if in the company of colleagues), in his search for fragile but tenable truths, which he always considers relative.

Mimesis? Its credentials have been revoked from a number of sides. The arts and crafts movement obtained a central and competing place in the sun after four centuries of neglect. In writing, drama, painting, and sculpture, those bastions of mimesis, artists came to think that representationalism was just one of their available resources, and perhaps not the most challenging or interesting at that. Appia and Craig altered the look of the stage. Schönberg broke with all "programmatic" elements in music, substituting the twelve-tone system of composition; and following him came the composers of aleatory music, which depended on chance arrangements. In film, the ideas of the traditional novel and drama held fast until the 1950s, when they were dealt a severe blow by Godard, Mekas, and the "underground" directors.

Look around now. Poetry becomes "concrete," increasingly graphic. In the novel, time and characterization are submitted to shuffling and dicing; plot and narration scarcely retain a foothold. Theater is the scene of ritual events and happenings. The upheaval grows more and more profound.

What about artistic technique? Surely that is still in season. But consider *objets trouvés*, the work of the primitives, which if powerful is often crude, and, above all, the work of artists specializing in life events or in natural objects that need only be "set in motion" or "arranged" for the desired result to be achieved. Certainly, technique in the sense of arduously gained skill has little meaning here, at least as intended by the academies of the past.

Great individuality has also grown doubtful, and, with it, the sacred or prophetic function of the artist. Is not the artist of today often a wistful jesting outsider, a mocker of his own pretensions and role who hides behind the technological appurtenances of the age? We can see Marcel Duchamp effacing his role and then retiring from art entirely at the start of this unassuming route that leads to minimal and conceptual art. We see the similarly modest individualities of John Cage, Merce Cunningham, Allan Kaprow, and the *nouveau roman* authors.

What of the art object? Surely *it* has not slipped from its acknowledged place in the triad! The answer is that while artistic activity still becomes objectified somehow, the appeal of immortality just is not there as it was. The work of art is often deliberately conceived by the avant-gardé to be ephemeral, sometimes disposable after one use, as in happenings. This changes the role of the audience profoundly. It is asked to contemplate less and cooperate more. Such situations, which occur not only at some happenings but also increasingly in fiction, music, and the plastic arts, are known as "open forms."

Some may protest that I have concentrated here on the most freakish examples of current unrest in the arts. But just the fact that these are the features attracting the most attention indicates, I think, that *the handed-down aesthetic model has lost its authority*. Also, the phenomena I cite have demonstrated a staying power, and their vitality forbids us to treat them as extravagances, as exotic hybrids. They have already changed the pattern of the evidence on which we base aesthetic thought, and they foreshadow only further change. We are required, accordingly, to ponder on the new aesthetic categories we think we might use — even if we may decide (as I do) that there is much in the transmitted (European) heritage that may be rescued and refurbished.

Towards a Transhistorical Definition

What I want to do now is develop an idea of art which can hold its ground despite the current crisis. Such a definition must run a gamut of difficulties. Artists will voice the strongest objections — they generally have a deep distaste for definition,

which they feel encroaches upon their independence of action. In my opinion, this
is erroneous, although some epochs of cultural history seem to confirm their fears.
Historians of the arts may also protest, citing the many different developments
in any given genre. I feel that this objection is also invalid, since the definition I shall
propose here is concerned with ultimate regularities and does not deny the special
characteristics of art at a particular moment.

Philosophers of art may have the deepest misgivings. The aesthetic school that
developed under the stimulus of Wittgenstein and especially of his last work, *Philosophical Investigations* (1953), holds that no real definition of art can be given.
This school argues that the definitions we use are arbitrary; we accept, according
to the "rules of the game," the proposition that a certain class of objects is to be
considered art, and we proceed to treat those objects in a specific way — which is
to say that we *ought* to regard them in this certain way, drawing delight from their
texture and rhythm, etc., without permitting ourselves a response which would
be appropriate to other kinds of objects, meant perhaps to impart information or
moral guidance or to perform a useful function.

In reply to this position, many other aestheticians in the analytical Anglo-American school say that in any given field we may encounter variability in the object
under investigation, but that this should not lead us to an utter distrust of definition. This opinion is shared by Janina Kotarbińska, who, in her very interesting
study "Controversy on the Applicability Limits of Logical Methods" (*Logique et
Analyse*, April 1965), has demonstrated the position of Wittgenstein and his followers to be too extreme. Her arguments are convincing to me, but they do not
exhaust the problem. Definitions are always historically conditioned; a new element may require that the definition be enlarged or perhaps limited. Art is not such
an exceptional phenomenon that the concept of art must continually fall prey to
ambiguity. If we were dependent entirely on logic, I could understand that this
would be a situation for panic; but I do not think that the methodology should or
even can be oriented by logical analysis alone.

An attempt at an authentic definition of art, founded on matters of fact, is both
feasible and necessary. It must be supported, of course, by the history of aesthetics,
considered in close relation to the history of culture. I believe that a feeling and
idea of art, common to diverse cultures, came about when art emerged from production and magic and that in the subsequent history of artistic creation the basis
of that rudimentary conception has remained, even up to the present. This rather
astonishing situation is perhaps owed in part to some "constants" in human na-

ture, but primarily to the cumulative effect of cultural experiences. Admittedly, the observer is likely to be most struck by the shifts in working artistic categories. But this ongoing process, with its psychological and sociological explanations, does not exclude the possibility of certain ultimate regularities (invariables). Neither unqualified relativism nor unqualified objectivism is admissible. If the idea of art, along with man and society, were to undergo *total* change in a given epoch, what right would we then have even to speak of a history of the "arts," and how could we dare to discuss their internal development?

A number of attempts to provide an adequate definition of art have been made. Most have gone wide of the mark, usually because they take a single side of the art object as absolute. I especially value attempts to approach art in terms of an entire range of attributes, and this is my own purpose. I now turn to what seems to me the first consideration.

A Structure of Sensuously Given Qualities A structure of sensuously given qualities is more than a precondition; it is the foundation for the concept of art. (We shall see later whether the structure of qualities is exclusively sensuous and is always directly given.) By structure, I mean in general a class of elements that comprise a coherent whole. The notion of a coherent whole needs to be clarified. According to the gestalt theorists (Wertheimer, Köhler, Koffka), the structural elements *do not* cohere as a "sum total." Rather, the attribute of overall structure absolutely conditions and determines the attributes of the elements. The general purport of the gestalt conception has been affirmed and developed from another angle by modern structuralists such as Hans Sedlmayr and Roman Ingarden. According to them, the structure exerts a fundamental formative capacity, to which the elementary qualities are subordinate. Ingarden describes it as a harmonious unity. In this sense artistic structures may be compared with organic structures. [1]

Another concept of structure is provided by those whose premises stem from information theory; Max Bense, for instance, whose most detailed treatment of the subject is in his four-volume *Aesthetica* (1944–60). In place of the traditional macroaesthetics, Bense proposes a microaesthetics based on determinate materials, that is, classes of signs that cannot be differentiated in terms of content and form. Each class constitutes one link of a given series; the elements of the classes have functional relationships with one another that can be stated in mathematical formulas. Here the structuring process is statistically rational; it is distinguishable from other physical processes in terms of the very slight probability whereby X or Y will crop

up. The artistic structure, like any other structure, is supplied with antientropic
signs. Its proportion — in the exact mathematical as in the aesthetic sense — is its
information.[2]

From these examples (which afford, of course, but a narrow glimpse into the
discussion)[3] the fundamental differences over the concept of structure as a basic
philosophical-aesthetic structure can be characterized as follows:

1. Is the structure an enumerable (and consequently quantifiable) system of discrete elements, or a definite qualitative system?
2. Is the structure, if composed of a qualitative system, something which can be
taken in only by an intuitive grasp of the whole, or is it accessible to analytic
modes of procedure?
3. Is the structure an ideal-homogeneous whole, or are its particularities more
clearly articulated in its so-called oppositions?
4. Is the structure comprehensible only in and through itself, or rather only in the
context of a larger system, of infrastructure or suprastructure?
5. If the character of the given structure is defined by a more comprehensive system,
the suprastructure, is this system then exclusively synchronic, or is it also diachronic?
6. Is the structure a logical construct, or is it an empirical given, in which case it
may be assumed that the structuring operation is historically determinate, that
is, congruent with the given cultural system in its diachronic as well as its synchronic aspects?

To each of these questions I would offer the same answer: only the second part
is to be affirmed. In my view, artistic structures cannot be reduced to quantifiably
rational classes, even if in the terms of certain systems this is procedurally possible and effective. It is also impossible to accept the intuitive understanding of
the whole, as Dilthey and the phenomenologists would have it, since this intuitive
procedure is not controllable. And the conception of Lévi-Strauss provokes doubts
because he acknowledges only synchronic connections between the system and
the structure, and, in his view, the alignment of the system with a set model may
be programmatically worked out, while, moreover, the model of any given structure
is rooted in the recurrent systems.

We may say this: every artistic structure signifies. Its significance results from
the given fundamental sign system to which it appertains. Simultaneously, however, every artistic structure is expressive, that is, one can explain it — in terms of
synchronic/diachronic norms — only by reference to the larger wholes which define

its modifications and its evolutionary rhythms. Hence I adopt here the standpoint
of Marx as he formulated his methodological theses and commentaries in *Capital.*[4]

I should add that artistic structures cannot be specified in terms of their particular character and their dependency upon historical circumstances nearly as precisely as they can according to the classes in mathematical set theory. K. E. Trangy
has said in this regard that the further we depart from logic and mathematics and
the closer we come to aesthetics, the more difficult it becomes to trace out firmly
the basic concepts (structure, elements, and the relations between them), and the
greater is the trend to apprehend the structure as a whole. All the same, Trangy
wrongly holds that it is harder than in other domains of humanities to locate significant, decisively dominant elements and relations in the structure of a work of art.
On the contrary; generally, these coherent entities possess a central focus and are
organized according to some defining main principle. The elementary qualities
enter it in differing orders of arrangement, to be sure, and in the most variegated
associations with one another. I shall have more to say of this in a moment. But
first a point that I believe more important must be clarified in the context of our
discussion of the idea of structure. I am talking of the view which holds that the
structure need not be harmonious. Erich Kahler has correctly pointed out that mis-
understandings can arise on this point, but he has not himself explained what
should be meant by harmony.

Of course, harmony might be said to imply the full agreement of all elements
with one another. Unfortunately, the concept of agreement is not precise, but it
is difficult to replace it with anything better. We can qualify and expand on it by
pointing to its contrary, that is, to discord or disturbance among the elements. In
saying that the elements are in a state of agreement, we mean to say that in a certain sense they are of the same kind, they possess like characteristics. They have
potency owing not to contrast but to similarity. The totalities put together of them
are generally static or barely dynamic. Such structures certainly have value and are
necessary, but just as valuable and necessary are disharmonious, dynamic structures. (We owe to Mieczyslaw Wallis the distinction between two kinds of values,
the gentle and the harsh, in which, of course, there can also be intermediate gradations.)

The problem of harmonious and disharmonious systems is linked closely with
the particularity of the *oppositions* that are characteristic of artistic structures.
In systems of the first type, opposition indicates distinct polar points of a composition (above—below, center—edge, right—left, etc.) or the unity of a whole evoked

by means of a dominant key, as against the multiplicity of constituent parts. In systems of the second type, the opposition is more clearly recognizable, for it assumes the character of a conflict. Two other circumstances permit us to speak of opposition as a characteristic trait of a work of art. The phenotype appears here associated with the genotype—the individuum belongs to a class of determinate objects and, at the same time, stands out from it. And inasmuch as we encounter old and new elements coming into collision with one another in a work, the synchronic system, which is a part of a diachronic system, testifies to the stylistic transformations.

When we speak of the structure of *sensuously given qualities*, we think of forms, colors, tones, graphic signs, black-and-white signals (on the filmstrip), movements (in dance), etc., which, within a great totality, comprise a totality of lower degree. Such a totality is at a lower degree as a result of the particularity of the single elements and of their partial systems; however, as a result of the association of elements and of the partial systems, and finally of the possible contrast, dissonance, and even contrariety among the elements, it has its *own expressive power*. Hence, the gravitational point shifts from the structure to the qualities which especially catch our attention, inasmuch as it is primarily the *sensuous* side of the phenomenon which holds us. In such cases we would be justified in speaking not so much of a structure but rather of hierarchically or nonhierarchically structured qualities. Yet it would be a mistake to stress either the qualities or the structure exclusively. The interrelation of these two moments is so complete that they cannot be separated from one another.

I think, for example, of the poems of Marinetti and of Mlodożenec, which are sustained chiefly by a complex sound-painting. These poets hope to liberate the word from syntax. They aim at an intuitively comprehended interrelation of words, and at times they achieve a coherent totality, determined by a peculiarly autonomous "syntax." In op art, too, the structure cannot be parted from the qualities. More than that—and of this I want to speak now—that coherence is directly linked with what is termed the relative autonomy of the work of art. When poetry is understood to be a specially ordered arrangement (a syntax or metaphor unambiguously differing from what prevails in the contemporary language system), when the principles of the Russian formalists are adopted and astonishment-exciting devices are employed with the aim of *freshening perception*, when Brecht by way of invoking the *Verfremdungseffekt*, "estrangement effect," outfits his actors in masks and demands that they play their roles with distance so that the sense of the *Lehrstucke*, "learning plays," will be emphasized—in all these cases emphasis is placed upon the structure with all its qualities, and the structure is set apart from the surrounding world, as something relatively self-sufficient.

I have underscored here *the double-sidedness of the configuration* to bring out the multiplicity of artistic structure and to note its characteristic attribute. This attribute leads us at a minimum, to stress the qualities and to distinguish artistic structure from any related structures. It must be asked, nonetheless, which *concrete properties* shall be ascribed to the structure, from among rhythm, symmetry, proportion, unity in multiplicity, or the balancing of elements which incorporates dissonances — in brief, any of those properties that are put forward as a nearer description of the aesthetic system. Every one of them seems important, yet not one of them can be considered a sufficient characterizing trait. Nor can any ensemble of these attributes be deemed perfectly characteristic of the work of art. We must proceed here with caution, because we are considering the most different sorts of combination, in different genres. Only all the traits together — and we have not by any means mentioned every one — provide the axiological attributes of a genre. They are the foundation for particular modifications in the individual works. As concerns the qualities, the situation is akin to that with structure. Diverse theories of art describe the qualities variously, especially in their concrete manifestations, such as sonority, vivacity, attack, or their opposites. Here every single work of art modifies the axiological traits of a genre.

The problem of the sensuous qualities is compounded owing to their universal compass. In the arts that function only, or primarily, through the word (literature, the spoken theater), the sensuous qualities are "transparent." In some poetic works we can still elaborate a phonemic-rhythmic configuration, as with the poems of Paul Verlaine, the "word-melodies" of Julian Tuwim, the "irrational language" of A. Kruchonykh and Velimir Khlebnikov, and the *Ursonata* of Kurt Schwitters. In prose, on the contrary, the graphic signs and the phonetic signs always express meaning, and a definite object world is built up through their aid. For this reason these qualities are termed *indirectly evocative*. We indicate their mediative function in the communicating of so-called literary images — not what Ingarden calls *Ansichten*, "appearances" (which cannot be parted from the fictive gestalt and the object), but rather the particularized phenomena and occurrences that the imagination asserts and that either have happened or are said to have happened. These, as we know, are structured by dint of narrative, action, fable, etc.

For certain rather exceptional readers the novel — like poetry — can be an eidetic experience, that is, they can actually "see," uniquely perceive (with all the senses)

the events and images while reading. However, for most of the reading public
(quite in accordance with the medium, which is basically noneidetic), only a certain
aura of semivisual or semiauditory correlatives adheres to the perceived complexes
of statements. Thus, through the meaning of the text and its commingling with
imagination, the perceptive response can, in some degree, be stimulated. Helping
to foster an almost total decline in eidetic possibilities has been twentieth-century
poetry, whose principle is almost the very opposite of *ut pictura poesis,* "let poetry
paint." The meaningful elements in it crowd aside the eidetic iconicity — proving
much more strong and efficacious than in the older, descriptive or narrative poetry.
The "images" spring from the collision of concepts; they are more implied than
explicitly stated. The concreteness of this kind of literature is due neither to rhyme
and meter nor to similes and other devices but to the peculiar texture of ideas in
metaphoric juxtaposition.

Indirectly evocative qualities, therefore, compose the foundation of the literary
structure. What concerns us at this point is not the linguistic matter, this graphic,
sonorous rhythmic medium, but rather the fact that the qualities that arise from
the *semantic* agglomerate afford diffused but intelligible representations of a sen-
suous-plastic world. On this account a unique atmosphere similarly issues to en-
velop the agglomerate.

In the history of aesthetics, this problem is discussed as early as Edmund Burke's
Philosophical Enquiry (1757). Broder Christiansen analysed the phenomenon in
his *Kunstphilosophie* (1901). His observations were carried further in *The Psychology of Art* (1925) by Lev Vygotsky. W. K. Wimsatt, Jr., vindicates and elaborates
the approach; he describes the hyperverbal relevance of the literary medium, by
which term he points to "the interrelational density of words taken in their fullest,
most inclusive and symbolic character."[5] The eidetic semantic world of the qualities fundamental to poetry and prose is just as crucial to producing the uniqueness
of this art as is the "empowered arrangement" which Roman Jakobson gives as
the crucial determinant. It is to be emphasized that while the semantic qualities
may be directly attuned to values of a mimetic type, they need not be. That they
bear reference to the external or the inner world is obviously not tantamount to
saying — any more than we would of the iconic signs of painting — that the content
is comprised of reflected objects or even that these are dominant. However, "content" motifs must as a rule be made a component of the fundmental structure of
semantic qualities, if by form we mean the directly, sensuously given.

The term "form" is, as everyone knows, one of the most abused in aesthetic discourse. Although it is inescapably ambiguous and vague, I cannot avoid it in respect to some crucial aspects of aesthetic problems. Because of the vagueness and ambiguity, I wish simply to state here that in other works (not translated into English), I have proposed that the term be applied within a specific context and in a specific sense: connected with its twin term, content. Now, with respect to non-representational art, I understand by content the means of expression, while form in this context is the organization (the structure) of this material; with poetry or song, content is what provides the pattern of meaning in the verbal media, while form is both the sound (or graphic) patterns and the organization of the material as a whole; with the representational arts, content consists of the ideas, persons, objects, events, and their relationships given by the iconic surface or the patterns of images, and by form we can understand the iconic surface, the patterns of im-ages, plus the organization of the material as a whole; and finally, with the applied arts (including architecture), I would suggest that by form we understand the tex-tures, the surfaces and their shape, while by content we understand the function. Here, the construction is usually regarded as a formal aspect too, except in the con-structivist version, where it becomes the content. With regard to the performing arts, I abandon the above terms and speak rather of "design" (e.g., score or script) and "execution," each of which in its turn possesses the aspects of form and con-tent. I do not discern material (the medium) as content in contradistinction to form, since all materials are aesthetically significant only as they are processed into the work of art or as they are emphasized (e.g., *l'art brut*, or noise in aleatory music), where they become means of expression and hence pertain to the content in the context of nonrepresentational art, as mentioned above.

One final distinction is still needed here: that of form as a *type pattern*.[6] This sense applies, however, only to special cases. Type pattern clearly is a *generical* notion; that is, it pertains to the peculiar *genre* of the work of art. When we speak, for example, of a sonnet or a mazurka, we mean an approximate ordering of the whole, including the means of expression; but when we speak about tragedy, or we specify that a novel is an adventure tale, already we are bringing in content as well as form to the given "type pattern," and our prior distinctions take priority.

I have left aside here the preliminary notion of *composition*, as it is, in fact, a definite particularization of form in the aesthetic meaning. I also have no space to dwell on the illuminating analysis by D. W. Parker, who discerned five chief factors of form (unity of the whole [organic unity], which in turn emerges from: a dominant motif; balance; thematic variation; and evolution). This scheme is beguiling at first glance, but in fact, it reveals no more than what I call the *particular valuational qualities* of which the ultimate form-value may be comprised. Thus, I cannot accept what I take to be the subcategories he proposes as the key traits of all art objects. Perhaps balance, alone, might be defended as a constituent valuational quality. Then, however, we would have to understand by "balance" any compositional concretization of a given ordered whole (and dissonance, looseness, even chaotic pattern might be manifest). Bur surely a dominant theme, variation, and evolution (a sequential, "dramatic" conception, also of spatial entities) provide contingent valuational qualities, dependent on how the particular artist might make use of them.

A Relative Autonomy of Structure Were we to restrict ourselves to the foregoing decisive attribute, we would be open to reproach for failure to arrive at complete definition. For we do encounter closed structures outside of art possessing the qualities that concerned us above—the surgeon's table with doctors and nurses standing round about it, a crowd of people suddenly running down the street together, a report or account of something that has just occurred. The gestalt theorists have tried for this reason to establish *Prägnanz*, "precise compactness," as the particular attribute of art structures. They hold coherent systems to be those in which no element is superfluous and none can be replaced by another. Beyond that, as Max Wertheimer has it, these structures have a much sharper tendency towards simplicity and regularity than other structures. Such terse structures thus appear to be harmonious only in the narrower sense, inasmuch as they evince a surprising uniformity of their elements and entail not merely a harmonious, but an actually functional unity. (Changing one element means changing another element.) Theorists find the affirmation of such a view seductive, but I doubt that it is confirmed in practice. We often talk about works of art without setting such rigorous requirements (we also grant recognition to disharmonious structures), while, conversely, far simpler systems can be found where the elements depend on each other in the tightest way, and these are not works of art. The terseness problem simply has no way to arise as regards the complicated structures of most works of art. If we really want to settle this issue, we must not merely draw a demarcation line between systems whose elements closely cohere with one another and systems where this is not the case.

Accordingly, the second characteristic attribute of art is in my view not so much a terse economy as a *relative autonomy of structure*. De Witt Parker and Erich

Kahler term it the fashioning of a *microcosm*.[7] This thesis might seem to contradict marxist views regarding works of art. For if we speak of a work as a microcosm, we may be charged with adopting the standpoint of extreme aestheticism, with proposing the absolute autonomy of artistic value. This is a hasty and a simplistic reproach, however, and cannot stand up to criticism. Parker and Kahler do not seek to divide art from reality. On the contrary, their characterization of the artistic structure indicates a macrostructure; they declare the sociohistorical order at a given time to be a tangible presence. The "microcosm" is not just genetically dependent upon the macrocosm, then, but it can reflect, or, in more cautious phrase, express it as well.

Lukács, in *Die Eigenart des Aesthetischen* (1963), adopts a standpoint which I have also expressed.[8] In the light of marxist historicism, I believe it is impossible not to accept the view that a work of art represents a "microcosm," not only in the mimetic sense, as a reflection of the macrocosm, but, above all, in the sense that by referring to the occurrence of artistic unities within a greater totality, one finds means to seek the determinants of these unities; whose one-of-a-kind status is only seemingly a paradox. These unities are somehow related to an authentic reality, and yet they function as though we had exempted them from reality. (Lukács has strikingly termed this an *An-sich-sein*, "being in itself," *in form only*.) Although they are in material substance or in use-value, for example, a part of our world, they are at the same time opposed to this world. They provide territories in which, quite apart from all their other possible functions (informational, moral, practical), these given systems of qualities, whether immediately sensuous or indirect and semantic, subsist in themselves. A fine example is provided here by functional objects, which are changed into works of art if outfitted with special outward attributes such as color and proportion beyond the requirements of their use. Even in times of radical constructivism or functionalism, in the architecture of Loos and the young Le Corbusier and in Bauhaus furniture, visual values of this nature have played a role.

We should also ascribe a relative autonomy in those cases where objects of everyday use or *objets trouvés* come to be looked upon as art. The dadaists and surrealists called operations of this sort *dépaysement* (whose prototypes were the *papiers collés* of synthetic cubism). It amounts simply to putting a given work or product in a context where, as a structure rendered conspicuous, it acquires an autotelic function. Picabia's inkwell, Duchamp's urinal, Rauschenberg's bed cease to be an inkwell, a plumbing fixture, a bed.

With pop art this problem becomes particularly important. Here we are in no way confronted with a return to figurative art, but rather with an effort absolutely to wipe out the boundaries between art and nonart. The magnificently got-up and consumed objects of everyday use, found in interior decors, in drugstores, or in shopwindow displays, are taken to represent a wholly proper domain for artistic activity. This applies likewise to the comics and advertising images in the works of Oldenburg, Indiana, Johns, Wesselman, and Lichtenstein. Of course, someone can ask whether we are not overly tolerant if we admit such productions to the realm of art. It seems they stem, as the cultural sociologists would have it, from a modern civilization that is determined by the mass media. The result is an onslaught of pre-fab, die-cut productions that may not claim the name of art, and a homogenized culture in which the easily grasped communication is king. However, I cannot regard this hypothesis about the emergence of pop art as the single correct one. Admittedly, the reliance of the art form upon modern civilization is too complete, countermanding its attempt to cast that civilization wholly into question. Other impulses are, however, essential to its appearance. Pop art is a reaction to the art of the avant-garde preceding it, especially to abstract expressionism. Hence, in a way it too takes up the whole problematic area which grew manifest in the twentieth century with the crisis of the concept of art. As I said earlier, this art is the expression of protest against a civilization which has made of art — even its most devilishly difficult aspects — a commodity.

In sum, there is no reason to deny pop art its status as art, its sublation of the boundaries between life and art notwithstanding. Its proponents are saying approximately: life can be aesthetic or not aesthetic; to gain awareness of this, one has to pick definite structures out from life. We think we are looking at objects from life, but they are differently organized, they are a mockery of life, or the poetry of their banal ordinariness is brought to the fore. What in a certain sense constitutes their own world of art is thus either maintained or asserted.

We can observe the very same process in another quarter. The mobiles of Calder, the constructions of Gabo and Pevsner, and the works of action painting impress us not as technical gymnastics, as engineering projects, or as simple, accidental, blindly active organizations of material, but rather as structures of sensuously given qualities having a relative autonomy. Here let it be said again that the moment of relative autonomy coheres with qualities that are so structured as immediately to seize our attention. Calling attention to structure plainly means, however, focusing upon its internal field, upon the autotelic qualities which function independently of the external world. Thus, the second attribute of art constitutes a *strengthening* of the first. This is no more true for the immediately sensuously given qualities than it is for the indirectly evocative, mediated (semanticized) ones. In literature, for instance, the indirectly given qualities are elements of a fictive world, constructed of course with the so-called vehicles of meaning. Moreover, a reflexive relation is in effect here; fields of qualities can be lifted the more readily out of their surroundings when they have a conspicuous structural organization.

In works of prose like those by Gide, Camus, and Max Frisch (*Stiller* and *Mein Name sei Gantenbein*), the autonomous structure rises on a footing of philosophical reflection. There are debates on the meaning of writing itself, ironical treatment of the author's own artistic vision, and discussions of the dubious identity of contemporary man, all this giving testimony to a most thoroughgoing skepticism. With Frisch it gets to the point where only external possibilities (not character) are seen in the forming of a human being. Self-consciousness has become the outcome of innumerable unknown variables which at any time may affect one's existence. The cinema offers similar phenomena: Fellini's 8½ on the one hand; the work of Godard on the other. Though intellectual reflection prevails, and thought represents the ground floor, as it were, this does not alter the artistic status, for the intellectuality here does not primarily serve the aim of cognition. It is one part of life which, in eluding the author or hero, calls forth in consequence self-sufficient thought and commentary and reflections upon itself.

The problem of the relative autonomy of a work of art is related to the question of space. Space has continued importance in terms of art's own world gaining a depth relief against the authentic background. In most cases we are speaking of the extrinsic, technical means of ascribing space—the contour of the picture in its frame, the sculpture on the pedestal, the acting on the stage, not to overlook the opening credits and "The End" in film. Space of this kind was made suspect by the dadaists and surrealists (Magritte, for example). In fact, the extrinsic denotators of space are not very important. Every work of art achieves its own genuine space strictly through the content of its special conspicuous structure, its intrinsic rhythm as evoked by the spatial, temporal, or spatiotemporal dominants.

A special role in the formation of intrinsic space is played by fiction, which with the aid of fable, characterization, and sequences of events creates an illusional world. And even though it is not certain where the fiction begins, the irreality of the narration demarcates it from what authentically was, or is. In the variety of reportage we deem artistic, from which all fable is excluded, the space is only to be had by means of a special language or particular construction. The conscious ac-

centing that is common to artistic experiment is another way of winning space.
For example, even those artists in the modern theater who have junked the fourth
wall (Eisenstein, Meyerhold, Piscator) have not been able to do without space in this
sense. When an actor walks into the audience or addresses the public directly (as
in Brecht's theater), these stylistic devices only modify the space. The effort indeed
is stronger than ever today to achieve the relative autonomy of theater, its functionality qua theater and not as an illusory slice of life whose accidental witness —
as it were — one is.

The Artifact of Skill or Virtuosity In European culture, but not only in it, art
has been defined on the whole as a distinctive form of activity for which one must
possess a special aptitude. What Thomas Aquinas spoke of as *recta ratio factibili-
um* was an unimpugned axiom until the twentieth century. But with the dominant
role of technology in modern civilization the axiom has lost virtually all credibility.
When it is possible with the help of an electronic brain to produce a black and white
diffraction spectrum upon a photographic plate — in other words, a synthetic
hologram — which, when appropriately illuminated, provides a full three-dimen-
sional image of the object that you can study from the most varied sight-lines and
perspectives, then we have a phenomenon where not even the technique of developing a film correctly is a problem, for the electronic brain (programmed, to be
sure) plays the crucial role.

Accordingly, as we come to describe the third attribute of art, we must consider
the modern experience with cybernetics and reformulate the classical thesis concerning techne, the special ability of the artist. There are two kinds of artifact —
the *direct* and the *mediated*. A direct artifact is one which requires human intervention (through the use of implements and certain skills), while a mediated artifact
is achieved either with the help of programmed machines or by an artificial organization of natural objects.

In Japanese *ikebana*, which is often cited as the classic instance of such arti-
ficed organization, flowers (and sometimes metal and manmade material) are arranged in a distinctive fashion, and impressive light effects are sought. Here we
have a *construction* of an artistic structure using raw material, the artist's intention
being to organize "naturally abstract structures." This interpretation applies mutatis mutandis to the *objet trouvé*, for here too the given formed object is shown —
structured — within a setting. However, the *objet trouve* need not, although it may,
provide an abstract pattern. If it is not, say, a piece of driftwood (akin to the raw

material of *ikebana*), but instead a much-worn pocket watch, for example, it will retain a semimimetic significance and have an effect rather like a pop art piece.

The artifact can accordingly be considered another attribute of art. Yet it is more dubious than the two previous attributes, since a raw, unworked object can be designated a work of art, with the act of structuring passed on by the artist to the perceiver. Also, the artifact entails a twofold understanding of the techne by which a work of art comes into existence. By techne we ordinarily mean artistry, skill, or virtuosity. We assume that *X or Y* must have a definite talent to approach a field to which one must bring a thorough preparation and, most important, some prominent individual gifts. But we must now also understand by techne the ability to program artistic tasks into a cybernetic machine. Definite talent is necessary here too, though of another sort, less individually predicated than in art. In a word, techne is not an attribute peculiar to art; it involves not so much the work itself as the means of disposition, the trained skill and capacity, the artist must have at hand if he is to make a work of art.

Individual Expression Having described artifact and techne as the third attribute of art, I come now to the fourth and last attribute, *individual expression*. If by this criterion we understood only the factual act of making, we should have to remain as wary of it as we are of techne, because it would then be a characteristic of the creative process and not of the work itself.

I am of the opinion, however, that individual expression is a feature not only of artistic creation but of the artistic product as well. In other words, we simply cannot accept that *X* will look at the world in a certain way, think this and that about it, in his own way select and accent definite phenomena, and that he will express *none* of all this in his work, which has only had—or to speak with more caution, partially had—this aim in being thrust into existence.

Of course the question arises: How is the individual expression in a work of art to be pinned down? It is not easy. I will return to this question; but first I must turn to a more urgent matter: Can individual expression be called an essential attribute of a work of art when it is not characteristic of such artistic productions as surrealist poems (e.g., "Calliope" by Ducrocq) or *objets trouvés*?

It is quite clear to me that in these works we are not confronted with any elements of individual expression. The artist hatches a programmatic concept, which is subsequently executed by putting together aleatory groupings of words or colors.

Yet the artist is involved to the extent of bestowing on the "ready-made" objects an artistic meaning and setting them off in some definite way. At the Cabaret Voltaire, the poet Tristan Tzara pulled newspaper snippets from his top hat and from them put together poems and dadaist manifestos. Tzara came near to achieving what has today been perfected by cybernetic machines. Using a kind of lottery, he aimed for the completely unexpected and, what is most important, an arrangement of elements without any personal intervention. Tzara did not give himself over *totally* to accident, however, since he himself made the choice of newspaper clippings and thus "encoded" poems. Surrealist practice is not dissimilar: automatic writing (much like action painting and jazz improvisation) is at bottom an expression of the stream of consciousness; it relies on accident, and permits the untrammeled personality of an artist (more precisely, the immediate creative process) to issue forth. We must understand in the same way Dominguez's means of painting, a method lauded by Breton as allowing the most intrinsic expression to a painter, who needs no longer adhere to the fixed principles of conscious, controllable invention. In both instances we have the composition of structures whose basic materials are expressive qualities: however, in Tzara's case the expression is, in large degree, a projection of what the perceiver brings to it, while in the second case the artist's intervention is primary.

This then is a gradual, rather than a qualitative distinction; but it is an essential one inasmuch as, for instance, we can similarly differentiate two modes in the contemporary happening. One mode has been located by American critics in the heritage of the collages and assemblages of Allan Kaprow; and these cannot be called pure improvisations, for the artist imposes his selections on the work rather strongly. The other mode is exemplified in the works of John Cage, which make maximum use of chance and unexpected elements and groupings. In both cases, the observer has to make out for himself the structuring of the work: They are both open systems. In the second case (the spectacles and ideas of J. J. Lebel are also representative), however, the spectators are more centrally invited to assert their own inventions within a certain schema. Events have been staged in which the totality of elements in the surrounding environment participate: form, light, movement, sounds. Merce Cunningham's dance company has taken part in such events, as have proponents of *musique concrète*. Art here becomes a means of playful enjoyment.[9]

I look upon individual expression as the most fluctuating of the attributes I have discussed, for in folklore, industrial art, and homogenized mass culture, as well as in the phenomena discussed above, it is frequently, if not always, impossible to locate it. The individual expression is usually embedded within the expressive *structure* which constitutes the work of art. I must add that the individual expression cannot be confirmed on the evidence of *one* work of art. A longer-term sampling is required for a disclosure of the peculiar stylistic attributes.

We might seek to connect individual expression with *authenticity* and *originality*, thereby stressing — rightly — the unusually powerful individual expression. What precisely these terms mean is not easy to explain. Works which manifest openness, sincerity, freshness, and immediacy, are often called authentic. But, how sincerity might be tested remains a conundrum; while freshness requires an element or an entire structure to be new or to imitate uniqueness. (Whether newness itself is individually expressive must be doubted; though it awakens interest, novelty all too often proves at last an empty vanity.) As for originality, it is plainly equivalent to singularity or uniqueness.

If I stress here the ambiguity in the concept of "artistic individuality," it is to make more understandable my conclusion. I find it unwise to reduce individuality as an attribute of works of art to newness or novelty, a concept that in turn needs more exact analysis; at a minimum, novelty surely means a different content or formal means than previously was expressed or employed. Novelty is a historical category; individuality is not. Novelty is an equivalent of individuality in just one sense, that each individuality makes its bow as "new."

From a *cycle of works*, from the global entirety of their structure, we derive a given number of properties that distinguish the particular artist from others. The roots of this singularity are not subject to a theoretical definition. We can point concretely to these properties; we can describe and even classify them in relation to stylistic attributes (theme, content, form) that predominate in the relevant cultural sphere. What differentiates the artist from the artisan is the *style* that is the property of the artist. This style can be discovered in the constituted structure, whereby further data accrued from the observation or reconstruction of the creative process prove helpful.

Technical perfection, I should say, is no standard of artistry; it is sheerly the result of professional capacity in a given artistic field, such as a skilled copyist or gifted counterfeiter must command to perfection. So long as van Meegeren understood brilliantly how to imitate Vermeer, he was a brilliant forger and no more. As his imitations increasingly showed their own strongly expressive properties, one could say that his work manifested an artistic mastery.[10]

If by the concept of individual expression we comprehend all of the foregoing, it will mean that we expect from the work of art at least a small degree of originality. Some aestheticians maintain that a good copy has its own status and also affords us aesthetic pleasure, that is, that we enjoy a faithful reproduction of a painting or a recording of a musical performance; they overlook, however, that what pleases us is the original, not the copy. While not wishing to impugn the pleasures of experiencing a reproduction, I wish to emphasize that through it the attraction of an original is what holds our attention; we seek experience of the original through all available means.[11]

My feeling is that the "fully" original works of art are those which carry to a rare degree of excellence the artist's individual attributes; originality may, in fact, be equated with exceptionally creative individuality. In other words, when we study authentic artists we find that *every one* imbues works of art with properties which peculiarly represent him. Some reveal themselves to the world; others discover themselves within the world. Still others are capable of discovering the world itself, whereupon they are often attracted to philosophy and science. But given all such differences, the attribute of individual particularity is constituent of all works of art. However, the term originality should not be used interchangeably with that of individual expression. While effecting some usually minor personal modifications, individual expression has to fall back on a common fund of artistic attitudes, emotions, thinking, and language. Originality may be understood to imply a more singular phenomenon in art.

In short, however much individuals may differ from one another, they still have much in common; the same applies to works of art, even in cases of the originality which signifies genius. In such cases, the work of art differs in both quality and degree from other works of art expressive of a given individuality. In works we cannot describe as being of genius, a transmitted mode of looking at the world is simply modified, a few stylistic devices are reworked, this or that theme undergoes a divergent treatment. In works of genius, the world is uniquely seen; an entirely individual style is exercised. In other works, individuality is largely an affair of particulars; in works of genius, the work is forged almost wholly in the individuality of the artist. Thus, a single sign, one trait, is often enough to distinguish the entire work from all others of its epoch and of past and future time. Genius and its unique products do not lend themselves to scalar weighing and measurement. A work of this magnitude cannot be more or less unique. There can only be a *different* concrete uniqueness or originality.

Originality cannot then be imputed to every work of art. We have thus come across an axiological attribute with whose assistance we will be positioned to describe hierarchies of objects that we have already discerned to be art.

Some Problems in Applying the Definition

Let me summarize. We call that object a work of art which possesses at least a minimal expressive structure of qualities and qualitative patterns, given sensorily and imaginatively in a direct or in an indirectly evocative (semanticized) way. These qualitative patterns and the definite structure enhance each other, building up an autotelic, relatively autonomous whole, set off more or less from reality while it remains nonetheless a part of realtiy. This object, I must add, is an artifact, in the sense that it is either directly produced owing to a given techne or it is the result of some idea of arrangement. Finally, this object is somehow related to the artist's creative individuality.

The axiological character of this whole that we call a work of art must be obvious and needs no further comment. What I should discuss further is the grouping of artistic values (and the valuational qualities that support them) which are pertinent to *all* art, as these can be distinguished from values and valuational qualities which pertain only to certain domains, kinds, and genres of art. This important issue must be taken up in a separate essay, where it can be adequately argued and analyzed.

I hope it is clear by my remarks about happenings that the term "object" should be understood here in a broader sense than in traditional aesthetics — the *process*, which has a beginning, middle, and end, is also a kind of aesthetic object.

According to this interpretation, the three earlier features are unquestionably necessary and sufficient conditions. The fourth and last, in the hedged formulation I gave it, can also be considered constituent of a work of art. Some avant-garde products do, however, erase the individual impress much as though art had returned to the primitive era when no institution of the artist existed. More broadly, we run into trouble with the idea of individual expression when dealing with the many able avant-gardists who take offense when this category is broached; all the same, even their anonymous gestures are individually expressive in some way. I should stress that my concept of expression is *not* centered on the intensity displayed, for example, by romantics, expressionists, and action painters. Moreover, in including individual expression, I do not claim that a work of art exists only in a single rendition. This singularity applies only to some arts, such as painting or "hot"

jazz; moreover, a solution to this problem depends on the answer given to ontological questions,[12] and the social context cannot be ignored in any matter of
aesthetic axiology.

On the basis of the definition of art proposed here, I think we may justifiably
conclude that art provides, as many have assumed, *a special mode of cognition of
reality*. We may say that the artist (within the structure of the particular fields of
qualities) presents his own special relationship to the world, and that the reader or
spectator monitors this relationship with approximate adequacy. This is to say only
that every work of art is imbued with manifold references to the world exterior to
it, and that, in its own fashion, the tachist abstraction or the purely musical structure is imbued with cognitive values as much as the genre painting or the literature
of the nineteenth century.

We must, however, differentiate among these cognitive values. Usually they are
linked in a more particular sense with elements proper to the representational arts.
There they are plainly in evidence and can most readily be verified. But let us consider such thoroughly modern and fascinating works as, for instance, the *Tractatus*
by Jerzy Krechowicz and Janusz Hajdun, performed in the Gdansk Plastic Arts
Theatre, or Kazimierz Urbański's film *Matter*. In the latter, matter is not depicted;
rather, a fantastic poem is created in which the continual volatility of matter, its
cycles and genesis—with ever more distinct forms emerging from chaos—come
before the viewer. This is certainly not mimesis, yet without doubt not only sensuous qualities are presented but their objective structuring too. This presentation of
the entrance of cosmic matter into our daily lives ever since the atom-bomb explo-
sions is the more remarkable in that the realm of physics is evoked with all the
gestalt of a quasi-reproduction, a quasi-scientific study. Hence, the special cognitive
values which are communicated are necessarily ambiguous. This characteristic
(it is often believed on evidence like this) seems a fixed trait of works of art in general. We should not forget, however, that philosophical works are ambiguous too,
as are scientific works more often than we may think.

The cognitive but not necessarily mimetic values of art that I have emphasized
do not constitute a separate and distinct criterion, it should be said, for they are
implicitly integrated in the structure.

My standpoint differs from one defended by many marxists. Hence, it seems of
use to demonstrate in some detail why it simply is not true—as is often maintained
on behalf of marxist aesthetics—that the imitation of reality is one of the residual
and constituent attributes of art. Such a thesis is nowhere found among the scat-

tered aesthetic remarks, observations, and analyses in the writings of Marx and
Engels. Nor does it follow from their methodological guidelines. One ought to be
convinced of this on the sole basis of the discussion in the *1844 Manuscripts* by
Marx of the emergence of art from the productive process. As for later marxist
thinking on this matter, we can distinguish here four distinct tendencies of thought,
which do not allow reconciliation with one another on all points. [13]

In Soviet aesthetics, which I examined in my work *Between Tradition and a Vision of the Future* (1964, in Polish), the view has until today remained preponderant
that the mimetic moment is conclusive as to whether a work will or will not be art.
Lukács is a supporter of this view; in contrast to contemporary Soviet efforts, however, he has brilliantly worked out and explicated his standpoint. [14]

Another course is taken by those whose spokesman in the Soviet Union has for
some time been Moisei Kagan. Their position is that the essence of the work of art
is to be looked for in its effect upon all of our psychic faculties; it remains unclear,
however, just what in the object itself is responsible for a particular reception. Perhaps Kagan is thinking of the individual world view that, as embodied in art, can
be expressed in the most various ways, including the representation of reality in its
broad scope and multiplicity.

Another position is represented by Christopher Caudwell, who holds art to be
an individual expression of sociohistorical and likewise generally human genotypes. [15] What shall pertain to art is, first of all, determined by the authentic emotional content, to which the author gives expression and which can entail varying
degrees of typification.

The fourth conception — one very close to my own — indicates as a constituent
attribute of art the formal (or nonmimetic) structure. This view was presented some
time ago by Max Raphael in "La théorie marxiste de l'art." [16] It has recently been
represented by Ernst Fischer in particular. I believe such a conception to be most
adequate to the general presuppositions of marxism. For instance, as I noted in
Chapter I with regard to art's origins, we can observe the formation of a special
structure, at once mimetic and formal, which Marx termed the measure *(Mass)*
which corresponds to the object. Later during the historical development, that is,
in the course of art's general and relentless autonomization, the formal aspect took
on an integrity of momentum immediate to itself, and detached, as it were, from the
original structure (which embraced mimesis too). This thereafter served as the
basic condition to every one of the arts, notwithstanding that such structures might
prove highly compliant to concrete innovations.

Let me return once more, however, to the definition I have proposed. No single
attribute, but rather the syndrome of all the attributes, permits us to describe a
given object as a work of art. The complementary system of attributes is alterable.
Only in some cases are we able to locate all four attributes unequivocally. There
are cases where all attributes, or some, are weakly accented. The first two attributes I consider fundamental and sufficient, though they do not occur apart from
the others. The expressive structure of qualities and the relative autonomy, in other
words, indicate a most marked individuality or else they are embodied in an artifact, as I have indicated. Accordingly, we are led toward an alternative definition.
It is not impossible that we shall want to speak of a work as art solely owing to
the weaker attributes (individual expression, artifact, and techne). Here then the
necessary condition would become sufficient. Yet in the light of our discussion,
such proposals must be rejected, for even though a number of objects do not immediately evidence all of our attributes, I see no reason to reject an encompassing
definition. At the same time, I am not enthralled to any codified prescription, for in
that direction lies a failure to come to terms with the object of study.

This projective, or regulative, definition leads to the possibility of ordering the
objects called works of art in a continuum. The attributes are interdependent, but
each can be stronger or weaker than, or equal to, the others. Thus, if we compare
the works within such a continuum, they can be said to be more or less artistic.
From our vantage point we can maintain, therefore, that even close by the zero-
point of the continuum, a minimum for a "good" work of art has been realized.
Here, unlike Beardsley, I do not distinguish a "good" work of art from a work of art.
Only in degree do I distinguish "good" works of art (i.e., their fundamental artistic
value). And unlike L. Arnaud Reid, in his study "Beauty and Significance," [17] I do
not distinguish ugly from nonugly works of art; either ugliness is a special and degenerate variety of the work (in which case we must deal with it in the framework
of our four criteria), or else it is connected with the axiological moments (poor integration, or not all criteria met) that enfeeble the artistry of the work. It thus appears
that we are brought back again to the continuum construed from the fundamental
works that we earlier proposed. L. Arnaud Reid sees ugliness as the absence of aesthetic value. This standpoint we have to reject as contradictory within itself. If an object is an aesthetic object, it then entails some part at least of that fundamental value.

The definition presented here can be applied to so-called marginal cases. When
we try to distinguish between artistic and nonartistic reportage, an architectural
structure and an ordinary building, an art photograph and a plain snapshot, we

come back again and again to the determinants I have described. A characteristic example among the older experiments is the work of Man Ray. His "ready-mades" are not common objects of use, although their intent was to abolish and transcend the separation of art from life. His well-known *Gift*—a household laundry iron with nails glued by their heads to its flat surface, so that they protrude—was stripped deliberately of its use function. The celebrated photographs (Rayograms) were not mere pictures but visual systems, where in a special way the previously unappreciated light-sensitivity of the material was explored. In a sense a similar *experimentum crucis* occurs today in such artistic probes as the silent musical compositions of John Cage and op art.[18]

The four attributes that I have discussed are fundamental axiological-aesthetic criteria, but they do not exhaust the list of artistic values. They should be viewed, rather, as groundwork values, which commingle to effect a coherent whole (i.e., the fundamental value), which is based primarily upon the first-named attribute. Since my definition is centered on this combined fundamental value, which appertains to all the arts, I have not directed attention to the *distributive* residual values, that is to say, those appearing only in limited sectors of art, such as the mimetic values germane to the representational arts (the realist category would be comprised here), or the functional values within the applied arts. On the whole, a typical structure in the representational arts is multilevelled, many-vectored, and requires a considerably more subtle analysis than do structures of the other arts (think of the structure of an Arabian carpet).

It remains to add that we have not treated from all sides the problem of expression as an aesthetic category, particularly the question of the various expressive values, and the peculiarly individual impact of the work of art as a manifestation of the creative process. The expressive values embody, in at least two cases, an internalized and self-substantiated value: first, as the symbol or sign of a psychological (but by extension, psychosocial) attitude, as, in music or architecture; second, as an accentuation of emotional factors (in all the arts).

The concepts presented here will not satisfy those who expect of philosophy an absolute precision. All the same, I believe we can make immediate operative use of these concepts, their ambiguities notwithstanding. Every science can precisely ascertain its underlying and its controlling concepts only up to a certain point. Of this Aristotle wrote long ago, in his Nicomachean Ethics. But perhaps it would be more apt to relate an anecdote passed on by Tranøy, who at one time devoted his seminar in Ljungskile to the concept of structure. To an aesthetician a mathemati-

cian spoke ironically, citing Wittgenstein's *Tractatus Logico-philosophicus:* "What
we cannot speak about we must consign to silence," to which the aesthetician
tellingly replied: "What we cannot consign to silence we must speak about."

I want to emphasize that the definition given here must be seen as an *open concept.* Art can so greatly change that the attributes I have discussed will not continue
to apply as a unitary group. Which attributes may have to be forsaken and which
new attributes may take their place cannot be known.

My aim has been to create a definition of the concept of art that would stand up
to contemporary critical and theoretical investigations. In this sense, the definition
given here rests upon a sociological substratum. Since any work of art is inevitably
a sociocultural phenomenon, the sociological aspect is inextricable from the substance of its overall artistic structure, appearing in all of its particular axiological
properties, which should then be interpreted in the context of the specific value
communication of the creator and the many-sided public. I have also tried to illuminate the problem from a more comprehensive viewpoint by giving attention to
earlier evaluations of art, to its history and the history of how it has been conceptualized since the beginning of human culture. In pursuing this historical and
generic hypothesis I sought for the attributes of art which in spite of continual modification, have stood up until today. I have harbored no illusion that my endeavor
would sweep aside parallel efforts, whether earlier or contemporary. I have failed
to present proof *more geometrico*—nor, on that score, will anyone else succeed.
At most I can appeal here to the historical evidence and anthropological data, as
gathered and sifted by students of the psychobiological constitution of mankind
and of the variables or constants that are manifested in human culture. The alternative can only be an evasion of the constraint of all definition. Admittedly, it is always possible that somebody will provide a better, more encompassing definition.
Should anyone assert that a work of this nature is entirely without meaning or
application, I have to ask him how it is that concepts such as atom, race, social
order, and psyche can be fixed, while when it comes to an artistic product this is
not deemed possible. It is significant that a large number of the scholars most influenced by Wittgenstein's ideas have decided that there is insufficient reason for rejecting aesthetics, nor can they find grounds for a refusal to seek the meaning of
art.

A final problem must be mentioned. My definition—not unlike every other definition in a similar framework—does not give a reckoning of each concrete value-
quality. That would have to be undertaken first on grounds of the history of the

particular artistic genre and its theorization; second, the critics in the field of the particular art are much better prepared to do it; third, concrete value-qualities cannot be fitted into a circumscribed "aesthetic alphabet,"[19] a fact which accords completely with the open character of our definition. In artistic practice ever-new qualities are produced, alloyed with one another, and transformed again. Aesthetics should acknowledge these new qualities without codifying them. The function of artists is to transgress all definitions, which are provisional in any case and represent, necessarily, a transitional solution. Aesthetics should prove ready, above all, to integrate these new value-qualities into the field of values earlier recognized as fundamental. And if this endeavor should turn out negatively, the aestheticians will have made a most important find, in the very fact of a complete incommensurability of the present and past. I do not believe, however, that such an incompatibility would occur. At any rate, it has not happened yet.

That we are living through a total crisis of values is a dubious "discovery." The not less important and useful assertion that what is, in fact, new today represents a creative continuance of the aesthetic tradition would be a likely result, were (optimally) the artists of every kind brought into discussion together and the full exchange of artistic, critical, and theoretical experience expedited.

Postscript 1967

Were I approaching the problem of definition today I would state, first, that expression as such does not constitute a firm attribute of every work of art, although individual intervention does. How expression and individual mediation are to be differentiated is a topic for an amplified study.

Second, I would give much more stress to the thesis that every work of art not so much "is" as "happens." In other words, every work of art actually occurs by a collaboration of the artist and his audience. The theatricalization of art is currently a major phenomenon. This is obvious in the happening, but it also occurs whenever art asserts an element of play. This ludic factor encourages us to speak of the quasi-ritualistic role of contemporary art.

Today's notorious "blurring" or "dissolution" of autonomous artistic structure indeed stems from the tendencies just noted, which encourage skepticism about, or even rejection of, the notion and practical desirability of techne, form, and expression. Conceptualism is but the final step on the journey "beyond" art. Collage trends in film (Godard) and musical form whose shape is challengingly nonchalant, without beginning or end, for the listener to hear or neglect as he wishes (e.g., recent experiments of Stockhausen) are obvious cases in point. Yet even in these striking instances, the arrangement of a whole, semi-isolated in space and/or time, cannot be given up; thus, it follows that a work of art without structure is unthinkable.

Finally, such interesting events as Genet's "theater within theater" (The Maids, The Blacks, The Balcony) and Robbe-Grillet's novel La Maison de rendez-vous must be analysed as the antipode of a ludic art. All the problems of an experience gained through the literary medium are highlighted rather than treated as transparent, harmless conventions. For Genet and Robbe-Grillet, there is no autonomous work of art existing apart from the perceiver, who is called upon more than ever to become engaged as a collaborator. The aesthetic experience here loses its contemplative character, very much as in the encounter with an art-as-play, and comes to be like a magical participation in the realm of comtemporary myths.

Quo vadis, ars? This nobody knows.

Notes

1. A convincing analysis of the phenomenon is provided by Ingarden in his book *Das literarische Kunstwerk* (Halle, 1931).

2. See Max Bense, *Aesthetische Information*, vol. 2 (Krefeld und Baden-Baden, 1956), pp. 32–51, and his *Programmierung des Schönen*, vol. 4 (Krefeld und Baden-Baden, 1960), pp. 17–32.

3. See also K. E. Tranøy, *Wholes and Structures* (Copenhagen, 1959); R. Bastide, ed., *Sens et usages du terme Structure* (The Hague, 1962); M. de Gandillac, L. Goldmann, J. Piaget, et al., *Genèse et structure* (The Hague, 1965); and J. Viet, *Les méthodes structuralistes dans les sciences sociales* (Paris—The Hague, 1965).

4. The same approach is taken in Lukác's notion of *Totalität* as a basis of artistic phenomena within a context of historical process, and also in Goldmann's hypothesis concerning the *vision du monde*. The conceptions of Lukács and Goldmann are, however, not as comprehensive as my alternative working questions in respect to the idea of structure. As a result of my discussion, I must reject as unfounded the effort of L. Sebag, in his *Marxisme et structuralisme* (Paris, 1964), to relate marxist historicism to a chance and subjective point of view which he would regard, moreover, as absolutely opposed to the system-creating tendencies of human thought.

5. See Wimsatt's article in the collection of essays *Aesthetic Inquiry*, edited by M. C. Beardsley and H. M. Schueller (Encino, Calif., 1967), p. 33.

6. Cf. D. W. Gotshalk, *Art and the Social Order* (Chicago, 1947).

7. See D. W. Parker, "The Nature of Art," *Revue internationale de philosophie*, 1939, no. 4; and E. Kahler, "What Is Art?" in his

book *Out of the Labyrinth* (New York, 1967).

8. See my study of artistic value, "O wartości artystycznej," in *Kultura i Społeczeństwo*, 1962, no. 4.

9. See the extremely interesting article by P. Restany, "L'art-jeu chasse l'art pour l'art," in *La Galerie des Arts* (February 1967), pp. 26–30. Art as play, appearing in our time as an emphasis more and more upon the activity rather than a result (the work of art), would seem an extreme case very like the painting of the chimpanzee Congo. Certainly we cannot accept without reservation Desmond Morris's thesis that the apes possess a sense of composition and a talent for calligraphy. In contrast, it is obvious that they exercise their energies in drawing and painting very much as they do in, say, gymnastics. It is this other sort of question—which brings out the important problem of the "artistic creativity" of the chimpanzee—that emerges from his painting's quite factual resemblance to tachism and aleatory products.

10. The notion of forgery is highly relevant to our discussion of individual expression. As concerns aleatory expression (e.g., jazz improvisations), forgery, *hic et nunc*, is excluded. Individual expression in the sense of a style or manner does, to be sure, entail the possibility of a counterfeit; yet not every forger can command individual expression. Therefore I distinguish artisan from virtuoso forgery. Forgery can so simulate an expression in the sense of originality, that the counterfeiter alone can accuse his work. Yet, by definition, originality eluded even the virtuoso forgers like van Meegeren or Dossena.

11. See the discussion in S. Ossowski's *Foundations of Aesthetics*, 3rd edition (in Polish; Warsaw, 1958), pp. 246 ff.

12. This problem has much in common with

that of the identity of the work of art, and requires a separate analysis. J. Margolis makes a striking distinction (*The Language of Art and Criticism* [Detroit, 1965], pp. 49–62) when he refers to more than one identity: thus, the work of Shakespeare can be treated as either literary or theatrical; this aspect differentiates music (the mere score) from painting (the one and original). The concept of "authentic" therefore has several meanings; it can designate: first, the entirely unique; second, the duplicable (from the original work, of course); third, that which we can adequately render from the score; and fourth, something that we can trace to the score's initial rendition. Authenticity as thus understood does not of course exclude the possibility that the rendition can be creative, not only in respect of adhering faithfully to the score but also as regards capturing its "spirit" or creating a wholly original interpretation. Ruby Meager in her essay "The Uniqueness of a Work of Art," *Proceedings of the Aristotelian Society*, LIX (1958–59), pp. 49–70, has further developed the many questions that are involved in the idea of identity. Not always is it sure, for example, which version of a work (e.g., El Greco's *The Healing of the Blind Man*) we should regard as authentic, and whether we are dealing with a copy when, say, Van Gogh imitates Delacroix, or Rembrandt and Rubens, Dürer. The problematic zone we touch on here has occupied Roman Ingarden for years. No one has penetrated the problems as deeply nor analyzed them in such detail as he. However, I want to declare my reservations concerning his basic distinction between the work of art and the aesthetic object. The reader is referred to my analysis of Ingarden's aesthetic axiology which appeared in *Estetika* (Prague), 1970, no. 1.

13. For discussion of the constituent attributes of art as considered by Marx, see my introduction to K. Marx and F. Engels, *On Literature and Art* (St. Louis, 1973). The conceptions here outlined do not exhaust, to be sure, every one of the solutions advanced until today. I have not mentioned the *Czelowiekowie denije* put forward by Gorky, some Soviet scholars' notion of art as an *ars operandi* or R. Garaudy's work *D'un réalisme sans rivages* (Paris, 1963), where art is considered not as an instrument for the cognition of the world but as a means to its appropriation through mythic-creative activity. Garaudy goes on to add authenticity and freshness as constituent attributes of art. I shall not further examine these efforts, inasmuch as the first two are overly general and the third is insufficiently clear if one considers that Garaudy holds every authentic art to be realistic. All these conceptions are tied in in some way to remarks by Marx.
14. See my essay "George Lukács' Universal Principle — Mimesis," in *Science and Society* (Winter 1968), pp. 26–38.
15. Christopher Caudwell, *Illusion and Reality* (London, 1938), and *Further Studies in a Dying Culture* (New York, 1949).
16. This essay can be found in Max Raphael, *Proudhon, Marx, Picasso* (Paris, 1933).
17. See *Proceedings of the Aristotelian Society*, XXIX (1928–29), pp. 123–154.
18. I cannot take up here the relevant question of the idea of aesthetic experience. It requires a detailed analysis of changes which parallel the modification in the idea of art. Let me only state here that the feeling of a heightened immediacy gained from the materials confined in and by the definite structure still remains as one of the distinctive features of this kind of experience.

The aesthetic attitude is attentive, because directed to and interested in the given field of sensory and imaginative data (directly or indirectly evocative). We may doubt, however, whether the aesthetic experience nowadays provides a "free play of psychic energy" — for the works of art so often either present difficult puzzles or direct us back into the perplexing and parlous environment. It is doubtful, too, whether we ever enjoy an equilibrium, an optimal homeostasis, since avant-garde products almost never appeal to the fullest powers of our spirits and direct themselves, rather, to shocking and mocking us instead of helping us (by whatever tragical rift) to grasp ourselves and the world about us. Among the experts and connoisseurs, too, the conventional response to modern art is one of a tense uneasiness — suggesting from another aspect that we need to modify our transmitted criteria and ideas. We can hardly doubt that what was treated as constituting the aesthetic experience in 1910–14 can no longer be accepted without serious reappraisal and a suitable alteration of this idea so that it corresponds to the extended domain of the arts in the 1960s. For a further discussion of this problem, see chapter 1, "The Criteria of Aesthetic Valuation."

19. Here I have in mind the very important fact that any definition of art as such can embrace the genetic attributes in but a most abstract form and, of course, the work of art *in individuo* not at all. Needless to say, each of the stated criteria appears in one or another concrete form; this being true especially of the first and last. The special quality of the particular criterion is not only a characteristic but is likewise derived from its association with the other criteria. This problem is described and analysed by R. Ingar-den in his *Experience, Artwork, Value* (in Polish; Cracow, 1965), pp. 128–136, 162–194. I share his position on major points, although I reserve until another occasion a discussion of some particulars.

Chapter 3

The Criteria
of Aesthetic Evaluation

Nobody, I am certain, will disagree with the observation that shifts occur in the valuations and evaluations that people supply with regard to art. Correspondingly, people change their minds about the frames of reference they employ, that is, about the reasons they are prepared to give for arriving at a particular valuation or evaluation. I do not suppose there will be disagreement about that, either; but what specifically do we mean by "frames of reference" and "reasons"? It seems we indicate a choice of characteristics—of traits, or sets of traits, which may be intrinsic, extrinsic, or both—by which a decision regarding value is made.

Let us go further and grant that the choice of criteria is generally made on quite relativist grounds. Our personal experience, as well as the historical pattern of such data, should confirm this statement. In generation after generation, the idea of *de gustibus non disputandum* is sustained. And yet is there a *conclusive* justification why anyone's taste should be thought invulnerable to dispute?

Let us consider a case concerning a recently fashionable topic, pop art. Anne asserts that pop art has been innovative, while her friend Joan responds that pop art is not really art at all. Anne answers that there are no "eternal traits" that define what a work of art must be, and whether or not an object is called art is decided strictly by certain people for whom it has a concrete social function in the given sociohistorical context. Joan rejoins that pop art is not characterized by the stylized autonomous harmony which many people believe is the essence of art.

Let us look in on another quarrel. Peter calls Jackson Pollock a giant among the American painters of this century, but John retorts that Pollock's reputation is inflated and merely transient. John defends this low evaluation by stating his belief that theme-presentation is an indisputable criterion of artistic value. Peter responds that the experts *he* respects think composition and the color mix are the fundamental values of art.

Such disputes, the reader will recognize, have a way of trailing off inconclusively. What is to dispose Anne or Joan, Peter or John, to give up a very righteous feeling with regard to her or his arguments? Each relies implicitly on a definite hierarchy of values, and each begins with, and goes little beyond, his or her previous disposition. The doctrine of *de gustibus* has often shown a terrifying ability to suppress systematic disputation in this way. Art history is indeed congested by such disagreements. Nonetheless, on the stock market of values, where some rise high and then quickly fall, some values do become sturdy blue chips while others continue to

The first version of this essay appeared in Polish in *Studia Estetyczne*, vol. 2 (1964). An enlarged version appeared in the Sarajevo journal *Pregled*, 1968, no. 4.

edge in and out of the market. Shakespeare was condemned, or else simply ignored, for about two centuries; then he gained a "universal" acclaim which has lasted to this day, although the reasons given for this acclaim are by no means uniform. El Greco was scorned by the prevailing standards of his time, but since the late nineteenth century his reputation has remained constant through the fluctuations of many modern schools. The art of primitive peoples was not appreciated until the cubists and fauvists came along; now their highly expressive masks and other artifacts are thought first-rate.

We should not permit ourselves to be dumbfounded by the widespread evidence of relativism in criteria. Human reality is continually undergoing change. Our common experience includes an art history of repeated renewals; but we should study the continual fluctuations to discover whether *some* valuational and evaluational standards are recurrent. If some are, which ones, and why? Certainly, when we speak of justifying reasons and standards, we are brought directly to the problem of axiological criteria. The gist of solving this problem, as I shall try to show in this chapter, is the judicious discrimination of our valuational and evaluational *procedures*. But before I come to a tentatively proposed solution to the axiological problem of procedures, I must undertake a brief excursus into the past.

Constituent Values, the Foundation for Ranking Works of Art

The attitude towards the axiological criteria of art which I have just now in effect been discussing is the *subjectivist* one. Those who adopt it often look back to David Hume as the founder of their school. That Hume was a subjectivist is not at all certain, however. His renowned essay "Of the Standard of Taste" (1757) begins, it is true, with a recognition of the variety of tastes and the difficulties involved in determining a proper criterion. Still, in discussing the permanent value of Homer's works, Hume said, "Some particular forms or qualities from the original structure of the internal fabric are calculated to please, and others to displease," and he continued, "It must be allowed that there are certain qualities in objects which are fitted by nature to produce those particular feelings."[1] Nor did Hume stop at this general comment. He bade the reader look for internal and external characteristics which might have a definite axiological relationship to beauty or ugliness. His concluding thoughts contain not a subjectivist but a relativist orientation, namely, a recognition that taste varies over time and space.[2] A full analysis of Hume's essay shows that his position was in fact antisubjectivist. He merely set aside for another discussion such difficult questions as: What is the nature of the ideal consumer of works of art? Is unity (implicitly taken to be an objective condition) the underlying feature of all works of art? Can we establish an identity of opinion among various generations as the sociocultural, intersubjective precondition for works of art?

A glance into the work of Kant is equally instructive. His philosophy is frequently cited with the aim of denying the possibility of the universality of aesthetic judgment. It is true that he held that aesthetic judgment lacks objective foundation, but we should remember that in some respects he agreed with Hume. In accordance with the principles of his transcendental philosophy, he argued that the constitution of our cognitive faculties is such that when there is unity of imagination and understanding (or imagination and practical reason) and also congruence of an imagined object with the organs of cognition, there can arise an aesthetic experience of the beautiful or the sublime.[3] If we recognize the natural foundations of our judging faculty, the antinomies of taste can be understood: taste is subjective but it tends towards being universal.[4]

The free play of our faculties produces Kant's famous *Zweckmässigkeit ohne Zweck*, "purposiveness without purpose," a property not peculiar to a given man or epoch, which results in aesthetic response not to particular colors or sounds but rather to forms, to unity in complexity. Thus, in a painting the artistically decisive element is the drawing, not the color; the latter makes its effect only through the senses.[5] Kant also argued that because of the constitution of the human mind (as he conceived it), things such as flowers and ornaments and musical fantasies (all of which are related to the category of free beauty, *pulchritude vaga*) please us in ways different from those of horses, people, buildings.[6] I cannot here pursue Kant's doctrine further, but may mention that paragraphs 30 to 40 of *The Critique of Judgment* develop these key issues. As with our exposition of Hume, the aim of this discussion of Kant has been to highlight one particular axiological tendency: the abandonment of subjectivism in favor of a belief in a comprehensible constant in human nature.

Hume and Kant were interested first in establishing aesthetic values and had less interest in ranking them. The question arises at this point whether evaluation, following as it does on valuation, is in every respect *dependent* on valuation. The response which would be given to this question by subjectivists and by relativists is obvious, for if we agree that aesthetic values are modified according to the person(s), time(s), and circumstance(s), we must logically admit that the *ranking* of aesthetic values will coincide with the valuational choices. What if we adopt a more

objectivistic position (relationism)? (Hume's and Kant's reservations point in this
direction.) Do we find ourselves compelled then to evaluate works of art solely by
referring to their valuational traits? This is the question I want to consider now.

Let us assume that we have used some definite criterion of aesthetic valuation
to say which objects are works of art and which are not. Next, we seek a criterion
which will allow us to differentiate among works of art as to their greater or lesser
value. In this way we distinguish the fundamental criterion, which *establishes*
value, from the graduating or scalar criterion, which *ranks* value. Now, in ranking
the value do we have to consider that the scalar criteria are entirely derivative from
the value-establishing criteria? In other words, is the statement that "X is better
(worse) than Y" merely an extension of the primary statement that "X and Y are
artistically valuable in such-and-such a way"? This identification does exist to
some extent, but I shall argue that it is only a partial basis for the evaluative operation. (It will also emerge that I allow for the role of *extraaesthetic* reasons in scaling
aesthetic objects and that I propose two other criteria as well.)

Before proceeding to a detailed analysis, yet another problem has to be considered briefly. Do the experts agree with me that a distinction should be made
between the valuating and evaluating procedures? We read in Hume's essay that
"by comparison alone we fix the epithets of praise or blame and learn how to
assign the due degree of each."[7] Hume did not work out the differences between
the criteria of valuation and those of evaluation; he did, however, note that works
of art may be more or less harmonious, and concluded that those creations are
superior which are without moral defects and religious exaggerations. The problem of the criteria of evaluation was not clearly addressed by Hume, then; and
Kant did not squarely treat the issue either. Paragraph 42 of *The Critique of Judgment*, long a bone of contention among scholars, suggests (in drawing attention to
moral ideas) that what is beautiful in nature should rank above what is beautiful
in art. Paragraph 53 alludes to a hierarchy of the arts and places poetry at the
summit. Another rudimentary approach to ranking turns up in the axiology of
Hippolyte Taine. In contemporary aesthetics, we may note, there is a continual
propensity to eliminate the evaluative moment,[8] the view being that any work of
art is characterized by its axiological singularity and that, consequently, comparative ranking is not only misapplied but also harmfully misleading.

A standpoint which supposes uniqueness to be the primary aesthetic value
seems indefensible to me. First, the assertion of uniqueness implies a comparison
made among objects belonging in the same class; and, moreover, comparison im-

plies at least some shared features which can be scaled. Second, though uniqueness no doubt must be taken into account when the aesthetic values of *X* and *Y* are weighed, we may certainly challenge the notion that singularity supplies *the* fundamental axiological principle which distinguishes a certain class of objects as art. My contention, which I shall argue for later, is that meaningful uniqueness is equivalent to originality, which is *not* characteristic of every artistic work. Third, objections to evaluative procedures stem overwhelmingly from the tacit or overt assumption that we grasp intuitively, without fail, the never repeated peculiarity of *X*. This assumption is arbitrary and must be rejected by anyone who does not share a belief in intuitive insight and the complete exceptionality of every work of art. Indeed there are numerous opponents of this one-dimensional axiological standpoint regarding aesthetic objects. The distinction I have offered is not stressed by them all, but in American aesthetics Stephen Pepper and Monroe Beardsley explicitly make this kind of argument.[9] Starting with the same axiological premises, however, they reach solutions to the problem of aesthetic evaluation different from mine. It may help to explain the divergence between us if I emphasize that my results are arrived at with an historicist methodology.

Since the valuational criteria were dealt with extensively in Chapter 1, I shall only recall here that I already discern a kind of propaedeutic scaling in the establishment of the aesthetic (artistic) values: These values as they appear in aesthetic objects will, if compared, prove to be graduated along what is in effect a *continuum*, some of whose elements will be more and some less artistic (aesthetic). Yet this initial aspect of ranking is not a procedure separate from the establishment of the characteristics of the axiological class now under examination; the evaluation proper commences only later on, when a continuum has already been confirmed on the basis of an ultimate criterion which has been chosen. For this reason, furthermore, I decline to make a distinction between a "good work of art" and a "work of art." The latter is always in some sense "good" even if situated towards the bottom of the continuum which comprises artistic values.

Let me stress that, unlike valuation, evaluation *begins* with the axiological criterion in hand. The set of qualities which characterize the art object may be assumed to provide the decisive reason to justify the ranking operation. In other words, if the strategy of valuation demands that we can only refer to *axiological-philosophical criteria* as the ultimate justification, the evaluational strategy allows us to refer to already available aesthetical-axiological data. (There is a problem complicating this statement, which stems from those evaluational procedures that do not derive from the set of qualities established as constituently artistic; I shall, as I said, explore this matter in the proper place.)

Problems in Quantifying the Constituent Values

How then are we to evaluate art? The initial, crucial operation in comparing and ranking artistic objects is the "quantification" of the fundamental artistic values already established. The creation that embodies the basic characteristics of art successfully and with a *greater magnitude* or *intensity* is the better work of art. [10]

Accordingly, if we desire to establish a hierarchy among certain works of art, we first must locate and acknowledge a common fund of data in terms of which they can be compared. The only fundamental areas of artistic value common to all sorts of art are *form* and *expression*, and we should therefore give the values in these areas precedence of consideration. Other major areas of artistic value—for instance, mimesis and the construction-function-form syndrome—are distributive, and we should give them primary attention only when assigning rank in the domains where such values are residual, in other words, in cases of representational art and of so-called industrial or applied art, respectively. Yet even with regard to the axiological fund which is both fundamental and common, the matter is by no means simple.

Let us observe a few of the complexities of quantification. Assuming that our standard of measure (in terms of magnitude or intensity) is legitimate, we can proceed to compare, say, the expressive value of one work with that of another work, in order to judge which of the two is the most fully achieved. We may perhaps find equality in the expressive quotients of the two works along with an unequal status in their degrees of integrated structural compactness. Or the reverse may be true: the formal achievement might be equal but the expressiveness different.

Some may think that I have reverted to traditional concerns when I carry quantification over to a domain such as mimesis or the specific functional values of an industrial (applied) art. For prominent here will be such evaluational guidelines as the *diversity* of elements and their *unity*, or the *identity* and *discrepancy* between form and content [11] or between form and function. [12] We could, alternatively, discuss such elements in terms of "formemes" or "iconemes" or—to go further with this terminology—"functemes." [13]

I have asserted that it is possible to make comparisons by referring to certain recurrent values, which may be defined objectively by the study of a sufficiently broad sample of works of art so as to note their common attributes. For example, consider the problem of evaluating the works of Aert de Gelder, Jan Lievens, Ferdinand Bol, and Bartholemeus van der Helst, as compared with the contemporaneous early works of Rembrandt. In this case the evaluation would probably be focused primarily on the expressive values, situated in a particular compact structure which has a particular mimetic character. Another type of application would be to the sustained work of a *single artist*, say, Mondrian between 1912 and 1920. In this case the key criterion would be the simplicity and terseness of Mondrian's compact formal structures. As a third example, Delacroix's works might be compared both among themselves, according to the criteria established in the artist's peak years, and then with examples taken from his predecessors and contemporaries, according to the criterion of the *romantic* expressional resources; or Ingres might similarly be studied and compared, situating him among his *classicist* companions.

Without question, Delacroix is notable for his expressive attainments and Ingres for his compact and elegant compositions. This leads to a most tantalizing question: Is there a way to make a comparative judgment of the two oeuvres? The answer must be no, unless a means could somehow be found to weigh the standard of expressiveness against the standard of formal structure. In the same way, Mahler and Scriabin can very likely be judged superior to their contemporaries in the composition of expressive, symbolical-metaphysical music. But how could we compare that standard with the very different standard established at the same time by the music of Debussy and Ravel?

It is my tentative view that great artists operate on an approximately comparable aesthetic level, although they develop disparate and noncomparable resources. The values to which they give body may differ from work to work in intensity and magnitude, but a lessened expressional quotient will be compensated for by a heightened formal organization, or vice versa. Even if we could assert that Joyce's *Ulysses*, with its diversity and vigor of language, incidents, and characters, is more expressive than Musil's *The Man Without Qualities*, while neither work excelled the other in formal perfection, we could not thereby conclude that *Ulysses* is the greater literary achievement. Musil's work can only be measured by its own extraordinary merits; it is, as they say, in a class by itself. *The Man Without Qualities* is a philosophical novel which deliberately achieves a highly artistic yet essaylike reflection on the crisis of twentieth-century culture. Its expressive and formal qualities are not those of *Ulysses*, or of any other novel ever written.

A similar case comparison can be made between Bulgakov's *The Master and*

Margherita and Sholokhov's *And Quiet Flows the Don.* The expressive qualities of the former are due to a unique blend of social satire and fantasy that ripples along under the deft control of the author's world view. The writing of this marvelous literary conjuror, Bulgakov, is neither more nor less evocative than that of Sholokhov, for *at this highest level of literary mastery, the only way to characterize the expression (or formal perfection) is according to its kind not its degree.*

In summary, a quantifying evaluation may be applied most rewardingly to distinguish the great masters from their lesser contemporaries in a particular place, time, school, style, and also to highlight the uniqueness of the peak achievements of the master artists. The reader may be annoyed by the idea of a quantifying approach to the work of Rembrandt, which set his entire artistic milieu in eclipse, or to Chaplin's early one-reelers, which will long outlive the ordinary slapstick film comedy of that time, objecting that the ineffable character of great art is impugned by a yardstick approach. But I do not use the term "quantification" in a literal sense. There are no calipers or sliderules to measure the magnitude, and no electronic sensors or binary calculators to provide a reading of intensities for the purpose of arriving at an appraisal of what is "better" in art. Let me entertain just two very restricted exceptions to this categorical statement: we may be able to measure physically, for purposes of artistic judgment, (1) certain *discrete* elements (such as colors, sounds, and shapes), and (2) the physiological *responses* which correspond to such stimuli and cofunction with them, partly by feedback. I will concede a literalness to the concept of quantification only with respect to such noncompound phenomena—and here I will allow even the possibility of a strict dependence of aesthetic qualities on the rudimentary data that are measured. Otherwise I have something different in mind.

I do not believe that turning up the electric amps for greater loudness can effectively transform a mediocre rock band into an excellent performing group. I do not think that psychedelic painting becomes better merely through the use of dayglo colors. The expressiveness that I speak of quantifying is not the unmediated result of the "strength" of the discrete, immediately given sensuous elements. However, neither is my use of the term "quantification" a mere metaphor; rather, my idea is that the *degree* of expressiveness or of formal perfection can be assessed by a direct apprehension.

Now, direct apprehension is a concept with a genealogy in aesthetic history, and I have already touched on it lightly in Chapter 2. I should only say here that the procedure is easily confused with what is called intuition, but intuition is more ambiguous and unreliable for it is theoretically unclarified in comparison with the direct apprehension of magnitude and intensity. I should note that individuals in the art public will without doubt have an *unequal capacity* for an adequate direct apprehension. (This aspect is elaborated briefly in Chapter 4.) In any case, even to the untrained amateur, the Barcelona architecture of Gaudi reveals an emphasis on expression rather than on formal perfection, as compared with the buildings of Adolf Loos, for example. Similarly, the exuberance of Whitman's poetry may be directly apprehended as being at an opposite pole from the restraint and delight in form of A. E. Housman's lyrics. And is not the looser, more vigorous form of Brecht's theater immediately apparent when compared with the delicately constructed dramas of Giraudoux?

My proposal of direct apprehension may seem to beg the test of empirical confirmation of magnitude and intensity. It may be verified, however, that quantifying judgments of art objects *are* achieved in this way and that they *do* possess a peculiar character by which any individual may try to check his own direct apprehension of a work of art. If a sampling of actual direct apprehensions of a given object brings out certain recurrences, then the empirical confirmation of the various personal quantifying procedures will have been achieved.

If there is a troubling aspect in quantification, as it is thus understood and applied, I would say it comes up in the distinction between form and expression. I consider the compositional qualities to be expressive and the expressive qualities to be compositional. However, when it comes time to distinguish value functions ("*this* is the formal dimension, *that* is the expressive side") then the task of discriminating for quantification becomes problematic, especially if we pass from nonobjective art to representational art, in which the expressive qualities also carry the burden of formal composition. I have a way of minimizing the confusion, which is to stress two distinct aspects of the apprehended structure: (1) the arrangement of the whole and the relationships among the elements—which I regard as the indices of form; and, within this, (2) the internal material—which is more or less expressive.

A final observation on this problem must be added. If we consider the avant-garde movement, especially of recent years, we cannot fail to note a calculated abandonment of both form and expression. In view of the aforementioned standards, applicable to art until just recently, shall we evaluate these new works as "worse"? I think that would be a mistake. The avant-garde premises have shifted the major tasks which artists face (and, by implication, those which we too must face) from the field of evaluation to the most primordial issues of valuation. We shall get nowhere by trying to compare the values of the best happenings with those of the works of Kandinsky; or the values of minimal art with those of the works of Mondrian. The interest of the avant-garde artist does not lie in the achievement of formal/expressive merit, but, rather, in the question of the mere possibility of "the art activity" under varying circumstances.

I might pull together this perspective on appraising art as follows: Evaluation presumes the existence of some quantum of expression and form, while its most propitious frame of reference consists of acknowledged works of art with a marked coherence of provenance and school, style, etc. It is, nonetheless, possible to evaluate artists of *diverse* periods and countries who have formal, expressive, or mimetic traits in common. Entire movements in different eras may similarly share parallel traits. Moreover, there are a number of characteristics that permit otherwise diverse works to be comparatively quantified—a common heritage, for example, as in the case of the influence of African and Polynesian sculpture on the works of Henry Moore, Archipenko, and Lipchitz. The analogical benchmark might be partly patho-psychological if one sought to compare, say, the paintings of Van Gogh and Ernst Josephson.

To this point, I have considered quantifications that are chiefly based on a single feature. Of course the actual quantifying procedure must be much more complicated. Still, from the simplified single-feature model we learn a crucial lesson: It is futile to compare the evaluations of two works which embody *incommensurable* (even if equally significant) values. In other words, the sets to be quantified must not be too unlike. The following points must be kept in mind as providing the most fully reliable basis for evaluation:

1. The works of art should be from the same period and place.
2. They should be representative of the same general trend.
3. They should belong to the same domain of art, and perhaps the same genre.
4. They should have common valuational qualities, since there are numerous ways to realize a given artistic value.

This last point carries further what I have said regarding form and expression as the most universal referents of evaluation; namely, that within their context we should discriminate the *kinds* of formal structure and the *kinds* of expression realized in particular valuational qualities. With these four points, we have an optimal blueprint with which to focus an evaluation. I should note that these discriminations may be (and frequently are) distorted by critics who seize on blatantly similar

traits and, wrenching them from the context for authentic comparison, leave no
adequate basis for assessing the tangible and necessarily complicated differences
of *degree*. It is wiser to skip evaluation than to make the needed comparisons in
a careless and crude way. We should respect an intricate complexity in the works
of two distinct artists which we find to possess some analogous values.

Even if we proceed with adequate caution, the comparative process is seldom
without foggy crossroads and frustrating obstacles. We shall conclude, for example,
that, on the whole, Terborch and de Hooch succeed about equally with mimesis
and compact integration; yet the works are so different in their expression as to
be incommensurable. And what of cases where the differences are not that great?
For example, the films of Fellini and Antonioni are successfully mimetic in different
ways: the Antonioni films are not laden with the baroque rhetoric that is typical
of Fellini. Yet we would find it difficult to defend any standard by which we might
compare their achievements with regard to the intensity or magnitude of expressive
values in their work. In the functionalism of the Le Corbusier and Gropius housing
projects (at Marseilles and Siemensstadt, respectively), we find an unevenness of
achievement. However, neither in the functional values nor in the expressiveness
shall we find a sharply decisive basis for ranking either more highly. Van der
Rohe's Seagram Building in New York City might be conceded an advantage in
terms of a painterly or sculptural value, but it could simultaneously be faulted for
functional imperfection.

Consider the case of X and Y which share the same (or similar) valuational qualities, with X being a shade superior to Y in expressiveness and Y having the comparative edge in formal balance (e.g., De Kooning versus Hans Hofmann, Dubuffet
versus Burri, Aalto versus Saarinen, Penderecki versus Lutoslawski, Robbe-Grillet
versus Butor). Here we can balance only tenuously the disparate superiorities within the works of art. We can treat the irregularities among quantification sets only
after we have arrived at such a solution-in-tension.

An important and difficult task for the historians of the different artistic domains
is to establish specific groupings of works of art and to provide reasons for them,
on the basis of which effective evaluations may be made. The task is the more
challenging when several domains of the arts are to be studied, which are pervaded
with the same style characteristics. That such studies are both feasible and highly
rewarding is confirmed in the work of many distinguished scholars. Indeed, the best
monographs on artistic geniuses make their most important contribution to general
aesthetics in this area. The outstanding artistic individuality is linked to a school

with which he shares common features. The genius is generally found to manifest the traits of the school to an unmatched degree.

I have underscored some of the difficulties in deciding on a fit evaluational approach, especially the risks entailed by different but equally significant axiological sets. I must emphasize that the requisite care and delicacy have seldom been applied, no matter how many warnings have been issued by aestheticians and philosophers. Criticism usually rushes forward, heedless of all warnings. It is easy to grasp why. Times of aesthetic crisis — when received ideas about art and beauty are in collapse, when the axiological strongholds are under attack — are alone capable of fully impressing upon critics the ultimate criteria of valuation and the relationship between the criteria of valuation and of evaluation. For the most part, critics apply the criteria of evaluation in place of valuation and do not realize the substitution. They speak, for example, of a work's perfection, excellence, or uniqueness, equating these qualities with constituent goodness. They are thus able to compare and rank all art objects (whether they are more or less art) without any problems or hesitation. An even more universal habit among critics is to treat *favorite* values or valuational qualities (those having an idiosyncratically personal or sociocultural bias) as the deciding evaluational standard; art objects are then compared and graded according to the presence and magnitude of these preferred qualities. Still another critical practice entailing neglect of the four points earlier outlined is artistic evaluation which refers only to the composition and response of the object's audience, and without pondering whether that response is predicated on the given aesthetic structure. (This comment is our first mention of the kind of evaluative process which is not based on quantification of the fixed constituent traits of art.)

The muddled evaluations I have mentioned (there are others too) should properly be turned back. They cannot, however, be ignored, above all because much of the critical opinion of the past and present is of this character. Of course, nobody should be forbidden to evaluate in his own fashion — not so much because of the resiliency that many works of art have shown against erroneous judgments, as because of the long and horrible history of the harm exerted by any kind of censorship. It is true that wrong aesthetic judgments seldom hurt the authentic work of art, and that where they do the effect is generally transitory. (Perhaps this also indicates the reason why a social unanimity is pursued in moral judgments, while there is a much greater tolerance for individual or group initiative when it comes to art.) Nonetheless, we may legitimately expect of critics that they will plainly de-

scribe their justifying reasons to themselves and to us. Thus, the most that should
be done to combat muddled evaluation is to encourage a more lucid methodology.

Does Any Category of Value or Art Exert Priority?

I shall now explore the widespread approach to evaluation which ranks works of
art according to whether a certain valuational quality or value appears which
merits a preferred status. I shall try to be definite whether or not the grounds exist
for such an *axiological hierarchy*. For example, is a creative work described as
applied art automatically inferior, by aesthetic criteria, to any other work which
(assuming a parity of expressiveness and compactness) offers some depiction of
reality? Or is priority perhaps due to applied art? Is form the primal value — so that
a deficiency of form would inevitably make a work of art inferior no matter how
expressively and mimetically well-endowed it might be? Or should the evaluation
simply look to the sheer abundance of the elements which constitute the artistic
structure?

It does seem to be true that painting has always been treated as more important
than the artistic aspect of dress and decor in the same period. This opinion goes
back to antiquity's doctrine that some artistic genres and themes outrank others
(usually they are said to be the more pure). Certain contemporary authors share
this opinion.[14] It does not appear to me that such a hierarchy of artistic values is
sound. In my view, the values of musical composition, for instance, do not *as such*
contest those of literary works. Nor do peculiarly musical or literary values *as such*
merit preference over the values peculiar to the Rietveld chair. Each artistic domain
implies and merits its own *distinct* criteria, as does each genre within the domain,
each peculiar artistic value, and each particular set of valuational qualities. The
criteria should correspond to the traits being analyzed and compared. Only within
the scope of that given frame of reference can the means be found to evaluate the
features of art.

We should look into another question which is related to the one above: Can
preference be assigned to the criteria of content over the criteria of form? This assumption of primacy appears in the history of marxist aesthetic thought from
Marx, Plekhanov, and Lunacharsky to Gramsci and Lukács. We can find an abundance of misunderstanding on both sides of the debate. A priority of content criteria
might prevail only in the case of representational art, and even here the subject
matter exacts a superior claim only inasmuch as mimetic elements determine the
formal and expressive aspects of the work of art. In other words, if the work fails

to succeed in terms of the mimetic criteria understood in this way, the structural compactness of the given whole is weakened. We should emphasize that, if attention to content criteria is joined to contempt for form or expression, what actually will be preferred are *non*artistic criteria.

What may be concluded is that the merits of works of art should be defined in the context of the distinctive traits of the given art domain and genre. Music should not be evaluated as a superior art simply because it is nonrepresentational. Nor should the novel be preferred as the better genre because it encompasses a maximum of transformed life content. However, counterarguments can be made. It can reasonably be objected that the unique work of art is potentially imbued with a wealth of *experience*, with a breadth and depth of referential data and patterns. Since this is so, why should not a painting by Rembrandt be compared with a brilliantly patterned Persian carpet? Why shouldn't Mahler be considered and ranked in a context including Kafka? I agree that the appeal to a fund of experience—of course objectified in a rich artistic structure—is not to be refuted.

Yet with this we must remember that what decides an axiological superiority is not the domain of art, the genre, or the given value *as such*. The architectural works of Nervi, Torroja, and Candella embody a much richer experience than do a lot of canvases painted nowadays. The tapestries of the Polish designer Magda Abakanowicz are often more imbued with thought than the average play performance. The songs of Joan Baez are more truly elaborated than numerous Hollywood films. Anyone can think of more examples, and they prove both that a hierarchy exists among the artistic values (corresponding to the intensity and magnitude of the evoked experience) and that the problem of judgment hinges on the discernment of *an ensemble of values*—whether purely aesthetic, or aesthetical-moral, or aesthetical-phisosophical, etc.—rather than deriving from a hierarchy of subject matters, themes, artistic genres, or the like.

Added Residual, Aesthetic Criteria: Novelty and Originality

Mention of the magnitude and intensity of the artistic vision brings to mind the question of the unique artistic personality. We pass, by way of this question, to a pair of additional criteria that cannot be measured by a quantification of established constituent elements. These additional criteria are *novelty* and *originality*.[15]

A number of theorists argue that we need not regard originality as a constant and constituent attribute of art. Against them, we might quote Kant—*The Critique of Judgment*, paragraphs 45 to 47—where he urges that art can be deemed beautiful inasmuch as it is the creation of genius and possesses originality. Kant's view is upheld nowadays by the school of Croce and by others who are oriented towards an empirical definition of art.[16] I think that originality cannot be equated with individual expression, a trait which *is* constant in art. Originality should be limited to a more particular and uncommon kind of expression.

While *individual* expression can and indeed must be assumed in the work per se, we shall only be able to discriminate originality-value *in a context*. By what procedure shall we single out this value? There must first be a determination of the individuality of the art object, which we discern, as I have said, by direct apprehension. Next there is comparison, in a twofold context: (1) with other works by the same artist (so that we may more fully grasp the particular qualities of this artist's singular production); and (2) with works by other artists (so that we may crisply demarcate these distinctive qualities from those discerned in others). Originality occurs rarely; because this is so, we tend to be on the lookout for the clues which hint of originality as we scan those traits of works of art that are indicative of individual expression. Some scholars want to restrict the term "work of art" only to those works which possess this highly unusual attribute. I think this a pointlessly narrow idea of art, and find it more valid to stress the fact that originality is an attribute that is highlighted when it is compared with other, nonoriginal attributes of artistic production—form, expression, mimetic content, or form-following-function constructions. Originality is, then, neither a set of given artistic qualities, nor simply an individual impress on the work of art (which we tacitly assume to be present); rather, it is an *extra attribute*—a quality of the qualities, that is, a specific trait which occurs infrequently among the constituent values.

Novelty, too, is a value distinct from the structural values which are fundamental and constant in every work of art. Being novel is not the same as merely being different. To be different is the hallmark of the value that I have called individual expression. Every work of art is different, for to some extent it embodies a distinct set of qualities. When we call a work novel, however, we imply a crucial further step: a break and departure, whether in the use of formal structure, expressive resource, mimetic theme, hero, or subject matter. Novelty, like originality, is a contextual value: it can only be discerned against an *historical* background, and it is a quality of the qualities.

How do we sharply demarcate the original from the novel? We could say that originality is observed in a *horizontal* framework, that is, in the context of a definite cultural system. Novelty's context is *vertical*, in other words, historically discerned. In both cases we have to consider the historical coefficient — in analyzing novelty, however, we have to consider the dynamism of civilization and culture.[17] The domain of art endures and also changes; what endures, however, is a tiny residue which has floated up from the ceaseless flux and the unrelenting competition. The criterion of newness stems from the human need to make and to perceive new contents and new forms. It is, accordingly, a primary criterion of evaluation among the avant-garde. The idea of novelty is central in approaching the plays of Stanislaw Ignacy Witkiewicz or Fernando Arrabal or the poems of e. e. cummings or Tadeusz Peiper. It equips us to categorize much of the value in D. W. Griffith's films, in Schönberg's and Webern's musical experiments, in Gordon Craig's plastic composition of the stage, and in Joseph Paxton's Crystal Palace.

Novelty lies in the decision to depart from the currently available resources of individual expression; its value cannot be quantified in terms of art's fundamentally constituent values *as such* because the issue is simply whether (and then, by how much) a given case of compact structure or expressive patterning or mimesis is new. In this criterion there remains still one possibility of quantification. I have said that novelty occurs in a context; that is, newness is relative to the familiar and popular. This gives us a standard of measure, which we may use on content, formal innovation, or materials newly incorporated by art (e.g., plastics, chemicals, and electronics). In any historical period some works of art may be *newer* than others and the novelty might be an aspect (extra attribute) added to some or all of the constituent values. The normal process in the history of art consists of the dynamic arrival of the new followed by its gradual assimilation until it has become a seamless part of the whole cloth of the available constituent values.

Novelty, then, may be quantified in relation to its degree of rupture with previous art history. No similar reference exists which would enable us to quantify the extent of originality. Art is original or it is not. Even if the originality occurs in a single constituent value, still, its uniqueness permeates the whole of a work and an oeuvre. The basis of originality lies in a distinctive way of viewing the world. We recognize the evidence of an exceptional artistic vision in a highly individual treatment of a certain value or values. We simply cannot measure this creative phenomenon by degrees; we can only state and point out its presence. Accordingly, the terms "better" and "inferior" do not apply.

The novel phenomenon may be duplicated, although the copy of the new will lack novelty (as our understanding of the historical coefficient will, of course, tell us); but *originality can never be duplicated.* Even the master forger Van Meegeren could not achieve originality (an authenticity)[18] in his art forgeries. The history of art reveals a long series of failures to copy true originality. In contrast, novelty is easily copied, and its duplicates gain favor with equal facility. Both categories are illuminated in Alfred Lessing's "What is Wrong With a Forgery?" (in *Journal of Aesthetics and Art Criticism* [Summer 1965]), although the author appears to oscillate between one notion of originality which reduces to novelty and is treated chiefly as a historical phenomenon, and another notion which is considered as an artistic phenomenon (e.g., Vermeer's specific qualities which even a virtuoso counterfeiter found elusive). These notions cannot be used interchangeably; and the more convincing one with regard to forgery is, as I have suggested above, the argument in defense of the highly singular character of originality.

In distinguishing between originality and novelty, we should give attention to still another question. Are these criteria mutually exclusive, or may they overlap? Can the presence of one heighten the value of the other? I should say at once that originality and novelty do often come together, especially in those artists who work with *new* form, content, or materials *in a unique way* (e.g., Brecht, Stravinsky, Gropius). From the standpoint of the historical coefficient, the originality of such artists is integrated with the avant-garde tendencies which they respond to and help advance. However, those who innovate in art often think that an avant-garde in problem-solving must automatically produce originality. Yet it follows from our analysis that not all the phenomena of an avant-garde movement will be original in any adequate sense of the term. It does not matter which innovating tendency we study: there will be an abundance of works of art which offer a novel departure from the established constituent values and very few which may rightly be called original. (Consider dada. It made a dozen reputations, but Kurt Schwitters stands out as the most representative innovator *and* the most highly individual artist. Marcel Duchamp, whose link with dada was but partial, can even be said to excel Schwitters.) Thus, in the "diachronic" dimension we find that some "synchronic" artistic structures urge themselves to the fore, and the result is that: (1) novelty may prove to be devoid of originality; (2) novelty and originality may overlap or coincide; or (3) original works may lack novelty.

Of course, in one sense it is true that originality is always novel; yet we must exert care not to overextend the idea of the new, which would happen if we made it coincide with creativity and the uniqueness we associate with it. Instead, I link novelty with the avant-garde. In other words, novelty is the externally radical aspect of the work of art, whereas originality is the internal, permanent character of the work in its most positive manifestation. By novelty the artist elaborates the basically collective dynamism of the transformation of art; by originality the personal articulation of his style is most fully realized. Both aspects contribute to the enrichment of human culture. However, the uniqueness of an individual artistic vision, if completely elaborated, appears to be the more enduring. The music of Maurice Ravel was original in this way without providing any kind of historical advance; and the same can be said of Alban Berg's *Wozzeck*.

Paul Klee was primarily an original artist and no avant-gardist in the way Man Ray was. The pictographs of Klee from *Schwankendes Gleichgewicht* (1922) to *Paukenspieler* (1940), ascetic and at the same time dense, reveal the avant-garde heritage of the 1920s, and yet Klee, just as much as Kandinsky and Miro, eludes comprehension in a framework of novelty. His creations afford an ineffable, enticing world of lyricism and fantasy which brings us close to the archetypes of human imagination and emotions. His exquisite communication alters what might otherwise seem inscrutable hieroglyphs into universally comprehensible signs.

The work of Dostoevsky provides another good case in point. We know from the critical studies by Tinyanov, Shklovsky, and Eikhenbaum that Dostoevsky should definitely not be regarded as an innovator. He moved among the avant-garde, yet he drew deeply on the achievements of Lermontov, Hoffman, Gogol, and his contemporaries in the so-called naturalist school. In this context his personal vision propels the originality of his oeuvre, as has been shown by Russian scholarship from Mikhailovsky to Grossman and Bakhtin. The result was a unique philosophical and moral drama composed of polyphonic patterns in anguished counterpoint: truths of reason vs. those of faith; history vs. psychology; and the continually disintegrating line dividing sanity from madness, the infinity of Christ's love from the tragedy of the human wasteland, the magnificence and helplessness of Good from the ubiquity and insidiousness of Evil.

Still another question can be raised: Is originality tantamount to *sincerity*? This is the view of Croce and some other theorists. Beyond doubt, sincerity is a trait in artistic processes. It is, however, a trait which eludes verification.[19] We have great difficulty even when studying an artist of our own time in learning if his comments relating to his work are distortions (even if unintentional) of the authentic creative process.[20] In studying work of an earlier era, the criterion of sincerity in creation becomes totally unprovable. Even if we could confirm the sincerity of a single work of art, could we infer a standard from its attributes which would enable us to evaluate other art? Can we even grant that sincerity confers artistic value? If we accept that proposition, all of the most amateurish "artists" will be very happy since surely the most distinctive attribute of their work is its sincerity.

At several points I have suggested that originality can be linked with breadth and depth of vision. "Vision" should not be taken to mean *only* some reproduction of the real world and the fates of men in it. Theodore Greene adopts the latter view, and is led by it to the untenable idea that "theme" is a decisive factor in artistic greatness, especially in literature, a domain which Greene admits is more congenial to his notion of originality than are those of music or painting, for example.[21] His argument thus presents us with another "special pleading" for the priority of one artistic domain over another. If correct, Greene's thesis would also provide a basis for a quantification of originality. In my judgment, however, we can find no more originality in Proust than in Vermeer, no more in Bartók than in Frank Lloyd Wright. These artists simply are original in different ways. Yet to conclude this is not to take away from Greene's wholly correct observation that a wealth and profundity of experience should be properly acknowledged where it is distinctly imbued in art objects. The criterion of originality is one mode of making such an acknowledgment. As we shortly shall see, nonartistic criteria also offer a relevant standard.

So far I have promulgated three scales for use in making comparisons:
1. the intensity/magnitude of the constituent values;
2. their novelty;
3. their originality.

Should originality outweigh novelty in a comprehensive evaluational scheme? Do scales (2) and (3) overshadow scale (1) in importance? Let us put the issue more precisely. If a given work of art has an edge over another work on the novelty scale, does it deserve higher estimation for this reason alone, even if the other work succeeds admirably in respect to the intensity of its constituent values? Similarly, is a more original work of art to be judged generally superior to any work which succeeds on scales (1) and (2) only? I do not see any implicit aesthetic grounds for affirming these propositions. The parallel scales we are using here must be used specifically; only in that framework can well-founded judgments be rendered. We may move to a comprehensive approach, that is, we may apply all three scales, *after* we first take pains to start with the constant and fundamental — the constituent — properties. Our procedural guideline will be similar to that formulated earlier with respect to criterion (1) only. That is, once we have found that all the given works of art fulfill criterion (1), and that one of the works is original, or novel, or both, we can then consider placing them in a hierarchy.

However, we must be exceptionally careful in this procedure, for, in fact, what we do here is to quantify the *apprehended* criteria in respect to one another, on the premise that the more of the value we have pinpointed, the better. As much can be said in disparagement of such operations as in favor of them. On the one hand, the amount of embodied values seems a fit measure, since we have previously made the reasoned assumption that the artistically constituent qualities (conjunctively or disjunctively) can be quantified. On the other hand, it seems inconceivable that we might find pairings of works where the criterion (1) is equally met all round, as a firm basis for the further comparison of criteria (2) and/or (3).

Moreover, even if we should accept such a pattern for the ranking procedure, I, for one, would have serious hesitations about labeling as "better" the work which can additionally be described as "new." The problem in dealing with originality is somewhat different. If we acknowledge originality as the decisive value in establishing a hierarchy of the given works of art, we must yet guard against the abuse of a strategy which transgresses aesthetics, that is, one which makes reference to some general axiology which we implicitly assume our audience will share. Beardsley has spoken, with respect to elementary aesthetic judgments, of a certain ultimate "area of undecidability." The present question is surely the type of case where the principle of undecidability should be invoked.

We now come to the crucial question: How are we ultimately to interpret and justify scales (2) and (3) as additional criteria of evaluation? Do we perhaps assume too much in presenting them as additional criteria? The case of (1) was simple. The quantified values (and valuational qualities), in view of our interpretation and ultimate axiological criteria, constituted the art object. These same values (observed as intensive to varying degrees) provide the criteria of evaluation. In contrast, novelty and originality are qualities which require separate interpretation and justification. Are they justifiable in themselves? That seems inconceivable. Then by what standard? We are put in a dilemma, and might easily be trapped into a vicious circle of assertion.

I contend that the way to regard novelty rightly derives from the *sociologically relativist interpretation.*[22] That is, the idea of the new in art essentially means that what is taken to constitute novelty will change as part of the constant change of aesthetic values. The value of the new accordingly has a paradoxical character: it is permanent only in the sense of a shifting and continual renewal. If we do treat

novelty as a continually recurrent, residual value in the context of sociological relativism, then it will be every bit as much an abiding criterion of *evaluation* as are the
constituently residual values of form, expression, mimesis, or the construction-function-form syndrome, for then one of our ultimate philosophical axiological criteria
will be seen to sustain the directly apprehended, historical case for this quality.

The justification of originality is much harder. Can we prove that this artistic
quality, which permeates the whole of an art object or oeuvre, is beyond doubt.
founded on any one of the five ultimate criteria in chapter 1? Presumably, the claim
could be made for objectivism in its singularistic version — i.e., stressing one single
element as providing a permanent foundation for beauty — that it gives strong support to the idea of this quality. However, historicists will retort that only the long-
term endurance of a given work of art, confronted with other works of the past,
present, and future, can make manifest what is truly original. Whatever the difficulty in deciding which philosophical-axiological orientation is most relevant, originality is undoubtedly sustained whether by the one or the other criterion and we
must accept it among the criteria of evaluational operations.

Added Nonresidual, Nonartistic Criteria of Value

We can now proceed on the basis of the three types of residual (i.e., aesthetic) criteria which I have formulated. I must, however, once again assert the need for care.
We must not make a complacent assumption that *nonartistic* criteria are necessarily
out-of-bounds. Let us in fact boldly acknowledge that many kinds of judgments on
works of art and of hierarchies for them are relevant. Among the most pervasive
kinds of nonartistic criteria are evaluations from the religious, political, and moral
standpoints.[23] Should the reader be astonished to find the pertinacity of these
standpoints affirmed here? Art is a cultural phenomenon and thus a functional part
of social life in many respects. The ire which my view might evoke would be mis-
placed. It would instead be helpful for a so-called formalist position to recall the
many milennia during which the formal characteristics of art (even the seemingly
purely ornamental ones) had a magical-symbolic significance. (In some cultures this
function has, in fact, continued to the present.) Knowing this, how can we deny
legitimacy to the nonartistic interpretations of art objects? However, this interpretation of art leaves a very important and suitable task to the aesthetician, who
should insist that the two kinds of evaluational criteria be lucidly distinguished
and forthrightly applied, and also should set the example. Undoubtedly, the aesthetician will respond to authentically artistic objects by emphasizing the criteria

that are residually fundamental to art; but this should not, of course, be done in a way that ignores or narrows the discussion about the larger context of interpretation.[24]

Thus, I will want to make clear that moral, religious, and political appraisals are axiologically relevant to art. I will add, however, that on occasion some of these judgments and hierarchies prove to be ideological in the constrictive sense of the term; they ignore, from their standpoint, the specific values of the work of art with its qualities and internal structure. Again, such judgments and hierarchies may incorrectly ignore all of the residual aesthetic values except one: A work's mimesis may alone be acknowledged. These are all departures from a proper and legitimate role for nonartistic criteria, however; and the marxists have defended that legitimacy in their debates with the structuralists.[25]

From the dim past until today, ideas of a moral, political, or religious character have been organic and sometimes fundamental aspects of artistic structure. They occur very commonly in literature, drama, and film; less often in painting, sculpture, and music. They frequently amount to a philosophical raw material for a creative artist. They may, moreover, prove functional in the sense that they set a determinate ideological direction and framework in which the mimetic materials can be successfully transformed. Where this is the case, we shall have grounds to consider the ideational contribution in our evaluative operation. The *artistic efficacy* of the ideas emerges from the quantification of the mimesis. One determines whether the mimesis has succeeded, whether it is large in scope, and whether it is intensive. Moreover, the mimetic measure of ideas has an extension to other properties; and the novelty or the originality of a work of art may be, in part, determined by this kind of ideological permeation.

Another related and frequently applied nonresidual criterion, only indirectly ideological, is that of *comprehensibility*. It is stated not by one class or interest group of society, but is the response of persons in many kinds of situations who experience the disparity between the creative artist's objects and the expectations of the consumer of art. The gap is frequently acute. It occurs in social systems where the cultural bulkheads between the classes have been upheld for centuries. It also occurs in circumstances such as we know today, where the artists are constrained to produce a commercialized or a neurotic or hermetic art.

There are changing and various reasons for the public's difficulties in achieving direct access to the arts; yet in no circumstances does the comprehensibility seem to me valid as an artistic criterion. It may surely be advanced as a nonartistic standard; but, when this is done, it must be with full knowledge of and respect for the demands which history shows the arts have the right to assert to assure their survival and growth. In other words, political and civic authorities should not be permitted to interfere with the residual criteria of art, although they may rightly do what they can to encourage a greater communicativeness in the arts. An inevitable tension arises between the wish to comprehend immediately and the likelihood that much new and original art will be baffling, at least at first and to many. Residual criteria must, nonetheless, be accorded their rights.

That originality is a major or the optimum characteristic of art may prove to be less than an invariant criterion; if so, it should be reclassified out of the residual values. A residual status has long been implied in the European tradition, but it has no comparable standing in the Asian or African cultural traditions, and this should alert us to its likely axiological limitedness. Even in Europe it only took a central place in the romantic era. We should note too that the recent avant-garde has had little avowed stake in the most ample expression of individuality as a significant value in its art. The masterpiece of a genius as embodiment of the hope *non omnis moriar*, has given way to Duchamp's irreverent gestures, minimal art, and happenings; the originality of the avant-garde has been redirected in large part to destructive confrontation of established values. In the place of originality, other cultures have held up canons and archetypes of art, often sustained over several centuries. The attitudes that lead to the creation of such works of art are very different from those of our society. Not the profoundly articulated personal vision of a created "rival world," but rather divine commandment, or a moral and social stability, is what receives evaluational precedence.

Do any other nonartistic criteria appear to lay a significant claim to cutting across class and other temporal and spatial demarcations? There are some philosophies of value which seek an evaluational synthesis, reconciliation, or overview. Such criteria have been posited by artists (e.g., Tolstoi) as to be explicitly promulgated. Some aestheticians, such as L. Arnaud Reid and Rolf Ekman, hold similar positions. Reid argues that art is "significant" only when it represents great human values.[26] Ekman believes the most important values in creativity are such criteria as sanity, balance, and life affirmation.[27]

Philosophical criteria seem reasonable and indispensable for art objects — but I still cannot call them artistic criteria, as do Reid and Ekman. It seems to me that Marx's general axiological approach offers the most cogent perspective for orienting the criteria suitable to aesthetics. Basic to this general perspective is the premise that problems of aesthetics cannot be solved except in the context of certain ultimate philosophical discriminations and choices. Given this premise, art's distinctive and yet only relatively autonomous criteria are seen to be dependent on the same facts that are fundamental in choosing and formulating a general axiology. It must also be added that among the fundamental data determining evaluational criteria are the data of *disalienational activity*. Elsewhere, I have discussed alienation and the artistic currents which point toward its being superseded;[28] I won't repeat the analysis here, but will just remind the reader that Marx's treatments of aesthetic problems were all formulated in reference to the problem of alienation. Anyway, wherever an evaluative approach does refer to nonartistic qualities in art, a tacit aspect of aesthetic valuation becomes manifest — that in this domain the ultimate criteria of reference are personal moral, political, religious and philosophical viewpoints. That is to say, our evaluative judgments hinge in matters of art on our philosophical views (i.e., our philosophy of value) and it is, therefore, inescapable that the criterion has to be sought not in the qualities singled out as the apprehended constituent properties of artistic value, but rather in the general axiological approach.

Admittedly, this conception of the nonaesthetic evaluative criteria implies that art may be judged from a big and internally contradictory range of individual viewpoints; and indeed how is the reader supposed to accept any "axiological calculus" which ignores the individual variable? Still, what emerges from a study of the spectrum of general axiologies is the hope and possibility of avoiding an axiological relativism — a form of relativism naturally encouraged by a highly varied and striated society. Inevitably, the relativist dimension is invoked swiftly and to great excess where the nonartistic criteria are discussed; there is much less of a check on the idiosyncrasies of conviction, and knowledge, and method. Yet we gain hope of clarification from the fact that here, as in other domains of value, the idiosyncrasies tend to cluster around a limited number of paradigms. The individuals of a given time and place do not differ as greatly among themselves as an initial glimpse at their contradictions might suggest. Besides, over the centuries the operative political, religious, moral, and philosophical viewpoints of evaluation — at least in our ethnocentric context — have proven remarkably stable; indeed, the possible range of approaches in each of these areas is finite and we can work towards their typology.

Even with this possibility stated we must still be impressed by the continual fluctuations in the way aesthetic objects have been evaluated.[29] This dynamic in the ranking procedure must be analyzed in terms of the characteristics of human nature and of culture. Although the range of choices open to the judging individual is limited, yet it is always in flux, with orienting traits continually receding or emerging, always being disconcertingly modified. For this reason, the domain of art and of art criticism becomes one great fascinating "axiological circus." This does not apply only to the nonresidual criteria of the nonaesthetic evaluation of art. We have seen earlier that a selective, biased preference may be extended to one or another single area, genre, value, or valuational quality of art. For instance, sometimes craft criteria of constituent artistic value may be exalted by an individual or a social group, and sometimes expression and originality, perhaps of a strenuously insistent character, may be urged to the fore; sometimes a seemingly artless representational art may be preferred, and at another time the purified formal structure may command the laurels. If today ugliness is the "in" taste, tomorrow it may be subtlety or the sublime or the camp or something else.

Nonetheless, the many justifying reasons for shifts in the ranking hierarchies will prove to be just concretizations and particularizations, which can be related to an adequately interpreted and justified system of the aesthetic evaluational criteria. Similarly, in the case of the nonaesthetic criteria the frameworks cited will be particularizations of the moral, political, philosophical, religious, or other schemata of thinking which prevail in the given spatiotemporal context. How could the justifying reasons not prove to be partial or variously accented? In its totality the axiological process is propelled by the fluctuations in art's paradigms; it is subject always to the imperatives of the here-and-now.

Synthesis and Application

It appears reasonable that we should grant a considerable justification to the nonaesthetic criteria of evaluation, and equally inevitable that these criteria will display a historical motivation and rootedness that renders them in some way and degree partial. We should not have to attribute a comparable indeterminacy to the residual (aesthetic) criteria of evaluation, if we bear in mind the cautions and distinctions stated earlier in this essay. In these axiological proceedings:

1. We shall remember not to overleap the boundaries of the *artistic* values and valuational qualities (i.e., we shall respect the *ceteris paribus*).

2. We shall take care to distinguish, on the once hand, the full-fledged, proper criteria of evaluation, and, on the other hand, the *subcriteria* which are mistakenly and notoriously advanced by so many laymen, artists, and critics—and sometimes also by aestheticians[30]—so as to legitimize their judgments on one of art's domains (e.g., film), trends (e.g., realism), genres (e.g., the grotesque), or valuational qualities (e.g., an insistent expressiveness). When a subcriterion is persistently overestimated, the evaluational distortion may have a personal or a sociocultural instigation; and, indeed, the insistence on a partial aesthetic paradigm may be admissible—it certainly is widespread—if we are lucid about the context in which we make this choice.

3. We shall not feel compelled to drop the nonartistic criteria. We will simply be aware that these are the *non*residual considerations and we will consider them in that light.

Now, point (1) is essential. Only when we have scrupulously demarcated the arena in which we shall propose comparisons, can we soberly hope to obtain reliable statements. Similarly, when we operate inside the boundaries of a single art, we take less risk of error than when we venture to bridge the differences among the arts. The risks are further reduced when within a single art we make our comparisons within a single style or trend, as our results can be more meaningful when drawn from commensurable empirical material. If such is our aim, making comparisons within the oeuvre of a single artist will assure us the best chance of minimimizing the variables and gaining trustworthy judgments.

It seems to me that the current scarcity of trustworthy judgments might be alleviated if, within the different art domains, task forces of historians and theoreticians employing adequately defined criteria were to confront the problems. I do not make this suggestion carelessly. A careless, untenable attitude—from a scientific standpoint—would be one which acquiesced a priori in the subjectivity or relativity of evaluations, while on the other hand, if subjectivism or relativism were ultimately legitimate, then we might forget all further systematic inquiry into aesthetic problems.

Suppose that the "axiological calculus" were patterned solely by individual preference (which is flawed and ephemeral) or by social convention (which enthrones whatever has fleetingly been termed an "art object"); suppose, accordingly, that a work of art is but a projection of transient and arbitrary human ideas and behavior. We should then have no basis for quarreling with any moral or political decree or taboo directed at art. We could not demarcate these pronouncements from the adequate criteria of aesthetic evaluation. Surely, too, such an attitude is irreconcilable with the attitude and findings of purposeful research, for— while not overlooking the most extreme avant-garde tendencies of the present— we may affirm that cultural history has elaborated a number of markedly sustained, autonomous modes of consciousness. Art structures have emerged and developed in the course of this historical process—and marxists should be notably prepared and adept in studying and explaining how and why. Similarly, marxists should have a certain edge in explaining why we seem today to be besieged by a questioning and undermining of aesthetic categories which have survived magisterially up till now—under the assault of such movements as impossible art or conceptual art.

Before concluding this essay I must point out that I have failed to deal with two questions which, though pertinent to this sketch of evaluational criteria, must be reserved for another occasion. These are: first, the problem of what gives the classical creative works, those which last, their enduring value; second, the problem of adequate criteria for the evaluation of the aesthetic experience. Still, a word or two on these matters may be in order. Let me outline the possible approaches.

The works of art we call "classics" are so defined by both artistic and nonartistic criteria. The latter are what fluctuate most and can spark the revaluation and devaluation of even the most "enduring" art objects. Undoubtedly, the artistic criteria also rise or fall in estimation, but they are less capricious, and it is surely from them primarily that the enduring character derives. Yet despite the flux in evaluations—despite the continually rehung "museum of the imagination," to use Malraux's phrase—we must, as I have argued above, acknowledge the special status of those axiological judgments which continually recur. Now, if we pursue the problem of "classic status" in this manner, we shall have to discriminate several types of the classic. Some are entirely formal in character; some will distill the experience and conscience of entire epochs; some will be historically excellent in both ways. I thus can offer no arbitrary assumptions regarding the substantial character of any so-called classic work of art. Each has to be investigated using some or all of the criteria of evaluation proposed here. Should a hierarchy be attempted among the works of classic status? I doubt it. They have been selected as fit for the highest rank, and they should be regarded as paralleling and complementing instead of competing with one another.

What about the problem of adequate criteria for the evaluation of *aesthetic experience*? Briefly, we would want to discover to what extent such traits of the experience as its *intensity*, its *integration* (the cooperation of all the psychic powers), and its *immediacy* respond to the objective features I have defined in this essay. I hope it has been tacitly clear throughout that we must be fully cognizant of the subject-object relationship. Where a choice has been unavoidable, I have opted to commence with analysis of the art *object*. Why? Not because I equivocate as to the principle; rather, because an approach, a strategy *must* be chosen. I am fully attentive to the axiological significance of the aesthetic experience — but I find it likewise axiomatic that within the subject-object relationship the work of art creates the audience, critic, or theorist, rather than the reverse. In other words, art objects generate the aesthetic experience, appreciations, and appraisals, and these all together lead finally to the evaluative activity.[31]

A treatment of the aesthetic experience would lead directly into a treatment of the *functions* of art objects. Indeed, we would need to discriminate early among: (1) the aesthetic functions which pertain to our quantified system of the fundamental constituents of art; (2) the aesthetic functions which pertain to novelty and originality; and (3) the nonaesthetic functions which are performed by the great majority of works of art.

One final caveat must be added. My proposed definition of evaluational criteria is *not* intended to be a system of axiological canons which is supposed to survive unaltered forever. I have no desire to issue an axiological fiat. I have only proposed some *historical* and *typological* generalizations that have empirical references (i.e., that I have derived from assessing the evaluational criteria proposed by a broad range of individuals engaged in varied activities, and, in particular, by persons with a pronounced acquaintance with the arts). I concede instantly that my formulations and proposals might very well be superseded by more defensible and comprehensive findings. I think, though, that these would have to be couched on a still broader foundation of sociohistorical inquiry.

Notes

1. *The Essential David Hume*, ed. R. Wolff (New York, 1969), pp. 372, 373.
2. Hume ends his essays with a statement that is captive to the taste of his time and country: that a depletion of humane feelings and of politeness and an excessive religious zeal pose a threat to works of art (ibid., pp. 380–383). This thought is contradicted by another of Hume's formulations, which gave him distance on the famous *querelle* of the seventeenth century: that a critic fails if he overlooks that a given author has addressed himself to persons of another epoch or nation and if he doesn't allow for and adjust the ensuing prejudices and viewpoints.
3. *The Critique of Judgment*, Introduction and paragraphs 8, 23, 26, 27, 29, 38. Among the main distinctions drawn by Kant between judgments about the beautiful and judgments about the sublime is that the former require both exposition and deduction because they are concerned with the form of objects, while the latter — because they are founded in human nature (the purposiveness of the will) and essentially involve states of mind — do not require any further deduction from a priori principles (paragraphs 30, 31). I must here leave aside even a succint survey of the chief and controversial issues of Kant's philosophy. It is clear though that Kant's aesthetics cannot be fully grasped apart from his two preceding *Critiques*. Specifically at issue here are the inconsistencies and ambiguities as to the basic faculties and operations of our mental endowment. (Cf. the highly illuminating essay by Eva Schaper, "Kant on Imagination," *Philosophical Forum*, vol 2, no. 4, 1971.)
4. Kant, *Critique of Judgment*, paragraphs 56 and 57.

5. Ibid., paragraphs 9 and 14.
6. Ibid., paragraph 16. Using similar arguments, Kant holds that regular geometrical figures cannot be a source of aesthetic experience, since the idea of regularity posits the intervention of reason (concepts of purpose) and prevents the free play of imagination (paragraph 22). The core of his thesis lies in these propositions: Aesthetic purposiveness based only on a given form has its counterpart in the freedom that inheres to the constitution of our cognitive faculties by virtue of their lawfulness. But this paralleling conformity as though to law which is brought about by our understanding and free imagination paradoxically occurs in the absence of law. The antinomy is solved because of the harmony which exists within the human mind just as the aesthetic transaction takes place. With important modifications the same notion applies to the judgment of sublime objects (paragraph 29).
7. *The Essential David Hume*, p. 375. In the next passage Hume points out the unequal levels of taste among different peoples, which results in different gradations (p. 380).
8. Cf. B. Croce, *Breviario di estetica* (Bari, 1913), chs. 2, 4. M. Dufrenne, *Phénomenologie de l 'expérience esthétique*, Vol. 1 (Paris, 1953), pp. 17–35. E. Bullough, *Aesthetics* (London, 1957), pp. 43–54.
9. Cf. S. C. Pepper, *The Sources of Value* (Berkeley and Los Angeles, 1958), ch. 13; M. C. Beardsley, *Aesthetics: Problems in the Philosophy of Criticism* (New York, 1958), chs. 10–12. The distinction is also accepted by K. Aschenbrenner, "Aesthetic Theory — Conflict and Conciliation," *Journal of Aesthetics and Art Criticism* (September 1959). The same direction is taken by R. Ingarden in his *Studies in Aesthetics*, vol. I (Warsaw, 1957), pp. 137–144, 173–177.

10. Cf. Pepper, *Sources of Value*, pp. 272–273, 288–299.

11. We mȧy cite the marxist tradition. G. Plekhanov in *Art and Social Life* (1912) offered two criteria of evaluation: the harmony of an idea and its form, and the truthfulness of an idea. A. Lunacharsky in his "Theses on the Tasks of Marxist Criticism" (1928) and "Thoughts on Criticism" (1933) also mentions an interest in formal structure, that is to say, in complex organization. In this tradition, the quantification of mimetic value is oriented to its cognitive and ideological aspects, and the compactness of the work of art is expecially considered.

12. This criteron has acquired more significance because of the entry of the functionalist concept into modern architecture and industrial design. Even should one argue that the optimal solution in this domain of art is an optimum correspondence among form, construction, and function, it must be acknowledged, first, that there are differing ways to realize the posited harmonious whole, and, second, that the three elements will be interproportioned differently in, say, an airplane hangar, a pants hanger, a Mustang automobile, a set of dishes, and a home interior.

13. I offer this projection on the analogy of the *mythèmes* spoken of by Lévi-Strauss in his *Structural Anthropology* (1963; French edition, 1958).

14. Cf. T. M. Greene, *The Arts and the Art of Criticism* (Princeton, 1940), chs. 24–25.

15. The phenomenon of genius in art was first formulated in this way by Alexander Gerard in 1774. In the same period, we may note, another notion of genius was advanced (by Edward Young) and was woven into the theories of romanticism (Novalis-Schelling-Coleridge). This notion looked on the genius as an "original," a unique phenomenon.

16. Cf. E. Kahler, "What Is Art?" in M. Weitz, ed., *Problems in Aesthetics* (New York, 1959), pp. 157–171.

17. Cf. the still valid analysis of this matter in E. Utitz, *Grundlegung der allgemeinen Kunstwissenschaft* (Stuttgart, 1920), vol. II, p. 370; also "Theses on the Tasks of Marxist Criticism," in A. Lunacharsky, *On Literature and Art* (in English; Moscow, 1965), pp. 19–21.

18. I use this ambiguous term here in place of originality, although their meaning is often the same. Authenticity is used in this context as an equivalent to genuineness, that is, an unfeigned artistic expression. The two other meanings of the term overlap my intention: authentic can also mean not forged and, in television or cinema verité, it can mean rendering the actual flux of reality.

19. Of course, it *is* possible to advance subjectivist or relativist interpretations of originality and novelty. The terms "original" and "new" might mean one thing to X and Y, something quite different to a group of Xs or of Ys. But I shall insist that these criteria be objectivized insofar as this is possible. This is done by considering them against a context of historically determined cultural structures. Let me emphasize, too, that we should try to analyze originality in the work itself, not in the creative process.

20. Cf. chapter 5.

21. Greene, *Arts and Criticism*, ch. 24, pp. 465–470. Even so, Greene seeks to avoid an equation of the value of a work with the artist's philosophy. We must consider — if I understand him — the scope of the questions posed by a work of art and not the substance of the answers.

22. For a description of the sociologically relativist approach to art, see chapter 1.

23. The earliest plainly nonartistic evaluations in European aesthetic thought are in the writings of Plato. In his *Laws* (Part VII, 801 D) he writes that "the poet should not create anything outside of the theme approved by the authorities as decent, beautiful, and good, and he should not bring his works before the public unless they were examined by a judge and guardian of laws and approved by them."

24. Cf. the analyses of nonartistic criteria in Beardsley, *Aesthetics*, ch. 12, and in J. Stolnitz, *Aesthetics and Philosophy of Art Criticism* (Boston, 1960), ch. 16. John Dewey earlier spoke of the so-called "confusion of values" in his *Art and Experience* (New York, 1934), ch. 13. However, none of these authors gives adequate treatment to the genuine conflicts between artistic and non-artistic evaluations. Marxists who have given detailed attention to these problems (Lenin, Lunacharsky, Gramsci) were constrained, owing to the mass cultural side of revolution, to give much significance to the criterion of *comprehensibility*, that is, art's capacity to communicate directly and effectively.

25. Cf. Roman Ingarden's way of dealing with these matters. He treats ideas as organic elements of works of art. However, he exhibits their aesthetic value only in the framework of the polyphonic system of the value qualities, thus ignoring their relations with the real, autonomous world.

26. Cf. L. Arnaud Reid, *A Study in Aesthetics* (London, 1931). The significance of works of art, Reid believes, should be deduced from their ideothematic values, which merge with their emotional and moral aspects.

27. Cf. R. Ekman, *Problems and Theories in Modern Aesthetics* (Malmo, 1960), ch. 1.

Also his essay "Aesthetic Value and the Ethics of Life Affirmation," *British Journal of Aesthetics*, vol. 3, no. 1 (1963), pp. 54–66.

28. Cf. my book *Between Tradition and a Vision of the Future* (in Polish; Warsaw, 1964), pp. 184–190; also my introduction to K. Marx and F. Engels, *On Literature and Art* (St. Louis, 1973); and chapter 9.

29. Cf. N. Rescher, *Introduction to Value Theory* (Englewood Cliffs, N.J., 1969), ch. 9 on the dynamics of value change. What Rescher says regarding the constant upgrading and downgrading of values can be applied, in the field of aesthetics, to any rescaling or reranking, on the basis of tacitly assumed ideas of the nature of a work of art and the corresponding aesthetic experience. However, at the moment of the "aesthetic earthquake" (such as we have seen occurring especially in the past two decades, although the opening of this process can be dated to the 1920s) the axiological shakeup touches the fundamental valuational criteria, and this becomes problematic.

30. Cf. New York University Institute of Philosophy, 7th, *Art and Philosophy*, edited by Sidney Hook (New York, 1964).

31. It is beyond question that the work of art most often preserves a certain residue of an artist's experience and that both the work and the experience must meet the condition of some degree of intensity and integration. Nevertheless, I do not accept the view that the evaluational criteria of art should be turned towards the connection of the work of art with the creative process behind it. If I took this as the center of my attention, I should have to address myself to the criteria of the creative process, and not to the criteria of the art object which have concerned me here.

Chapter 4

Valuation and Evaluation from Plato to Kant

The problem of aesthetic judgment emerged rather late in European aesthetic thought. Plato and Aristotle did discuss some criteria of evaluation; but neither gave consideration to the criteria of *value* as these are reflected in the act of appraisal. The relativity of the ideas of beauty and ugliness did provide a theme for the Sophists (particularly in the anonymous treatise *Dialexeis*), but they did not try to analyze the propositions on which this relativity was based. The problem of the validity of aesthetic judgment was treated more fully by those Stoics who, following Aristotle and Diogenes the Babylonian, stressed the sensuous character of the response to beauty and art as the basis for value judgments. A further step was taken by Alhazen and Vitello in their remarks on sensations and perceptions, and the conditions conducive or prejudicial to the perception of such qualities as beauty and ugliness, but they stopped short of the question of aesthetic taste and judgment.

It is remarkable that the Renaissance failed to introduce any new consideration of the question of how beauty is perceived. Its poetics and art theory concentrated on the artistic process and the possibility of knowing the essence of the empirical world. Alberti and da Vinci stressed the importance of what they called *concinnitas* and *mimesis*; they seemed to lay little difficulty at the door of valuative and evaluative criteria. Even Dürer treated the problem of appraisal only incidentally, though he devoted much concern to his search for the measure of beauty.

Indeed, the issue which here concerns us did not begin to mature until attention was finally focused upon the subjective aspect of the aesthetic process. This new perspective can be traced to the seventeenth century, to Leibniz's notion of aesthetic experience as a vague knowledge of perfection and the contemporaneous French treatments of aesthetic taste. The focus was shifting towards epistemology and psychology; Leibniz and Baumgarten opened a road that runs directly to Kant through their analyses of the key question of whether perception is intellectual or emotional.

Another road leading to Kant started with the eighteenth-century British school of aesthetics, which grafted certain French ideas to its native tradition. The British school, under the influence of Leibniz, considered aesthetic taste to be a specific psychical state, and repeated the French formula of a *je ne sais quoi*; unlike the German school, however, it associated taste not with some cognitive process, but rather with a process akin to the action of the instincts. Some eigh-

A shorter version of this essay appeared in the *British Journal of Aesthetics* (October 1966).

teenth-century English writers do, in fact, refer to an "aesthetic instinct." The Frenchman Bouhours, almost a century earlier, had stated that what reason subsequently discovers, is first infallibly suggested by taste; and Dubos would later speak of the sixth sense on which proper aesthetic judgment is founded. At the same time, taste began to be understood as the faculty of discerning not only the *good* but also the *better*. We find this problem posed in France by Chevalier de Méré and Montesquieu, among others, and in England by Hume, Burke, and Gerard.

The predominant concern at that time was to describe beauty's counterpart as a specific psychical faculty, demarcated to be sure from the domain of reason. Since we no longer share this concern, we believe that the especially valuable conviction of these men was their notion that a well-developed taste requires not only sense, feeling, and imagination, but also sound judgment. A concomitant idea which is also important for us is that taste is by no means random and unique. However, there was no more agreement then as to the conditions for the universality of taste than there is today. La Motte, Shaftesbury, Hutchison, and Home maintained that sense and feeling were the primary, if not exclusive, foundations of agreement in aesthetic appraisals. Others (for example, Hume, in his classic essay "Of the Standard of Taste") suggested that similarities of judgment in matters of art and beauty are determined not only by similarities of nature, but equally or even preponderantly by social conditions acting through tradition, cultural patterns, and acquired attitudes.

Such is the historical background of Kant's views; and it is with him that the history of this problem really begins. Kant's approach to aesthetic judgment is based upon the philosophical foundations laid out in his *Critique of Judgment*, and I shall here attempt to single out the main points relevant to this topic.

The domain of aesthetics, Kant held, lies between that of the intellect, which is concerned with regularity in nature, and that of the practical reason, which postulates the idea of freedom. The aesthetic domain is rendered operative through the judgment (a reflexive, not a determining faculty), which seeks to establish general principles for particular cases. Now, the act of judgment predicates a congruence between cognitive activity and the design of nature, and it regards this harmony as *relative only to the human subject*. Thus this design, or, more exactly, the purposiveness, is given purely subjectively and formally, without any directed purpose, in an image of the given object which is immediately associated with a feeling of pleasure; and this image is in no way at odds with the intellect as the faculty of understanding. The appreciation of beauty is characterized by this harmonious and free play of all psychical faculties. Kant says that the ability to formulate a judgment based on this pleasant experience constitutes what is called taste. The judgment of taste is not a cognitive judgment — its reasons are merely subjective. The existence of the object is irrelevant: for what counts is simply contemplation, in which a state of pure and disinterested liking is achieved. As this liking is impersonal, it has to include (without any mediation of concepts) a claim to universality, and here lies the crux of the problem. The universality of aesthetic judgment is founded, so Kant maintains, on *the constitution of our cognitive faculties* (part I, section 9). The peculiarly aesthetic pleasure arises not from an object of imagination only, but rather from the harmony of imagination and intellect. In this way the *sensus communis* will arise from a subjective necessity (the object *ought* to please everyone, since I approve of it according to my judgment), and not from a cultural unanimity established among different peoples and different epochs (section 17).[1] Aesthetic judgment, accordingly, is not such that it can be supported by arguments that would compel others to acknowledge its soundness. Yet although *privatgültig*, it makes a claim to universal acceptance. Kant discusses this antinomy (sections 56 and 57) as a pairing of propositions, one of which locates a substantiation for taste in concepts, the other of which does not; and he provides an extremely simple resolution. Each of the propositions uses a different definition of "concepts." The concept which Kant says constitutes the authentic basis for aesthetic judgment refers to the subjective purposiveness of nature, to the suprasensuous substratum that lies at the foundation of appearances.

I do not find Kant's argument convincing, mainly because he relies on a transcendental method and purely deductive operations (sections 30, 31, 38), while repeatedly impugning the empirical procedures to which he nonetheless resorts when discussing pleasure as the basis of taste. Kant flatly and consistently rejects social conditions of judgment, but, while substituting for natural determinants some unexplained and a priori patterning of cognitive faculties, he nevertheless vacillates between a psychological and an epistemological interpretation. Therefore, the object is wholly determined by the subject; in other words, beauty and the sublime are determined by taste — which yet does not seem to be explicable in purely transcendental terms. Finally, wherever Kant discusses those aesthetic judgments that draw on intellect or reason (section 17, on the ideal of beauty; or section 42, on the superiority of natural beauty over artistic beauty), he is forced to declare that he is stepping beyond the field of taste — since his inclusive thesis is that the aesthetic judgment is wholly a matter of taste, with taste being a specific faculty based on imagination and feeling.

Yet Kant's misconceptions are highly instructive. They marshal a wealth of ideas, and they evince a methodological maturity in posing the problems. We should note well that the problem of taste, so easily solved by Kant, is in any case only apparent. If we reject the transcendental method, we shall find that differing preferences cannot be considered logically contradictory. After all, we do not consider one person's liking for champagne to be inconsistent with another's preference for cognac. Thus, the de gustibus maxim should no longer frighten and discourage us, since we may talk about a contradiction in aesthetic judgments only where a difference arises concerning the same object and the same attributes of that object. Even so, Kant's solution of his antinomy involves a discovery of importance: Uniformity of experience should not be sought in a concept; rather, we may most usefully investigate whether the human natural and social reality encourages a uniformity both in experience and concept. Undoubtedly, this presents a difficult and complex question, involving as it does the "constants" of the human species and of its history. It would be helpful, also, to rephrase the Kantian antinomy to focus on the contradiction between what is unique and what is general in the aesthetic act and in its objective counterpart; and thus to discern what is really particular to these subjective and objective elements and what is shared by them with other members of their specific class.

However, my critical digression notwithstanding, the fact remains that Kant's analysis brings to light all the main themes of this chapter:
1. the subjective character of judgment, which, nonetheless, seeks for an objective verification in human nature (if only in the constitution of the cognitive faculties) or human culture;
2. the locating of values (e.g., beauty and the sublime) as the foundation of judgment;
3. the universality of the possible elements of aesthetic judgment (above all, the opposition between the intellect and other faculties)—this being an aspect of objectivity.

Even Kant's omissions in the argument prove instructive. If writers of the eighteenth century were capable of raising the problem of aesthetic judgment, it was because doubt had already been cast on the a priori existence of a metaphysical Beauty. They were, however, still incapable of making any clear and precise distinction between judgment and value, and, more importantly, between an elementary discrimination of value (with appraisal as its counterpart) and a judgment concerning the degree of value. Kant himself was drawn into making evaluative judgments, but apparently without being aware of their distinctive character. We find that the same trouble befell Hume before him.

One other point is to be noted, which in the context of Kant's aesthetic system may seem surprising, but which is for us extremely valuable. In section 41 he writes of the empirical interest in beauty, which he links to the social drive and the history of culture. He had to scuttle this line of reasoning to sustain his philosophical consistency elsewhere, yet in this brief passage he indicated, with understanding, a status of value that was to be explored and articulated in historicist doctrines from Vico, Diderot, and Herder through Hegel, Marx, and Taine.

At this juncture our brief survey may be closed. After all, it is not with the history of the problem of aesthetic judgment that I am concerned here, but with the debates today in progress. Yet a look at the background seemed essential, not only to introduce some of the specific questions, but to demonstrate the complexity of the problem.

Now, there is an obvious difficulty involved in using the term "objectivity," which, in the history of European thought, has borne various meanings in connection with taste and aesthetic judgment. I would tentatively distinguish at least three senses of the term.

1. "Objective" can refer to an independence from any subject, or, strictly speaking, from the process of cognition. In this sense the physicist says that a positron or neutron is objective. Of course, nothing is *knowable* without a knowing subject; yet this sense of objectivity involves not epistemological but ontological questions.

2. "Objective" can refer to a dependence of the subject on the object that conditions knowledge, as is the case, for example, with sense-data. Redness and heaviness present something that has firm ontological foundation, though this "*something*" does not exist without the human subject. We may, thus, call redness and heaviness "*dispositional properties*" of reality, understanding that these potential qualities are specifically actualized only in relation to the species *homo*. (Whether these qualities are responded to in a similar or perhaps identical way by other species of creatures does not interest us here, for the question brings up no novel arguments or counterarguments.) It is clear that the term "objectivity" in this sense has an epistemological character.

3. "Objective" can refer to a sharing by many people—be they a single population group in a particular epoch or the whole of mankind. The second meaning of "objectivity" implied some universality in the attitudes of subjects. In the third meaning this aspect of universality prevails, embracing not only cognitive data (sensation, perception, concept) but ultimately also the emotional and conational aspects of human attitudes.

I shall try to point out that the question of the objectivity of aesthetic judgments can be solved by taking into account the second and third meanings of the term. There are three questions that must be answered if we are to frame the problem properly: What is the structure of aesthetic judgment? What are its varieties? What construction should be put on the notion of objectivity with regard to these varieties and perhaps with reference to the structure of aesthetic judgments? Before we tackle these questions, however, there is still a preliminary problem to be solved, namely, the relationship between taste and aesthetic judgment.

The Dispositional Taste Response and Aesthetic Judgment

In distinction from the definition suggested by eighteenth-century aestheticians and adopted by Kant, by "taste" I shall here mean a certain disposition and the actual experiences connected with it, which are *not* identical with aesthetic judgment. This disposition belongs to the sensibilities and the imagination, which produce a specific and immediate response to some objects or qualities in a context which might be termed "aesthetic." The actual experiences connected with this disposition depend on the individual, on the given situation, and on the objective referent. At any rate the experience which I call the response of taste is not of an intellectual character. Different persons are endowed with different degrees and also with different kinds of aesthetic sensitivity; some may be sensitive only to literature, or painting, or music while others may be sensitive to several kinds of art and natural beauty.

I believe that aesthetic sensitivity, while rooted in our natural constitution, is to an equal degree a cultural phenomenon. It has developed in the course of centuries and is universal·in the sense that a person lacking any taste whatever seems to be exceptional or even abnormal. Any such hypothesis about the genesis and character of taste is, of course, as difficult to verify as speculation about the origin of mankind. We can agree, though, that taste is both a social and natural phenomenon like all other patterns of human cultural behavior. The opposed extremes (postulates of the existence of taste as an aesthetic instinct or of the complete absence of a natural basis for taste) should be dismissed because they both lead to overstatement and are both famished for lack of evidence. No anatomical research has yet come up with an "aesthetic gland" or any other physiological basis for an immaculate, spontaneous immediacy of aesthetic experience. If a person can distinguish one picture or composition from another, this must ultimately be ascribed to his education and good memory. If he discriminates between "worse" and "better" works of art, this must also be attributed to assimilated standards of aesthetic value, recollected observation, and effective intelligence. Even the ability to distinguish fakes from originals must be the outcome of cultural indoctrination.

However, there is no genuine sensitivity which can be acquired only and mainly by training, habits, and routine. Some individuals seem especially gifted in discerning slight yet distinctive variations, whether as beholder, reader, or listener. There is nothing mysterious in this fact. We do not puzzle ourselves if A has weaker eyesight than B, or if B is physically stronger than A. We admire the gifted wine-taster, or the person whose olfactory capacities surpass the average human potentiality. Aesthetic taste, accordingly, should be considered primarily dependent on the natural power to grasp visual and auditory nuances and variations (just to keep to the two so-called higher senses traditionally singled out in relation to the realm of art) of any object submitted to scrutiny. This also applies to the capacity (conditioned by the individual's constitutional makeup) to articulate the peculiarities of a design and find out, more quickly and precisely than could other individuals, what changes or shifts have occurred in the artistic structure (aesthetic object) he is examining.

This does not, let me once more emphasize, allow us to postulate an aesthetic sensitivity functioning in an isolated and pristine way. Knowledge influences sensitivity as much as sensitivity influences knowledge. Imagination and emotions caught up in the experience of taste — let the former be constitutionally as robust and lively as may be conceived — will not remain impervious to the lessons of the environment, space, and time. As Marx argued persuasively more than a hundred years ago, the human senses are molded by social praxis and correspond to given historical circumstances at every stage of human evolution. With this idea always in mind, we have to acknowledge the fundamentally natural prerequisites of taste. That is why taste, as it is here conceived, cannot be well-founded though it can possibly be learned if the propensity is lacking; refined taste, about which so much has been written since the eighteenth century, is simply taste manifested and cultivated in favorable circumstances. Personal taste can and generally does succumb to outside influences to the point where no individual differences are in the end discernible; that is, people with different dispositions (as to their kind or degree) respond to the same objects or qualities as aesthetic stimuli. If individual sensitivity is therefore elusive, it is much easier to discern the general "taste" of an age or a community. Above all, the phenomenon of supraindividual taste reveals a feedback mechanism, since individual dispositions are influenced not only by the taste responses of neighbors but also and most often decisively by prevailing aesthetic judgments.

By aesthetic judgment as distinct from taste I do not mean a psychical act of an intellectual character that is ultimately a purely psychological statement. Rather, I mean a proposition which stems from a basic process of this character but which ultimately formulates an appraisal founded on certain more or less objective reasons. The logical structure of this kind of proposition may be an object for investigation in itself, but that would take us beyond our present concerns. Suffice it to say that in the experience of appraising, judging, and estimating—and in contradistinction to a taste response—rationality and a cognitive emphasis are manifestly conspicuous. Aesthetic judgment may, but need not, be the continuation and the climax of the experience based on taste. In fact, aesthetic judgment need not follow from any genuine experience but may be "borrowed" (i.e., constitute a mere copy of an opinion formulated by somebody else). It should also be stressed that taste need not always result in a verbal expression of the experience (as opposed to mere gestures or facial expressions signifying approval or rejection).

Aesthetic judgment can thus be more or less remote from the experience based on taste. It seems to be closer if it is rendered in the form "X is likable," which is parallel to a psychological statement such as "I like this," since both of these utterances are an expression of a still vivid or only just receded experience. Of course, such statements may also be borrowed and should thus never be accepted at their face value. Aesthetic judgment proper is more remote from the taste experience, since it invokes some objective reasons to justify why "I like this" or, to restate it, why "X is likable." In this instance thought processes are intensified and the initial existential propositions to the effect that such are my feelings or that such are my sentiments towards the given object yield to implicational utterances or even to comparative formulas describing my experiences as compared with the feelings of others or describing the qualities or objects actually experienced as compared with those experienced on other occasions. In each of these latter cases, aesthetic judgment is an appraisal, that is, a statement ascribing for certain reasons some values to the experience, to its objective counterpart, to the adequate relation between them, or to some context in which such a relation might appear. According to this conception, a distinction must be made between an appraisal which refers directly and solely to the qualities and objects considered as aesthetically valuable, and a comparative evaluation confronting such immediately experienced values with some others and rating them. The former is an appraisal in a broader, fundamental sense, because it constitutes an element of *every* aesthetic judgment. Thus, I have arrived in my considerations of taste and its interrelations with judgment at a preliminary though barely outlined discernment of the basic varieties of aesthetic judgments. I shall now turn to the problem of the objectivity of taste and aesthetic judgment in general.

I have defined taste as a specific individual experience which depends on particular dispositions in particular circumstances. The difficulty that now appears is how to transcend the private, intimate, and unique response which precludes agreement if not, indeed, communication. Both Kant and the aestheticians preceding him attempted to overcome this deadlock by referring to the universality of the aesthetic experience. Could it be proved that taste is either some aesthetic instinct or a function of some definite construction of our cognitive faculties, a solution would be at hand. I have, however, questioned both these notions. Thus only two alternatives remain: either we give up taste as the determinant of the ultimate objectivity of aesthetic judgments, or else we consider some other suggestions. We must examine the latter possibility before we can be satisfied with a negative conclusion, for there is another naturalistic hypothesis available which is different from the instinct hypothesis. This is the gestalt conception, which refers the essential identity of taste, despite the possible emergence of some accidental differences, to the identity of the objective qualities presented by a particular branch of art or by nature. (In this context, I assume that the taste experience should be considered as the cornerstone of aesthetic experience of any form, no matter how rich and complex its elements. This strategy of approach is not without peril, since much aesthetic experience, especially in relation to present-day avant-garde art, is highly intellectualized. Nonetheless, for the present discussion my tentative formulation will be adequate.)

Such an assumption, supported by social and historical arguments in favor of common constant foundations for the cultural experience of mankind, would lead us towards an emphasis on the peculiar structure of objective elements which may validly be designated aesthetic. Taste would then constitute the reflection of some such structure, instead of being the single creative force of aesthetic reality. It would be subject both to this structure and to those general laws of nature and society which tend to maintain the universal pattern and balance. It is easy, to be sure, to find objections to such an hypothesis. Some critics charge that gestaltism and similar conceptions beg the question, empirically, and that they offer a kind of "aesthetic phlogiston" in place of scientific explanation, since human history is continually changing, so that the relativity of individual taste is matched by the relativity of group tastes predominating at any given period. Accordingly, since we have no sufficient grounds marshaled here and now for resolving the respective claims of objectivists and relativists in favor of either, we have to keep this hypothesis in reserve.

There are, meanwhile, some other possible positive answers to our inquiry. For instance, it might be argued that taste is an intuitive faculty zeroing in on what German idealistic aesthetics calls *das Kunstsein* — the essence of artistic phenomena. This view seems, however, both arbitrary and contingent on an act of philosophical faith. It might also be argued that objectivity is restricted to a single community or era, on the assumption that while human nature rules out the possibility of common tastes, history does not, if only within strictly demarcated periods and groups. In other words, what is here treated as objective is an individual taste which has been constrained and regimented for immersion in the taste of the group. This is, however, not an hypothesis but a simple statement of sociological fact. Beyond this, it is not clear why the view developed from such a statement — that successive but *different* and perhaps even opposed or contradictory aesthetic judgments rooted in group tastes are all equally objective — should be termed objectivist. This is a thinly disguised version of relativism, for all these judgments either refer to the same objects or offer varying conceptions of what "beauty" truly is. In studying these and other claims to comprise my second alternative — and for a systematic inquiry, see the typology presented in chapter 1 — I have effectively arrived at a negative response to my basic inquiry: in short, there is no recourse left except the reserve hypothesis, according to which taste is to be regarded as a consequence of natural and social laws.

In each of these versions taste means a certain kind of *choice*, for the term refers to a person's dispositions or habits towards some *thing* which constitutes a proper object of liking. However, an orientation towards an object does not in every instance constitute the essential content of an aesthetic experience, for one may *merely* like the object (i.e., without an aesthetic transaction occurring). Taste means —according to the hypothesis I have held in reserve—a choice directed towards and set upon certain definite values, as well as a reliance on them.

I now turn to the first of my two alternatives, to see whether and in what sense objectivity may be imputed to the aesthetic judgment itself. Because judgment is the result of an intellectual process culminating in a verbal proposition that is available to logical analysis, it should be much more objective than mere taste could ever be. On further thought, however, this notion turns out to be deceptive. The simplest aesthetic judgment of the kind "X is likable," may, as was pointed out earlier, be no more than the counterpart of "I like X"—an appraisal referring to one's private sentiment. The proposition "I like this," considered as purely descriptive of an immediate or just receded pleasure, provides no aesthetic judgment at all, for it lacks any justification or criteria for taste. Even so, those who utter such statements generally lay stress, whether they mean to or not, on aesthetic *satisfaction*, thus attributing a peculiar merit to their experience and delimiting aesthetic value as a peculiar pleasure.

On what this peculiarity may be founded is hard to conjecture, since the aesthetic hedonists and emotionalists offer notoriously vague and evasive replies. I suspect that even today they perpetuate the French seventeenth century *je ne sais quoi*, which at its origin was a promising and stimulating mistake, but in the nineteenth and twentieth centuries only obscures the chief issues for investigation. Incidentally, I am very far from denying some peculiarity of aesthetic sensations and emotions. I would gladly defend the tentative term "peculiar satisfaction" if the experience being discussed were also closely related to the specific, semiautonomous, coherent structures of sensuously given, intense data (and probably to other data imparted by such patterns). By "closely related," I mean anchored in and evoked by such objectively entrenched sets of qualities. This, however, is precisely what the hedonists and emotionalists contest and challenge. In any case, if we acquiesce in the dubious conception of "aesthetic pleasure," we would have to agree that aesthetic judgment is an entirely subjective matter. If, however, the statement "X is likable" is not reducible to the expression of sheer private liking, the question follows: Why is it that the object or its properties (or both) engender this peculiar joy that we call aesthetic? Why is X worthy of special attention? We are faced then with the same question which we encountered in considering taste: On what grounds must aesthetic judgment be founded for its objectivity to be guaranteed?

The simple answer—that taste supplies this basis—returns us to the reserve hypothesis. Accordingly, the only recourse for constituting and corroborating aesthetic judgment is to propose and employ some definite criteria of value as the basis for appraisal and evaluation. Again, as in the case of taste, there appear the same mutually exclusive and scanty possible solutions between which a choice must be made. I have rejected as self-contradictory the notion that aesthetic judgment is only a statement of feelings, for then judgment could only be deemed objective if it were additionally assumed that in all mankind given qualities and objects evoke similar aesthetic responses, or that all human beings react aesthetically in identical ways and, by their responses, create the aesthetic objects. This would return us to the hypothesis of universal taste as an instinct or as a separate cognitive faculty. Moreover, we would have to support such an assumption by the additonal assumption that a given experience will gain adequate and identical expression in judgments formulated at different times by different individuals with different cultural backgrounds.

It might also be maintained that aesthetic judgment is objective if either actual or potential consent exists among many persons within a strictly delimited cultural context; but this kind of objectivity is equally dubious. If at some time t it is urged that some work x is unaesthetic and at another time t' it is deemed a masterpiece, or if a taste T belonging to some group g champions an aesthetic ideal sharply opposed to an ideal asserted by a group g' which lives in the same time and has a taste not differing from T, then these pairs of judgments and ideals can hardly be considered objective. The only objective fact here is that in each judgment *something* is valued by *someone* as aesthetically relevant. Instrumentality of judgment is, however, by no means identical with its validity or soundness. What has occurred here is a simple substitution of "We like this" for "I like this" and once again there are no firm grounds of objectivity.

The root question can now be put thus: Do we refer our judgments to a set of consistent individual experiences, or is there something beyond these experiences that determines the judgment in a manner independent of circumstances? In short, the objectivity of judgment depends on the objectivity of values, and aesthetic judgment depends for its status not only on its subject (which is obvious) but also on its object. Thus, the distinctions between taste and judgment are of a psychological and epistemological character, while from the standpoint of axiology their difference disappears. In both aspects there arises at the outset the problem of seeking the proper, most valid criteria or standards for an appraisal. In discerning the objectivity of taste and judgment, some reference has to be made to the objective qualities which stand in some definite relation with the subject who responds to them. M. C. Beardsley[2] pointed this out when, in his discussion of the variations of taste and judgment, he touched on the variations of reasons. He remained undecided at this point, however, although he leaned toward an improved instrumentalist solution.

Going a step further than Beardsley's illuminating analysis of pros and cons, I would suggest that it could be concluded that a necessary condition for being able to say anything at all about the objectivity of aesthetic judgments is the existence of certain natural, social, and cultural regularities which combine to fix some biologically and culturally stable ways of selecting aesthetic objects as peculiarly coherent structures and of producing objects called works of art. It is evident now that the anthropological hypothesis developed in my discussion of taste and since held in reserve emerges as the only remaining possibility if we are empirically oriented in our research. A competing hypothesis, which makes a strong claim for the objectivity of aesthetic judgment, alleges that an appraisal, or *Wertantwort* as the Germans designate it, intuitively responds to aesthetically valuable qualities or to certain values, which are given once and for all and await discovery. This proposition should, however, be rejected as absolutist; its reference either to eidetic intuition *(Wesensschau)* or ultimately to experience solely by means of introspection, renders it unverifiable, as it hardly allows for any intersubjective consent.

The Kinds and the Degrees of Objectivity

Although my discussion has shown, I hope, that when all else has failed we may found the objectivity of judgment on objectively comprehended values, yet none of the questions raised earlier has been adequately answered or dismissed. Aesthetic judgments are made with reference to various patterns of value and enter into various relations with them, so it becomes necessary to distinguish their different kinds as well as their different degrees of objectivity.

The first problem that must here be raised concerns the logical status and structure of aesthetic judgment. The argument has been made — at least from Leon Petrażycki through to Ayer, Wittgenstein, and their many disciples, chiefly at Oxford and in the United States — that appraisals are not genuine statements. A genuine statement is either true or false: its truth-value may be tested by reference to the reality described by it. Appraisals have, according to this standpoint, a different structure; they do not assert, but only persuade and exhort. They merely express a sentiment which the speaker wishes to impart to others. This kind of message cannot possibly be referred to any empirical data, its only authority being its own proposal which it seeks to make persuasive. What is the structure of an appraisal? It is an assertion that "X is aesthetically valuable." (The phrase "aesthetically valuable" may be replaced by various other descriptions depending on the speaker's opinions on art and beauty.) It is another kind of appraisal which announces that "X is a masterpiece" or that "X is rubbish." Such a proposition as to the work of art's merit or excellence is called by this school an evaluative one and is considered to have even less persuasive force than does a simple inter-pretation of values. The latter is always to a high degree arbitrary so that an evalu-ation which is based on it must necessarily be even more so.

This extreme position has, however, been eroded even within the neopositivist tradition itself. Factual statements and appraisals are no longer held to be different in kind, but only in degree according to the various proportions of cognitive and emotive-conative elements involved in them. A proposition of a given shape (e.g., "this is a good table") may in one context be understood as a purely factual state-ment and in another as a pure appraisal. Yet there is still support for the theory perhaps most cogently argued by Charles Stevenson,[3] that appraisals are pre-dominantly of a persuasive nature, exhortations to prefer particular objects and qualities which have been chosen and recognized as valuable. Maria Ossowska[4] has stressed that this quasi-imperative character of appraisals reveals their weak-ness as factual or descriptive statements. She believes that, though they can be substantiated on the ground of certain accepted assumptions, they cannot be verified since no one has yet precisely and reliably shown any stimuli that are creative of value.

Is this line of argument convincing? Its most remarkable feature is what Os-sowska has called "accepted assumptions." It talks about the logical structure of appraisal only after having predetermined what the values are. This proves that, whatever the logical structure of appraisals is, the main issue lies else-where. The works of the Anglo-American and Polish schools of semantics set forth the proposition that the philosophical or, more precisely, axiological viewpoints explain whether objectivity can or cannot be attributed to some types of proposi-tion, while logical and formal considerations are of but secondary aid on this issue. In this respect, the Oxford philosophers' abandonment of neopositivist extremism seems symptomatic.

The structure of an appraisal obviously differs from that of a purely descriptive statement. If we did not admit this, we would have to acknowledge all elements as valuable and all attitudes towards them as evaluative. If I say, "This is round and red," and then add, "It is expressive, dynamic, and interestingly constructed," it requires no analysis whatsoever to see that these two propositions are entirely different, as the latter one expresses overtly an emotional involvement, a kind of "committed-to" attitude. This does not mean that appraisals lack any empirical justification and that they are totally unverifiable. Characteristically, this approach is questioned by English aestheticians from Oxford and some Americans of kindred views[5] on the grounds either of the uniqueness of artistic values or of the impossibility of defining the objective identity of a work of art. Both these objections must be considered as extralogical in character and both have been rebutted in the course of later discussion. The objective identity of a work of art can be determined in both its physical and its historical aspects,[6] while the uniqueness of values requires only a proper judgment but does not ban universals.

However, the most important point is that, instead of reducing aesthetic qualities to unaesthetic ones such as color, shape, or texture (though this is admissible in the extreme cases such as *musique concrète*, *l'art brut*, or happenings), we must consider the aesthetic qualities themselves as susceptible to description and not only to persuasion. For instance, it is hardly reasonable to try to deduce the aesthetic value of a poem merely from the kind of words used and their arrangement (if we exclude such extreme examples as dada verse or the Khlebnikov and Kruchonykh *zaumnyi yazik*), but we can describe and analyze its metaphors and key words to justify our evaluative "persuasion." Furthermore, what is aesthetically valuable is usually a suitably ordered ensemble or set of elements and not a single quality. Such a set or gestalt is doubly dependent, first on the neutral properties and secondly on the beholding subject; the gestalt is subject to description and there is no doubt as to its axiological character. The many analyses presented over the last decades by such scholars as Ingarden, Pepper, and Arnheim (deliberately selecting philosophers of differing schools) have abundantly proved the strength of this position.

Since it is not the formal-logical structure of appraisal, but, rather, the interpretation of value that is basic in determining whether any judgment is or is not objective, it seems obvious that the various kinds of aesthetic judgment are dependent on what values we apprehend and how. I am adopting here a distinction between the criteria of appraising (or valuating) and of evaluating, which I have set out and defended in chapters 1 and 3.

Criteria of the first type serve to determine kinds of artistic value; those of the second type serve to compare and rate works of art. The primary aesthetic judgment concerns those values that have been established as artistic. Let me remind the reader that, of all the possible solutions to this problem, I have found the historically oriented one to be the most adequate. It is to some degree consistent with those tendencies in Anglo-American aesthetics (as represented by Morris Weitz, Joseph Margolis, Frank Sibley) that deal with art as an *open concept*. According to this view, the catalog of qualities which may acquire artistic value is never complete, and the future creations of artists are unpredictable. However, unlike Weitz and others, I believe that the concept of art is definable on the basis of the past history of artistic endeavor and of the aesthetic awareness of humanity.

Not only human nature, but also and predominantly human culture, accumulates and perpetuates solutions corresponding to certain formal structures (gestalten) and to other artistic values involved in these structures such as expression, representation, etc. A primary aesthetic judgment is objective insofar as it relates to a legitimate artistic value. The proposition "X is aesthetically valuable" is an elliptical form of the judgment "X is valuable for such and such reasons," with appropriate criteria of value performing the role of ultimate reasons. Yet the reason revealed through the proper criterion is, in fact, a fundamental axiological category affirming the given character of aesthetic value. Artistic value or, more broadly, aesthetic value requires a specific and detailed justification, usually composed of a cluster of second-order reasons which particularize the applied criterion. An appraisal or valuation involved in such a judgment may, however, ignore value, and in such a case the judgment is deficient and impure. A judgment that fails to point to a value is either quasi-aesthetic or not aesthetic but psychological, moral, political, etc.

The syntactical and logical structure of the primary judgment now being discussed is by no means unambiguous. It may express various intentions; that is, its points of reference are not always the same. Propositions of identical shape must be considered for their meaning and not for their structure, that is, from the semiotic and not the syntactical point of view. The primary judgment is a particular proposition if it refers to some individual value as actually given and embodied in some artistic (or, more generally, aesthetic) object. Some aestheticians, especially those of the phenomenological school, consider this the only aesthetic judgment proper, as no other kind penetrates the genuine and unique essence of an individual object. However, this object is only a specimen of the class of objects, called works of art, which fulfill the same axiological requirements. Hence, the primary judgment may refer to values in an exemplary manner; that is, it may point out something common to a whole group of works of art and not something peculiar to one of them. The Italian phenomenologist Guido Morpurgo-Tagliabue has called such a judgment an "essential" one (giudizio essenziale). I prefer just to call it general to avoid the notion that a particular judgment misses the "essence" of its object.

Another ambiguity in primary judgment is revealed when the proposition "X is beautiful" can be understood as saying either that a certain object is valuable or that aesthetic value belongs to an object. The first meaning seems to be entertained by those who consider values as transcendental, as the modes of being of objects; the latter, by those for whom values are accidents. These positions seem to be reconcilable if one associates aesthetic value, as I do, with the specific structure of the qualities of the total object that are given both in a sensory and in an extrasensory way.

To conclude this discussion of the primary aesthetic judgment, let me remark that certain particular properties, or aspects, or patterns of the artistic value which constitutes its basis have often in history been treated as canonic, that is, as unchangeable and irrevocable. In these cases aesthetic judgment becomes normative and regulative. (Morpurgo-Tagliabue aptly calls it giudizio rettorico.) It is then deficient because it relies on criteria which unwarrantedly establish some transient or partial specifics of the artistic value as absolute.

I have distinguished between primary and secondary judgment, the latter being evaluation proper. Evaluation treats of a series of works of art or aesthetic objects and ranges them according to the degree of their fulfillment of certain criteria. These criteria are based on a set of artistic values that have been established as fundamental. In different patterns these values emerge with differing intensity and prominence. Aesthetic evaluation is thus objective insofar as it relates to those values, discovers and confronts them, and invokes the criteria of degree for its justification. Evaluation also commonly appears as an elliptic proposition: "X is better than Y," meaning "X is better than Y because of such and such reasons." In its balder form the proposition is a mere existential statement of

some hierarchy of values with reference to their degrees or to their kinds. The rating
of artistic and aesthetic values surely requires a more detailed justification —
although I should stress that the reasons acceptable in such operations have already been specified (i.e., the artistic constituents are already affirmed; in other
words, the axiological particulars are at hand to exact their implied demands). Why
then must our justifications be elaborated? Above all, because the artistic values
presented to our estimates exist on multiple levels and in multiple dimensions,
which may prove to be independent or interdependent. Another necessary point is
that the evaluative judgment calls for both a particular and a general appraisal,
since, without grasping what is common to the objects evaluated, it is impossible
to weigh up their comparative values, while, without perceiving what is unique
and peculiar to each, it is impossible to reveal the appeal and strengths of the
object which stands out of its class.

   Evaluation thus appears as a complicated cognitive process in which appraisals
may overlap. It is even more vulnerable to deforming influences than is the
primary judgment. Even taste depends on a choice according to some definite
preferences and its operation is influenced by aesthetic judgments. These, if they
are primary, reflect a decision as to what is and is not artistic; they appraise
their objects with reference to fundamental values. In the secondary judgment,
the concomitant appraisal of value is often directed by irrelevant considerations
and the aesthetic motivation is often obscured or even lost. In such instances an
evaluative judgment no longer deserves to be termed aesthetic and, accordingly,
cannot be accurate (or adequate) in the sense here suggested. Secondary aesthetic
judgments may also prove defective if they compare objects which are incompar-
able as to their respective values. Here, too, their adequacy is obviously distorted
or destroyed. It is not my intention, however, to enumerate all the possible dangers
to which the evaluation proper is exposed. I only wish to show that objectivity
of this type of comparative judgment also rests on values and their complicated
and multilayered interrelationships and patterns, and that it is easier to attain an
objective appraisal (valuation) than an objective evaluation.

Recapitulation
It is time for recapitulation. The problem of the objectivity of aesthetic judgment
raises difficulties first of all because of the ambiguity of the term "objectivity"
(a difficulty which is not confined to aesthetic discussions). My analysis has brought
out, I trust, that there are at least two meanings of this term involved in axiological

reasoning. In one case, objectivity means universality or, strictly speaking, universal agreement, while in the second case it means truth-value. According to the latter meaning, aesthetic judgments should be treated as logical statements, but a great number of aestheticians and logicians hold that they cannot meet this demand. Aesthetic judgments — as we are told by the representatives of the analytic-linguistic school — concern emotions and conations and, even if they refer to some objective qualities, there is no possibility of verifying them by means of measurement operations. Thus the only objectivity that is available to axiology depends on a "universality" which may be confined to one social group or one culture or may be spread over many cultures or even the whole of humanity (with the same sort of gradation being applicable to the temporal spread).

My point of view is, however, different. I have proposed a solution which goes against this sharp distinction between truth-values appropriate to logical statements and no-truth-values appropriate to axiological judgments. Chiefly, we must remember that axiology has a field of study different from that of physics, biology, or even history. The sciences deal with *neutral* facts which have to be stated independently of the way they are perceived. Axiology deals with values, that is, with *subject-object data*. However, this granted, I still do not see any firm ground for maintaining that only if these data are measurable will they afford a criterion of truthful statement. I have tried to argue for another distinction, one between universality based only on shared tastes and opinions (which in my scheme does not go beyond relativism) and universality that has its foundation in the relational equivalence of subjective and objective conditions (traits) observed in the aesthetic process. This adequacy might be explained by the constitution of *homo sapiens* and the historical praxis of men who repeat their experiences and so, among other things, reaffirm the aesthetic invariants. In this case the criteria of objectivity — universality and truth-reference — coincide. [7]

I am aware that the problem of the objectivity of aesthetic judgment has been barely outlined here. I have failed adequately to defend my "reserve" anthropological hypothesis to which I have had to resort over and over again because of the major significance of the criteria of value and of evaluation. It is in this sense that Maria Ossowska seems to be right when she says that the truth or falsehood of valuative and evaluative judgments is generally proved by reducing them to some accepted assumptions. I think, however, that she is wrong in her contention that they are unverifiable, since these assumptions may be more or less empirical. No doubt aesthetics, being a philosophical and not a strictly scientific discipline, leaves more questions moot than the history of literature or the theory of social development. Throughout the humanities, verifiability is a more difficult problem than it is for physics or even astronomy. Nothing ultimate can really be said in philosophy, if one foregoes the dubious joys of *Gedankendichtung* — a thought process colored with poetic license. The domain of values probably presents the greatest barriers to verifiability. The chaotic, misleading, everyday usage of terms and ordinary practical setting produce an exceptional confusion for axiological discourse, for discerning implicit attitudes towards valuation and evaluation, and for axiological praxis. This is the experience of aesthetics no less than of the general theory of values.

The critic, the artist, and the man in the street all aspire to bring home the aesthetic lodestone, while the aesthetician is treated suspiciously as, at best, a bumbling spinner of theories. Yet it becomes his task to take into account all the aesthetic *idola fori* and to discuss them thoroughly. It is he who has to confront patiently the old aesthetic categories with the emerging ones, and to seek the continuity in the discontinuity. If he is eager, as he should be, to check his own procedures again and again, to seek out the results of every competing school (even if they refute his own premises and conclusions), to avoid consciously the temptation to systematize the aesthetic sphere once and forever, and always to stick to the evidences of life and of the painstaking advances made by the exact sciences and by psychology and sociology — in this case, the aesthetician's philosophy of value might grow more sure. The assumptions he accepts will then be defensible to a considerable extent, even though there can never be any assuredness of total accuracy.

My aim in this chapter has been, in part, to point out that the most secure way out of the troubles inevitably associated with the issues of taste and aesthetic judgment is what I term the historicist solution. This approach does not neglect man's natural dispositions, but it emphasizes that nature was culturalized in man's social history. I believe that the hypothesis which I assume as basic can, therefore, be fairly well tested by biopsychological, social, and historical data so that the aesthetic judgments based on it can be indirectly verifiable, in proportion, as well.[8]

There are several problems which I have only skimmed. For instance, the question of preference and of choice as constituent both of taste and of the primary and secondary judgments needs a separate analysis. This question has been interestingly treated by C. I. Lewis and several American scholars still follow him.[9] The problem of evaluative judgments has also not been developed, though they

call for at least a twofold analysis. It should be asked, first, whether the fundamental primary judgment does not imply a latent evaluative judgment (i.e., rating
the objects accepted as works of art according to their being more or less artistic
within the limits of the given continuum); and, second, whether the cognitive operations involved in a detailed comparison of more than one work need to be studied.

There remains also the problem of whether evaluation is based only on quantification (i.e., a presumed "magnitude") of values which are understood as primary
values. In chapter 3 I tried to show that rating, that is grading or scaling, is
founded also on other criteria (originality and novelty). All this, however, demands
a thorough and painstaking investigation of aesthetic values and their patterns.
It is owing to their complexity that two differing judgments concerning different
aspects of the same object may be equally objective. Yet if this is a self-evident
statement, there remain much tougher problems, such as the relations of "particular" values (Beardsley's term) to one another and to the whole: Do they prove
aesthetically operative in every context? I side with Ingarden in saying that we
are still at the initial stage of exploration of this aspect.

Finally, in respect to Kant's antinomy of taste (which we may take on into the
problem of aesthetic judgment), problems of major importance appear — such as
the private character of individual taste, its social aspects, and also the uniqueness of a particular aesthetic judgment and its applicability to classes of objects
(or what we have called its exemplary side). Possibly, these are not insoluble antinomies but dialectical oppositions which do not necessarily lead to contradictions.
(In such matters Morpurgo-Tagliabue speaks of the *paradigmaticità* of aesthetic
judgment.)

I have sought to emphasize in this chapter, first, that the problem posed in the
title is demonstrably and intimately linked to the issue of value and is dependent
on the orientation to that issue. The reason for this is that the initial appraisals,
without which valuational judgment would not come into existence, are begun and
established in the very same process by which the values are constituted. Of course,
this also happens when new values and new appraisals, mutually interrelated,
emerge. Second, my aim was to show that the notion of aesthetic judgment turns
out to be ambiguous. A close analysis was needed to detach it from taste and bring
out its various types, accordingly modifying the way in which the deceptive term
"objectivity" is usually understood. Whether I have suceeded in presenting a sound
or tidy argument is another matter.

One final question of interest is the relationship between the objectivity of aesthetic judgment and that of ethical judgment. Opinions on this issue, too, differ. Maria Ossowska has drawn up a suggestive comparative table of aesthetics and ethics on this point.[10] She concludes that there is a higher standard of competence in aesthetics, since it is here easier to detect the "value-creating stimuli" or objective qualities, since aesthetic objects appear in isolation from their environment. I must admit that I do not find this conclusion entirely convincing, flattering though it is to my specialty. In fact, aesthetics has been struggling for years with the notion of an ideal observer and can still find no way out of the vicious circle in which either the ideal observer is determined by public taste and judgment, or else some values are first acknowledged as artistic and whoever expounds them is recognized as a final authority. Aesthetics, thus, has continual difficulties with its standards of value and judgment, and competing views still leave the field contested as it has been for centuries.

However—if I may be allowed to venture into rather foreign territory—ethics does not by any means seem to me more exposed to subjectivity of judgments or to universal claims of competence. Moreover, it is from Maria Ossowska's work that I have learned so much regarding moral values and judgments that I feel the justification of their objectivity to be by no means a hopeless task. Additionally, I believe that the same anthropological hypothesis (based on marxist historicism) is applicable to both ethical and aesthetic judgments. However, I incline to agree with Stuart Hampshire that while ethical judgments are expected to be objective, no such demand is put on aesthetic ones.[11] Disagreement in the former is socially dangerous, while aesthetic quarrels are thought harmless. If we add the reservation that there have been historical periods in which dissent in matters of aesthetics was not tolerated, Hampshire's view may be accepted insofar as it is pragmatically sound.

There is, indeed. no social pressure to undertake a defense of objectivity such as I have here presented. Yet it does not follow from this that such attempts are otiose. It is possible that people conform in their ethical judgments to avoid social dysfunction even though these judgments, as Ossowska has pointed out, always depend on different and conflicting philosophies. Conversely, it may be to maintain mental balance and avoid boredom that they differentiate their aesthetic values and judgments even though these are more uniform than we tend to suppose.[12]

Notes

1. I leave aside here Kant's distinction between the judgment of beauty and the judgment of the sublime, which involves a delight of the imagination and the practical reason. To demonstrate the antinomy in Kant's idea of taste it is enough to analyze his judgment of beauty.

2. M. C. Beardsley, *Aesthetics: Problems in the Philosophy of Criticism* (New York, 1958), ch. 10.

3. See C. L. Stevenson, *Ethics and Language* (New Haven, 1944).

4. See M. Ossowska, *Podstawy nauki o moralności* [The foundations of ethics] (Warsaw, 1955–1963).

5. See W. Elton, ed., *Aesthetics and Language* (Oxford, 1954).

6. Cf. the work of C. I. Lewis, Roman Ingarden, and Georg Lukács.

7. (Note added in 1971) This essay was written six years ago in polemics with the neopositivists; it nonetheless acceded to their assumptions with regard to the logical status of aesthetic judgment being in part "crippled" due to its assertive-normative character. Were I attacking the problem today, I would develop my own analysis in a more consistent manner, by arguing that the logical status of aesthetic judgments as compared with that of so-called atomic statements is not weaker but merely *different*. We can easily conceive and argue for the notion that any proper aesthetic judgment is a kind of proposition if we interpret its logical status by means of the explanation-procedure. In other words, what must be done is to introduce into the explanans some additional assumptions, specifically *the cultural code* (its scope ranging from limited population and time parameters, to geographically and temporally transcultural parameters) which consists of the given system of beliefs, opinions, paradigms, and norms, not ignoring the rules of language adequate to the expressed ideas, emotions, etc. Such additional assumptions allow us to define a universe of elements pertinent to a proper aesthetic judgment. In this formulation, the basic elements of the "universe" can be extended to what I term aesthetic invariants. In this way we can state that the kind of objectivity peculiar to aesthetic judgments implies their truth or falsehood and that this truth-value, in turn, implies a specific logical status in what they say. In stating this, I draw on the most recent marxist-structuralist inquiries of the Polish scholars at work in the Poznan circle.

8. This "reserve hypothesis"—which I have found no alternative but to advance as my operative hypothesis—obviously needs close analysis in numerous details. I want to sketch here some fundamental operations which could prove the validity of the hypothesis. First, there should be full-scale study of man's transition from a creature nearly indistinguishable from other animals to a social being (in terms of labor, or production and its implements, as well as of language in relation to emergent intellect). We might find some features of the human biophysiological makeup which remain continuous through the process of exteriorizations, that is, which are affirmed again and again during man's gradual mastery of the external world through techne. Skill as an aspect of art is an apparent constant. A second constant would seem to be the aesthetic structure (understood relationally, that is, with both the subject and the object as "adequate" data), which was caught up in the production processes and magical rituals, and gained an initial degree of autonomy only later, probably in the late neolithic period. A third apparent constant is the relatively autonomous status of the aesthetic structure. Such structures undergo many changes and modifications in the course of history but the core traits seem to recur. Accordingly, I believe some cultural universals of mankind might be affirmed and I am not persuaded by the anthropological skepticism of, say, M. J. Herskovits (see *Man and His Works* [New York, 1948]).

9. C. I. Lewis, *An Analysis of Knowledge and Valuation* (La Salle, Ill., 1946), chs. 14 and 15.

10. Ossowska, *Podsawy nauki o moralności.*

11. See Hampshire's essay in Elton, *Aesthetics and Language.*

12 In addition to the works quoted in the text, my reading for this paper included the following: K. Gilbert and H. Kuhn, *A History of Esthetics* (Westport, Conn., 1954); R. Bayer, *Histoire de l'esthetique* (Paris, 1961); W. Tatarkiewicz, *Historia estetyki*, vols. 1, 2, (Wroclaw, 1960); F. Schümmer, *Die Entwicklung des Geschmackbegriffe in der Philosophie des 17. und 18. Jahrhunderts*, Archiv für Begriffsgeschichte, vol. 1 (1951); R. Ingarden, *O poznawaniu dziela literackiego* (Lvov-Cracow, 1937), chs. 4 and 5, and his papers for the aesthetics congresses at Venice (1956), Athens (1960), and Amsterdam (1964); G. Morpurgo-Tagliabue, "Gusto e giudizio," *Rivista di Estetica* (September–December 1962) and "Fenomenologia del giudizio critico," ibid. (January–April 1963); S. C. Pepper, *The Work of Art* (Bloomington, Ind., 1955); R. Arnheim, *Art and Visual Perception* (Berkeley, 1954); G. Lukács, *Die Eigenart des Aesthetischen* (Neuwied, 1963); S. Ossowski, "O sub-

jektywizmie w estetyce," in *Festschrift for T. Kotarbinski* (1934), and *U podstaw estetyki*, 3rd ed. (Warsaw, 1958); also essays on aesthetic concepts and questions of value or evaluation published in various journals by M. C. Beardsley, M. Weitz, J. Margolis, and F. Sibley from the late 1950s until 1965 (when this paper was originally shaped).

Part II

Artistic-Cognitive
Values

Chapter 5   Expression

Expression is widely reputed to be an aspect of the work of art which is as mysterious and elusive as it is attractive and compelling. Indeed, many scholars have given up or put off the attempt to encompass this problem with discursive analysis. Whether intimidation, deferential admiration, or plain healthy skepticism is the cause of hesitance, I think we certainly may share the emotion but need not let it make us give up the task. My approach is to proceed by clarifying the most significant ways in which the phenomenon is found and the term is used.

This analysis will show, I think, that the need to come to grips with expression is even greater than believed; indeed, some usages treated here seldom get attention, let alone sufficient acceptance. There is no doubt that the warnings against abuse of this term have been widespread. Philosophers, psychologists, and artists, whose purpose is to comprehend the aesthetic practice of the past and present, are aware that the chief cause for the obscurity of certain ideas of expression has been the question's complicated status. Surely this acknowledged complexity is the ultimate reason for the general rejection of any single, unequivocal definition.

Unfortunately, many scholars of today's ascendent linguistic-analytical school are so intent on avoiding error that for clarity's sake they insist on a disentangling logical analysis, with the matter at issue relegated to a secondary status. In the last twenty years, several distinct attempts have been made to give expression a single, unified definition that would be simple yet so lucid as to render the present diversity of definitions superfluous; all these endeavors have been unsuccessful. Why? I dare say because all shared the failing of reductionism.

My approach will be different: First, I shall try to disentangle the meanings of the concept, and, following that, I shall inquire into precisely what the aesthetics of the past and the present has found most significant in the data of expression. That is my major plan, but there is also a secondary aim, which emerges from an awareness of one of the pitfalls especially prevalent in my approach to aesthetics. In the marxist tradition the terms "expression" and "mimesis" have frequently been treated as though they were interchangeable and indistinguishable. In the next chapter I will show that there does exist a complicated yet close relationship between mimesis and expression. The phenomena may in a sense coincide, they may overlap, or they may simply complement one another—depending on the variety of expressiveness that is used and on the context in which the phenomena occur.

The most fundamental coherence of the categories of expression and mimesis will be found to occur with regard to the sixth meaning of "expression," as the term is analyzed in this chapter.

Characteristics Shared by All Definitions of Expression

Common to all of the different varieties and meanings of expression is the fact that *although the sets of qualities, as manifest traits, occur in the art objects, their effect is virtually psychic and as such they find their referents in the human subject.*[1]

The expressive qualities — with their specific feeling-tones, their own "physiognomy" — have usually been described by the term "tertiary" to distinguish them from what are termed the primary (measurable) qualities and secondary qualities (color, sound, etc.) of the object. Whereas in the case of mimesis the work of art is demonstrably connected with the outside world, in the case of expression the connection is with the inner world of both the artist who conveys the expressive "message," and the recipient who submits to the experience of the evoked expressiveness.

The chief difficulty that must be discussed in this respect has to do with the artist. He makes an object which is to provide a semipsychical mediation between him and his audience, and we readily assume that he must be entirely sincere, that he is attempting to tell us what he has genuinely felt. Yet it is beyond doubt that artistic "sincerity" only in extreme instances approximates the sincerity achieved in intimacy or exhibitionism. Nor have we sufficient reason to assume that the expressive quality is always and precisely adequate to what was experienced by the artist in his creative process.

If it is possible to speak of any correspondence here it would be between the artist's assumed *intentions* to present this or that psychic state (though they may fail to be embodied) and the semisentient characteristics of the given work.[2] Thus the only "sincerity" that is of interest to aesthetics is that which pertains not to a man making confessions but to an artist who determines what and how to "confess." The expressive relationship between the work of art and the artist is thus intransitive and asymmetrical: Insofar as we reliably know a good deal about the artist's personality, the vicissitudes of his life, and his immediate allegiances, we are entitled to pass judgment on the expressive traits of his production as they possibly correspond to his temperament and character; nothing of the kind can, however, be attempted in the reverse direction. There is necessarily an investment

by the artist in the work's expressive features, but the nature of that investment
is irrelevant; it does not matter whether the artist expresses genuine or feigned
emotions. Alone of importance are our assumption that he intended a certain
presentation and our decision as to whether he succeeded or failed.

At this point, I must stop for a moment to dwell on this issue of intention, which
is rather crucial in considering whether the artist's expression conveys what he
feels (sincerity in the form of intimacy) or what he has chosen to convey (sincerity
in the artistic sense of congruity of idea and execution). I do not subscribe fully
to the notion of "intentional fallacy," although in most cases it does have a bearing.
Even in other cases where we have documents against which we may check the
artist's actual project of execution in the effort to discover if he intended to express himself in a certain way (Flaubert's comment "*Mme. Bovary c'est moi*"; the
elderly Rembrandt's self-portraits; Modigliani's *Jeanne Hébuterne*), what nonetheless concerns us is not the work's relationship to the artist's experienced intentions but, instead, the *intentional* psychic state embodied *in the work*. Even
in those cases where we can speak of verifiably genuine prior intentions to create
a certain work in a specific manner, nonetheless this pursuit leads along a slippery
road that takes us away from the work of art itself.

Yet it may be argued that in such instances we might understand the expressive
features more fully when they are referred to the artist's biography. This could be
seriously urged with regard to Rembrandt, whose tragic sense of abandonment, of
being made to face the terrible wrath of God is fully documented. It would be hard
to make a comparable case for Modigliani's picture, for neither the beauty of Jeanne
nor the painter's passionate love for her can be confirmed in the expressive dimension of the work. However, even if we could make statements about the works of
Modigliani, Flaubert, and others similar to the one we have just made about Rembrandt's self-portraits, my major argument would remain intact and central: The
expressiveness of a work of art is sustained by its own composed elements and not
by its relation to the circumstantial emotions or even the creative goals of the artist.
If the work lacks expressive appeal to observers who know nothing about the artist,
then it is a failure in its artistically expressive aspect.

Thus, in responding to the expressive traits of a given work, we can and should
assume only a hypothetical intention on the part of the artist to express this or
that. With this formulation we make allowance for the inevitable transaction between the artist (considered whole, as a given human, creative personality) and his

work, yet we prohibit any reverse inferences. I shall make no definite statements about the intention, its content, and its fulfillment; I shall, rather, adopt the standpoint of the public, which observes in a work of art some intentional, semisentient data. Whether the artist's genuine emotions or even his true intentions are revealed remains a problematical but separable matter. We should bear these findings in mind, since, when artistic qualities are described as expressive, we frequently tend to take it for granted that their semisentience has some direct relationship to their creator's psychic life.

We should, by the way, distinguish between emotions of the artist which are occasional and due to chance and which are only rarely transmitted to his works, and emotions which are central to the artist's temperament and character and which may be said to provide an expressive "signature." I believe no one will question the role of the latter (their function is recognized in the third variant below and is emphasized in the fourth). With regard to this "signature," we note again the ambiguous role of the artist's intentions for a given work or for his oeuvre as a whole. The role and uniqueness of an artist must be determined largely—and sometimes exclusively—from a study of his works and not from his biography or his occasional remarks.

There is still a catch here, however, as my conception seems to eliminate entirely the spontaneous subconscious or unconscious expression. To this objection I would reply that I do *not* eliminate the subconscious or the unconscious in the creative process, although I am inclined to interpret the latter as basically a rationally controlled operation. The interrelations between the artist's unconscious and the work of art I find revealing for the psychological explanation of the creative personality, but much less so for the interpretation of the work of art.

From these reflections it may readily be seen why the art *object*, with its expressive properties, must be given the primary scrutiny as the mediating entity between the artist and his public. In mentioning the public, let me stress that expression entails not only the bestowing of certain semisentient characteristics on some data and their arrangements, but also the *evoking* in human agents of some authentic, sentient phenomena by means of those semisentient properties. Figure 1 roughly illustrates the result.

The recipient is more or less actively cooperative; that is to say, to some degree he also imbues the work of art with semipsychical qualities.[3] This interaction hinges on three factors—the expressive qualities of the work, the human subject,

THE ARTIST   THE WORK   → THE RECIPIENT
(or PERFORMER) ——————————→ OF ART ———   for whom
who imbues   which has ← ——————— the qualities
the work of art   expressive   prove evocative
with certain   features
semipsychical properties

Figure 1.

and the circumstances. It is important here to distinguish natural objects and nonartistic human artifacts from artistic objects proper, since in the former two cases
the recipient's proper activity may be much more extensive.

The "Empathy" Theory

Expression is defined encompassingly by some authors as the empathic projection onto objects of images, feelings, and ideas, where the objects are usually
exemplified by natural phenomena. This point of view is not wholly without merit;
but as a fundamental explanation it has to be regarded as anachronistic. Admittedly, I ignore the various divisions of the empathy school in this very abbreviated
statement, which reflects the extreme formulation of the theory, and which, in fact,
amounts to a more securely argued version of the "pathetic fallacy" which is associated with John Ruskin.

The paradigm of this standpoint can be found in the work of Theodor Lipps and
Vernon Lee. Lipps argued that, by virtue of the human capacity for empathy *(Einfühlung)*, the contrariety between the self and the aesthetically enjoyed object vanishes; what we enjoy in that object is ourselves *(Ich Qualitäten)*, our free spiritual
vitality which we have projected onto the perceived and contemplated dance movement, work of architecture, depicted landscapes, etc. He stressed the "inner imitation" by which we involuntarily imbue the given object with our creative powers,
since the artist's or the performer's activity is basically (i.e., metaphysically) not
different from ours, the audience's.

Lipps did *not* believe that there is a complex, specific connection between sense-
feelings (which would absorb an object's structural features) and the operations
of empathy, and he influenced Vernon Lee to adopt a similar standpoint. She did
question her mentor's notion of empathy as the projection of a metaphysical ego,
and she saw greater importance in the conjuncture of the qualities of the perceived
object and the activity of the human subject. However, she admits no contribution

of a positive stimulus to the transaction by the object's "physiognomic traits." She goes as far as to protest that empathy must not be confused with "inner mimicry" (sympathy). Lee asks us to assume, then, that the animation of the inanimate—for example, of the rising contour of a mountain—is the product of our imaginative faculty, and that it lacks any correlative stimulation such as the particular "physiognomic features" of the mountain might produce.

On the whole, then, the basic theory of aesthetic empathy does notice the existence of objective qualities and assert the evocative powers of the artist, but it stresses basically the spiritual projection of the self which alters aesthetic experience into para-aesthetic or creative experience. In terms of figure 1, empathy theory attributes to the feedback from the recipient to the work of art an arbitrary character. The evocative quality of experiencing art is all supplied by the recipient-subject, while none of the evocation is assigned to the object as such. The theory has been analyzed so often by so many authors, that there is no point in giving a detailed critique here. Most vulnerable at the points its proponents think decisive, this version of expression seems unbalanced and, thus, the least helpful.

The Expressiveness of the Artistic "Material"
A second version of expression looks not to the free projection of an imagination but to the properties which are indigenous to the medium of a particular art. It asks: What are the attributes of the selected means of expression, that is, its *materials*? These "captive" properties can consist of tones (characterized by intensity, timbre, pitch, and duration), colors, etc. The finest exposition that I have found of this interpretation of expression is in Karl Aschenbrenner's *Coherence in Art*.[4] Aschenbrenner's work speaks of "tendative powers" inherent to the media themselves. The artist impresses his vision on these media only by employing the tendative powers in a definite context. The public, for its part, responds to the semisentient characteristics in the context of the whole pattern while attending to the potentialities of the medium. This version of expression represents the extreme opposite of the empathy theory. What the elementary instrumentalities convey is deemed more important than what the recipient adds. Little remains to the artist other than the exercise of judicious selection. In terms of figure 1, the object's evocative effect is here overstressed and the input of both the artist and the public is underrated.

From this kind of discussion we may begin to doubt whether the traits called expressive are truly of a tertiary nature. The hue, saturation, and intensity ascribed to a given color — that is, the so-called secondary qualities, here seem to provide in themselves a significant expression; the same might be said of the so-called primary qualities (e.g., the pitch of a tone). According to the original formulation of the concept,[5] a tertiary quality was a feeling-tone which seemed a property of the object. The notion was subsequently developed to place emphasis on certain *felt qualities* of the aesthetic object. In this sense the expressiveness of the materials could be associated (assuming an inherently tendative medium) with a tertiary character, inasmuch as the feeling-tones are stimulated. Yet if we think in terms of artistic wholes, this entire distinction among primary, secondary, and tertiary qualities may seem unfortunately complicated and pointless. We should then probably speak instead of an integral, seamless expression which includes such evidently physical (that is, primary) elements as the motion in dance, the contour of a building, the prosodic and metrical traits of poetry, and graphic composition. Thus, it seems possible to accept the second interpretation of expression up to a point, for it does rightly guide our attention to the coexpressiveness of the medium (material). In combination with the next variety and interpretation of expression, this "material" standpoint provides us with fundamental valuational qualities.

The Expressiveness of Structured Patterns of Qualities

Expression can also be seen as pertaining chiefly to particular qualities which are invested into a given material context, and are arranged so as to bring out some peculiar attributes and effects of the material. The crucial aspect here is the establishment of many-sided patterns, such as domination and subordination, emergence and recedence, simplicity and intricacy, compactness and looseness, repletion and depletion, harmony and disharmony, rhythm and arrhythmia, swiftness and slowness, monotony and variety, contrast and sameness. All the patterns are commingled in the whole to provide a manifest character which projects delicacy or crudity, exuberance or calmness, elegance or assertiveness, gaudiness or restraint, subtlety or ostentation, and so on. When we discuss these characteristics, we ascribe them as semisentient qualities to the given artistic wholes. This is not to say that we find a literal refinement, crudity, and so on; rather, we respond to their feeling-tones, as is exemplified by a highly complex and hardworking musical composition which may yet offer us the physiognomy of a simple and even idle moment.

Expression as a structured pattern of qualities is seen especially well by comparing the works of Pollock and Miro, Stravinsky and Hindemith, Kurosawa and An-

tonioni, Moore and Giocometti, Saarinen and Le Corbusier, St. John Perse and
Essenin, Isadora Duncan and Jerome Robbins. Undoubtedly, these examples invite
the charge of having been randomly drawn from our century with an eye to expe-
ditious contrasts. Quite so. However, the memorable and even blatant contrast is
often the most enlightening.

With regard to the structure of specific qualities I can say that:

1. All works of art are to some extent expressive.
2. The more artistic the object, the more expressive it generally is, in its own peculiar way. (Note that "expressionist" art, discussed below, is not regarded as
   inherently better than other kinds of artistic expressiveness.)
3. Expressiveness of this kind is especially noticeable in cases of nonobjective art.
4. Representational art is also expressive in this sense. (Note that in saying this I
   do not rely on anything that is explicitly described or depicted as emotion or its
   nonartistic outward show in this form of art.)

This final point needs further development. Painters of the Italian High Renaissance certainly represented emotional symptoms of their subjects, but it would be
difficult to argue that these pictures are very expressive. The paintings of El Greco
and the self-portraits of Rembrandt and Van Gogh, however, are highly expressive,
owing not so much to the features of the represented subject as to the way in which
the paint is applied: the colors, textures, and lines of composition. To take examples
from other media, the expressiveness of Yunichiro Tanizaki's short novel *The Key*,
like that of Masaki Kobayashi's film *Harakiri*, has little to do with the personality
of the hero, who is perversely obsessed by his sexual frustration, but depends on
the way the tale is told. Tanizaki achieves an aesthetic patterning which is pervaded
by ethical tact, refinement, and crystalline clarity. Another case: The title character
of Peter Handke's theatrical work *Kaspar* is a modern, Rousseauian simpleton imbued with a certain distinctive expressiveness — but the primary expressive dimension is the language employed in the play, which the author toys with ingeniously
and insidiously. Language, the rudimentary vehicle of social life, becomes the butt
of the cosmic joke and the chief specific subject matter of the play.

At this point, I should directly consider the problem of the artist's individual
style or manner and its equivalents in the art object. The more such objects we
have from him, the more we can observe to what extent he reverts to the same or
similar arrangements of his materials and media. It thus becomes easier to detect
his "signature," his singular patterning effects, within the expressive result. (I shall

return to personal expression and the latitudes in which it operates in discussing the next two variants of expression.)

What is the significance of this third variant in terms of subject-object relationships? The expressive traits are here entrenched in the object itself. The implications of this solution are brought out by the gestaltists, and Rudolf Arnheim especially, with great skill. The artist supplies those properties of the object which possess semisentience, and it is through these objective properties that he evokes feelings in his public which are more or less similar to the emotions that he experienced in his creative endeavor (or, to be more exact, the emotions that he intends should carry his artistic "message"). The imminent status of expression gives the character also of the "symbolism," by which I mean the meaningful aspect of the particular qualities and especially of their patterns. "Symbolic" meaning depends on the conceived correspondence between the pattern-forming mind and the patterned status lent to both inanimate and animate worlds.

Do we learn from gestalt theory with sufficient explicitness and persuasiveness whether the artist's expressive signs, implanted in the art object, gain a commensurate emotional and meaningful response from the public? The complexity of the problem demands a separate study, but I do feel that we should be rather skeptical towards the answers provided by the gestaltist school. However, regardless of the disputes in progress concerning the genetic background, and whatever the ultimately most convincing hypothesis, we shall certainly have to acknowledge the fascinating, even astonishing phenomenon of the seemingly psychic qualities that inhere to some art objects.

I am emphasizing this third version of expression because of its centrality. The more so because it is related not only to the feeling-tone of particular qualities and their patterns but also and ultimately to the achieved *artistic whole*. In a word, the given work of art is in some way expressive of more than its concrete attributes; the achieved total expression is the "polyphonic" result of the consonance or dissonance of the commingling feeling-tones. No serious aesthetic inquiry today can pass it by, as can be demonstrated by reference to Mikel Dufrenne's *Phénomenologie de l'expérience esthétique* (1953). I believe that this version is essential to understanding the variety and richness of expression as artistic value. There is no limit to the possible concrete, inherent "physiognomies," which might range from abstruseness to crystalline clarity, intricacy to simplicity, suavity to crudity, consonance to dissonance, monotony to brilliant charm. Integral to the traits of the entities are often multitudinous specific sets, or patterns, of valuational qualities. Even if a scholar were to make a catalog of all the patterns or qualities and how they could be concisely pinpointed or infallibly achieved, I doubt he could do it. Indeed, it is hard to pinpoint the precise relationship between the valuational qualities (and their patterns) and the varieties of the expressed physiognomies. This trouble in describing any stable and reliable correspondences may help to encourage the widespread view among aestheticians that the expressive values are ineffable.

There is obviously no contradiction between what I have just written and my earlier judgment that the medium (materials) may prove inherently expressive due to some distinctive properties. I do not see how we can deny the expressive appeal which is inseparable from the established tone of certain instruments (a violin or flute) or the texture of some substances (wood or metal) or certain rhythmic meters (iambic or spondaic). The warm and the cool ranges of the color spectrum are widely accepted. Musical annotation assumes a similar expressiveness: andante, presto, vivace, con brio, etc. Yet it seems no contradiction to insist on the primary hegemony of the expressive composition (the entirely given formal structure). As I remarked while discussing the second version of expression, the medium (materials) will rarely appear to claim pride of place as the exclusive or even foremost valuational quality. Usually, it is incorporated and modulated with other dimensions of the given artistic whole. Even if the material proves foremost in some simple patterns, we will find trouble in ascribing to it a definite, single expressive value. Harsh and high-pitched notes (tones) can produce feelings of terror, anxiety, or just displeasure. Warm colors can evoke a feeling of joy or perhaps boredom. A room interior dominated by aluminum may give us a slight frisson, a sense of irritating fragility, a soothed lassitude, or perhaps a dull exasperation. In all of these cases, the ultimate expressive evocation undoubtedly derives from the totality comprised by the qualities and the structure plus the context in which the artistic whole functions.

Interpretive Expression

Expression may also be understood to refer to the singular characteristics of a particular dance or music performance; that is, to those characteristics inherent in the process-like "objects" that are achieved through interpretation and that are consequently derived from the idiosyncrasies and the creative method of the particular performers.

We must be careful here again to avoid equating expression with the spontaneous, intimate experiences of the dancer, violinist, pianist. The expressed feelings may simply be feigned; or (as in the case of theatrical acting, where the Stanis-lavski technique, with its psychophysical exercises is especially pertinent) they may be deliberately stimulated so as to induce the para-authentic experience. Often a performer can perfectly duplicate a certain pattern of embodying a particular work of art in performance after performance. There is ample reason to believe that this is *not* due to the artist's having brought his expression into the tightest possible relationship with what he genuinely experiences. Performers, it may be observed, are capable of growing as "cool," as distant from the "object" they are producing for us, as is the painter, composer, or playwright.

We should likewise be clear about the *bifurcated* character of the expressive per-formance-object. Inherent in the nature of the expressive qualities of this sort of work of art is a constant process of remolding. An exact "replica" of the enduring matter of the work is a fatuous notion; a rote duplication of earlier successful per-formances is all but impossible, and probably undesirable. The specificity and idiosyncrasy of each successive performance — the individual touch, the manner and style — modifies the expression that is implied by the musical or the dance score and, at the same time, confirms or even enhances some of the expressive traits of that score.[6] We praise in their own right the interpretive styles of a Heifetz or a Richter. However, we also seek in their interpretive performances the expres-sive characteristics we know exist in the compositions they play.

The expression of a theatrical performance presents a more complex problem, and I shall focus here only on the artistic personality of the play director. (Let me stress that I use the term "personality" only to indicate the particular and distinctive traits that are manifested in the work of an artist.) We may agree that the approach of Olivier or Brook to Shakespeare is undoubtedly expressive, and where the direc-tor or stage designer is guided by a developed philosophy of the theater (as is true, for instance, of Craig, Appia, Brecht, or Lebel) this expressiveness may well appear to be increased. The director's expression necessarily has a different em-bodiment from that of the dancer or violinist, since he does not usually appear in the actual performance. This circumstance prohibits any encompassing statements about *the* expressive quotient of the theater director.

The productions shaped by some directors do display a complete control. Where this happens we see a collective, unified performance, and nothing short of this can entirely realize the director's expressive vision. At this degree of integration, theater, like music and dance, may be analyzed in terms of *ensemble* expression. We should not forget the protracted collective assimilation and preparation of artistic ideas which alone conditions ensemble expressiveness. In such cases, the expressive coherence and intensity of the ensemble becomes at times more con-spicuous and more decisive than the original invention, that is, than the individual expression of the initiator. Common to the Peking Opera, the ballet of Jerome Rob-bins, the Moscow Art Theater under Stanislavski, the Berlin Ensemble of Brecht, and the Grotowski or Bread and Puppet theaters, are coherent and distinctive com-positions of expressive performance qualities. A unique collaboration must pervade the work of the companies—even if ideas supplied by one person have organized the ensemble's expression.

The Expressionists

In the preceding notions of expression, every art object or performance has offered a potential case for discussion. We turn now to a version which has restricted ap-plication. Its relevance extends just to one particular class of works—those that may be variously described as dynamic and harsh, highly intense and dramatic, pervaded with dissonant elements, skewed to the morbid and ugly and fugitive. Normally, we find this class of works (and performances) contrasted with works expressive of a static harmony and a concordant beauty. The latter, it is argued, are impersonal achievements while "expression" (in this understanding of it) is proof of a deliberate eschewing of self-control and a wish to embrace the dynamic and the spontaneous.[7]

This special version of expression was particularly fostered by the so-called expressionist movement in art, which encompassed the work of the *Brücke* and *Blaue Reiter* groups, Wedekind, Strindberg, Benn, and Mahler. The tendency flour-ished primarily in Germany and Scandinavia. However, we should not overlook the antecedents and legacy of the school. Some philosophers wish to apply to this propensity of art the comprehensive name romanticism. I do not care for that term in this context, since it applies more aptly to a specific era in art. Yet the propensity itself does exist and, moreover, is permanent; there is a long line of artistic realiza-tions which show expressionist traits. The artistic pendulum swings to reinforce this propensity at times when social stability is weak, when civilization is starting to shake and religious (metaphysical) syntheses are being dispersed by the urgent problems of the day. It should also be noted that a preference for the works of art in this legacy may emerge entirely apart from any concrete interest in the art's themes—in its social and psychological conventions and its metaphysical content. A taste for expressionism may develop on the basis of its inherent organizing expression.

In order to correlate this version of expression with the approach I have used in the other versions so far discussed, I should probably speak of its being manifested to a certain degree instead of being categorically different. I should probably speak of the "more intensively expressive" traits which appear in some art objects — such as paintings by Van Gogh, Rouault, Soutine, or Chagall; surrealist poetry; Gaudi's buildings, Witkiewicz's novels and plays — as compared with some others. To use this formulation, of course, does not eliminate but, rather, qualifies the restricted sense of this version of expression.

The Expression of Psychosocial Equivalents
The last version of the concept of expression that I shall discuss involves psycho-social equivalents. Here, the art object is studied in relation to the sociohistorical material abroad at the time and place of the work's origin, which has been internal-ized, experienced, and felt by people then living, and transformed into correlated expressive attributes by artists. Here, in other words, are the expressive equivalents of social moods, intuitions, beliefs, strivings, and opinions; every work of art is, to greater or lesser extent, treated as a symptomatic and emblematic depository of the life of society, including especially its mythology and its ideological conventions, which, having given rise to feeling-patterns, function back and forth across the in-definite boundaries of the rational and the irrational. The artistic personality is here considered as a mediator between these ubiquitous but diffuse attitudes and psychosocial patterns, and a work of art in which certain correlative expressive attributes appear. The activity of the artist points in two directions: to the materials of historical experience and to their expression in art; to the artist's what and why and also to his how. We must not confuse this version of expression with any of the others. It considers the work's particular qualities so as to refer them to a collective social subject, and in doing this it discovers an historical objectivity in the expres-siveness itself. Here, the expression is not only a palpable stimulus to aesthetic experience in the recipient; it is also a manifestation of a sentient world antecedent to itself.

It is essential to note that this idea of expression is not confined to the rendering of the aforementioned moods, intuitions, beliefs, goals, and opinions; it also extends to some extent to the description of overt behavior, to the extent that this behavior corresponds to the internalized sociohistorical data. Thus, patterns of life style are themselves considered "expressive," that is, potentially adequate to convey the inherent social psychology. This version of expression thus draws on both internal and external phenomena.[8]

What is the marxist view of this problem? As I indicated at the start, the terms "mimesis" and "expression" have generally been used interchangeably by marxist writers, following the precedent of Hegel and Taine. Plekhanov provides a significant case of this confusion of terms; and his influence on early Soviet aesthetic thought was decisive on this issue, as on others. However, as a legacy it has had a lucid defender and explicator in George Lukács. Both in his early writings and his late major work *Die Eigenart des Aesthetischen* (1963), Lukács, drawing on the work of Wilhelm Dilthey, sought consciously to reconcile the identity of the two categories; that is, he subsumed my sixth aspect of expression within his universal category, mimesis. He accordingly (and arbitrarily, I find) proceeded to outline the presumed mimetic character of music, dance, architecture, landscape gardening, and the applied arts. I cannot go into my reasons for differing with Lukács here;[9] however, I should like to point out that in my view the nonobjective arts are unquestionably expressive—and it is precisely through their expressive traits that they relate to the social world at the time and place of their origin. Nor is psychosociological expression absent from literature, theater, or cinema; but here, it is chiefly projected through the representation of the social psychology of the characters of the fiction.

Here, then, are two aspects (representation and expression) of a single viewpoint holding that the experience of a given society can be rendered in nondiscursive, artistic "messages." These aspects are generally complementary and tend to confirm the social meaningfulness of art because, whether congruent or confluent, both have their referents in the substratum of a specific place and time ("climate" is the common, vague word for it) which is pervasive in the style of both art and life. In the representational arts, the two aspects may merge, and we then find that an expressive manner (or style) which describes (and typifies) emotions, has been organically united with mimetic description and realistic typification (as for example, in Stanislaw Przybyszewski's novels, Strindberg's plays, or Van Gogh's *Chair* or *Shoes*).

A difficult question must be faced here: Why should reality be granted to a *collective* social subject, and why should it be presumed capable of being the emotional progenitor of the expressive qualities of a work of art, when I hung back from attributing a definite relationship of this kind with regard to individual experiential data? Is this not a double standard? I think not. There seem to be solid reasons for linking expressiveness with a social substratum. First, let me recall that although I did not reject the possibility of a correspondence between the expressiveness of the art object and an artist's genuine experience, I said that the emotions *putatively* intended by the artist, that is, those actually found embodied in his object, are of much greater importance. Moreover, impressive evidence is at hand from many sources to substantiate the statement that no artist can divest himself of ties with the substratum, or act independently of the climate containing him as he grows to adulthood, lives, and works. It should also be noted that the social feelings at issue here, that is, the climate suffusing the work of art, consists not so much of the subtle, more elusive and marginal emotion in the context of the society, as of the popular conventions, the shibboleths. In a word, this substratum—which of course does not exclude the other modes of expression—consists of the modes of thinking, feeling, and behavior displayed in the "public theater" in which all must be actors to at least some degree. (Perhaps the ancient category, *decorum* best suggests the applicable frame of reference.) The artist may use these resource materials as expressive building blocks, with a number of varieties of intention: at times he totally identifies with the building blocks; more often he adopts a certain distance from the more publicly acknowledged modes of social feeling. However, precisely in order to communicate his own *intended* emotions, the artist will need to rely to some degree on the use of the recognized community expressions of feeling.

This interpretation somewhat parallels the hermeneutic idea of a direct connection from the *Zeitgeist* through a mediative artistic personality to the work of art. There is one aspect of the hermeneutic approaches—*Verstehen durch Nacherleben*, understanding through empathic experiences—which may be accepted if freed of the irrationality which is its implicit nature; this is the view which states that, in order to understand fully a work of art (and its context), we must reconstruct the contemporary modes of feeling, striving, and so on (together with the predominant mystifications, and the artist's individual response to and solutions in this climate). Marxism makes major use of this approach.

Almost certainly, the work will prove to have no simply deciphered and direct causal relationship to the given social psychology. A great number of artists bury their social feelings, distort them, try to elude them; but these strategies should be taken into account as an analysis is developed. However, whether the emotional expressiveness is genuine or is feigned by the artist, whether he attributes it to himself or to certain others—none of this matters for the present analysis. The artist may have his buried, distorted, elusive relationship to the publicly shared emotion of his time; yet the imprint of the collective social subject will be registered. Art is in every case symptomatic, for the artist's subjective response is never purely idiosyncratic; it always hinges on the given collective social subject, either positively, negatively, or evasively.

What can now be said of the relationship alluded to at the start of the chapter between mimesis and expression? I said then that the two categories have a close and complicated relationship: they may coincide, or overlap, or simply complement one another. If what I have said in the preceding few paragraphs is correct then so was that opening formulation.[10]

Conclusions

In my opinion, version three (relating to formal and material valuational qualities structured into a comprehensive pattern) and version four (relating to interpretive performance) — both of which emphasize the artist's "handwriting," that is, the expression peculiar to him — seem to be the fundamental aspects of expression. Version one, as I have tried to suggest, does recall to us the part played by the recipient's empathy in some cases of expressiveness (especially in relation to nature, as in the case, for example, of landscapes imbued with a significance through our moods); but it is outdated in its basic claim for universal application. Versions two, five, and six, while disparate in application, seem about equal in weight: from the morphological point of view we must pay attention to the expressiveness of the media (materials) of art; from the stylistic point of view we must take an interest in whether some expressive properties are more expressive than others; and from the point of view of artistic genesis and function we must take an interest in the psychosociological expressiveness of art (here there is a link to the related issue of the comparative meaningfulness of art).

The aim of this essay has been deliberately modest. Certainly there are other substantial points of view on expression that did not fall within its scope; they all, however, seem to be derivative in one way or another from the six concepts here distinguished. I fully realize that these six deserve more ample consideration. They require further clarification, quite possibly some correction, but certainly development and elaboration. If the reader finds any hint of definitive statement in the essay, I urge that he excuse it as a slip of thought and pen. Finally, among the issues not grappled with here which are, nevertheless, basic to the elucidation and proper rating of the concepts treated, I must call attention to the whole (and perhaps crucial) question of the genesis of artistic expression — its favorable conditions for emergence, its process of interiorization and then exteriorization, the place of nature and of social history in generating and evolving the expressive symbols, etc. Onto these obscure passageways, I have not even opened the door.[11]

Notes

1. Nelson Goodman in the excellent third chapter of his book *Languages of Art*, (Indianapolis, Ind., 1968), has done much to dispel the occult aura clinging to the idea of expression. He and I agree that the problem of expression is basically distinct from that of the depiction or description of the world, although we use differing methods to treat the question of the latter, denotational operations. I accept and mean to build on Goodman's statement that expression is a "metaphorical exemplification," by which he indicates an insentient property that is invested by a symbol, which has a sentient frame of reference.

2. In this sense, we should distinguish between artistic expression and ordinary expression (an example of the latter is a smile as a sign of genuine joy). In ordinary life the only parallels to artistic expressions are the so-called professional signs of expression, and, insofar as we find a diplomat, lawyer, or other professional "intending" (acting) these expressions, we are reminded of works of art.

3. An interesting question which cannot be dealt with here concerns the character of the emotions which are experienced as aesthetically expressive. I assume that in most cases the recipients really do feel an authentic sorrow, joy, pain, or delight. I understand why the Aristotelian notion of catharsis is part of the foundation of European aesthetics, for art may so move us that it returns in dreams or otherwise haunts us. Nonetheless, the emotions do differ from those in ordinary experience. Their ambiguous status derives from art's *virtuality* (or more narrowly formulated, its fictionality). Due to this characteristic, Coleridge's notion of suspended disbelief is also relevant to the emotions aroused by the cinema, music, poetry, etc. This is not so much a function of the presence of given expressive traits, as it is a characteristic of aesthetic experience on the whole.

4. I am indebted to Professor Aschenbrenner for allowing me to examine his ingenious argumentation at the manuscript stage. Other works that refer to this point of view are: T. M. Greene, *The Arts and the Art of Criticism*, 3rd ed. (New York, 1952); D. W. Gotshalk, *Art and the Social Order* (Chicago, 1947). The wealth of examples supplied in these books relieves me of the need to mention others.

5. Cf. B. Bosanquet, *The Distinction Between Mind and Its Objects* (1913); S. Alexander, in Encyclopedia Brittanica, 14th ed.

6. This is not the place to analyze the "personal touch" of a painter or writer, although these too, of course, have the potential of a uniquely expressive style or manner. In the visual and literary arts, however, the individual expressiveness is rather directly and fully imbued into the ultimate art object. Only as a secondary question will we perhaps be drawn into discussion of the idiosyncratic latitude of the literary or painterly artistic process. In the performing arts, for obvious reasons the processual idiosyncratic expression is a question high in priority. "Processual" means here "interpretive"; and, to be quite clear, we should note that a *twofold expression* occurs. Our attention is focused on the question of the extent to which the interpreting artist preserves and at the same time modifies the primordial expression which is the musical score or the stage or film script. If he *improvises*, however, then the expression that is achieved in the process of performance falls under our third category. I might add that sometimes the reverse occurs, yielding results treasured by the student of such matters. By this I mean an ably *expressive description* of some person's *interpretive* performance. A famous case is Proust's interpretation of the violin concerts of Venteuil. We may recall too Proust's expressive account of Elstir's painting in which he first stresses its expressive qualities. What we have here, then, is a two-layered, intensified expression — Proust, the writer, representing the work of his fictive heroes, the artists — within a single coherent entity (object).

7. In my view, this notion also forms the basis for the viewpoints of certain contemporary avant-garde artists who claim programmatically to turn away from "expression," even while the critics who examine their work tend to emphasize the differences among individual practitioners (even the most impersonal of them) and persistently find traits that should be termed expressive. A good current example is minimal art. Its founders and practitioners, as well as sympathetic art journalists and critics, say that minimal art is nonphysiognomical, flat, technological, linear and geometrical, architectonic, etc. (Cf. G. Battcock, ed., *Minimal Art: A Critical Anthology* [New York, 1968].) Some minimalists proudly relate their work to serial, systemic thought. Forerunners are claimed in Duchamp, Malevich's suprematism, and constructivism. However, the Battcock book also brings out that many supporters of Kenneth Noland, Barnett Newman, Ad Reinhardt and Tony Smith do find their minimalism expressive. Direct acquaintance with the works is confirming; for the act of making "cool" art devoid of symbols and individuality in itself serves to imprint a feeling-tone. Harold Rosenberg and Richard Wollheim allude to this oblique expressiveness, when they see connections between minimalism and dada or mention its conspicuous gesture. In the present framework of analysis, version three and especially version four are applicable.

8. The concepts of Wilhelm Dilthey may well be judged useful in the discussion of psychosociological expressiveness. See also, for example, E. A. Lippman, "The Problem of Musical Hermeneutics: A Protest and Analysis," in S. Hook, ed., *Art and Philosophy* (New York, 1966) pp. 307–335. Lippman refers the significance of musical symbols to a community of understanding and emotion. He locates an ultimate basis in nature for the human tonal experience; however, he stresses, and calls primary, the importance of sociocultural conditions. Lippman finds these to be the source of the multiple meanings in a given work of art, as well as of the variety of styles, and the predominance in a given period, of certain trends.

9. Some of the points at issue are treated in my essay on Lukács in *Science and Society*, Winter 1967.

10. This essay was finished in 1970. I later read Alan Tormey's *The Concept of Expression* (Princeton, 1971). Tormey excellently defends the third version of expression presented here, which is oriented to formal properties. I have only praise for his discussion, and also for his argument, very like my own, that mimesis and expression should be distinguished, since the portrayal of expressive actions is not tantamount to expression proper (cf. pp. 53–55, 138–139). However, in chapter 4 and 5 Tormey finds to be unwarranted the imputation of artistic expressiveness to the intentional state of the individual human subject; he presumably would thus reject the imputation to a collective human subject. I do not find enough validity in his counter-arguments to justify a negation of versions six and four in my analysis. What is Tormey's case? He shows there is no way to *disprove* that the expressive physiognomical qualities of a given work of art have direct reference to analogous intentional states that are experienced by artists. (All the same, Tormey himself cites the case of Carl Nielsen to demonstrate that a depressed musician can produce a humoresque.) Yet both his proof and exemplification are insufficient. Why?

First, there exists a body of literary proof (especially apparent, perhaps, in the cases of romantic irony and the so-called *Kunstlerroman* where the author's alter ego is the hero) to show that the artist's *creative* experiences do have a direct effect on what he may express in his work.

Second, it even is possible to introduce some irrefragable examples in which the expressive properties of a work of art clearly have their direct source in the artist's experiences — in what he very possibly truly felt and, in consequence, what he intended to objectify as a creative reality. One such instance is Adam Mickiewicz's desperate longing for his homeland embodied in his epic poem *Pan Tadeusz;* or, more recently, E. M. Forster's posthumous novel *Maurice* dealing with homosexuality, which was the author's own anguishing problem.

A third, the *absence* of any guarantee that the imputations will be well or ill founded may have mixed implications. In other words, the impossibility of disproof doesn't exclude that the correlation does exist!

Fourth (and here I refer the reader to a fine discussion by Tormey in chapter 2), we do indeed impute behavior to certain intentional states, if the referable data can be observed in complex patterns that conform to our hypotheses. Since this is so, why can we not say the same for artistic expressiveness? This is especially true where the pattern — documents left by the artist or his associates — confirms that the artistic expression has a plausible relation to the expressive psychic character. If this line of argument is correct, then the proper conclusion is that the equivocal ambiguities of "expression" are irreducible — and in addition that version six should be retained.

11. Of importance for these questions, besides the gestaltist view, is the Jungian hypothesis, which sees expression as shaped by the archetypal mythology of mankind. An interesting conjecture is set forth by Harry S. Broudy in his essay "The Structure of Knowledge in the Arts," in R. A. Smith, ed., *Aesthetics and Criticism in Art Education* (New York, 1966), pp. 23–45. Broudy discusses "imaginative schemata" that give rise to aesthetic experiences, and to symbolic expressiveness in particular; he sketches a genetic explanation which relates both to the natural human situation and to man's nurturing in society.

In the marxist literature, particularly Soviet, on the question of the genesis of expression, a sociological explanation is usually advanced, although a natural propensity that generates expression is not wholly excluded. In the Soviet musical aesthetics of the 1920s and 1930s, when a theory of expressive qualities formulated by Boris Assafiev prevailed, the natural side of expression was widely acknowledged and analyzed. Recently, a few marxist aestheticians (among them Ernst Fisher) have revived the issues centering on the origins of expression, and have emphasized the affinity of the expressive traits in art and magic. Indeed, it is reasonable to hypothesize that the major source of motivation for expression is the impulse to animate the inanimate, combined with the peculiar response to a likeness (*similis simili gaudet*). Thus we too, in our civilized state, find it "natural" to respond to the objectified semisentient qualities.

Still another pertinent theory concerns the habits that we pick up and retain while forgetting their origins. It is, for instance, in this way that we come to associate certain qualities with the fears and joys that fascinated us in childhood; when grown up we find these same qualities fearful or joyful and do not quite understand why. This theory is, however, not adequately incisive; it helps in determining neither what it is that makes us respond in a particular way nor why this response occurs.

Are the expressive associations that we internalize merely accidental and circumstantial? Are they dependent on given here-and-now social situations and our corresponding behavior? Are they perhaps based on a capacity or propensity for animistic magic? Or on some inborn schemata? Are they perhaps constituted by a *patterning* of reality which, while modifiable in particulars, is confirmed and entrenched by continual mutual exchanges among human agents and finally comes to be based on a common semiotic stock and praxis, shaped in turn by a centuries-long cultural tradition which has some regularities that may be "universal" (i.e., shared throughout the species)? In short, are these expressive traits of a transient or a constant character; and, if constant, then to what extent are they of a natural or a cultural origin? The phrasing of this final question can help us remember that the problem of the genesis of aesthetic expression cannot be resolved short of working to

solve the question of the origins of human culture and art in general.

Chapter 6

Mimesis and Realism

Mimesis as a Cognitive-Artistic Axiological Category

Semiotic interpretation has invested aesthetic discourse not only with a new terminology but also with new problems. The semiotic character of the art object and the interaction between *signifiant* and *signifié* are questions which have been thrust into the foreground and have become the focus for discussion of such issues as: the linguistic or quasi-linguistic nature of the artistic message; the autonomous structure of the art object and of its referents, if any, outside its own reality; the denotative and connotative function of a sign message; and the relationship between "form" and "content." It can be seen from this short list that the semiological set in aesthetics has by no means banished the traditional concerns. If anything it has lent them a fresh vigor by extending the area of argument with the addition of new perspective, as is made evident by the controversies over connections between art and language in the strict sense, their similarities and differences. This debate, set in motion in Paris by Roland Barthes and enlivened by Christian Metz's studies of the film message (cf. his *Essais sur la signification au cinéma* [Paris, 1968]), has spread within aesthetics. A particularly stimulating contribution has come from Mikel Dufrenne, who devoted the second half of his *Esthétique et philosophie* (Paris, 1967) to refuting the view that art can be regarded simply as *langue*. Though the following remarks are tangential to that field of discussion, I must acknowledge my great debt to the authors just mentioned; and I have likewise profited from the three-volume collection of essays issued by the Tartu, Estonia (U.S.S.R.) study center, *Trudy po znakovym sistemam* (1964–67).

The subject I propose to discuss is a venerable one. Indeed, many aestheticians would call it outmoded. The semiologist may well find it hopelessly incongruous, not to say repugnant, for I intend to treat mimesis as an axiological category. Nevertheless, there can be no doubt that there are parallels with the semiological investigations of the signification of works of art, particularly in their denotative aspect. The student of aesthetics does not, we should note, apply himself in the first instance to the matter of *signifiant* and *signifié*. These two aspects of the sign, which in the case of art (as Metz and Dufrenne would presumably agree) can only be separated out in the abstract, are apprehended by aesthetic analysis through

The first part of this essay (on mimesis) appeared in *Semiotica*, vol. II, no. 1 (1970); the second part (on realism as a kind of mimesis) appeared in *Wśṕółczesność*, May 1970, and in English in Jean G. Harrell and Alina Wierzbianska, eds., *Aesthetics in Twentieth-Century Poland* (Lewisburg, Pa., 1973). Both parts have been reworked and expanded.

valuation of the integral sense of a work. Be it added (and concurring again with Dufrenne) that this integral sense cannot be established without relating the work to the reality beyond it. Nonetheless, the questions asked by aesthetics differ from those of semiotics not only in wording but also in substance, being directed to the following points:

1. Can mimetic value be specified, and if so, how?
2. Does mimetic value of itself determine the artistic achievement of the object of which it is an attribute, or is it dependent on other values?
3. Does mimetic value enrich the total artistic value of the work, or does it collide with other specific values to the impairment of complete aesthetic satisfaction?

The Varieties of Mimesis The literature on the subject of mimesis is, as in almost all cases connected with the history of aesthetic concepts, a lesson in ambiguities. The nuance which Erich Auerbach lent to this category in his book of the same title need not trouble us here since the author himself, no doubt advisedly, avoided a precise definition of the basic topic of his study. The three great traditions which relate to mimesis in European aesthetics — the Platonic (representation of appearances, or of what is sensuously given in reality itself), the Aristotelian (representation of the essences of things), and the Democritean (representation of the actions of nature) — are still current today. The endurance of the first of these can be detected not only in contemporary art doctrines predicated on the close imitation of aspects of the objective world (which usually means some variant of naturalism), but also in those like op art that call for a running record of everyday experience. The Aristotelian tradition leads to the kind of aesthetic system today embraced by Lukács, who gives perhaps the supreme example of such an approach. The Democritean tradition reaches through the Renaissance idea of *natura naturans* to contemporary structuralist ideas. According to Lévi-Strauss and Barthes, *l'activité structuraliste* involves a patterning and modeling of structures in accordance with rules derived from the surrounding world. Outside of these three traditional heritages, mimesis turns up — often enough without the term being used — in the latest theories of cinema, in their references to illusion being pushed to its utmost limits not only through the employment of moving images but above all through the evocation of the vagaries and confusion of the flow of life, this sense of the here-and-now being attributed quite rightly to the mechanical means of reproduction used.

Of the formulations just cited, the most problematical is the legacy of the Democritean tradition, since it is to be doubted whether men imitate the "actions" of nature. If they sing or build it is because they are a part of nature and predisposed to certain concomitant modes of behavior. Should the mimesis of molding a vessel in the shape of a shell or of carving an axe head to look like a beak be offered in evidence, this is something which could equally well point to mimesis in the Platonic or Aristotelian sense. To put it another way: When we refer to the veritable actions we stretch the meaning of "imitation"; where the term is feasible it refers surely to an outwardly perceptible simulation of "appearances" or of whole structures.

There are likewise some formidable snags in the attribution of mimesis made by the theorists of "nonfigurative" art. To contend, as they do, that nature is represented in the works of Malevich or Kandinsky in the 1910s, or in the abstract arrangements of color in Pollock, can hardly be regarded as more than a metaphor. However, the cubists could legitimately claim that they were observing nature, since their movement did not make an extreme break with the depiction of reality. In other words, we can talk of some version of mimesis as long as artists have retained some conception of nature, even if they have discarded its Renaissance model. Nothing, however, supports those critics who are wont to supply their own metaphysical justifications to a composition. Even if we do find such metaphysics coming from a painter himself — Mondrian, for example, maintained that the geometrical, rational reality of his pictures mirrors an ideal, horizontal-vertical order in the world — it is fair to ask whether there is any corroboration for such a belief. Again, if the idea is that an artist like Pollock is giving utterance to his anxieties in the violent collisions of colors, lines, and forms, we have to consider whether this is not a matter of expression rather than mimesis. Finally, those who adduce the resemblance between some works in the abstractionist canon and photographs in biology or physics textbooks forget that this is not conclusive evidence of a process of reproduction. All it need mean is that the artist has been influenced by science exhibits, or that a kinship of sensation and thought between the scientist and artist has brought about a parallelism of the matter communicated.[1]

It is possible that some (though doubtless not all) modern artists derive their "abstract motives" from reality itself, that is, that they are concerned with a study of color, form, and space relationships. There is, however, no way of authenticating these points of reference even if they sometimes are there. The difficulty is that mimesis can be judged not on the basis of the supposed intentions of the artist but only by the artistic structures. There must be some bare minimum of mimetic elements in them for this category to be applicable.

Illusion in Art The most extreme version of mimesis involves reproduction with a special apparatus. At once the question arises: Is there such a thing as the perfect likeness, and would it, in any case, provide an artistic value? If we consider the cinema's "reflection" of reality, we cannot help but conclude that it is not an absolutely exact reproduction since there is an inevitable process of distortion: in the first place, the visual and audio recording is still less than perfect; second, the image registered on the celluloid is two-dimensional; and third, even when color is used, there is always a certain unmistakable artificiality to it. None of this vitiates the notion of a "copy" as the term is used of the figures in a wax museum or the dummies in a shop window. However, a moment's reflection is enough to make us wonder whether even these are the examples of replicas that they appear to be. After all, the whole point of a dummy is to create the illusion of something being what it cannot be.

Where the same result is sought by pop art, we might speak of it as a mock-up which mocks; for the point, made as though between quotation marks, is to improve our sensitiveness to the goings-on in ordinary life. Indeed, pop art is not oriented to any hope of total illusion but rather to byplay at the borderline between fiction and the phenomena of the present cultural context. The larger aim (where we may speak of one) is not to create an artificial aesthetic realm corresponding to the world's data; it is to "aestheticize" our encounter with life's flatness and ugliness. We should, accordingly, expect no experience of illusion with pop art, or, at most, we should expect it only in the initial phase that sets up our subsequent and central response.

Yet there are many kinds of illusion. Some can be classified as belonging to a sensory dimension, and we may treat them as pertaining to the constant features of human response; others rely on individual idiosyncrasy; others still on the responses of whole groups, strata, nations, cultures. To what extent and in which sense is art (or at least its representational heritage) truly dependent on illusions? Does any resemblence whatever to the world we know (whether inward or outward, whether the object of description or of depiction) involve us in, or merely in, the make-believe attitude? Ernst Gombrich devoted a whole book to proving that art is based on illusion, and that its degree depends on prevailing cultural stereotypes and the anticipations associated with them. He argued that it is a mistake to say, for example, that Constable's paintings are a truthful likeness of the English countryside; a close comparison of *Wivenhoe Park, Essex* (1816) with a photograph of the same scene demonstrates beyond doubt that Constable did not reproduce his subject. Nor indeed, according to Gombrich, did the photograph.[2] All art depends on certain conventions, on knowing as much as on seeing, and the two processes are inseparable.

Gombrich's argument outraged the gestaltists, and no wonder, for it was a direct assault on their theories. In the dispute between Gombrich and Arnheim, I side with the former when he says there is no such thing as an "innocent eye" which perceives the world spontaneously, unguided by culture. However, there seems to be no need to go to the same extremes as Gombrich, whose fascination with the "sociology of knowledge" à la Mannheim and Popper led him to dismiss, luckily with less than complete consistency, any tenable concept of nature whatsoever. Did he not himself make the point that Constable's pictures bear more of a likeness to the English landscape than do the free-hand sketches drawn by children?[3] Also, a comparison between the painting and the photograph of Wivenhoe Park is no more interesting than a juxtaposition of the latter with the original, for we are dealing with a continuum whose limit is the landscape itself, frozen, of course, in a particular instant of history, the further stages being its various, more or less faithful, renderings.

Thus, it is not the case that the ultimate test is the cultural context and the projection of our anticipations. Even though our habits of looking at art and our standards of judgment have changed, we have a tendency, which Gombrich himself concedes and proceeds to examine, to interpret even a picture like Mondrian's *Broadway Boogie Woogie* (1942/3) along mimetic lines. In my view there is slender justification indeed for this example, unless we make the rationalization that the painting represents the rhythm of the streets of New York. What is more instructive is to match the instance of the Constable against certain illustrations reproduced by Edward Fry in his anthology of cubism: the photographs of the houses in L'Estaque painted by Braque in 1908 and a view of Horta de San Juan which we know from the Picasso painting (1909). Undoubtedly there is a perceptible element of mimesis in these pictures, but we need only glance at the Constable (and its original) to see how much more emphatic it is there by comparison. Fry also juxtaposes photographs of W. Uhde and Daniel Kahnweiler with Picasso's portraits of them (1910); if certain resemblances can be made out in a pinch in the former case, there are none whatsoever in the latter.

Mimesis and Film Thus, if art involves "illusion" in Gombrich's sense of the word, the mimesis attendant on its creation still requires closer definition. Might the reproduction provided by the cinema be as much removed from *Wivenhoe Park* as is the Constable painting from Braque's *Maisons à L'Estaque?* In stressing the highly reproductive nature of film, theorists have usually settled on the observation that it alone among art forms is capable of capturing the flux and haphazardness of life. Yet it is revealing that in neither theory nor practice has the idea of absolute spontaneity proved viable.

In the twenties, Djiga Vertov, editor of *Kinopravda* and author of *Kinoglaz*, preached the supremacy of documentary over dramatic-psychological art due to its maximum objectivity, among other reasons. However, if we look at his first manifesto, *We* (1922), we will at once see that the creational factor stole to the forefront of his thinking in his call for a cinema which was to set its sights on "the new heroes" and penetrate revolutionary processes. His paean to "dynamic geometry" also betrayed a specific cast of thought. By 1926 he was openly advocating the editing of selectively observed facts, while in 1930 he recollected in an interview for *Kinofront* that he had practised a patently purposeful and rhetorical art, that he had been interested not in imitation of the fortuitous but in the "enthusiasm of facts."[4] This was also the temper of his films *The Sixth Day of the World* (1926) and *The Eleventh Year* (1928).

Another emphatically mimetic theory is developed by Siegfried Kracauer in his *Theory of Film* (he uses "realism" synonymously with "mimesis"). Kracauer held that the proper function of film is the direct reflection of the stuff of life as revealed in all its tumult, a communication of the physical reality of the world.[5] He was thus led into the awkward predicament of being forced to debar tragedy from the cinema and to uphold broadly the Lumière "line" to the exclusion of Méliès and the whole avant-garde. What is more, while conceding that even the documentary approach must embody a creational germ, he arbitrarily sought to fix a point at which "creation" becomes inimical to film. Beyond this point he placed not only avant-garde experimentation, but also any kind of philosophical or ideological intrusion by the artist; yet in his conclusions he flew in the face of his own argument by praising some highly deliberate, socially concerned, intellectually imaginative films (for instance, the work of Eisenstein, Chaplin's *Monsieur Verdoux*, Kurosawa's *Rashomon*, Bergman's *Wild Strawberries*).[6] If we set aside the central dilemma in Kracauer's theory—the unresolved contradiction between the principle of reproduction and the patterning of the material of film—and examine his constructive analysis, we will find a partial truth of great consequence. This is his demonstration that film can give a more profound and convincing picture of the real movement of life, its fortuitousness, its welter of events without beginning or end that knit almost unassisted ("raw material," "found story") into fragmentary, unpredictable strands of fiction that intertwine and overlap. Mimesis in the sense of the reproduction of reality by means of a film camera is, therefore, a specific value which cannot be reduced to other types of representation.

This is the crux of the Andre Bazin's argument, in *Qu'est-ce que le cinéma? Ontologie et langage* (Paris, 1958), that ever since *Citizen Kane* (1941) the cinema has approximated the open-endedness of reality, its indeterminacy and mystery. Bazin's analysis of the evolution of the cinema shows, nevertheless, that mimesis in the sense of a registration of the authentic, inchoate course of events and the physical reality of the world is not a property of all films, while the rise of television has taught us that it appertains to other art forms as well. The demarcation between these arts is here immaterial; what we are interested in is a version of mimesis that cannot be described as the simple duplication of recognized realities, but that amounts, rather, to their *reproduction*, insofar as film can preserve, despite the shift from one frame of reference (reality) to another (art), the texture, space-time structure, and rhythm of change of actual persons and events. If art can indeed impart the illusion of communing with reality itself, it is here at its most potent and complete. From what has been said, however, it will be understood that the illusion is produced not merely by the camera's ex tempore recording of the hurlyburly of life but in equal measure by the controlling hand of the artist. However self-effacing, his presence is revealed in the camera angles, the casting, the organization of takes and sequences, etc. In short, the film artist transforms—in Ingarden's phrase—the material for a work into the material of a work.

The points outlined here have been very thoroughly explored by Christian Metz. His analysis of the difference between the impression of reality given by the photographic material and the impression fabricated from this material by a fictive reality (*diégèse*) roughly approximates the distinction I have drawn between a mimesis of sensory appearances and mimesis involving a reproduction of the flux of life and its haphazardness. By "*diégèse*" Metz means something more precisely understood than the "image of reality" with which Bazin had replaced the "reality of the image" achieved by editing and construction. Film fashions a near-real but imaginary world, and so is intensively related to, and simultaneously at odds with, the actual material of cinema, with all that is contributed by the *signifiants*, and with what is denoted on the most immediate plane of the work. The cinema, Metz says, invariably preserves "*la mondité*," but at the same time it keeps transforming this mimetic material, rising above it not only as a result of a film's intrinsic connotations but also in the denotative aspect. Willy-nilly, *diégèse* is involved in the generation of discourse. Thus, Metz is fully alive to the internal dualism of film, dispelling the dilemma that defeated Kracauer. He does this by making mimetic value — my term, not his — only one of the elements, however cardinal, of film art.

Not that the film director who pursues mimesis should entirely try to subordinate himself to the fortuitous either. Very often a work of "illusion," in the sense of the utmost verisimilitude, is achieved by a deliberate and judicious artifice. De Sica's *Umberto D*, which Kracauer so admires, was no documentary. The aspect of resemblance was very carefully planned and followed through. This provokes us to question whether reproduction is an *artistic* value only to the extent that it is the outcome of the artist's intention, or whether artistic value also adheres to the undoctored image of reality. The first alternative runs foul of the generally accepted rule in aesthetics that the artist's intention cannot be said to provide the corroboration of mimetic or any other value. If we are to go by the work itself, however, the second possibility must also be discarded since its standard of value is the accuracy of representation of a kind expected in a trial record or a report with strictly informational aims.

The case for unadorned, documentary mimesis being an artistic value might be made if we assume either that reality itself is of artistic value and the director and his camera are merely intermediaries, or that the act of reproduction as such attains it by sheer technical excellence. Neither of these conjectures seems tenable if we expect mimetic value to possess a specific character. The point is that in the first case — quite apart from the debatable assumption of "beauty" that exists outside art (the whole course of aesthetic study suggests that art is the soil in which we cultivate aesthetic responses to natural and social phenomena, extrapolating the artistic standards of a given period) — the most we could agree to acknowledge would be a derivative value, a sort of surrogate. If we say that a specific value lies in the perfection with which the reality is reflected — the feature we distinguished in the second alternative — we are then talking about the attributes of reproduction rather than the end product or, to be more accurate, we are transposing the properties of the former on to the latter. In any case it is by no means obvious why the quality of the reproductive process should redound to its aesthetic merit. Since machines excel human beings at this activity, and a skilled craftsman will similarly be more proficient than someone who is out to create something new and personal rather than duplicate what is already there, the second alternative as such must also be struck from the list of aesthetic pluses. Reproduction should only be regarded in terms of artistic value in strict relation to syntagmatics, the specific marshaling of the elements expressed in the "language" proper to cinema (Metz shrewdly observes that film is *"langage,"* not *"langue"*). In short, the reproduction to be found in a newsreel has primarily a cognitive value. If invested with an artistic message, however, that value can no longer function on its own; that is to say, it ceases to be anything unless organically embedded in a *parole* (the term used by Metz). If this holds for cinema and television, it is a fortiori all the truer of mimetic works in the traditional fine arts or literature.

The Cognitive-Artistic Value   We must, thus, regard mimesis as an axiological category which requires a semiological interpretation. A work that possesses the attribute of representation assumes sign status because of something that lies outside it. However, this semantic relationship is embedded in the semiotic system constituted by the structure of that particular work, the idiosyncratic fabric of a given medium of expression. It might be said then that mimesis is an artistic value to the extent that it enriches a work by means of truthful relationships to the external world.

The concept of "truth" is used here principally with regard to the denotative function (in both *signifiant* and *signifié*), while "enrich" is intended to underline the fact that "artistic truth" is not as such constitutive of art, being contingent on other fundamental values with which it interlocks in an indivisible nexus. The term "denotation" is often used in an unclear way by philosophers. I define it to indicate reference from a given sign (or ensemble of signs) to a model or models in the real world, a reference which is generally of an iconic character (iconicism also extends to sound patterns in extreme cases of onomatopoeic analogues) or rendered through a verbal medium to which some relatively stabilized idea-image is attached. To denote thus means to use depiction or description to represent something as having certain determinate characteristics, although, as I shall try to bring out below, representation may also to some extent be schematic or distorted (e.g., it may include "phantasmata"). It is the resemblance to the acknowledged model which provides the focus for the representational object.

I must once more stress that producing a resemblance to something is not equivalent to copying, it is not sheer make-believe. To hold that the experience of illusion ensues from a maximal blurring of the possible distinctions between the given sign and the thing represented, is to speak of something other than the experience of a work of art. I am brought back here to a point I sought to make previously: Since mimesis obviously has a denotative function, it can achieve artistic status only as it coalesces with the fundamental artistic value, in other words, with the expressiveness of the so-called formal structure. The more achieved and conspicuous the fusion, the greater is the artistic value of the mimesis. Sheer denotation may equally well be characteristic of a diagram, a traffic sign, an auditor's statement, or a prize-fight gong. Even a photographic approximation requires something "extra" to be termed artistic photography. However, let me note that, once fused into the total artistic structure, mimesis provides a new aesthetic dimension which some critics and artists quite arbitrarily and prejudicially overlook or deny.

These questions are central to John Hospers' *Meaning and Truth in the Arts* (1946), which is still one of the best studies of mimetic values (there given the blanket term of "representation"). Hospers makes it plain that those who deny that such values pertain to art are unable to distinguish a merely illustrative function of the work from it symbolic content, which is sustained solely by colors, lines, sounds, words, and their meanings. In other words, while causing the specific substance of the work of art to disappear behind a mimetic theme, they proclaim, contrary to all experience, that only combinations of sense-perceived elements or semantic units without any referents in reality can form the aesthetic stratum.[7] Hospers' proposed distinction between artistic values in a "thin" and a "thick" sense seems most apposite, at all events more to the point than the misleading suggestion that "formal values" alone are proper to aesthetics.[8] He added—and this corresponds with what I have argued in slightly different terms—that the boundaries of mimesis cannot be fixed in any hard-and-fast fashion since the different arts continually shift on a continuum from representation to nonrepresentation.

When Hospers proceeds to substantiate his case with specific examples, he makes another point which seems most helpful to a clarification of our argument: The demarcation between the representational and nonrepresentational arts cannot be set according to an identifiability of the relationship to the external world that would require verification in specific realities, in a specific original.[9] This proposition accords with the idea of artistic truth which Hospers says is inevitably oblique and vague ("truth to," as opposed to the "truth about" of science). The category of mimesis embodies the sui generis, dual status that infects the whole work; it does not forfeit its cognitive nature since it directs the attention to something beyond the work, nor is it reducible to purely informational value. Artistic "truth" is predicated on the presence in some form of material counterparts (in the case of iconic signs) or symbolic analogues (in the case of conventional signs) in external reality; at the same time it is so elusive a quality that it cannot, even when its raw material is language, be formulated in a statement that can be scientifically validated.

Mimesis and the Fanciful Can we then regard as mimetic the work of Bosch or Méliès, say—to keep to arts which work through iconic signs? Does the appearance of grotesques within an artistic structure rule out representation of the world? For instance, if we see stones flying about the cinema screen, firing at flowers from catapults and then being assembled by the breeze for a meeting, will we say that reality has been represented in such an erratic flight of fancy? Hospers rightly extended the province of mimesis with the argument that reference to concrete originals is not its sole possible condition, although it is clear that in portrait or landscape painting or in the historical novel such a requirement might be in place. In the cinema a correspondence between the "material for a work" and the "material of a work" is all the more certain in view of the mechanical reproduction involved. In all these cases, however, it is assumed—at least tacitly—that the real world manifests itself in art through a likeness of both objects and occurrences. If we go further and allow mimesis to embrace fantastic images of reality, are we not committing a violation of reason as well as terms? I think not: fantasy and fable do not float entirely free of reality; the stones and flowers in my example are not make-believe, nor is what passes between them or the course of the action. What is startling—and inclines the adult mind to metaphor—are the properties invested in the stones, and it is this that produces the distortion of mimesis.

Here we approach a new problem which I can only mention in passing, that of symbolism strictly so-called. All I shall say is that the category of mimesis does not in itself explain the symbolic function of a work. Mimesis is its foundation but the interpretation of symbols can only be made in reference to certain historically determined semiotic rules.

Since nothing has yet controverted my assumption that mimesis varies in kind and degree, I would suggest calling the work of artists like Bosch, Chagall, or Méliès "mimetic-in-part" and, taking this idea a step farther, treating many of the paintings of Klee, Miro, or Picasso as examples of a "semimimetic" reality. Much as it may still be denied by some, there is no disputing the mimesis of such works as Picasso's *Girls of Avignon*, *Three Musicians*, and *Guernica*, Klee's *Conqueror*

(1930), or Miro's *Siesta* (1925); by comparison Klee's *Waverer* (1938) or Miro's *Head of a Man* (1931) are only putatively mimetic, while the compositions of Mondrian from 1914 to 1919 or Wladyslaw Strzemiński in his "unism" period are amimetic. As I have emphasized, it was these works which Mondrian held were a proper representation of reality (a view incidentally still ardently upheld by Hans Jaffe, one of the leading authorities on *De Stijl*).

The Scope and Limits of Mimesis Therefore, it is clear that the grading of mimesis and the demonstrating of its aspects does not go far enough. Mimesis always relates to reality; we must, therefore, define what we mean by reality. It should by now be clear that the field of reference for mimesis as I understand the category is our *reality, both natural and social, as made up of concrete objects, events, processes (internal as well as external, when the former are described or depicted), and situations, appearing in various segmentations, in certain inward and outward relationships, in simple or complex structures.*

I am aware of the epistemological and ontological pitfalls of such an oversimplified model. The problems with which Gombrich wrestled in his book concern not only the process of perceiving the world but also an overall analysis of the development of human knowledge. When he says that we interpret as we perceive, he is touching on an issue that goes beyond the limits of psychology.

Every act of knowing is governed by at least three things: the object on which it fastens; the subject in the sense of the generic capacities for apprehending the world; and the current state of knowledge. There is a fourth point — individual modification — which, crucial though it is to an account of the creative process and aesthetic response, can be passed over here. Those three basic conditions are enough to reinforce my earlier argument that mimesis is not the passive copying of reality in the manner of a mirror. In reproduction no less than in semimimetic works, imitation is accompanied by a certain creative element. However, Gombrich, as well as other writers like Francastel and Strzemiński, have drawn far more extreme conclusions from such subject-object conditioning concretized in an historical context, since they question the meaningfulness of any single concept of reality on account of its being modulated by the degree of visual awareness or, in broader terms, being a projection of a sum of human knowledge. The trouble with this case is that it absolutizes the active element in human perception.

Leon Chwistek, whose position in the arguments on this subject seems symptomatic, rightly stresses the plurality of the realities among which we live. However, if we scrutinize the four types of artistic reality he distinguished (the reality of things as seen in the ordinary, normal way—naïf art; of things as discovered and described by science—the Renaissance pattern; of impressions—impressionism; and of the imagination—the avant-garde since fauvism and cubism), the first point to strike us is that each of them is in some way mimetic. They owe this quality to the presence of objective elements. In everyday reality, and also in the sphere of impressions and imagination, there is at most a distortion of these elements and their interrelationships. The obvious question which springs to mind is which of these realities is the most mimetic, and the answer would be what Chwistek calls "physic" reality. The term is a misleading one, however, even though it accurately places the antecedents of this model of reality in science. The snag is that it is concerned not with the depiction of atoms and neutrons, but with things as seen macroscopically, in the way they impinge directly on our vision. Now it may well be wondered whether such perception is indeed "ordinary" or "normal," considering how differently it has been recorded by primitive culture, for instance, or that not so long ago Picasso's paintings were, despite their palpable mimesis, almost universally decried as the antithesis of representation. Doubts of this kind might be answered by saying that, although mimesis has been variously interpreted in the history of culture, in the cases of both primitive art and Picasso we are dealing with bodies of work which contain mimetic elements.

We need only specify exactly what is meant by the "objective" reference of art to reality to make this proposition acceptable. Such an agreement will not be secured simply by means of a terminological convention. It is surely significant that primitive peoples were intent on representing the world of objects even if they distorted them and that Picasso retained its components though abandoning the Renaissance formula of perspective. Although reality is variable, being dependent on the communal perceiving subject, on altering stereotypes and on fiats that x is true and y untrue, it still contains certain common features. Their absence would preclude communication between people and ages. It is this reality, that is, one founded on certain macroscopically perceived constants and at the same time modified by individuals, social groups, nations, races, and periods of history, to which the category of mimesis should be referred. In short, my case for the mimetic properties of art does not in any way imply a commitment to the anachronistic psychology which maintains that sensations, ideas, and their associations combine to reflect at an ever higher level objectively visible realities. Mimesis is predicated on a constancy of perception anchored to anthropological principles, to a treatment, that is, of the objective world angled to the recurrent modalities whereby people enter into active intercourse with the world. However, mimesis cannot be accommodated by the narrowly empirical bearings of an atomizing psychology which sees the outside world as a welter of instants submerging the identity of both perceiver and perceived. Mimesis requires at bottom a *projet*, to use an existentialist term, a composite view of realities which, by a feedback, it reaffirms.

Accordingly, the reality to which the artistic sign refers is not, nor can it come to be, as verifiable as is scientific research. This is true, first, because, as has already been pointed out, it rarely corresponds to some concrete original; second, because the subjective factor is clearly prominent; and third, because the value sought by the artist is seldom a carbon-copy similitude — the reality of nature is always presented through a filter of social reality. In the case of iconic signs, the painting, sculpture, or film can be compared to the original subject while the cultural context which helped guide the artist's attention to that particular object and encouraged him to see it in a particular way can be, as it were, understood.

A fine example with which to develop this argument is Akira Kurosawa's film *Rashomon*. This splendid work has unanimously been interpreted as the artistic equivalent of the philosophical debates of today concerning the relativity of reality as it is perceived by different individuals. What we experience in the film are three versions of a single event, with no one version capable of being singled out as the definitive account. Nonetheless, some common points recur in all three versions of the dramatic events and they all have the same mimetic amplitude (the persons, the setting, the details of the scene, etc.). This may appear too easy a defense of my standpoint, but it suffices to remark that this and other Japanese films, and Indian films too, which in many respects we find exotic and strange, are yet communicative and allow us to respond with recognition to their fundamental materials (which are undoubtedly of a mimetic character). With this fact in mind, we may take *Rashomon* as a relevant parable.

As another example, take the recent discussions among semiologists concerning the syntagmatic and paradigmatic dimensions of film. (See the work of Barthes and Pasolini.) The problem of nature *versus* or *cum* culture takes on very high priority in these discussions. The crucial issue may be formulated as follows: While it is true that we recognize the structure of a work of art owing to cultural paradigms (the "Western" adventure; the Samurai tale), it should also be obvious that there is some potential both in the objective world around us and in our human capacity for perceiving the world which gives us access to the fundamental planes of every

movie, letting us discern the fantasy of Walt Disney from an acutely realistic rendering, a genuine human face from its distorted mask, and so on. Of course, the
only wise solution of the issue must be to state the interconnection of the cultural
and natural aspects. The same is true of the traditional fine arts.

We can always anticipate natural foundations to mimesis. As I dwell on a landscape by the seventeenth-century Chinese painter Tsia Che-piao, I fail to perceive
as much or with as wide ramification as would a native appreciator. One has to
learn to grasp the structure of such a work in a dynamic, processual way so as to
follow the artist's itinerary on the vertical scroll from the bottom-right. Yet anyone
must recognize the contours of trees, of a bridge spanning a river, of a shelter in a
valley, of a lowering mountain. Similarly, a Chinese viewer would harbor no doubts,
when shown Giacometti's bronze *Public Square* (1948), that the weirdly elongated
figures represent human beings, nor would he fail to discern that Mondrian's *Composition in White, Red and Yellow* (1938) is amimetic, while Rouault's *Homo Homini
Lupus* (1944) represents a person against the background of a dramatic landscape
with a blood-drenched sun. It might be objected that the Asian peasant could well
understand the Giacometti scene as a gathering of ghosts, or that an African native, for example, could read into the Mondrian a landscape, and that he might fail
to grasp Rouault's depiction if the death penalty in his culture does not involve
hanging. These reservations cannot be treated lightly; yet what is stressed in each
of these instances is either a lack of basic relevant knowledge, or the superimposition of irrelevant knowledge. It is my argument that, where shared knowledge may
be assumed (and the third-world peasant is increasingly lettered; he knows more
and more about the death penalties that other cultures mete out), the responses of
various individuals will be more or less similar. In my Giacometti example the spec-
tral interpretation would, paradoxically, confirm that human beings have been
recognized, and that the mythical world of an afterlife is consistently modeled on
apt earthly experiences.

Mimesis and the Semantic Signs of Literature Difficult as may be some of
the problems in the visual arts, it would not do to finish with mimesis as such without confronting the even greater complexities of those media which employ the so-
called conventional signs. Whatever else the representational arts may have in
common, there is no denying that they differ quite markedly as they relate to their
raw material. In poetry or fiction, it is the denotative function which again provides
the source of mimesis. However, just as the mediation of signs is never detached

from the linguistic context, from the cultural tradition or the aesthetic consciousness, so denotation cannot be divorced from connotation, least of all in the *signifie*.
A work is composed of signs and, indirectly, of their meanings, and, by virtue of its
particular syntagmatic organization, it constitutes an interverbal reality furnished
with simple or complex semantic components that combine into a superior structure. What are its points of reference? Ingarden's answer, and that of the formalist
schools (in Russia down to 1926 and the American New Criticism) is that there are
none in external reality. This seems quite incompatible with the evidence of the
novel. It is revealing that as the interests of the Russian formalists shifted and they
turned from the analysis of poetry to prose, the question of "*syuzhet*" began to
engage Shklovsky and Eikhenbaum — their studies of instrumentation, linguistic
(nonrational language) and lexical elements yielded to investigations of subject
matter. [10]

   The subsequent history of this doctrine, especially in its Prague version, has
shown that the idea of examining the message of a novel purely in terms of an
isolated syntactic-semantic structure in which only the interplay of words and the
meanings glancing off them matter will hardly pass muster. The work of Mukarovsky, an active disciple of the structuralist school, is instructive here. Ever since
his report to the 8th Philosophy Congress, one of the cornerstones of his aesthetic
views has been that every work performs two functions simultaneously: one autonomous; one communicative. Out of this duality comes the special tension in the
structure of the work and its perception. On the communicative level, he has placed
all the story elements *(umeni tematická, obsahová)*. [11] In his studies of poetic language, particularly that of fairy tales, he has emphasized that not only the semantic whole, but also its components, have as much a connotative as a denotative
strain. Each element of the work appears in relation to another and in consequence
the meanings accumulate, though each word and sentence points to a reality outside it. The denotative aspect of the sign has a static nature, the semantic dynamic
being carried by the connotative one. The antinomy between the two yields the
peculiarity of the messages of novels and poetry, though it is much more evident
in the latter. In this way we have crossed into the realm of poetry, and here too it
seems feasible to talk of elements of mimesis. Mukarovsky treats the fable, nonetheless, in the same way as any work of poetry and, mutatis mutandis, would proceed similarly with the nineteenth-century novel in which plot is all-important (the
construction of a reported reality apparently in process of unfolding) or with fiction
in which a narrator's account or a dialogue structure is uppermost.

My earlier distinctions compel me to grade mimesis also within the province of conventional (symbolic) signs. In suggesting that the denotative nature of the work be made the basis of mimesis in literature, I am not simply acknowledging that one of the properties of all nouns is to designate. On that score, any piece of verse could scrape by as mimesis, unless avowedly nonsensical, like the poems of Aleksei Kruchonikh or the jingles which Stanislaw Ignacy Witkiewicz interpolated into his plays. As I see it, mimesis is a quality inherent in the whole of a work, in that specific property (the "higher meaning structure") which makes the connection to the more complex patterns in the reality beyond. These higher meaning structures are invariably inventions—of objects or persons and their relationships, of events, situations, some developed theme, and so on, depending on the genre of poetry or prose concerned. Only secondary in this respect are such questions as: the substance of the message itself; the degree of independence of its particular elements; the tense, person, and "purity" of the narrative voice; or the possible interaction of pictorial elements with sounds and meanings.

All that matters here is the degree of mimesis obtained in accordance with the rules of syntax as they affect both syntax and meaning. Consider this passage from Miron Bialoszewski's *Grey Eminences of Rapture:*

The stove too is beautiful
It has tiles and grillwork
It can be ashen
       silver
       grey—almost drowsy . . .
especially when
it shuffles sparks
or when it dies. . .

It is obvious that this is significant verse, that it uses verbal signs to animate surfaces just as iconic signs do in the visual arts. When we come to the out-and-out wordplay of a poet like Khlebnikov, however, we find mimesis evaporating in the clash of dissociative semantic segments. In such a case the collision of the images evoked by the common nouns and the whirligig of meanings they set spinning make it more rewarding to analyze the relationship between the creative subject and his work rather than that between the welter of signification and external reality. Even when semimimetic elements appear in Khlebnikov's verse, as, for example, in *The Spell of Laughter* ("laughers laughing laughs who laugh laughily"), they

are still eclipsed by the linguistic experiments and instrumental acrobatics. When—
to move away from poetry—we read Simone de Beauvoir's comments in *La force
de l' âge* on her own writings, *Les mandarins* among them, it is hard not to be
struck by the affinities between the autobiographical and the fictional elements.
Although she emphasizes (and rightly so) the difference between authentically
experienced and imaginary reality, the degree of mimesis which pervades her
novel seems quite notable in comparison with so much other contemporary fiction
(e.g., the work of William Faulkner).

It would be tempting to conclude that in poetry mainly the depictive *(ut pictura
poesis)* tendency, and in prose mainly the narrative (epic or diaristic) tendency,
dominates or is all-pervasive and sets the manifest pattern with respect to the
mimesis. These are, in fact, prevalent modes, and the artistic techniques which do
bear on the mimetic rendition of the reality. Nonetheless, these conclusions must
be tempered by two major reservations:

1. Depiction or description, in the present context, means something quite other
than description in a scientific sense. A sociologist who prepares a report on the
voting pattern or the crime rate in San Francisco, *describes* in a mode quite different from that of a poet or novelist. The poet will view San Francisco through the
I-subject; the fiction writer understands the city through the modality of his characters. This is true even of the historical novel; in Sienkiewicz's *Quo Vadis*, for instance, Rome is described otherwise than it was by the Roman historians of Nero's
day—it is treated in a fictitious frame of reference.

2. A prevalence of the descriptive tendency conditions an *enhanced*, or heightened, literary mimesis but does not in itself constitute that distinctive characteristic.
Here again, as in the nonverbal media, we should see mimesis as extending further
than the phenomena customarily so labeled. Mimetic elements can be glimpsed in
lyrical novels and theater pieces as well as in lyric poetry; and the fantastic setting
of fairy tales or of science fiction makes sense only within a context of mimetic
plenitude or paucity. In short, the literary "higher semantic structures" are dependent on more or less ample "mimetic substructures." Elimination of the mimesis
occurs only in the most extreme, exploratory, and inventive efforts to elude the
conventional sign-syndromes. It is symptomatic that this has so far happened almost solely in poetry, whereas in prose the single instance I have so far noticed is
the recent practice of the *Tel Quel* group (e.g., *Nombres* by Phillipe Sollers, *Circus*
by Maurice Roche), in which the semantic and syntactic patterns of language are
calculatingly distorted. However, it seems highly dubious whether these works

should be called novels. I think that the explications provided by Jacques Derrida, a leading *Tel Quel* theorist, in *La dissémination* (1972) legitimizes my doubts. There is, likewise, good reason to assert that "concrete poetry" is basically not poetry. Its factual value is one of graphic and sound patterns; and, considered from the viewpoint of literature, it raises a significant artistic gesture of protest against poetic dogma; but this is a rebellion which has already crossed the frontier beyond poetry.

Mimesis and the Rendering of Essences Although cognitive values have been traced in all the varieties of mimesis examined here, I must now add that they only come into view in this way when we focus on the Aristotelian tradition (among those distinguished at the beginning of this essay). If the idea of mimesis is directed at the essence of things, it comes to be a medium of knowledge on a par with science or philosophy, or even superior to these, according to some aesthetic theories which maintain that it plumbs the *haecceitas* of objects, people, and events, capturing as well the basic meaning of historical processes. If the concept of truth in the philosophical sense can be extended to artistic perception, this is an aspect from which the latter merits analysis. Mimesis thus described appertains alike to the visual arts, literature, cinema, or theater. Whether literature digs deeper into the essence of reality than does painting, and cinema more deeply than either, thanks to the potency of the medium of mimesis, is a question I shall pass over here except to say that I feel it is wrongly put. All these arts have the power, each in its own way, to get to the heart of reality. Of course, they do vary in the range of their explorations, but no evidence has yet been produced for ruling that the broader the area of reality covered by an art form, the deeper its fathoming goes.

Mimesis as the representation of the essential features implies a substantial modification of our way of talking about the relationship of art to reality, the idea having undergone a shift of meaning which makes it more apt to talk of the *transmutation* rather than the reproduction of reality. Mimesis in the Aristotelian version surely postulates an active process of perception in the sense of a highly selective attitude which generalizes through particulars, compressing complex processes into concrete situations and a multiplicity of social types into a single exemplar.

In a discussion with the Paris semiologists, principally Barthes, Mikel Dufrenne has made the point that there is no factual basis for a belief in the absolute autonomy of the work of art. It is, of course, possible to consider the signification of a work solely in terms of its syntagmatic content; but it should be realized that such an interpretation is bound to be truncated. In an essay on literary criticism which argues the need to elicit the sense as well as structure, Dufrenne recalls Husserl's *Sinn-von* and very properly underlines the dualism of meaning of all artistic communication. I quite agree with him when with certain echoes of Mukarovsky's semiotics, he opposes the reduction of a work to a system bearing no relationship whatsoever to external realities and protests against the idea of criticism solely as a meta language for testing *les validités* (Barthes), unconcerned with the establishment of any kind of verities. Nevertheless, Dufrenne seems to couple his insistence on the communication through the work of art of truth about the world with a dismissal of mimetic values. The difference between his position and mine hinges, at bottom, more on philosophy than on aesthetics. In his dispute with semiological structuralism he comes down on the side of the subjective sense which the artist lends to his work, that is, his idiolects which embody a singular style. Here, too, I can endorse each of his propositions; what I cannot accept is the way he is led in his emphasis on the primacy of the expressive qualities to put mimetic values beyond the pale of art. His standard work, *Phénoménologie de l'expérience esthetique* (Paris 1953) explains why he has taken this course: Art, he writes, like science, though in a different way, gives coherence to the chaotic matter of reality. The world *(le monde)* is not reproduced but created in relation to an existential design and to *l'affectif*, which is given a priori. Thus, if art represents anything, it is only to the extent that it expresses the attitude of the artist who objectifies through *les sensibles* what is basically unreal. Accordingly, if I take issue with Dufrenne it would not be in terms of aesthetics, since we would be arguing about the basic premises and conclusions of the phenomenological-existential theory, of which he is a leading exponent. It should be emphasized here that views of mimesis as an aesthetic and axiological category do have their roots in the holder's philosophical system, as can be seen from the case of Dufrenne which I have advisely cited. For that matter, this is not unexpected; my whole point has been to show that the concept of mimesis embodies a certain (explicit or implicit) view of reality in the argument for a greater or lesser correspondence between a world being portrayed and its reflection in the work of art. Accordingly, while I believe the artistic process to be of a subject-object nature, this does not mean that I disown Dufrenne's claim for expression, which is an element of every work of art. Where we part company is over the philosophical judgment which induces me to maintain that mimetic values can and should be separated from expressive ones, and that, in the case of works of a certain aspect, the former are more conspicuous.[12]

Summation So Far In the foregoing pages I have tried on the one hand to bring out the varieties of mimesis and on the other to answer the questions posed at the beginning. In summing up thus far the following points might be made:

1. Mimesis is an artistic category involving a specific type of value and never appearing in isolation. This value springs from a truthful, that is, analogous representation of external reality, here understood as a complex pattern of elements (statically and dynamically given, usually taking the form of concrete animate or inanimate objects and their interrelationships, all occurring within a given space-time continuum) registered macroscopically and as adequately as the state of knowledge permits. These elements also embrace inward reality where it affords the artist's model up to the same extent as the behavior of specific persons and the world of objects. In other words, a literary account of someone's happiness or a portrait of a sad expression are as much a mimetic theme as a description of Paris in Balzac or Zola, or Michelangelo's statue of David. It must be emphasized that in talking of analogues in art I consider their referents to be not objects in general, since that would include colors or combinations of colors, but objects in the verifiable form of "bodies," animate or inanimate, which have certain inherent qualities and are associated with states, events and, above all, the relations between them. Thus the first step in grasping what mimesis means is to select for it a universe with definite characteristics. [13]

2. The mimetic sign is truthful in the sense that there is a correspondence between it and the reality signified (iconically or conventionally). The degree of this correspondence varies and is the standard for distinguishing the different kinds of mimesis graded along a continuum. (a) The continuum begins with the vestigial equivalence which we have called "semimimetic" because of the difficulty of reconstructing the phenomenal structure from the content of the work itself; [14] the dominant patterns of the semimimetic work are also decisive in bringing about this fantastic cast of the whole. (b) A different and fuller correspondence occurs when only some elements belonging to an artistic object have a completely recognizable relationship to external reality (this concerns appearances in iconic art principally). (c) A third variety of mimesis is the direct, integral reproduction of appearances, as in the visual arts primarily, or indirect reproduction by means of certain semantic wholes, as in art forms whose sole or predominant material is language. Representation of this type is not uniform: it runs all the way from maximum fidelity to the outside world to extreme formalization or schematism. All reproduction is to some extent, however minute, schematic, but the fuller the treatment of external

realities, their components and relationships, the less obvious this schematic structure is. (d) A special kind of mimesis is the representation of real life in all its flux
and inconclusiveness. The camera makes cinema and television capable of producing images in which the appearances of persons and things, situated in the context
of space-time mobility and change, transmit the rhythm of reality itself to the work
of art. (e) Finally, there is the mimesis which is concerned with essences, a kind of
transmuting representation which may accompany any of the preceding varieties. [15]

   This continuum of five varieties of mimesis is constructed on the basis of the
artistic-cognitive criterion of the identifiability of the reality depicted and the penetration of its fundamental attributes. If I were to adopt a purely artistic point of
view—that is, if I were to consider the augmentation of the creative factor—the
scale would be arranged differently; it would begin with reproduction, go through
the representation of appearances from utmost fidelity to marked distortion (or
schematization), and culminate with the antipodes of semimimetic art and art
which is directed towards essences. It should be stressed that this growth in the
creational factor is not the only measure of the enhancement of artistic value. Another criterion might be the degree of structural consistency. However, it is obvious
that cognitive-artistic value and purely cognitive value do not increase symmetri-
cally. At any event, neither of these scales admits the possibility of treating mimesis merely as a copy of reality. Even the concept of reproduction is not a mechanical
duplication of the outside world, but an exploration of its authenticities.

   While we can talk—in the case of a mimesis based on appearances, semiappear-
ances, or imitation of the rhythm of life—of a representation either in a faithful
or a distorted form, mimesis in the Aristotelian sense should be described as transmutation, since it seeks out and visualizes the meaning of reality. In this kind of
mimesis the subjective factor is cognitively most active. In the case of semimimesis,
on the other hand, the subjective factor is directed away from apprehension of the
outside world. This issue has come up before, and I showed then that resemblance
or similitude, although it is the chief aim of representation (the denotative function),
is yet artistically insufficient by itself. Recently, conceptualist-minded artists have
presented us with such moot cases as plain pictographs or seismograms, which
they tell us are works of art. Here we are wholly beyond mimesis and into an extreme gesture of the avant-garde intended to debunk a cultist attitude towards
art and the art market.

   3. Mimesis, being an integral element of the whole artistic structure, can be sepa-

rated out only in the abstract. If the work is representational, mimesis subsists in its entirety; indeed, the formal and expressive elements through which mimesis has been achieved become, as it were, transparent. In consequence, there is generated a twofold tension: (a) between the semiotic situation in itself and the semiotic situation which points outwards to nonartistic reality, and (b) between the pattern of formal elements which commands separate attention and the overall artistic structure which reabsorbs and neutralizes it. The first antinomy has been the subject of frequent and perceptive analysis by Mukarovsky. It has recently been emphasized in the work of Julij Lotman, who approaches art objects as structures of dialectic opposites: the virtuality of the world as represented in the object contrasts with the reality of the object per se, the resemblance of the object to something real contrasts with its fictional status, and the syntax of specific elements building up an inward rhythm contrasts with the semiotic design which appeals outwards to both author and recipient.[16] The second antinomy was long ago examined in a classic inquiry by Roger Fry. Analyzing Daumier's *Gare St. Lazare* he drew attention to the way in which the plastic and mimetic values were at the same time meshed and in competition with one another.[17] Due to the semiotic context, the problem of the cultural coefficients of mimesis is no less fundamental than is the presumed natural human potential for recognizing the substance of a represented world: in fact, the former molds and modifies the latter. The rendering of mimetic traits always follows a particular code within the sociohistorical (environmental and circumstantial) setting. In the case of primitive art, for example, the modern viewer demimetizes what the original social group readily experienced as a pictogram. Another, if tricky case is provided by the stereotyped movie, to which many fans will respond "over"-mimetically. A sophisticated viewer will take the formula western or detective film for relaxation; the naive audience may treat it as being true to some life which they cannot experience directly and may, therefore, discuss it seriously.

4. In the works now under consideration, *signifiant* and *signifié* tend to disrupt the unity whose inherence to art was so justly emphasized by both Dufrenne and Metz. The point is that there is a field between the denotative and connotative functions which polarizes as much as it unites them. The unquenchable antinomies I have indicated in mimetic works enrich their fabric, but if they grow too sharp they fracture the structural whole and detract from the value of the work. One instance of this is when illustrative motives overrun a work and turn it to moralizing or propaganda. Another equally jarring example would be aggressively obtrusive

accentuation of the devices used to organize the artistic structure. From the view-point of mimesis, the former case is of greater interest. I have assumed that mimetic value is not to be referred strictly to some concrete prototype, although in certain genres and in certain works such an eventuality cannot be excluded. Nevertheless, artistic truth is generally understood not as a duplication of here-and-now facts, but as an approximated or generalized representation of the specimens of a given class and the relationships between them. The closer mimesis approaches to the exact reproduction of particular occurrences, objects, or persons and the familiar interactions between them, the nearer it comes to purely documentary art. The further it moves away from this, the closer it draws to fantasy and the obscuring of the genuine relationships between people and objects.

5. Mimesis has been called an artistic-cognitive value and this emphasizes its sui generis nature. Cognitive value, however, is not an element of mimetic works alone. It resides in all art if only by virtue of being a special type of communication implicating the artist on the one hand and the structure itself on the other. Still, mimetic works seem to have a quality lacking in others — the ability to refer not only to themselves and their authors, but also to the reality they denote. This is why any account of mimetic values must give a special place to their cognitive amplitude — which is after all the source of that oscillation within the sign structure noted in the third of our conclusions.

The ideas which I have developed in the preceding pages depart from the argument I set out in an earlier essay "Le réalisme comme une catégorie artistique" (*Recherches internationales à la lumière du marxisme*, no. 38, 1963). Nowhere is this more true than in the treatment of the semiotic nature of the work of art, which, in that essay, I viewed in the light of traditional semantic analysis, but which semiological research has now shown to require thorough reappraisal. It is quite clear that I was wrong to argue that the universal sign-like characteristic of works of art is solely a matter of each of them being a token (or index). I can also now see that the division into semantic and nonsemantic signs is rather antiquated since some kind of cognitive meaning attaches to every work of art; any inquiry into these problems should thus be shifted to the complex relationships between denotation and connotation, between syntagmatics and paradigmatics. Indeed, the main lingering problem in the analysis of the category of mimesis (as of the category of realism) seems to be that we must establish the paradigmatic elements which allow us to accept a corresponding (analogous) relationship between the work and what

may be regarded as not only its basis but also its model. Of course, this is not paradigmatics within the strict meaning of Saussure's *langue*, but in the sense of cultural stereotypes which in a given context govern the reading and interpretation of
a certain semantic content. That culture does determine our understanding of nature needs no further explanation; it is, I may simply emphasize, a question of cardinal importance in apprehending mimetic values. The point was brought out in
the second volume of *Trudy po znakovym sisteman* by V. Toporov, L. Zhegin, and
B. Uspensky in their examination of the space composition and design of paintings
from the Buddhist and Byzantine spheres of art. The fact that the artist nonetheless
tries "to return to the self and to nature" despite the codes laid down by a given
culture is an indication, however, that transmitted paradigms do not ultimately
constitute the foundations of art.[18] This still leaves unanswered the question of
when, in what circumstances, and in which arts, the depreciation or the upgrading
of mimetic values is evidence of spontaneous urges on the part of the artist to overcome the existing paradigms and when it, in fact, perpetuates them. Studies along
these lines seem to go beyond semiology, though in such matters, too, it may well
shed light on aspects of our subject which are still shrouded in obscurity.

Realism as a Mode of Mimesis
Marxist aestheticians have not reached a consensus in their understanding of the
notion of realism. The opinions now current, however, all agree that it involves a
transmutation of reality. What does this transmutation mean? In my view, the idea
of realism includes the selection of real phenomena, the extraction of their characteristic and typical features, and the representation of these traits in a "condensed"
way that directs attention to deeper meanings, that is, to the coherences which include and yet transcend the surface appearances of phenomena. Further, the transmutation of reality implies an organized formal structure, whose limits are indicated and whose traits are nourished by a particular subject matter; which is
absorbed by these so-called content values and which, in turn, lends an autonomy
to these values in relation to the world of their real referents. Artistic activity in this
dimension attains a twofold domination of the world: psychosocial and technical-
material. I have said elsewhere (in controversy with André Malraux) that this application of the term realism is tantamount to "creationism."[19]
  Is my notion of creationism opposed to what the reader may have thought of as
the definition of realism? This would be reasonable only if the reader were to understand realism in terms of a certain nineteenth-century mode of fiction and its

manifestos, which do, in fact, seem incongruous with the artistic methods and creative advances of the twentieth century. However, more and more present-day marxist authors are turning decisively away from that anachronistic concept of realism.[20] Accordingly, the artist is understood to imitate not so much *natura naturata* as *natura naturans*. He contributes to the creation of the social reality even while he is created by it. However, to regard realism as an artistic category presents us with complexly involved problems. I cannot here offer an exhaustive analysis, but I should like to offer a tentative outlining of my point of view. Once again, I regard what I wrote on this topic in 1963 as inadequate.[21] I believe the following remarks are much more responsive to the problems.

Higher Semantic Structures The question of realism cannot be posed correctly if we have not initially defined what is meant by "mimesis"; especially since realism becomes at times virtually reduced to mimesis. Indeed, an intermediary realm exists between mimetic art and the art I have classed as realist. However, as carefully as we can we should demarcate realism within the context of mimesis for analytical purposes. I shall want to do this in light of the example of modern aesthetic thought and practice and, moreover, with an awareness of the sharp differences among the core philosophical attitudes (and even among the specifically historiographical orientations) discoverable in art. Realism, then, is a distinctive category, which invokes (as does mimesis) a relationship of analogy; it is chiefly distinguished however, not by a stress on the form and exterior look of objects, or on the vigorous and helter-skelter unfolding of developments, or on the intricacies of the interrelations of objects, persons, and events, but, rather, by attention to typical moments, in other words, by an evocation of some essential aspects of reality. Obviously, this decisive kind of *analogon* or correspondence relationship does not exclude other criteria from being applied to realism. However, other criteria are not indispensable to the artistic constitution of realism. Realism and also other modes of mimesis can be spoken of as artistic categories only in the sense (and to the extent) that they link more or less effectively (i.e., intimately and organically) a content and an ensemble of expressive means with a represented segment of the world. This is to say that we have not an interpolated, indigestible cognitive structure that happens to be situated in a work of art but, instead, a representation (meaning-structure) which is imbued with the fundamental elements that we term art's "language."

This seems to be a notable characteristic of art: its media and specific means of expression have, as it were, the faculty of absorbing the conveyed content, and vice versa. Perhaps it might be retorted that the "language" is always crucial, even in the case of symbolical-mathematical formulas. This is, in fact, true; clarity and consistency do hinge on the manner in which a thought is conveyed. Nonetheless, outside of the artistic domain, the vehicle of the message is to a great extent interchangeable, or else it is entirely transparent (as in logic or mathematics): the emphasis always falls on *the communication* of the given idea. However, art is constituted by *the communicated idea* with the indivisible whole being irreducible. Here, then, the language is no mere "garment," it is the integral "body" of the artistic message. A further sense of language must be also emphasized. This is its aspect which the French semiologists term *"parole"* — the idiomatic, personal way in which the artist's ideas are presented. The contemporary avant-garde often sidesteps this idiomatic utterance, preferring a deliberately anonymous expression of the artist's problematic situation. Nonetheless, the very fact of a peculiarly individual language (which is termed one's own style) best elucidates why the cognitive relation of the work of art to the world is inseparable from the artistic structure as a whole. For the cognitive value is here fused with so-called formal and expressive values, and more than that, this whole is suffused by an individual valuative approach, heightening the subjective (both personal and social group) perspective towards the objective reality.

Lukács spoke of this feature of art as anthropomorphic. By the means of a sensuous and expressive medium, an individual tries to capture the totality of the world around him (with himself at its center) and to recreate it with the self-contained totality of a poem, novel, painting, or musical composition. In every case the work is composed of a system of signs which, in a way apt for its medium, asserts two simultaneous fields of reference: one field interior and closed, the other exterior and open. A tension results between the structural (syntactic-semantic) plane and the structural-semiotic plane, in other words, between the form-and-content of the work on the one hand and the form-content syndrome and its sociological referents on the other, and we may say that this antinomy, which is characteristic of all mimetic (including realist) works, is paralleled by a tension between the represented (virtual) world and the representable (real) world.

Closing in on the problems of realism, I must say something further about linguistic (literary) signs. These seem, on the face of it, less adapted to the functioning of mimesis (and realism, of course) than are the pictorial (iconic) signs, which quite directly facilitate the choice of materials and the shaping of the analogy-models.

Literary signs are accepted as meaningful only by common consent, that is, they are conventional. Given the linguistic tradition, the moment in that tradition, and the attendant cultural context, it is possible to find in the conventional (literary) sign its *significant* function and also its denotative function. To the conditioned or determinate character of the denotative function, we owe the possibility of a mimetic and likewise a realist category in the arts and also the possibility of describing a variety of denotative properties along appropriate scales. It seems impossible to discern any principles of mimesis (including for realism) through isolating and studying the semantic elements. Failure has met the research into the cognitive content of literary works which tries to analyze the logical value of the propositions, whether one by one or in combination.

The attempts of the Anglo-American analytical school (e.g., Weitz and Margolis) are characteristic. To date they have not succeeded in deducing the represented world through the method of distinguishing purely predicative propositions from other propositions which they discern as fictional. To speak of "implied truth" and "implicit meaning," and to categorize it as a kind of truth differing from that of the sciences, simply does not follow from the logical analysis of, say, a sequence of utterances by Mr. Pickwick or perhaps of the dialogues between Sherlock Holmes and Dr. Watson.

How then are we to embrace and surmount the total meaningfulness of these complexly interconnected and ramified unities, especially in their reference to extra-literary reality? It appears that we must make up our minds to admit certain "higher" level "semantic figures" or "semantic systems," to use the terminology of Polish authors with a structural-semiological orientation. In other words, the unit of analysis must be the character, the character grouping, the leitmotif, the action, etc. (along with the interrelations among these elements).

I must also say a complementary word about how the *analogy-model* of a literary work may be discussed. Take this proposition: "A man descended by a twisting street towards the steps which lead into the largest square of the city." We may surely examine the link to reality of this language unit *in abstracto;* in other words, as a proposition which lacks a concrete amplifying and determinate context. However, it seems difficult to speak of a mimesis *as such* when such propositions are met away from a larger representation, that is to say, apart from a more extensive semantic totality. We have in that sentence a relation of reference, which asks for a greater context. In a pictorial work, any selected fragment will yield a sufficient relation of reference if it has distinct contours and a relation of analogy to objects

or persons in the real world. Not so in a literary work, where the entire structure
has more or less to provide the context for the reference.

Consider the case of a mimetic painting, a landscape. What parallels it as a proposition? Not the statement, "A tree stands on the shore of a river." A paralleling
proposition would be one which defines the subject of the painting, for example,
"View of a Bank of the Vistula River Near Warsaw." (Mimetic value, I should add,
is never the result of a recognition of "proper names," for even in an historical
novel or a work of artistic reportage the real persons and events are transmuted by
being set into a fictive world which, as Roman Ingarden has remarked, generates its
own objective logic. Any literary work makes a new patterning of the represented
world and employs, accordingly, "common names.")

I cannot discuss in detail here the structural difference between prose and poetry,
a problem which is pivotal since, in the twentieth century and especially in poetry,
there have been notable modifications in the semantic functions (cf. chapter 2).
Nor can this be the occasion for fully discussing the ultimate ontology of the literary
work: the peculiar status of its depicted world. I may, however, remark as follows.
The depicted world can be constituted solely by means of propositions (though it
cannot be reduced to a sum of semantic propositions and sequences); and it cannot
be considered apart from the given linguistic and cultural tradition. In this way,
fictions clearly reveal their semiotic dependency. The ontology of a representational
world derives, then, from the broader ontological world of the cultural context;
but to this I must add that a fictive world differs from nonfiction in this context
because of its peculiar code. On the one hand, the fictive world is a creation of the
particular consciousness that endows it with meaning and value; on the other hand,
the fiction transcends that consciousness. It might be said (to use Husserl's term
in a modified way) that every fictive world partakes of an intentional character, or
(to use a different angle of approach) that the full mimesis of which I speak is realized only because of the code and rhythms of a fictive world, but that the fictional
structure, in turn, is viable only because of the mimetic potentiality.

I have perhaps stressed overly the distinction between iconic and linguistic signs,
and it will lend some balance to reemphasize that both kinds are translatable from
one culture to another.[22] That the differences which sequester the iconic and linguistic conventions do not stop communication does not mean that the cultural
context lacks an effect on the way we apprehend realism or mimesis in general.
Rather, we cannot accept the idea of *adequatio res et intellectus* as indiscriminately
applicable. On the contrary, within a given social context some relationships of

analogy can be apprehended *outside* the prevailing code or convention which determines the way the artist must relate to reality and the reality to which he must relate. The only "convention" which cannot be dispensed with in this respect is that which has emerged in human cultures on a natural basis. Mimesis, accordingly, has its appeal through what is generic in the culture — and thus in nature, through the mediation of the culture.

The *Analogon* of Realism Now realism is distinguishable as an artistic cate-. . . .
 assumed a different aspect, however, and from the end of the sixteenth century, gory from other forms of mimesis because its analogy-model may, although it need not, be solely composed of the mimetic elements. I mean that, on the evidence, a realist creation can include aspects of fantasy — and the expressed conviction that God, angels, devils, tree-spirits, and other such things exist. The crux or principle, I repeat, is that certain selected social, psychological, or psychosocial phenomena are epitomized by realism; and such epitomies may (have to) be expressed also with distortions or an upending of the real objects and persons and their relationships. As examples, I think at once of the powerfully imaginative typificational achievements of Dante's *Divine Comedy* or of the Polish romantic school. The *essential*, we see, takes full control of the gravitational center.

It should be unnecessary to add that I suggest no version of "essentialism," which is the view that certain qualitative moments (and perhaps their systems) may be discerned, either eidetically or discursively, which make it possible to say once and for all how phenomena come about. By "essential," I only mean what may be empirically apprehended in a context of natural and historical regularities.

These empirical and recurrent traits of nature and history as grasped at a given time are what entitle us to discriminate objects, actions, processes, and relationships from one another (always, of course, in a relative framework). Undoubtedly, the ultimate choice of historical criteria of the essential leads us to social philosophy (and ideology) for justification; and we shall discover quickly that, if broad agreement on the idea of mimesis is hard to come by, we can scarcely hope for a consensus regarding the concept of realism. The neo-Thomist, the existentialist, and the marxist have basic philosophical differences, and these differences have a determinate ideological dimension. Accepting that we cannot achieve a broad concord in regard to realism, we should also overtly acknowledge that behind the aesthetic judgments lie differences in philosophical tenets and, most commonly, also in ideological bias.

For the marxist, realism chiefly involves the social domain, or, more broadly, the psychosocial field—and within this perspective, natural phenomena too can be regarded as "essential," that is, as highly significant for the persons living in a given time and place. For the idea of the "typical"—traditionally linked by marxist thought with realism—always takes a functional definition within a framework of historically determinate human praxis. The philosophical assumption (*Weltan-schauung*) cradling this concept of realism is that "the real" is entirely in the context of the material universe (*diesseitig*), accepting that the context by no means precludes religious faith, "unreal" images of reality, "mythologizings" of innumerable kinds, the conviction that the individual is the sovereign reality, etc. Accordingly, the question which I start with as a marxist when confronting a realist work is not, "What about this individual artist, who has certain philosophical or political beliefs about the world?" but instead, "What are the essential phenomena as this work envisions them, and to what extent do the criteria of 'the real,' psychosocially and sociohistorically considered, sustain or explain the judgments active in the work of art?"

Principles of Realism in the Twentieth Century I do not place much store in the scholastic controversy which seeks to declare whether the realist should depict just what at bottom predominantly *is*, or instead what is *emergent* in the developmental processes, however presently exceptional it may be. Apt as a comment on this debate, I believe, is an observation by Marx in the third volume of *Capital*, that many varied versions of the typical (or of typification) are useful and feasible in the context of an epoch. We may use the marxist notion of realism, accordingly, in attempting to answer the question: Typical in what respects?

It would be hard to withhold the description "typical" from works as obviously diverse among themselves as Kafka's *The Trial* and Gorki's *The Mother*, Sholokhov's *Virgin Soil Upturned* and Hemingway's *For Whom the Bell Tolls*, Mikhail Romm's *Nine Days of the Year* and Fellini's *8 1/2*. In each work there appears a social structure which is treated encompassingly (as a totality); and, within the limits set by this structure, different kinds of standpoints of consciousness probe the crevices and cruxes of the historical moment.

Kafka, for instance, is at once critical of alienation and its tragic victim-witness. The French marxist Roger Garaudy was quite right to reject the condemnation meted out to Kafka by Soviet aestheticians. If, indeed, by "realist" we mean one

who sheds light on key phenomena in a particular sociohistorical setting, how are
we to refuse the realist title to this genius? We *do* require an author to be more
than the stoneblind victim of the processes that engulf him; and if he is to master
in imagination the events occurring around and including him, he must arrive at an
interpretation that somehow *transcends* these processes. Kafka is successful on
both counts. (In contrast, it is doubtful whether the *nouveau roman* authors sustain
the critical distance needed to survey the situation in the world which is their subject matter effectively.)

What of the Fellini film? It uses excellent dramatic means to study the artist as a
problematic and preoccupying theme. At least since Gide's *The Counterfeiters*
such autothematism has been well established in fiction. With the novels of Alain
Robbe-Grillet and Nathalie Sarraute the focus shifts to the making of a metalan-
guage, fused with the narrative line but primarily aimed at enabling self-commen-
tary by the mind that composes the text. The project is as illuminating and successful in the very best examples of the *nouveau roman* as it is in *8 1/2*. It must be
emphasized, however, that Robbe-Grillet, for example, does not say anything relevant to the reality context to which he still refers. Conversely, Fellini does not simply
and at length affirm that the *how* of discussing and composing reality has lately,
for many, taken priority over presenting the *what* of reality. He proceeds instead
to depict the displacement as itself a revealing integral symptom of our present
value crisis. The problem of artistic practice is knitted into the encompassing social
practice. Accordingly, as was Kafka in another time and context, Fellini is a critical
realist. In Fellini we see beyond doubt that the great realist is a "creationist" at
the same time; not content with providing a bare description of social reality, he
brings various perspectives to bear on it, which enhance the artistic stature because
they reveal and they transmute it.

A mere chronicle or improvised reportage cannot be regarded as an art object.
In contrast, even the works of art termed naturalistic must include some generalization, that is, a selection or combination of key or secondary phenomena. As an
example, consider the rudimentary mimesis that is found in eyewitness television,
home movies, and the still experimental home videotapes (the apotheosis of all
this is the chronicle *An American Family*, shown nationwide on American educational television in 1973 with great audience response, and notable for its sociological data but not for its artistic composition). Yet even here some evidence of at
least a selective attitude usually appears. Still more is *realism* distinguished by the

attitude with which it regards reality; an attitude which — rather often resulting in a portrayal implicitly at variance with the artist's expressed political, philosophical, and religious convictions — not only is selective, but (this is decisive) merges with and "gets inside" some essential processes of the social world. In this way artistic realism may at times contribute, through its audience, a certain impetus to the further transformation of social life.

The empathetic-creative integration with the social processes (which need not be primarily gained through activity, but may be vicariously achieved) is, in my opinion, indispensable to the realist method. This is a primary reason why it is so difficult to achieve an artistic typification. On this basis it appears necessary for a realist artist to get energetically involved with comprehending many aspects of the world as it is, the better to extract and to condense organically what is recognizably "typical" into an *analogon*, a "rival" world whether fictional or nonfictional. The classical German aesthetic school spoke of the typical as *das Besondere*, or *das Allgemeine im Einzelnen*, translatable as "generalization drawn from individual traits," and also as "individual traits that imply generality." One or the other emphasis may be appropriate, depending on the given typification. A continuum of possibilities from the especially general to the especially particular occurs within the criteria of the realist school.[23]

At the same time, this involvement in the social world, whose various aspects he is probing, will frequently provide the realist artist with a critical means of going beyond that "given" social world. What I mean is perhaps most clearly demonstrated by the practitioners of socialist realism in its early, authentic version. Such realists might often come to a deliberate creative decision to affirm (and hopefully assist towards full emergence) those aspects of social reality which they believed could and should be furthered. How would they do it? Chiefly by means of scourgingly critical portrayal of other, backward or apathetic yet typical aspects of reality, which set a brake to the developing human potential. (My reason for distinguishing between periods and modes of socialist realism is set out in chapter 7.)

Realism in Past Eras I have outlined the central principles of realism with reference to examples from the twentieth century. The same criteria of typicality and encompassed perspectives are relevant to the works of other eras. In ancient times realism had a mythological and in medieval times a theological skeleton. In line with my criteria, Homer and Dante achieved classical works of realism. The context and the patternings of human cultural consciousness were changed by the era of Shakespeare and Cervantes and again by the era of Molière and Lessing. Decisive in each differing social context, however, is the correlational "adequacy" between the literary work and typical traits of the sociohistorical structure. As for the artistic mediation, it must rely on, and be achieved in terms of, the *prevalent* cultural patterns (with all due allowance for idiosyncratic modifications by individuals). By this I mean the patterns of consciousness that are characteristic of the given social whole and that dominate (with variations along a continuum) all institutions and conduct, all customs and life-styles, all modes of thinking and feeling.

Further, in light of the factor of transformation in the characteristics of realism, we may look in every instance for the sociohistorical dynamism. This processual understanding of an incessant flux of established but fading traits, which are integrated with and yet in tension with developmental or novel elements, enables us to discern the specific rather than the abstractly postulated character of the typical. It also allows us to see definitely that social history tends to foster certain patterns of consciousness rather than others, and that, on this basis, *social history itself is tendentious* in its essential direction; there ultimately appears a latent (or manifest) directed dynamism of history that is beyond the control of individual will. I mean that, beyond the occurrence of change-sequences, certain permanent transformations occur which do lead in turn to something definite. A roughly vector-like movement forward can be detected, and in this sense the ideas of progression and retrogression are sensible and even indispensable.

However, these generalizations supply no premise for dogma-oriented talk declaring, say, the priority of a positive hero over a negative hero. The crux of realistic representation is whether the heroes (of whatever description) or the circumstances (whatever they are) have been conceived to reveal the fundamental conflicts of the given time and place. For the same reason — if one thinks seriously about it — the question of whether sociopolitical events should have the top priority is secondary. The essential events of an era can be approached from many different sides: frontally, as, for instance, in the novels of Balzac or Tolstoi (who for this reason were celebrated by the marxist classical authors); or indirectly as with Goethe's character Werther, who is a very typical middle-class German of the eighteenth century, or Diderot's sentimental dramas, which typify the prerevolutionary French *tiers état*. Pushkin's *Eugene Onegin* caught the social patterns of the upper class of its day; and a generation later Gogol's *Inspector General* bitingly

satirized the rotten and crippling Tsarist bureaucracy. In sum, the central problems
of the time can be as characteristically revealed through a depiction of the habits
and social psychology of a single social class (ascending, descending, or in its full
powers) as through a portrayal of open class conflict, with its political and ideological articulations.

   The same is the case for figurative (representational) painting and sculpture,
which is fortunate, since the art patrons of history often commissioned their own
portraits, and their intentions often guided the solutions which painters and sculp-
tors found for their problems. (It should be noted that this usually occurred with
more than halfhearted compliance from the artists.) Nonetheless, the range of realist portraiture extends beyond the likenesses of monarchs and princes by Van Dyke
or Velazquez and of bankers by Matsys. The realist tradition is also defined by the
etchings of Hogarth and Goya, and the paintings of Goya, Daumier, and of David
both before and after 1789. All of these examples are related (no matter how differently the ways) to the decisive social and political realities of their times. Perhaps still more interesting are works by the Dutch still-life painters and by the
fifteenth-century Italian landscapists, which presage the future dominance of the
urban bourgeois patriarchate and the decline of feudal power. I cannot expand on
the visual arts here, and must refer my reader to L'Absolu et la forme, my polemic
with the philosophy of art of André Malraux, for an elaborated presentation of
this field of realism.

Realism and Alienation What does demand attention here is the question of
whether the achievement of realist art always requires a critical and even hostile
attitude to the "mother's breast" of the social reality into which the artist or the
writer is born and raised. Formulated in this way, on the basis of evidence already
presented, the answer clearly has to be no, realist portrayal needn't be antagonistic to society. The statues of Phidias and Myron are not, the *Canterbury Tales* of
Chaucer are not, the portraits by Franz Hals and the novels by judge Henry Fielding
are not. Nor are the (early) realist works about the October Revolution. Our dominant modern idea of critical realism should not cause us to overlook the fundamental change of attitude among artists — and the traits of realism — which accompanied the rise of capitalism. Leave aside for the moment the folkloric and plebeian
artistic traditions. It is then possible to agree that up to the sixteenth and seventeenth centuries, the principal artists all shared in the dominant, ruling-class con-

sciousness of their times; we can search from the Renaissance all the way back to the Altamira and Lascaux cave depictions of preclass society without finding any objects of art which "dissented." The bust of Queen Nefertiti did not, nor did the sarcophagic bas-reliefs of the Egyptian dynasties, the Ajanta shrine sculptures, or the Chartres or Bamberg cathedral sculptures.

Two tendencies of history in the modern period altered this situation for art generally and for the realist method in particular:

1. As capitalism established new relations of production, the inherent social conflicts broke out, as Marx described, and the pace of socioeconomic development
   accelerated, with both the tempo and the instability creating an unprecedented
   skepticism about matters that had once seemed settled or natural.
2. By the end of the eighteenth century, the artist's role had begun to shift towards
   that of the social outsider.

This latter transition was very slow. We can perhaps see in the figure of Hamlet the start of the alienation of a once-consenting art. It is tempting to see him symbolically as the first modern intellectual, displaced by the skepticism that wedges between his traditional sense of duties and privileges and the social core which had held people like him fast since cooperative species life began. However, I dare not compare Shakespeare to his character; at least, not too closely.

We might more reasonably equate Cervantes with his adventurers Don Quixote and Sancho Panza. Both (for different reasons) are displeased with the class in power and the social climate. Sancho Panza emerges from the long-abused masses and displays the earthy wit that enables the survival of the plebian poor. The Don of La Mancha has grown restless with the faded cloak of privilege which fails to comfort him in a new world of mercantile habits. Quixote, like Janus, looks both back and forward in history to seek for utopian satisfactions. With such a cast in his major novel, we may be certain Cervantes was antagonistic toward his era. Yet artists continued on the whole to acquiesce to the social hegemony from the fifteenth to the seventeenth centuries.

Only in the nineteenth century does an institutionalized breach appear, clothed in the ragged and motley colors soon understood by the social classes as "the Bohemian way of life." Meanwhile, the breakdown of the aristocracy, that traditional class of patrons, continued apace. The industrial and merchant capitalists devoted themselves to further accumulation, to the comparative neglect of refined pleasure or status display. With their old footing eroded, artists were little encouraged to pledge allegiance to these new social pillars. To argue that the "outsider" writers, painters, architects, and so on were capable of stripping themselves of illusions and prejudices would be ridiculous. Yet as the contention in society rose, we can see beyond any question that their loyalties wavered and grew ambiguous. Before the dawn of the twentieth century the increasingly anxious and skeptical dwellers in Bohemia had felt the ancient, class-anchored status of their calling grow socially indeterminate.

I have briefly surveyed the sociocultural evolution of the artist's trade (omitting many aspects and nuances) with one single aim: to give perspective to the modern artistic consciousness as the context, premise, and mediator of critical realism. The indeterminacy of that situation and its correlated awareness have fired in many artists a fierce thirst for utter independence. Others have no less bountifully committed their awakened sense of freedom to an historical idea and an immediate program of social transformation. Such artists include Mayakovsky, Brecht, Neruda, Guillen, Aragon, Meyerhold, Siqueiros, Leger, Eisenstein, and Pasolini. Each has made his own distinct choice of a life and creative method. A personally defined Communist commitment is coupled with a critical attitude towards official doctrines.

If this sketch is accurate in its essentials, then we may conclude that the differing frames of reference of ancient, medieval, and modern society have been accompanied by some distinct (particular) standards for the character of realism. The realists of antiquity and the middle ages display not even a trace of critical distance from society. Yet it is precisely this critical distance which becomes the telltale dimension and criterion as we come nearer to the present. At the same time, while the breakdown of former certainties and the experience of the emergent, alienating conditions grows more excruciating, the temptation also grows to "find an easy out," that is, to market a remunerative banal art, supported in turn by a clever and interesting yet necessarily conventional career within the increasingly "established" bohemian or even "left-wing" tradition.

Those artists who take realist depiction seriously travel a more difficult route: they attempt to become part of the cutting edge of their culture and to probe deftly and deeply the aching or cancerous nodes of the day. I need scarcely add that artists in socialist-based countries are by no means so touched by grace that they can afford the luxury of effortless transportation on the coattails of history. The institutions they encounter require the continued vigilance of a critical realism.

Events make clear beyond any doubt that advances in technology may enhance, among other means, the capacity of institutions to be cruel. The trend towards technocratic efficiency and cooperation in production and distribution that was

enthusiastically and seductively envisioned by the American socialist Edward
Bellamy in *Looking Backward* (1888) has, in fact, entrenched a frequently nightmarish bureaucracy whose methods are often those of complacent tyranny. Indeed,
an incessantly critical orientation towards the world is an imperative resource of
the modern sensitive and thinking individual. No artist and certainly no realist can
venture to conceive that his context is exceptionally privileged.

In this appraisal, the features of realism emerge as historically dependent on the
awareness of the contingencies of the human situation. Realism is moreover increasingly bound up with the broadening of the social and political scope for acting
on those contingencies. Artists and other creative intellectuals have more and more
joined in revolt against the vestiges of an institutionalized inhumanity; the realist,
accordingly, takes pains to witness what is problematic and especially what is
hypocritical and fraudulent. Realism also comes ultimately to embody—owing to
this same broad and long development—that wealth of human potentials which,
however often oppressed, maimed, and defeated, can never be wholly lost due to
their irrepressible, Promethean source. Just here I should perhaps stress again that
the interpretation I provide is premised on a definite philosophy of history. My
orientation stems from the marxist heritage, which emphasizes not a fatalistic acceptance of mechanistically interpreted social "necessities," but, rather, the human
person as the potentially creative historical factor.

I want to emphasize that the division of the critical from the earlier, noncritical
epoch of realism is no better than approximate, and needs closer study and verification. I am also certain that the distinction and shift is more relative than absolute, and occurred along a protracted and subtle continuum. The same might
be said with regard to the transition of more recent critical realism to a transcendent, even "utopian" mode. I certainly do not want to imply a low opinion of the
aptness and achievement of recent, well-observed, yet not especially rebellious
realist attitudes; and I also note that more distant periods offer many attractive
portrayals of a disalienated world which are in a nostalgic vein: Shakespeare's
mellow island at the eye of *The Tempest*; the fantasies that animate Cervantes'
characters; the idyllic isles of Watteau; the visions in Goethe's *Faust*, Part II; or
the Surrealist dream in our century. Yet with all the qualifications stated, we must
still recognize the emergence in the last century of an unprecedented trend towards
"thinking-about-today-in-the-light-of-tomorrow," which we can understand as
the extension and development of a recurrent concern by realism for the inherent
tendencies of transformation in social history. If this aspect of realism has become

more compelling, it is because we have all grown more aware of history's pitfalls and seductive mazes, past which human beings sometimes try too bruskly to direct their steps.

Final Clarification and Prospects It will be clarifying to compare the fundamentals of realism as distinguished above with the idea of realism discussed by Roman Jakobson in an interesting essay of 1921 (included in Todorov, *Théorie de la littérature*); a similar idea is presented in the work of Roger Garaudy and André Malraux, and it purports, simply, that realism should be considered to occur as a property of every creative work which is new from the standpoint of the extant social situation and artistic conventions. What happens if we accept this argument? We must then accept all innovations as "realism" regardless of their sociohistorical content. "Realism" would then be juxtaposed to the continuation of any existing convention in art. What is more, *all* "realism" would be accordingly given high marks, since the achievement of novelty has been lent a positive connotation in itself. There is a certain attraction to this viewpoint; and we cannot quickly dismiss it because, as already noted, there is enough ambiguity to the function of realism in marginal and in emergent contexts so that we cannot simply foreclose its possible manifestation as novelty. However, at the same time we must try to avoid superficial, trivial, or eccentric uses of the term. From the marxist standpoint there is little basis for equating the idea of realism with artistic novelty in a given historical context. Realists indeed may rely on time-honored means of expression; and, conversely, the mere fact of producing a realist novel in a "new" era does not guarantee a positive achievement.

Let me restate the traits of realism as I distinguish it:

1. It is a conception which implies a philosophical orientation with ideological ramifications.
2. It interests itself, to be sure, in the fundamental traits recurrently operative in human culture; that is, it seeks what is "essential" to social life (there is often controversy about what is essential).
3. It assesses social life in an historically concrete and socially relative interpretation, which assumes not a fixed human nature but, instead, a dialectical emergence of new modes of consciousness on the basis of semistabilized contradictions.

Thus, whatever degree of human universality may emerge in realism ("truth to human nature"—the Anglo-American aestheticians who write of realism apply this term extensively) has its premise in a developmental perspective which respects the continually changing historical contexts and contents of the human species. Such matters as love, death, success, and failure, recur, but they are continually modified; the persons and circumstances of "the real" and hence of realism are transformed. This kind of human universality may at times be represented through mere mimesis. Some might even argue that its unadulterated, complete representation can *only* be mimetic; yet a knowledge of works of art suggests that merely mimetic representation is, by comparison, flat, unevocative, incomplete, puerile. Again, however, an intermediary zone occurs between realism and other kinds of mimesis.

If I have been clear enough, the reader will see how the demarcation of mimesis of other kinds from the mimesis which concretizes realism is founded on interpretation with a philosophical and sociohistorical basis. However, I should also say a word here about how realism—both as artistic practice (method) and as artistic doctrine—relates to the tradition of artistic methods and programs (in the two final notes to this chapter I go into it a bit; let me say something here in an expositional fashion). My 1963 essay "Le réalisme comme une catégorie artistique," which I have already mentioned, pointed out that in the range of aesthetic doctrines, realism occurs between *idealism* on the one hand and *naturalism* on the other. The idealist (Zuccari, Bellori, etc.) have proposed an artistic program in which an "inner design" is sought out; their artistic procedure is chiefly regarded as *cosa mentale*. Naturalism (with Zola as chief spokesman even today) argued that empirical data must provide the primary orientation for the artistic method. Now, this juxtaposition of the doctrines may furnish a schema of some usefulness, and that is precisely what I said in 1963; however, I must now add that it is an antiquated and insufficient clarifying device: we must, instead, seek the tensions experienced by each artistic method, that is, study the praxis which results from the use of a working generalization of one or another kind. I have already done this for the realist method, in describing a "continuum" from the historically specific to the historically abstract.

What of naturalistic praxis? Its working generalizations have only an oblique contact with social history as it develops. The human being is considered a fixed entity with eternal problems of love, death, hatred, sorrow and the like, and naturalism may assume (as in its nineteenth-century formulation) that man tends above all else to an animal and biological fate. Another variant of naturalism, quite comprehensible where there is no context of historical or other extensive thought, locates the human being in an intimate community where chance details cause epiphanies of far-reaching effect.

At the other extreme of working generalization, idealism (a kind of rhetoricism) as an artistic praxis starts from abstracted ideas of man in his relationships. The specifics of history drop out while ideas move onward of their own impetus; the key figures are spokesmen of concepts to be proven. This didactic plan may so hamper a work as literature that it becomes more an essay or inspirational sermon; or what presumably should have been a figurative painting becomes only the illustration of a concept.

Today, literature displays a tendency to allegorical devices and to parables with an archetypal outcome which often eliminates the living hero and the experienced event. This seems to me one symptom of an increase in *schematic* working generalizations. Why should this artistic shift have occurred? Perhaps most importantly because the avant-garde has started to question the semiautonomous, sensuous status of works of art as such. The *realists*, however, remain ardent believers in the function of the semiautonomous, specifically artistic objects.

It may be replied that today even realists often seem to bring in allegory or parable. That is true, but when they do, the telling of the tales still occurs in a social and historical matrix; as a matter of praxis the schematized understanding merges with a "content" of collective experience, imparting a pervasive philosophical irony and grotesquery. I can mention two Polish authors, Stanislaw Ignacy Witkiewicz and Slavomir Mrozek, who integrate their quite unmistakable outlooks with a sociopolitical environment. Witkiewicz deploys the tragic and farcical characteristics of Poland between the two world wars; Mrozek draws attention to some surreal if not absurd aspects of the Polish socialist experience. This is representative for the wing of modern realism which relies on its knack for philosophized expression.

Realism also continues to draw for positive gains on a "you-are-there" method, with results which often have the force of immediate experience, and also on the naturalist practice of lending animal traits to some characters. In both cases, it is the context of the artistic whole which is decisive, not the particulars of the artistic presentation. Zola's practice has often been more influential than was his doctrine, and despite their vaunted biologism, his novels are strongly laced with social criticism, a tradition which points, for instance, to Edward Albee.

I hope I have demonstrated this about my schema of artistic techniques: what we should look for first is not the presence of a *doctrine* of idealism, naturalism, or realism, but, rather, the kind of artistic *praxis* that predominates. A given device may serve a particular limited, productive purpose. Meanwhile, a pervasive working generalization, which stresses either the sociohistorical patterning of experience or the specifics which frequently are perceived as the products of chance or fatality, can set the commanding aesthetic tone.

I have shown that typification is ultimately opposed to a perception of reality as either fatalistic or dominated by chance; yet the demarcation of realist from other kinds of mimetic portrayal is so delicate that both techniques are often found deployed almost inseparably. Although typification is a flexible, capacious technique, there are limits to its digestive powers. These limits were to a considerable degree clarified by Lukács in his numerous essays on realist practice; however, his acumen left him when he came to the literature of the avant-garde. His artificial barring of the avant-garde was disputed by Ernst Fischer and Roger Garaudy. Both marxist critics demonstrated that Kafka and Joyce were as much involved with typification (each in his own frame of reference and on his own terms) as was Gorki or Thomas Mann.

I agree with this assessment. Appropriate for a fully adequate treatment of the problem would be a broad, specific, multileveled analysis and interpretation of all the pertinent and disputed works. In painting the same analysis and interpretation might serve to dispel the controversies around "modernism." We might, for example, study the realism of Rouault, which *is* a realism both despite and, in some ways, because of his devout Christianity, as compared with the realism of Buñuel, which is based on a "Christian atheism" obsessed by visions of the obscene and the holy. Another stimulating angle of approach might analyze, say, the works of Kafka and Giacometti for their intimations of rebellion.

Having just come to this starting point, I must draw to an end. Alas, everything that could be managed within this overly compact chapter has been of a theoretical character. Yet I must take a last moment to tell the reader that I should not have attempted a defense of realism along the foregoing lines if, indeed, I did not find that realism could in this way be established as a definite artistic category, with its particular equivalents in the immediately given objects of art and literature which afford us the concrete cognitive-artistic values.

Notes

1. Cf. L. L. Whyte, *Aspects of Form* (London, 1959) and G. Kepes, *Structure in Art and in Science* (New York, 1965). None of the scholars (or the artists from various fields who appear in the second book) contributing to these works find any evidence of scientific discoveries being directly imitated in twentieth century art. However, they all do emphasize the dependence of art on science (not, incidentally, a feature of our age alone). If the debts are particularly heavy in the twentieth century, it should be added that it is not only on art that science has exerted a potent influence. It should also be noted that both books sensibly underline the point that the presence of these dependencies is neither exclusive nor dominant. The overriding trait is the parallel trends in art, science, and philosophy towards a new vision of man and his relationship to nature. An interesting analogy of this type between mathematics and painting has been drawn by M. Porebski in *Kubizm* (Warsaw, 1966) and between cubism and phenomenology by G. Habasque in *Le cubisme* (1959). It is also a fact, as Duchamp among others has corroborated, that the futurist representations of the rhythm of movement were based on the time-exposure studies of the French physiologist E. J. Marey.

2. E. H. Gombrich, *Art and Illusion*, 2nd ed. (Princeton, N.J., 1961), pp. 53 ff.

3. Ibid., pp. 299ff. The same approach was developed on this question by Nelson Goodman in the first chapter of his *The Languages of Art* (Indianapolis, 1968). I concur that the visual perception cannot be predicated on the pristinely innocent eye, wholly without dependency on cultural stereotypes. It now seems even commonplace to state that we do see or hear phenomena under the impress of our prior knowledge of the world, and, therefore, that our perception commonly undergoes some modification. Yet no sufficient arguments are advanced either by Gombrich or by the scholars he cites, to dispute the existence of a "normal vision." Of course, psychophysiological permanency cannot be defended as against all cultural paradigms. It seems, rather, that the psychophysiological considerations induce a certain skeletal "symbolic communication" that is common to mankind. We must, however, distinguish between symbolic systems relevant merely to a given time, place, social grouping, and so on, and cultural factors which are permanent in their recurrence. (For example, for the unicorn to have a new recognition and fascination in every generation, it is necessary, among other factors, for every individual born to have some knowledge of an animal and of the closest actual species.) Goodman states (p. 33) that "nature is the product of art and discourse"; I should add that it is in this sense that we undertake the classification and characterization of most objects and their relationships in a habitual way. These habits eventually become so ingrained in us as to overleap historical and ethnocentric factors. Basically, then, we can only "imitate" nature inasmuch as certain tendencies of our perception remain constant.

Let me incidentally note also that my usage of the term "denotation" differs from that of Goodman. Representations of a unicorn or of a character such as Mr. Pickwick are denotative even though neither exists. In each case there is a cluster of prototypes sustaining the representation. We can refer to a model of a human being or an animal (the more general framework of abstraction) and (at a more specific level) we can further point to some mimetic traits of the rhinoceros and hippopotamus in the image of the unicorn, and to certain typical features of the middle-class nineteenth century Englishman in the image of Pickwick. I also differ from Goodman in my use of the term "realism," which I locate in another dimension. His emphasis is right in part: in the idea that a likeness depends on the given culture and its semiotic systems, as well as on the conventions of realism in the given period. However, I qualify his emphasis for several reasons:

1. As I have just indicated, in part a likeness is *not* reducible to cultural stereotypes.

2. Although I agree that realism isn't at all a matter of the faithful rendering of an absolute and constant reality, yet it still may have correspondence to some sociohistorical constants; and here the conventions or "standards of representation" would mean more than merely a canon for depicting or describing reality, as we can proceed through the semiotic paradigms to discern the basic problems of the time and place, the modes of thinking and feeling which reveal the whole social fabric.

4. Cf. D. Vertov, *Statyi Dnevniki, Zamysly* (Moscow, 1966), pp. 45–48, 94–97, 122–124; or *Film Culture*, no. 25 (1962).

5. Siegfried Kracauer, *Theory of Film* (New York, 1965), pp. ix–xi, 12–23, 33–40.

6. Ibid., pp. 262–311.

7. Prior to Hospers a similar interpretation was outlined in W. Abell, *Representation and Form* (New York,‛ 1936) and T. M. Greene, *The Arts and the Art of Criticism*, Part III (Princeton, 1940). Later came M. Weitz, *Philosophy of the Arts* (Cambridge, Mass., 1950) which followed corresponding principles. All of them emphasize that the aes-

thetic surface (that is, the ordered material of a work composed of the elements rudimentary to a given art) does not account for the whole wealth of artistic values. Another excellent argument supporting this position is provided by Goodman in *Languages of Art*, chapter 6, where he lays stress on art's cognitive values. Goodman insists that we should be continually attentive to the "symptoms of the aesthetic" (syntactic density, semantic density, syntactic repleteness, exemplification). However, he urges discernment within the context of an artistic whole of the particulars of representation, which he holds must be imprecise but not ineffable.

8. Cf. J. Hospers, *Meaning and Truth in the Arts* (Chapel Hill, N.C., 1946), pp. 13–14, 108–110.

9. Ibid., pp. 23 ff.

10. Cf. T. Todorov, ed., *Theorie de la littérature (Textes des formalistes russes reunis)* (Paris, 1965), and V. Shklovsky, *Khudozhestvennaya proza: Rozmysleniya i razbory* [Artistic prose: reflections and analysis] (Moscow, 1961).

11. Cf. J. Mukarovsky, *Studia z estetiky* (Prague, 1966), pp. 85–160. See also the distinction drawn by Max Bense, in his *Aesthetica* (Baden-Baden, 1965), between two types of artistic sign: *Zeichen von Etwas* and *Zeichen für Etwas*. The latter corresponds to my notion of mimesis.

12. This same problem appears in a different version in the attempts to universalize mimesis as a category applicable to all arts. A revealing example of such an interpretation can be found in G. Lukács, *Die Eigenart des Aesthetischen* (Neuwied, 1963), where at the same time he accentuates the principle of the representation of reality and shifts the emphasis to what he calls "Ab-

bild des Abbildes" in relation to music, architecture, and landscape gardening. This "*gedoppelte Mimesis,*" as he puts it, is really an expression of collective states of mind objectified in a given work. Such a view is, of course, a far cry from that of Dufrenne. Lukács' position has its roots in Diltheyism. Nevertheless, in both cases, utterly opposed though the aims are, expression comes unexpectedly to supplant mimesis: Lukács quite simply substitutes the former for the latter in the instances just mentioned. If, however, we are willing to treat music and architecture as amimetic arts (in keeping with Dufrenne) it is, among other reasons, because in such arts as literature, theater, film, or figurative painting, mimesis forms a basic component of their axiology. To argue against Lukács (universalization of mimesis) might, therefore, be to argue against Dufrenne (elimination of mimesis).

13. I do not take colors as such into account because they cannot have a recognizable mimetic correspondence to a referent model in external reality, but only to color in general. It is true that painterly technique includes the term *couleur locale*. This is in contradistinction to, say, the Byzantine approach or the impressionist and postimpressionist experiments with color. We tend to forget that our "normal" way of seeing and rendering colors is in conjunction with the objects they adorn. In short, the blueness of the sky is different from the blueness of water, the pink hue of the rose is different from the pink nose of somebody with the sniffles. The same remarks apply to movements and shapes. This is one reason why the dance, which suggests objects or events and their relationships, is so fascinating. Oriental dance even has evolved conventional scorings of movement. Similarly, the

great mimes (e.g., Marcel Marceau) have learned to express themselves semimimetically. There seems to be less of a troubling problem as regards sounds. Their onomatopoeic usage is rather rare and extraordinary. Incidentally, a single sound is incapacitated in this sense; there must be a sequence of sounds to imitate a birdsong (Beethoven) or a speeding locomotive (Honegger). The noises introduced in avant-garde music by Varese, Cage and the "concretists" are not mimetic signs, their aim is rather to erode the boundary line between everyday life and art patterns.

14. This statement should not be taken to mean that the artists who contrive at a semimimesis have no concern for the mimetic result. A widespread opinion up to the present holds that the element of mimesis in some avant-garde art is only a feeble pretext, a mere expedient. This canard dies hard. In fact such avant-gardists as Picasso and Klee continued to refer to real phenomena as they sought deliberately to stress the full aesthetic significance of *deformation*, that is, of their promulgation within the modern European heritage of a trait endemic to Oceanian, Asian, and Mexican primitive art. We may also see modern semimimetism as heir to the archaic and medieval achievements in our tradition (with what expressive results, the reader may consider). A related point, which I think even more important to state, is that the human figure, and other objects, did not enter neutrally into the work of Picasso or Klee. Both artists positively sought this kind of iconography as one way to express their grasp of the world. Mimetic elements might also be used, of course, as a decorative element (and they were only so used by a number of followers of the avant-garde pioneers). This fact does not cancel the justness of our continuous scale running from semimimesis to the most profound mimesis.

15. We bring in realism under the blanket term of mimesis due to certain crucial common features, hinging on the *analogon* representation, that is to say, a peculiar, cognition-oriented correspondence between the artistic structure and the extra-artistic reality. However, realism — as I shall later explain — differs basically from mimesis, with respect to the philosophical justification. The idea of mimesis as such refers to generic traits perceived through human praxis (communication of all kinds, including behavior); while realism is a concept dependent on definite notions of the character of historical processes and their ultimate regularity.

16. Cf. J. Lotman, *Lektsyi po strukturalnoy poetikye* [Lectures on structural poetics] (Tartu, 1964), pp. 18–29. Lotman undertakes a semantic (and model) analysis of the likeness relationship between art and reality (pp. 30–40).

17. R. Fry, *Some Questions in Aesthetics* (1926), quoted in *Transformations: Critical and Speculative Essays on Art* (New York, 1956), pp. 20–23.

18. Cf. Metz's essay "Le dire et le dit au cinéma: vers le déclin d'un vraisemblable," in *Essais sur la signification au cinéma*, pp. 222–244, and Dufrenne's remarks on artistic individuality bursting through the confines of a given code of meaning (*Esthétique et philosophie*, pp. 103–112, 133–158).

19. See my book *L'Absolu et la forme; L'esthétique d'André Malraux* (Paris, 1972); earlier editions were published in Polish (Cracow, 1966) and Italian (Bari, 1971).

20. I discuss this question in *Between Tradition and a Vision of the Future* (in Polish;

Warsaw, 1964), chs. 3 and 4, where I offer a critical commentary on the viewpoints of Soviet scholars. See also, among Polish studies, the works of Henryk Markiewicz and Stefan Zólkiewski, and, among other studies, particularly those of Ernst Fischer and Roger Garaudy, and Georg Lukács' *Die Eigenart des Aesthetischen*. Lukács' position seems the most persuasive, since he is the first to have brought an analysis of such thoroughness to the peculiar nature of artistic cognition (*das Typische als das Besondere, Allgemeine im Einzelnen* — the typical as the special and the general in the particular) and such scientific mastery to an analysis of the mimetic phenomenon as it is tied in with the formal foundations of art. (In this book he describes the latter as a *Für-sich-sein*.) Nonetheless, Lukács mistakenly — in my opinion — broadens the mimesis concept to include all of the arts, as part of his judgment that mimesis is a constituent property of art. Moreover, he opposes (however consistent it may be with his premises) avant-garde tendencies, which he sees as undermined by decadent traits. In *D'un réalisme sans rivages* (Paris, 1963) Garaudy rightly defends the connection of the avant-garde with realism, but his analysis of realism is inconclusive. Garaudy describes, as factors contributing to realism, the *conscience de ce qui manque* and also the will to partake of *l'acte créateur d'un monde en train de se faire*; possibly he is influenced in this by Sartre and by Mikel Dufrenne (*Phénoménologie de l'expérience esthétique* [Paris, 1953], Part I, ch. 4, and Part IV, ch. 3). He blurs art in general into realist art, I believe arbitrarily. I do, however, agree with Garaudy's consideration of art as being at once myth and cognition, that is, as being a project which transcends and supersedes the existing reality while at the same time offering fundamental knowledge of that reality. Even so, Garaudy forgets that this "mythical" or "utopian" feature is not a constant one, not constituent, even for the past two centuries. In other passages, Garaudy states that another determinant of realist art is labor, a proposition which is overly vague. (Does he refer to an artistic remaking of reality, or some general operational artistic deeds?) At any rate it would be exceedingly difficult to resolve into a coherent unity the visionary, technical, and cognitive aspects of such an analysis of realism (as I sought to demonstrate at greater length in my essay "Garaudy: antynomie prometeizmu" [Garaudy: The antinomies of Prometheism], *Wśpótczesność* [Warsaw], 1967, nos. 10 and 11).

Other instances that seem to me to present an abusive usage of the concept of realism are: Lucien Goldmann's interpretation of Robbe-Grillet's *Les Gommes,* as well as his other interpretations of the *nouveau roman* that accept the works' "realism" on the basis that they express (are representative of) an absolute reification; and the recurring idea in contemporary art theory that a nonfigurative art is the more profoundly realist. The error in the latter case lies in the notion that the structure of cosmic matter is being reflected in what is only superficially "abstract" art. As for Goldmann, he holds that the homology between the economic structure and the structure of the literary world is a prime criterion of value. However, the homology criterion (even supposing the reified world of Robbe-Grillet is the counterpart of the technological reification of today) must prove arbitrary in many cases.

Moreover, this kind of mimesis takes no account of the social consciousness which resists the devastating fetishism in our time.

The creators of the "new novel" consider themselves realists, it is true; they at any rate employ this notion in the sense of an overthrow of stereotypes and conventions, in the sense of a fresh and direct apprehension of the world. Whether we are thus presented with new content or with new forms, or both at once, is not clear. Probably, the latter solution is favored by Robbe-Grillet and by Nathalie Sarraute, whose views differ in other respects. In any case the uncertain aspects of this proposition are not what concern me now. Despite the polyvalence of the term as examined here, it would be difficult to accept a definition which would categorize as realist a literature that creates its own independent reality, or that assumes that, while the world *exists* to be sure, it is the "point of view" defined by the hero which gives it *meaning* in every case, or that, finally, treats human beings impersonally, as but objects emergent from chaotic flux.

21. In the essay "Le réalisme comme catégorie artistique."

22. By extension, it appears to me that to explicate the mimetic properties of art we need not rely on an older psychology which bifurcates the cognition process in terms of two separate units (subject and object) and mechanically totals up the sensations, representations, associations, etc. Rather, we may proceed, by developing the assumption that human perception — due to anthropologically recurrent (cultural invariants) factors — is remarkably stable. As noted in the first chapter, perception is *active*; that is, in ways dependent on prior social experiences, it is selective and interpretive of the given here-and-now reality. At the same time, perception is determined by the common human condition (for, although each person individually filters the stimuli, the choices and the decisions involved are largely predicated on the sociocultural context) and also—and here of most pertinence— by the recurrent aspects of the social praxis of the human species. Mimesis—as I explicate it—correlates primarily to this latter frame of reference. This understanding of perception is corroborated (as is the finding about mimesis) by the most recent scientific experiments.

The conclusions of existential phenomenology also lend support to my understanding of mimesis, which is predicated on the marxist notion of certain invariants that confront human praxis. Precisely if man perceives the world situationally, in active encounter with it (being able to perceive the field of objects in a synthetic manner, and reaffirming his human *projets*, in large measure thanks to the reiterative nature of the train of situational patterns), mimesis then would appear most credible as an artistic category appealing in a similar fashion to individuals from diverse cultures and from different epochs. This is a problem I deal with at full length in my book *L'Absolu et la forme*.

23. There is, in this case, a continuum because, while the general traits prevail in some realist works (hence the notion of individualized generalization), in others the particular traits predominate, making the variant notion, generalized individualization, applicable. Of course, the optimal and ideal sphere of typification is that where the *Allgemeine* and the *Einzelne* comprise an entirely organic and compact whole. This happens with the great masterpieces of realist art. However, works of individualized generalization (e.g., the plays of Friedrich Schiller) tend towards a kind of art we may may term schematic and abstract, while realist works of generalized individualization tend the other way, towards naturalism (Zola is an example). Of course the notion of a continuum should not be reduced to our two extreme instances selected more or less at random. It is meant to indicate the diversity of realism. (See the discussion of this topic with reference to Lukács' views in G. H. R. Parkinson, ed., *Georg Lukács* [New York, 1970], especially in the essays by Mészáros, Pascal, and Parkinson.)

Chapter 7

**The Vicissitudes
of Socialist Realism:
A Little Lesson in History
Which Should Not Be Ignored**

Art and the Theory of Art

There are obviously only three distinct possible relationships in time between art
and theory: either the course of events precedes theory, or they develop in combination, or theory anticipates the appearance of the new artistic current. This temporal factor is quite fundamental to the relationship between the two phenomena.

In the first case, the art theory introduces nothing new to art, and serves only
to explain an artistic process that has already flowered. At most, largely through
critical studies, it helps the public understand the new works unexpectedly arising
in the field of art, and plays the role of popularizing these new works, in the best
sense of the word.

In the second case, the art theory elicits and crystallizes new artistic phenomena,
defines their significance and depth, gives us the philosophical, social, and historical
key to them, and demonstrates the ways in which they are new and different from
previous phenomena. In this case, theory and art develop on a par. Very often the
same person practices both, sometimes availing himself of the former in his creative
revolution, sometimes of the latter to affirm his conceptions.

In the third case, theory becomes the dominant mode. It speaks of what should
be, indicates the path that it is necessary for art to take, and leads art to that path,
deaf to all objections and protests. When it adopts this approach, theory always
manages to find a certain number of obsequious zealots.

This classification is simplified; very often the cases are entangled, or one of
them ends by metamorphosing into another. Nevertheless, the history of art and
the history of thought do provide many examples of these basic patterns. Aristotle,
in his *Poetics*, speaks of the long historical process of development of classical
tragedy and Greek comedy. Da Vinci and Dürer advanced a new art and at the
same time a new aesthetic theory. Diderot and Lessing proceeded in this same
manner two centuries later: they attacked Boileau, Corneille, the Abbé D'Aubignac,
and Gottsched, who, fortified by Aristotle's *Poetics*, had fossilized dramatic art into
a dogma. Similarly, in the sixteenth and seventeenth centuries Lomazzo and Zuccari imposed certain canons on the plastic arts. Toward the mid-seventeenth century the French Academicians, led by Le Brun, succeeded them, and in the eighteenth century it was the turn of the neoclassicist Mengs. There are countless
examples; in each generation at least one of the relationships is asserted as valid.

This essay is based on my preliminary study of this topic, "Against the Prophets of Catastrophe," published in *Mys Filozoficzna* [Philosophic Thought], 1957, no. 3. It was translated by S. Alexander and
published in *Diogenes*, no. 36, and is here published with some modifications and a 1972 postscript.

A study of the more or less parallel courses of the histories of art and of aesthetics shows that when art has marched on the very heels of artistic theory, or
to the same rhythm, artistic theory has had a positive effect in stimulating artists
and society. In the third case, theory—generally the result of an artistic current
already out of date—has prescribed rigid rules to art, and, in order to cut a figure
as epigones, its proponents have condemned newly made works. Such theory—
dogmatic by nature—serves as a brake on the development of art, offering the
public false, limited, and obsolete criteria of appreciation.

The third case often occurs in connection with what is called academicism. The
academies were launched in Italy in the sixteenth century and were supposed to
promote discussion in the inner circles of artistic groups.[1] These institutions quickly
assumed a different aspect, however, and, from the end of the sixteenth century,
they have served to set up rules—a hierarchy of subject matter, the priority of
certain formal means of expression—and to enunciate the *quantum* of science indispensable in order to be considered an artist *sensu academico*. They have, in this
manner, transformed living and fruitful art theory into doctrine. Their merit in con-
ferring a social status on the artist ceases to have any significance when compared
with the wrongs they have committed in setting up codes for the creation of art,
for, as soon as any doctrine became official, not only in the artistic but also in the
social and political sense, it was bound to become corrupt.

Moreover, it is not by chance that academic doctrines had the official, cultural,
and political support of absolute power (originally through the might of the Medici,
later—and more importantly—in France). These doctrines were openly conformist
to the spirit of the court, favorable to the status quo of social life, or at least not
very dangerous from the social point of view due to their decayed idealism and
their reliance on assertedly immutable models. When David rebelled, in terms of
his kind of classicist art, against the social and political order of his time, he undermined the Academy of Paris.

A striking example of the corruption of aesthetic doctrine is provided by the
Jesuit domination of art during the period of the Counter-Reformation. Academic
doctrine had merely issued decrees; here, the politically dependent aesthetic doctrine went to the point of interdiction. Academic doctrine pretended that it alone
possessed the privilege of truth; politically dependent aesthetic doctrine made of
this truth an inviolable taboo. Academic doctrine punished art which departed from
established canons by subjecting it to scorn; politically dependent aesthetic doctrine threatened, in similar cases, direct or indirect reprisals. The latter is, therefore,

a phenomenon which has much more to do with the police than with culture. The Council of Trent ordered the unleashing of a merciless battle against heretical art; from then on, painting depended strictly on the Holy Scriptures.

Does all theory end in time by becoming distorted and molded into doctrine? Does all corruption of theory derive from the fact that it depends on political power? It is very dangerous to reply here, *ex promptu*, to questions that should be examined under all their historical and national aspects. Nevertheless, it remains true that the chronicles of artistic and aesthetic ideas (e.g., Lionello Venturi, *History of Art Criticism* [1964], or Katherine Gilbert and Helmut Kuhn, *A History of Esthetics* [1954]) lead us to the conclusion that all art theories gradually succumb to a tendency to doctrinization, and that there has been corruption whenever there has appeared the more or less despotic domination of a privileged social group.

The acceptance of Renaissance theories of art by the school of mannerism and the Jesuit Counter-Reformation would seem to indicate that the emergence of doctrine does not always compromise the principles of art. An art theory might be correct, and yet a doctrine may be derived from it which is no more than a lot of unjustifiable and false directives.

Contrary to widespread opinion, the number of aesthetic solutions is limited. All theories may be summed up in a few essential and juxtaposed theses, which are already present in the works of the pre-Socratics: the beautiful representing the order of things in the cosmos and the Beautiful representing the inner order in an artistic work; the Beautiful which is the reflection of reality in a work; the Beautiful perceived by the intellect and the Beautiful as the pleasure of the senses; Creation born of inspiration and Creation which is the child of skill (techne). The artistic theory of the Renaissance reverts once more to Aristotle's conception, transmitting it, enriched, to Diderot, Lessing, and Herder; and these theories lead through diverse nineteenth-century aesthetic currents — romanticism, critical realism, naturalism — towards the conception of socialist realism.

The aesthetic theory of the Renaissance correctly demonstrated that: artistic methods are methods of research; art requires technical competence as well as imagination and knowledge; there is nothing which should not interest the artist; art is as agreeable in terms of sensation and emotion for him who creates it as for him who perceives it; to be an artist is to plunge oneself into the quest for truth and to work towards the establishment of laws of taste and aesthetics; there is no beautiful work lacking an inner balance of all its components.

I may be told that these are generalizations without any deep foundation, that they are, in fact, so foundationless that I might just as readily proclaim and demonstrate their contraries. Indeed I might, and arguments of this sort have often been used. It is necessary, however, to check the correctness of these aesthetic principles according to other criteria; we must neglect the distortions resulting from corruption, and consider what made the works of art which gave life to these principles fruitful, comparing this concretized aesthetics with the arguments of the opposed aesthetics.

Thus, there are always two tendencies present in the history of aesthetics. Art theory advances, modifying and enriching its results with the rational examination of art. Continually reflecting concrete circumstances, it emphasizes new discoveries in art, discoveries of a scientific, aesthetic, and social nature, interlinked one with the other. However, after a while, theory coagulates into doctrine. Its principles slough off as catechisms; instead of guiding art, it orders it. In this doctrinaire incarnation, theory begins to resemble those "aestheticizing" moralizing concepts which are opposed to it, and which confuse art with science.

Where there is social and directly political subjection, corruption is a less regular occurrence than is metamorphosis into doctrine.[2] By imposing a theory, and declaring it to be the *only* valid one, the ruling class justifies the application of the punishment of ostracism or, in cases of insubordination, physical force. All these postulates and prohibitions issue from an Institution headed by bureaucrats, who are thereby elevated to the rank of supreme connoisseurs of art.

Is Socialist Realism an Invention of the Devil?
A brief excursion into the history of aesthetic thought will permit us to view socialist realism in another light than that of the polemicists who up to now have had the last word. Socialist realism is part of the *best* artistic and theoretical inheritance of the past, despite all the distortions which recent historical circumstances have forced it to undergo. It started a new art, nourished on new social, political, and cultural ideas. It responded to questions and moved in the forefront of the needs and aspirations which life, not intellectual speculation, was engendering. Then, as the new works were born, they were analyzed and confronted with those of preceding epochs, and thus a new aesthetic theory crystallized. This theory is not of the type that outruns artistic facts; it is the balance sheet of what already exists. Why should Gorki be judged from the point of view of 1956 when the historical circumstances of his work were altogether different? Gorki's theoretical efforts

were, in fact, much closer to those of da Vinci, Dürer, Diderot, or Lessing than to
those of the defenders of a lying and toadying art.

Everyone interested in the subject knows that magnificent art works were created
before 1934 and that the Soviet Union was at that time the inspirer of new experiments in form and content. Those who connect the birth of socialist realism with
the year 1934 have no respect for the current of history. First of all, the *artistic*
aspect was already underway much earlier. There are those who would even place
it in the period around 1906, when Gorki's *Mother* appeared. Second, the *theoretical* aspect, although only formulated at the time of the first Congress of Soviet
Writers in 1934, also dates back to the earliest years of the Soviet Union.

Thus, that argument is false which would have it that it is possible to determine
whether the theory of socialist realism is good or bad according to the artistic
products that follow its proclamation. What we must do is exactly the opposite.
To know whether a theory is correct, we must confront it with the creative works
which have determined its aesthetic pronouncements; and, in this particular case,
there are universally recognized masterpieces.

We might refuse to apply the term "socialist realism" to the creative work of this
period before 1934. There are those who propose other terminology: "art of the
socialist epoch," or "socialist art." However, this is not merely a quarrel over
terms. The burden of proof that "socialist realism" is an inadequate term falls
upon the adversaries and not the partisans of the expression. What do its adversaries tell us? They admit that socialist realism, in its initial conception, and not
after its bureaucratic corruption, is *not a style* and should be defined as such. Thus,
this realism did *not* initially preach any prefabricated poetics, although it is now
often reproached with having been taken as a "creative method" which led eventually to a stylistic norm and to rules concerning the construction of a work, and
which also imposed a certain norm of interpretation, that is, a way of seeing, of
understanding, and of appreciating things in a manner conforming to historical
and dialectical materialism, according to the latest meaning given to it.

Conversely, the opinion according to which realism[3] is, above all, *an attitude
towards reality* is justified, although it has not been demonstrated with precise
analysis. Certain thinkers interpret the term in this way. Thus, Stanislaw Ossowski
declares there is realism "where there is a search for artistic values on the plane
of correlation between the work and the object represented."[4] Ossowski's realism
is provided with cognitive values. Roman Ingarden emphasizes the same thing,

although indirectly, through an analysis of the various ways of apprehending the truth of a work.[5]

In 1917, new social conditions arose and, with them, the life of man was completely changed, including his ways of being, thinking, feeling, and wanting. Different relationships among people were born, different problems took on importance, and different ideas were formed. A new social ontology determined a new philosophical, scientific, and artistic epistemology. The artist synthesized these trends into a historical truth which was the essence, at the same time, of his own individual quality. He shared this characteristic with his contemporaries, for they also thought and wanted the same things, or almost the same things, as he. The term "realism," therefore, deserves to be retained for reasons other than that of tradition. It is the counterpart of the realism of past centuries, a realism that was quite as *engagé* as that of Gorki, Sholokhov, Mayakovsky, Eisenstein, Pudovkin, Vakhtangov, Deni and Moor, Deineka, Pimenov, Pietrov-Vodkin, and Grabar during the initial fifteen years of socialist reality. We might search for another name for their creative work, but I doubt that a better one could be found than that which they shaped themselves, and which, subsequently, was so unworthily compromised and slandered. The essential question is not "Is the name correct?" but "Does there exist a group of common factors in the best creative work of this epoch, and does this group of common factors distinguish this creative work from that preceding it?" In my judgment, we can respond to the latter question in the affirmative.

Before the thirties, an open struggle between different artistic trends went on in the Soviet Union. There were those who defended the prerevolutionary positions. The majority, however, acknowledged a new reality and expressed their acknowledgment in various ways.

We may find rational ideas and ideals just as much in the different efforts of the Proletcult, of Dziga Vertov, of the Fexy, of Meyerhold's and Vakhtangov's theater, of the group "The Four Arts," and of the *OST* painters, as in the despotic plans of *RAPP*, the comprehensive writer's organization set up in 1928. The ideas and ideals led, if sometimes with many zigzags, to the birth of masterpieces of socialist realism. Although different artistic groupings contested with one another, they all held the conviction that the creation of an ideological and revolutionary art was indispensable. They were motivated by an awareness of poverty, famine, and toil, as well as a pride in the victory won at the Winter Palace. They lauded the heroism of those who had been the first to construct a new world, who had been alone and besieged, but convinced that they would soon succeed in convincing all

humanity to travel the same path. The new hero of the time was the popular
masses; and the problem of work came to the forefront. Some wanted to create a
new plastic art in the factories, to popularize the sense of beauty in the streets and
workshops; others were fascinated by easel painting and its sometimes lyrical,
sometimes epical, modes of expression; but the arguments of both camps reckoned
with, and on, a new public.

It is notable that the new experiments in form in the Soviet Union during the
first ten years after the revolution were always backed up by social and political
arguments. Their creators wanted these experiments to serve the revolution, reflecting its essence and helping to create a radical transformation of taste in aesthetic matters. Obviously, it would be absurd to assert that all the works created
during this period were realist in the sense that the word "realism" was given
around 1932–34. Nevertheless, diverse artistic currents — the cult of the machine
(the beauty of construction), the cult of the social masses, the cult of politics-as-
the-guide-of-art — were fused into works which will last in the history of art: Mayakovsky's poems; *Potemkin; Storm over Asia; And Quiet Flows the Don; Forward;
Lyubov Yarovaya;* posters by Deni and Moor; graphic art by Favorski and David
Shterenberg; revolutionary painting by Deineka and Pietrov-Vodkin; sculpture by
Shervoud, Shadr, and Moukhina.

I do not intend to attempt a listing here of the aspects of realism which allow
us to call it socialist. Undoubtedly, we are dealing with a cluster of aspects which
might be extended, and cannot be set up according to arithmetical rules. The features that I mentioned above suffice, it seems to me; they may all be found, although visible in different degrees and in different contexts, in Soviet works of the
epoch of rapid transition.[6] Socialist realism was not an invention of the devil, tend-
ing to destroy artists who claimed their right to the most elementary independence.
It was, rather, a product of life, a reflection of truth expressed in myriad ways,
and often subject to exaggeration — there were as many manners as searchers (or
groups of searchers), but their vision and form were always intended to satisfy
the millions of people who were then opening their eyes to art.

Before proceeding to recount the gradual emergence of the theory of socialist
realism, I want to dwell for a moment on a problem still troublesome to many
scholars of the subject. The issue is whether the turn in Soviet cultural policy which
occurred in 1932 — the date is generally contrasted with 1934 — did not already
mark the beginning of the end, the start of the downhill slide for artistic achievement. The argument which fixes on 1932 usually states that, before this date, there

were competing artistic groups, none of which had the decisive approval and power of the Party behind it, while with the gradual rise of socialist realism to the level
of artistic dogma (starting in 1932) the party gained total control over the artists.

I find that this interpretation departs from the historical data and, moreover,
neglects the dialectical background. First, we must remember that the last genuinely
unbridled discussions of art policy took place in 1925–26. A central instance of
these debates was the one sponsored by the Press Department of the Party Central
Committee (May 9, 1924), devoted to cultural policy in matters of literature. The
chief speakers were Aleksander Voronsky, editor of the respected *Krasnaya nov*,
which published many nonparty but sympathizing writers; and Ivan Vardin (pen
name of I. V. Mgeladze), for the pugnacious *Na postu* group which sought the
meeting and which wanted full party control of literature and decisive backing
of proletarian artists against the *poputchiki* (fellow travellers). It is interesting to
note that Trotsky, Bukharin, and Lunacharsky sided with Voronsky. The Party
Resolution which came out of the discussions was a compromise. "*Na postu*" was,
however, still chastised for seeking to vulgarize and monopolize policy according
to its lights. The June 1925 Resolution of the full Central Committee of the Party
took a similar stand.

What happened in the following years? The leverage shifted towards the *Na
postu* position; its proponents terrorized literary life, slandered Voronsky, caused
Zamyatin to emigrate, humiliated Pilnyak and pushed Mayakovsky toward suicide.
Given this setting, the official and unofficial Party declarations of 1932–34 were
remedial and positive; only this fact can explain why they were received so widely
among artists as an improvement of the situation. Simultaneously, of course, these
declarations opened the possibility a now-centralized terror. The Party could usurp
the last remnants of the artists' autonomy if it chose. The handwriting was on the
wall for the avant-garde movement in Russia, which was now labelled ultraleftist.
However, for any student of Soviet culture in these years it must be clear that the
opportunity for experimentation had been dwindling since the mid-1920s.

Programs Derived by Artists from Their Work

To study the formation of the theory of socialist realism, we can turn to a mass
of sources — for example, the collection of documents concerning the Soviet plastic
arts in the years 1917–32 in I. Matsa, L. Reinhardt, and L. Rempel, eds., *Sovietskoie
iskusstvo za 15 liet. Materialy i dokumientatsia* (Moscow-Leningrad, 1933). We
may here trace the main lines of development of the first decade of Soviet plastic

arts in the manifestos issued by the various artistic groupings, in the events involved in the birth, development, and decline of these groups, and in the facts about
exhibitions and art instruction. The outline of the following five years is more superficial, and the work is not lacking in lacunae even with regard to the first years.
Nonetheless, the volume constitutes a very rich vein of authentic data. The chief
editor, Ivan Matsa, although an eminent art critic, contents himself with a very
modest contribution; he prefers to present a picture of the times through brief introductions to each of the three parts of the book. After analyzing the materials presented, I am led to the following conclusions:

1. During this period, Soviet art was always accompanied by theoretical reflections. That is to say, each group sought to justify its practice with a program.

2. The program of socialist realism was present from the twenties on, though
it had not yet been defined by that term. Artists spoke of "revolutionary realism"
or "proletarian realism." Such groups as *Novaia Organizatsia Zhivopistsov*, *Krug
Khudozhnikov*, *OMCh*, *OST*, *Oktiabr*, which had been partisans of easel painting
and monumental frescos, put these ideas into practice. Even where the program
was not fully realized, it was articulated.

3. The members of *AChRR*, a group continuing the traditions of the *pieried-
vizhniki* (travelling exhibits), also made use of these ideas as "heroic realism"; the
interpretation, then, was highly flexible.

4. These ideas were not utilized when it was a matter of applied art (with the
exception of the *RAPCh*), for it was believed, correctly, that they were as strong as
their subject only in the case of an art representative of reality.

5. The theory of socialist realism as it was understood in 1934 took up ideas
which had been promulgated from before the birth of *RAPCh*, that is to say, concepts stated by the *poputchiki* of the groups *Oktiabr*, *OST*, and *OMCh*. The most
varied, and often contradictory, elements—on the one hand, the doctrine of communicativeness, and, on the other, the doctrine of continuous formal experimentation—enter into this theory, put forward, we should note, after a defeat for sec-
tarianism. Without amounting to the proclamation of a new era, this theory did
constitute the balance sheet of fifteen years of bitter disputes over the determination of what proletarian art should be.

The argumentations and artistic programs in this collection prove that the interpretations and the consequences of these ideas were being worked out well before
1934. The theory of socialist realism—as the facts testify—was put together gradually, in combination with the irregular development of Soviet art during the first

fifteen years of its existence. These historical facts also point out some weaknesses
of the theory, such as the fact that the term was borrowed from literary theory and
could not be extended to all domains of art.

Even in terms of the literary programs, beginning with *Krasnaya nov, Na postu,*
and *RAPP,* the premises and conclusions were not unequivocal. Different and conflicting currents within the larger trend of a literature committed to the side of the
Soviet state, produced such formulations as: the spontaneous cognition of the
Soviet reality must be primary; or, literature must be a class weapon based on
dialectical materialism; or, a committed proletarian writing will "infect" the feelings
and thoughts of readers by means of its subtle sociopsychological fictions. The
latter position, bolstered by the ideas of Tolstoi and Plekhanov, was urged by *RAPP*
ideologists, who laid the foundation for the theory of socialist realism. However,
the remaining conceptions were also incorporated into the program of socialist
realism which was advanced by Zhdanov.

It is incorrect to say, then, that the Zhdanov theses of 1934 amounted to an
arbitrarily imposed code. They only represented a generalization of the same kind
as the theoretical generalizations of the twenties. They were so lacking in precision
that the *Oktiabrists* and the members of *OST* would have been able to subscribe
to all of them. The codification of the theses as a closed system took place later;
for the plastic arts, only in 1945.

From Lenin to Gorki and Zhdanov in 1934

Gradually, as the art developed, so too did both the programs derived by artists
and the theory of socialist realism. Meanwhile, what was the status of inner-Party
attitudes? Many scholars have, of late, emphasized a demarcation of the era preceding Lenin's death in 1924 from the following Stalinist era. It is quite true, as I
have already indicated, that the last wide open party debates on cultural policy
took place in the year or two following Lenin's death; but it would be wrong to
speak on this account of an arbitrary imposition of dogma or a turnabout of principles during this era of transition. It would be more appropriate to contrast the
views of the Lenin circle with those expressed at the First Congress of Soviet Writers
a decade later. I shall later discuss the fundamental differences between the Lenin
and Stalin eras as these ultimately emerged. First, and so as to deter unwarranted
conclusions, I would like to indicate some principles of Lenin's cultural politics that
pointed towards socialist realism. The corruption of this theory into an adminis-

261   From Lenin
to Gorki and Zhdanov
in 1934

trative formula was only conditioned by the epoch that followed. Its later form was
almost entirely in contradiction with Lenin's aesthetic theses.

During the years 1917–24, Lenin, although primarily concerned with political,
social, and economic problems, very often expressed his opinion with regard to
cultural matters and indicated his view of the possible new roles of culture in socialist society. Above all Lenin aimed for the *popularization* of culture. That is why
he attacked the adepts of the *Proletkult* who were ignorant of the cultural heritage
of the past. That is why he emphasized several times that the proletariat, unlike
the Roman *plebs*, wanted not an amazing or modish "circus" but a serious art,
in the best sense of that word. That is also why Lenin demanded an art that could
be *understood* by the masses. The sympathy that Lenin felt, on the one hand,
for literature like that of Gorki and Barbusse, and, on the other hand, for the then-
famous plan of "monumental propaganda," is another reflection of the propositions he maintained. We also know, from his discussions with Clara Zetkin, that
Lenin neither loved nor understood contemporary art.

Lunacharsky, an art critic very sensitive to literature and a connoisseur of all the
new artistic currents of his time, defended the ideals of the avant-garde and thus
laid himself open to sometimes heated debates with Lenin.[7] We need only examine
Lunacharsky's works to realize, however, that despite the often very serious tone
of his polemics with Lenin, they defended exactly the same basic aesthetic principles.[8]

During the years 1926–29, while still Commissar of Education, Lunacharsky
conceived of himself as the executor and continuer of Lenin's policies. I do not
believe that his views sprang merely from the official post he occupied. On the
contrary, I am certain that his opinions were the result of reflection, the personal
debates he was in the habit of having with himself. In "The Cultural Tasks Which
the Working Class Must Assume" (1918), he early took up Lenin's ideas. Here
briefly is his reasoning: A proletarian culture exists. It results, and will continue
to result, from those artists who have become involved in the revolution and the
building of socialism. Their art is an art of struggle; and soon it will also be practiced by workers and peasants, who will begin to narrate their experiences, much
as Gorki and Martin Anderson Nexö have done.

Lunacharsky wrote in "Art and Industry" (1924) of the aesthetic pleasure given
us by clothing, furniture, dwellings, machines, and the look of streets. He dreamt
of a world soon to come, in which two brothers, the artist-technician and the tech-

nician-artist, would create the conditions necessary to revolutionize aesthetics. That was an idea in the marxist tradition which Julian Marchlewsky had stated before the October Revolution; and, in the first years after, it was very popular among the Soviet intelligentsia. The plastic arts were to influence the surrounding world, organize space in the widest sense of that word, *coexist with man* in his everyday life, and turn aesthetics right-side round. Lunacharsky was, therefore, on the side of those who are for contemporaneity and who seek above all to give art an applied character, directly relating it to architecture.

However, Lunacharsky also approved of the *AChRR* group in its objection to modern "autonomous" art. It is notable that artists of the Cézannist group *Valet Karo* and of "The Four Arts" group passed into the *AChRR* group without the least pressure exerted on them. The *AChRR* group could count on Lunacharsky's favor because its followers were creating a revolutionary art, an art of the era, comprehensible to the public and very popular. In "On the Value of Formal Art" (1926), Lunacharsky disavowed academic epigonism as much as cultivated decadent art. He recognized the formal value of experimental art but asserted that, under the circumstances, it was possible to bedazzle people without being able to satisfy them. Above all, he declared, the hunger of the contemporary public must be appeased, and appeased with new nutriments. However, until the new forms for the new basis of things appear, "it would be better to make use of Turgenev's and Pushkin's classic language rather than an indecipherable language."

Such were the opinions of a man who made war with Lenin to defend the rights of art and the right of formal experiment, the man who popularized expressionism, cubism, futurism, and purism in his writings, and demanded, in 1926, in a fine speech entitled "Let Us Be Careful Vis-à-Vis Art," that an appeal to the current aesthetic level of the masses should not be used as a basis for the rejection of difficult works of art which will at some point in the future be comprehensible by and easily accessible to everybody.

On some questions, Maxim Gorki's opinions were unlike those of Lunacharsky; Gorki had no use for a Western European contemporary art whose principal (and decadent) aim seemed to be to seek new means of expression, for he held that a popular art should above all bring forth a proletarian art. However, it is significant here to note the way in which the opinions of Lunacharsky and Gorki both led towards the 1934 formulations.

Some of Gorki's aesthetic opinions were arrived at before the October Revolution. In his 1909 study "The Annihilation of the Individual," he contrasted the optimism and sense of collectivity stimulated by folk literature with the sense of loneliness and decay evinced by the works of Sologub, Artsybashev, and Kuprin. If he proposed folk literature as a model, it was because he found it optimistic, healthy, and moral, speaking the same language as the masses, expressing thoughts and sentiments similar to theirs. It was not a question of mechanically imitating the style but of adopting a comparable moral attitude. In "The Self-Taught" (1911) and "Introduction to the Works of Proletarian Writers" (1914), he emphasized that literature must represent the truth of life, and the writers best able to represent this truth would be those arising from the formerly oppressed classes.

Many of Gorki's postrevolutionary speeches already foreshadow his 1934 report. I will cite only the most important. In "On the Proletarian Writer" (1928), he wrote that the new art must poeticize collective work and must take cognizance of the fact that man is capable of the most beautiful deeds and that he can influence the flow of history, inspiring it with the most beautiful human ideals. The same year he declared in "How I Learned to Write" that romanticism was no more than a simple reaction against realism on the part of those who saw life in the large, that is to say, those who saw man, how he desired to live, and what his ideals were. In "On Socialism Realism" (1933), Gorki contrasted bourgeois literature, dominated by selfishness, the quest for material pleasures, and the war of all against all, to humanist literature, dominated by a striving for the common good, for social well-being in preference to personal comfort, and for interpersonal coexistence on the basis of rational and cordial friendship.

Was that the universal opinion? No. Gorki's personal opinion then? No, not that either. In his articles, Gorki was expressing the aesthetic opinions of the majority of Soviet artists. These opinions were born of the tempestuous discussions which, over a period of more than ten years, had revolved around the basic question: What must the art of our epoch be, and does existing art truly correspond to contemporary needs?

In 1934, Gorky and Zhdanov drew up the balance sheet of these discussions. Let me here cite the key ideas of their reports.

Gorki: "Myth is an invention. To invent means to extract the essence out of any given combination and transpose it into an image. In this way realism is born. . . . If to this essence one adds, following the logic of hypothesis, what one would like to see achieved, and introduces it into the created image, then one obtains romanticism, which is the foundation of myth and is very useful for its revolutionary effect on reality. . . .

"Work must be the principal hero of our books. It is that which must fashion man and shape him to the demands of modern technique. . . . We must learn to treat work as a creative art.

"Socialist realism claims that to live is to act, to create, to continually develop in man his most personal gifts in order that he may triumph over natural forces . . . to assure his happiness on earth. . . ."[9]

Zhdanov: ". . . The line must be well-known in order to be able to represent it honestly in literary works — not in a scholastic, superficial manner, not in the style of objective reality; it is necessary to represent reality in its process of revolutionary evolution. . . . That is precisely the method, in literature, and in literary criticism, which we call the method of socialist realism.

". . . Yes, Soviet literature is tendentious. . . ."

". . . To be an engineer of human souls is to have one's feet solidly rooted to the soil of reality. . . . Our literature is firmly set on the hard ground of materialism, but romanticism is not beyond its ken; only, it is a question of a romanticism of a new type, revolutionary romanticism.

". . . You have a choice of weapons. Soviet literature is able to make use of all kinds of weapons — forms, styles, and methods of artistic creation — to exploit their diversity and the richness of their forms."[10]

In my opinion these statements may be summarized into three cardinal propositions:

1. Contemporary life, in all of its aspects, provides the subject matter of art, and it is the artist's role to prove responsive to this subject matter. However, artistic truths are always of a personal character, and they must result from individual discoveries. The artist arrives at his truth through a synthesis of contemporary facts; he either estimates existing reality or involves himself in the future by detecting new phenomena. These truths are tendentious because reality is tendentious; and the artist is fundamentally obliged to choose between past and future. (Zola had wished to be a passive chronicler, but to make an honest account of events he found he had to speak out for socialism.) Anticipating socialism of necessity involves intuiting the form of the future human personality and depicting its incipient stages in the setting of the present. Thus, the developmental person or model is not merely an invention of the theory of socialist realism.[11]

2. *Engagé* or ideologically progressive art can rely on the expressive means that best suit the artist. If the doctrine of realism has anything to say with respect to

the specific means, it is only that artistic form is desirable and efficacious from the ideological point of view, since it gives a kind of translucence to ideas.

3. An art fulfilling conditions (1) and (2) has not only a positive aesthetic but also a positive moral effect. This effect is not without importance because art can thereby help us to understand life better and to live better.

It seems to me that I have not abused my rights of interpretation in the above exposition, and, if it be true that such ideas may be drawn from Gorki's and Zhdanov's reports, then these reports are completely acceptable. They take up again the excellent aesthetic tradition extending from Aristotle, through the theoreticians of the Renaissance and those of the Enlightenment, to the Russian revolutionary democrats. Whoever might consider the tradition bad, will, nevertheless, concede that this aesthetic reappears with implacable regularity at every decisive turning point in history, every time new social principles manifest themselves. It is an aesthetic which also distinguishes our epoch. I will not deny that its main ideas are presented in generalities; it is that which gives them both their strength and their weakness. Today we know that it is the weakness which has taken over.

Institutionalization of the Doctrine

The First Congress of Soviet Writers marked a turn away from the promulgation in some quarters of the slogan "with us or against us," that is, from the increasingly orthodox fashion of dividing writers into marxists and nonmarxists which generally accompanied the practices of putting art and political ideology on the same level and attempting to stifle any criticism of events in the Soviet Union.[12] However, some of the formulations in Zhdanov's report already foretold that those who thought of opposing the inducements to orthodoxy would run into difficulties.

Zhdanov pressed the proposition that Soviet literature possessed an avant-garde quality because it was engendered in an avant-garde society. This thesis was false; it put in question the law of the unequal development of art and of society which Marx had earlier advanced. It was in the name of this thesis that the Hungarian Jozsef Revai "demonstrated" in 1950–51 that Lukács was not a marxist aesthetician.

This thesis would have it that not only was Soviet literature automatically better than the classic literature of past centuries, but also that contemporary bourgeois literature was decadent and deprived of all value. Therein lay theoretical oversimplifications which were to lead to dangerous practical consequences. A bulk-

head sealed against any penetration of the art practiced in Western Europe and
the United States, a state of suspicion and scorn for whatever came from beyond
our camp, served only to diminish socialist culture. Furthermore, Zhdanov uttered
his ideas in a tone and way which rendered them decrees. He spoke not only of
what was but also of what *should* be. A theory of art which goes from description
and synthesis to the setting up of norms supported by terms like "must" and "necessary" is skirting the abyss. From this point it is but a short way to the command:
"Here is what is permitted and here is what is forbidden."

However, in 1934 these aspects were not as perilous as they were to become
later. The evolution of socialist realism toward its "institutional" version was gradual. A date which might serve to mark the definite dominance of this "institutional"
version is the year 1936. To be more specific, this point of no return was marked by
the article "A Chaos of Sounds Instead of Music," published in *Pravda* in January
1936. The subject of this fulmination was Shostakovich's opera *Lady Macbeth of
the Mzensk District*.

What strikes us in this article is that, instead of entering into a discussion with
the artist, it simply pronounces an anathema permitting of no appeal. Moreover,
the principles of realism, feasible and discussable in terms of the representational
arts, were, without an offer of justification, carried over into an attack on the expressive characteristics of the musical score. It was official now that socialist realism was the only tolerated artistic current in the Soviet Union. A limited group of
people were granted the privilege of deciding what was socialist realism and what
was good or bad art. This small circle had had conferred upon it the right to represent the aesthetic opinions of the entire nation. It is not astonishing, therefore,
that Zhdanov referred to this article at a conference of Soviet musicologists held
in 1948 under the auspices of the Central Committee of the Party. The year 1948
was the epilogue to what had begun twelve years earlier.

Lenin had mentioned in his writings the possible intervention of the Party in
matters of art, but he never spoke about forbidding experimental art. Lenin had as
much confidence in artists as in the mass of the people. This confidence stemmed
from his belief in the irresistible and persuasive advances of socialism. Lenin wrote
that one could not be independent of society but that the socialist regime would
permit artists to choose freely. In Lenin's time socialist realism was not the only
current, but one among many artistic currents. Lunacharsky defined Lenin's policies
vis-à-vis art in the 1926 article mentioned above, in which he recommended be-

having with great prudence every time it came to a question of deciding the value of a work of art.

In "On the Freedom of Creation in a Socialist Regime" (1918), Lunacharsky gave the impression that the artist would be free as a bird. This view derived from his conviction that artists, aware of society's new needs and deeply involved in the new life, would abandon intimacy ("everything which is secret, interior, personal, untranslatable into any language") for rational clear art marked by personal sentiments but dedicated to the common cause. He knew at the same time, to his great regret, that certain creative artists would find it very difficult to set themselves upon the path of socialist art. His article ended with these words: "Before reaching the socialist paradise, perhaps we shall have to rest for some very bitter time yet in purgatory."

The main documents of the Zhdanov period—the small volume containing Zhdanov's speeches and the resolutions of the Central Committee of the Party concerning literature and art from 1946–48—prove that Lenin's point of view had been abandoned. Ideologically progressive art became synonymous with making propaganda for everything good, while omitting to mention anything else. Even if Zoshchenko's and Akhmatova's writings did deserve to be severely criticized, it should have been necessary all the same to tolerate their existence. The mainstream group of writers—Katayev, Paustovsky, Fadeyev, Ehrenburg, Olesha, Tvardovsky, Inber, etc.—should have been able to continue producing different kinds of creative work. Zhdanov would, however, allow no tolerance. He launched and sanctioned the principle of monopoly around a single official idea.

Muradelli's opera *The Great Friendship* was accused as a pretext to subdue what was called the "formalist coterie." Suddenly one learned that it was forbidden to practice a modern art because it was addressed only to an elite. What were the formal models which became, instead, *de rigueur* for Soviet art? The *mogutchaia kutchka* in music, the *pieriedvizhniky* in painting, Tolstoi and Chekhov in literature. Although it was not maintained that one must comply with the ideological principles underlying the creative works of the nineteenth century, the artistic language of that time was openly imposed, under the pretext that it was the only language which could be understood by the masses. Moreover, those who dared to defend different opinions in art were accused of subversive activity. Zhdanov spoke as a dictator in 1948; he used epithets instead of relying on arguments.

Thus were the principles of socialist realism transformed into their opposite.

The doctrine of truth became a doctrine of Byzantine prostrations before inviolable commandments from the highest authorities. One had the right to see what was good and to dream how that might become better still, but it was expressly forbidden to take notice of what wasn't going well. Thus, literature and art, seeking to avoid whatever could not be praised, lacked truth.

The theory of the diversity of genres, styles, and forms was changed into a theory that served as apologist for a single style. "Epigonism" was openly cultivated. Art was conceived of in an academic and conservative manner. Experiments in new forms were looked upon as diabolical inventions because they were also being carried on by contemporary bourgeois artists, who were damned by definition.

Finally, the theory of the moral influence of art was replaced by the theory of the submission of artistic ideas to the political aims of propaganda and agitation. There was no question of culture but only of the politically extolled social cult.

This doctrine—let us call it Zhdanovism—did not admit of any other aesthetic interpretation. Nor was its activity limited to the field of culture; politics supported it and was thus able to menace recalcitrants not only by barring their road to livelihood and glory but by subjecting them to repressions. Every artist had his supervisor, an institution charged with seeing to it that the artist did not choose any "false steps." There were factional specialists in publishing houses, editorial boards, and agencies to guide the decisions of the creative artist and to point out to him the right road—and the risky spots. An entire hierarchy of aesthetic overseers was put to work. Everybody, from the critics to those representing the final court of appeal, helped to implement the administrative mills. Every theoretician, furthermore, had his supertheoretician and every critic his supercritic.

The Sources of Corruption

I would distinguish two dimensions to the corruption of the theory of socialist realism: one heteronomous; the other autonomous. The first led to the events so many times discussed since the Twentieth Congress of the Communist Party of the Soviet Union. The second has to do with laws immanent in the development of aesthetic theories. These sources were not independent of each other. For Zhdanovian theories to achieve such interiorizing power, both causes had to be active simultaneously.

External sources which directly contributed to the corruption of the Zhdanovian doctrine were:

1. the conception of socialism as built and already achieved and impeccable;
2. the conception of the intensification of the class struggle;
3. the conception of art and literature as phenomena fully subordinate to the same social rules and interpretive procedures as politics.

Zhdanov's idea of socialist realism as already achieved (see his speeches of 1934) implied that there already existed in reality more than a developmental model; there was, in fact, a fully worked out and immutable model for aesthetic representation. This ideally beautiful world in turn justified the call for a kind of Platonic realism in literature and art. Then, alleging the intensification of the class struggle as a pretext, all art "alien to the socialist camp" (as the phrase then went) was calumniated; those carrying on experiments in our own camp were distrusted, and a cleavage was then brought about between Soviet culture and the rest of contemporary culture. This doctrine was no less Platonic than the one preceding it, for it substituted, in place of an enemy who could be recognized, a frightful enemy, entirely invented from head to foot. Finally, the last of these ideas debased art and science to the level of *ancillae politicae* which implied the same discipline vis-à-vis authority, the same duties, the same tactic, the same elasticity in abandoning former positions to occupy new ones, and the same criteria of judgment as in political questions.

What were the immanent causes of corruption? I wrote earlier in this chapter that art theories tend by their natural evolution to gravitate towards dogmatism. However, in the case of socialist realism, this would not have been able to occur so quickly, and in such a way, without the intervention of the external factors. It is also to these external factors that we must attribute the eventual resemblance of this doctrine to that of the Jesuit Counter-Reformation.

I also discern another immanent cause that helped to speed this transformation: the fact that the aesthetic institutions were founded on the implicit priority of the educational function of art. According to the 1934 definition, the educative influence must spring from a work's truth and its beauty *stricto sensu*. However, this theory was formulated in so imprecise a way that it was easy to reverse it. Here is the reasoning on the point as one finds it in Gorki and more precisely in Zhdanov: It is important to educate our public because truth and beauty are its birthright; the artist, however, is not the proper one to determine the ultimate character of this truth and this beauty. That duty falls only to the supervisory group acting on behalf of the people. How could this interpretation have arisen, contrary to the more elementary aesthetic principle, long honored in Russia especially, which

might be formulated thus: "To utter the truth in the most beautiful possible form"?
Here is the principle as it came to be understood: "To educate by means of art in
as communicative a way as possible."

It was not a question of a conscious plot by the enemies of socialist culture; nor
even a plot by high functionaries with limited ideas who did not understand that
the truth of beauty and the beauty of truth always have had something to teach,
and that one could shape the public by such means as well as by means of ugliness
and lies. Here are the real causes of this situation: first, the fear of unveiling the
entire social and political truth, coupled with the assumption that art could influence thoughts, sentiments, and public action in an immediate and lasting way;
second, the fear that honest art, irresistibly borne toward discovery, in subject
matter as well as in form, would remain incomprehensible to the masses; third,
the fear that a handful of thrown pebbles might cause an avalanche.

The first of these causes is entirely external. The difficult conditions in which
socialism was being built provoked continual tension. It was a matter of not dis-
couraging people, of not permitting distrust and doubt, and art was made use of,
among other expedients, to attain this goal. The fear of being criticized with regard
to shortcomings led to the political terror.

As for the second cause, the conflict between the avant-garde tendencies of
artists and the backwardness of their public is a permanent characteristic in history.
However, this split nowhere else attained so *dramatic* a character as it did under
the socialist conditions in the Soviet Union. There the masses were particularly
backward and the artists, finally free to devote themselves unconditionally to the
search for new forms, made rather rash use of their experimental practice.

Lenin was aware of this conflict and he defended the masses; he demanded
that art be modern and comprehensible at the same time. Lunacharsky struggled
with the same problem. Sometimes he tried to resolve the dilemma by giving satisfaction to both parties; at other times he followed in Lenin's tracks. For example,
in his article on Derain (1927), despite his great admiration for the artist, he expressed some reservations with regard to the modernism of his work because he
found it devoid of revolutionary elements and not very "accessible." According
to Lunacharsky, in order to be understood by the masses an artist must make use
of the language of classical forms, the language used by Michelangelo, Tintoretto,
and Rubens. Before him, Gorki had condemned Dostoevsky in the name of the priority of the educative function of art. Zhdanov, at the time of his attacks against
Zoshchenko and Akhmatova, declared that an art which is content to criticize can-

not be pedagogical. He refused to approve the "formalist" group exemplified by Shostakovich because, he said, they committed the sin of false originality. Music of genius is always accessible to everybody at first hearing, he affirmed. The music the "formalists" were writing was degenerate because it was strange to the Soviet people and difficult to understand.

From Lunacharsky to Zhdanov, then, the same arguments recur, and what gave them birth was a genuine social conflict. This conflict was sharply etched in the speeches of Mao Tse-tung at the forum of artists and writers held at Yenan in May 1942. There he asserted that the only criterion to be kept in view is the culture of the workers, peasants, and soldiers, that is, that in interpreting life and truth in artistic language one must, above all, take account of the audience for which it is destined. Mao did distinguish two types of artistic recreation, one very easy and the other more difficult, but he declared that the duty of the Party is, above all, to popularize art and not to elevate it excessively. He thus openly favored *utilitarianism* (according to which the value of a work is to be measured above all in terms of the public response it finds) and resolutely set *political* above *aesthetic* criteria.[13]

The Party and the Artists
The thesis of the priority of the educational function of art is bolstered by the thesis of the directing role of the Party in the field of art; and, reciprocally, the direction of the Party seems that much more indispensable in the field of art to the degree that artists are aware of fulfilling ideological functions. The Party "defends" the masses against any art that does not choose to be communicative, and guides the artists lest they should lose contact with the masses and fail to confront the more important problems, that is, those most useful from a social point of view.[14]

None of these doctrines, all closely interconnected, seem correct to me. I understand Party "direction" with regard to art in an entirely different way. The priority of the pedagogical function strikes me as deadly to any rational aesthetics. If the Party has a legitimate role, it is to be a source of inspiration and partnership, rather than a political organizer. To intervene in matters of art with the authority of a regular tribunal or court of appeals, even with the best intentions in the world, is to harm artistic growth.

The Party leadership has the right and the duty to discuss problems with artists. However, this discussion must have the character of a freely argued polemic conducted among equals. If a work of art seems harmful, let another artist or critic, Party member or not, speak up and justify the criticism. Let the accused have the possibility of defending himself. Let truth be revealed in public discussion. Judged in this way, a work of art submits its worth to proof in the face of society. If, on the contrary, it is the leadership of the Party —composed of eminent persons, but specialists in matters quite different from art — who decide whether X is socialist realist or not, then the situation becomes perilous. It is all too easy to make random judgments and thus create havoc. Even if a connoisseur is found in the group of politicians, everything is not settled. Once a mistake is made, art pays for it in time and expense. Today, it seems to me, the widespread consensus is that a group of Party leaders cannot represent the aesthetic aspirations of an entire people.

If we interpret Party leadership in matters of art as it has been interpreted up till now, we inevitably arrive at the doctrine of the priority of the educational function of the work of art. This is a risky doctrine in terms of aesthetics, because these rigid norms make it possible to excuse all kinds of inadequacies in a work just so long as the work keeps its compact with an ideological point of view. Moreover, even the genuine ideological commitment of the artist may be displaced by a merely tactical agreement with the latest officially proclaimed "Party line." History demonstrates that the least durable and most circumscribed aesthetic systems are those depending on the priority of the pedagogical function.

The educative influence of a work derives from its content values integrated with its structure and aesthetic values *sensu strictu*. Each artist has a personal way of discovering the world, of giving it proportion, form, and color; he judges, stimulates, and obliges us to think and rethink about certain aspects of things, whether it be by recalling them to us or by making us discover them; he charms us by his language and composition. Therein lies the essence of the moral function of art. This function can only come from creative freedom. The artists must be aware of this freedom, must feel it *instinctively* and cling to it. Creative work truly serves the cause of the Party if it represents the truth of life in adequate aesthetic forms —and not if it merely follows Party directives step by step. If socialism is the most humanist regime, it is because it can create the most tangible and favorable conditions for the creation of this art. If the masses are to be educated, they must have not only communicative art but also —and perhaps I should say especially— difficult art.

The theory of socialist realism, in my opinion, does not at all imply that the teaching role takes priority over art's other functions or that Party authorities must have the last word with regard to art criticism. The artist and the public play coequal parts in the great process of evolution and need no mediators. The artist's work is ultimately the expression of that evolution and, insofar as it is so, it educates both artist and public.

Altogether, socialism as it has been so far practiced and experienced is in need of further study. I do not know if I have succeeded in this chapter in the task of extricating the theory of socialist realism from the Zhdanovian cocoon that has enveloped it. Let us hope that Soviet scholars, who are in the best position to know the source materials, will write a history of art capable of proving that the essential elements of this theory have remained unimpaired.

The theory of socialist realism must be an "open" theory. By this I mean that it must be ready to enter into controversy with other modern theories with regard to such problems as have here been set forth; and it must stand comparison with new artistic phenomena. This comparison must rest on the principle of nonaggression, that is, it will not be simply a question of affirming, *per fas et nefas*, that every work of value is socialist realist or that every socialist realist work is an artistic phenomenon of high value.

Postcript 1972

I have no doubt that the foregoing part of this chapter carries the imprint of the time when it was written, which was the Winter of 1956. As the reader will easily gather, I was involved in the polemics over what should be meant by the concept of "socialist realism." Why did I get into the discussions over this question? On the one hand, at that time the very thought of a socialist realism was under vehement attack from some Polish critics (and I should remark that many of their pens had been used prior to October 1956 to subscribe blindly to everything which issued from Party headquarters). On the other hand, their Soviet counterparts were content to defend socialist realism in a merely hagiographical manner.

Given this situation, my own emphasis—and I concede that today's reader may find it less inclusive than he might desire—fell on the theory's *emergence* and, in particular, its relation to an artistic evolution which, more than simply antedating the developed principles of socialist realism, indeed interacted with and encouraged numerous variously convergent reflections on its artistic practice. I focused on a few carefully selected theoretical and critical texts—the most pivotal as I then believed (and still believe). If, for example, I referred to Zhdanov's and Gorki's speeches of 1934 to the exclusion of Bukharin and Radek, it was not so much because the latter names were then on the Index (as they still are), but instead because of the substantial agreement among all the spolesmen. Bukharin's speech far surpassed the other official reports at the Congress in terms of intelligence, breadth of scope, and sensitivity to poetry, yet it embraced the same principles that I analyzed in my 1956 essay.

I have decided to leave the foregoing text substantially unchanged, for I believe the views there set forth are still fundamentally correct, though the stress of the argument is now dated and insufficient. The reader may, moreover, judge to what extent my pioneering study has been subsequently validated. The intervening years have given rise, particularly in the Soviet Union, to many essays concerned with socialist realism. However, few successful attempts have been made to dig into the real course of evolution, and the earlier standpoint has prevailed, corresponding to the trend towards so-called re-Stalinization.

In 1972, the theory of socialist realism still remains a sacred cow. Nothing can be said that is genuinely critical with regard to its vicissitudes and the emergence of Soviet literature, fine arts, and music. Equally resurgent has been the opposite, equally extreme, view: that of antimarxist Western scholars who will not admit to seeing anything sensible or valuable in this artistic current. They treat socialist realism exclusively as an official, vacuous doctrine imposed on writers, painters, and composers by an authoritarian regime. In consequence, whatever they approve of they discuss as more or less a departure from socialist realism. Both of the extreme approaches, I feel, are mistaken. Accordingly, the 1956 essay, in my view, continues to perform a corrective function in the present context.

Nonetheless, there were issues I did not take up at all which now appear to me to be pivotal for the study of the integral and ongoing evolution of this doctrine. In sum, my central thesis above is: the body of theory which came to be called socialist realism arose gradually, as a natural outcome of the literary and artistic experiments which should be dated to as far back as the work of Martin Anderson Nexö or Gorki's *The Mother* (1906). It is perfectly evident, however, that the development of both the artistic tendency and its counterpart in theory (not to mention the interplay between them) has had a primary dependence on the socialist reality.

Now, the crucial point with regard to this fundamental fact is the extent to which the Soviet artists (especially the writers) were able to render equally the positive and negative sides of the system-in-the-making, and, similarly, how much they were able to testify to the strivings to overcome defects or reversions before they might become mortally dangerous to the socialist ideals. It would prove highly fruitful to adopt such a perspective and in its light to rewrite the history of Soviet literature and the other domains of art. The approach has yet to be applied. Those "inside" the Soviet cultural establishment are either apologetic or teleologically blinkered, behaving as though the present moment were a pinnacle to which all the meandering previous roads were destined to lead by a route of distortions or mistakes that were, moreover, inevitable. Those who stand "outside" the Soviet culture seem so totally biased they can scarcely credit that many (and among them major) artists who were involved in the Soviet reality were neither bribed nor terrorized to do so, but grew to be spontaneously and sincerely committed.

Let me then try to sketch some elements of such an approach.

The Bourgeois and the Transitional Novel   The chief point at issue in the presocialist novel, as Lukács has superbly demonstrated in his *Theory of the Novel*, is the problematical individual. (I would only add to this thesis that, in the best of these works that oppose the containing social reality, a possibility does appear for the hero to attempt to transcend the situation in a search for lost, genuine values.)

In the socialist framework, the theme of the problematic individual could not but be continued, but the angle for the study of the conflicts shifted. The individual now came to be regarded in his transition from a rejection of the new era, through a time of Hamlet-like doubts, to an ultimate commitment. Much of the most enduring Soviet literature deals with this theme. Novels which give excellent and typical examples were written by Olesha, Leonov, and Ehrenburg, while the model fiction treating this transition, as nearly all agree, is Alexey Tolstoi's *The Road to Calvary*.

However, the new epoch also called forth another kind of hero, not explored within the bourgeois novels studied by Lukács. This hero was the peasant whose entire world was shaken by the revolution. Pilnyak's novels deal conspicuously with this subject matter; while the paradigmatic work representing the torments suffered in the countryside during these years is Sholokhov's *And Quiet Flows the Don*. This epic novel points, moreover, to a definite outcome to the epoch of shattering transition. Where the heroes of A. Tolstoi not only grew reconciled to the Soviet reality but actually began to participate actively in it, Sholokhov's chief hero, Grigori Melekhov, was defeated — yet the Soviet reality advanced to new achievements.

The conflicts portrayed by these modes of fiction — involving intellectuals or peasants who resisted the new social system — were revelatory of considerable historical truth. Meanwhile, the peasant authors adopted, for the most part, the stance of fellow travellers, seeking to strike an inward truce with a reality that was not entirely comprehensible or acceptable to them. Such tales, then, have a thematic gravity that is not identical with the core themes of socialist realism. Examples are abundant: Trenyov's *Lyubov Yarovaya*, Fadeyev's *The Nineteen*, Ivanov's *The Armored Train*, Furmanov's *Chapaev*, Makarenko's *Pedagogical Poem*, Ostrovsky's *How the Steel Was Tempered*, or the more symbolic and very paradigmatic drama by Vishnevsky, *The Optimistic Tragedy*. In such works we do see the main trend of the socialist-organized artistic vision; however, the characteristic that I have mentioned as the crucial point for writers functioning in a socialist reality is, to a large extent, lacking or unfocused, and that is an awareness responsive to the negative aspects of the new epoch.

Works in the socialist mainstream for the most part treated the negative side as something wholly exterior, pertaining only to the prior circumstances against which socialist men and women had to act. Negativity was solely attributable to the obstinacy of outlived social forces, which might continue to intervene or to present obstacles, but which would only temporarily hold up the advance of the revolutionary program.[15]

"Insiders" and the Negative Side of Reality: Babel and Mayakosky Hence, we must further scan the literature of the revolution to define instances where writers who were completely identified with the socialist purpose and active in it — let me call them "insiders" — were yet sensitively open and alert to the defects and dangers which the postrevolutionary era carried within its own forces. Now, if we do structure the pattern of a developing Soviet literature as I have here outlined, it seems to me that two great authors will deserve special attention for fulfilling this function. They are Vladimir Mayakovsky and Isaac Babel: Babel for his collection of stories *Red Cavalry*; and Mayakovsky particularly for his satirical play *The Bathhouse*.

Red Cavalry seems to be one of the most adequate and deeply felt portrayals of the experience of the revolution. The savagery and ruthlessness it vividly portrays are justified not only with respect to civil-war norms but also and especially in terms of a response to a past of horrors: the recollected centuries of oppression, hunger, poverty, and ignorance imposed on the masses. The author encourages us to try to consider even the most nightmarish, inhuman bloodshed from the standpoint of the just passions of exploited people. However, Babel the revolutionary enthusiast is also Babel the penetrating ironist: the swift revengers of past mischief are inarticulate, the movement forward is anarchical movement, and the elemental drama of redemption resounds like a warning bell. We are very far here from the mystique that permeated Blok's *The Twelve*, which portrayed "the red terrorists" as the apostles of a new Eden. Babel espouses the ideals and ideas of socialism with all his being; there is no doubt of that. Nonetheless, he scrutinizes the messengers of his hope with no trace of dreamy self-deception or religiosity. Seeing the still backward masses with his clear vision, Babel realizes that there can be no guarantee that socialism will ever become fully embodied.

The completed image that Babel gives us of the revolutionary carnage is reminiscent of the articles published by Gorki during 1917–18 in *Novaya Zizhn*. Gorki was then at odds with Lenin; he argued with foreboding that the tide of anarchy could only incite the Bolsheviks to ever more dictatorial steps. In other words, Babel's vision, like the political editorials of Gorki—speaking from the inside of socialism and in the name of its aims and ideals—presents a warning for the fate of socialism, which has as its reference the political immaturity of the masses. It seeks to forefend the iron dictatorial rule of a tight circle of professional revolutionaries.

Red Cavalry, of course, does not harangue: "Look here, to destroy is much simpler than to build." This is a trivial insight and, beyond any doubt, not appropriate to times of revolutionary upheaval. No, another much more fundamental and serious issue is paramount here: the destroying grows thoughtless and becomes perilous even to the avengers when the masses, who alone can sustain it, lack a constructive self-awareness. Insofar as the masses do lack this quality, the stopgap of a bureaucratic authoritarian regime becomes inevitable. Lenin most ruefully experienced this realization in the last years of his life.

Mayakovsky's play offers a case which is complementary to that which Babel implicitly demonstrated. Mayakovsky attacks overtly the genus of the Soviet bureaucrat and the cynical or hypocritical slogans and phrases that hide the vilest careerism, incompetence, and isolation from the masses. *The Bathhouse* might be called the first (albeit satirically exaggerated) portrayal of the coming Stalinist regime which would be built on double-talk and ruled by degenerated new-style managers for whom "socialist ideology" had become wholly dissolved within a banal conformity. Lenin, who was not favorably disposed to Mayakovsky's futurism due to his own traditional tastes in art, nevertheless praised the sardonic Mayakovsky poem "In Re Conferences," critical of functionaries who confused and complicated the discussion of serious matters by endless futile chatter. *The Bathhouse* was another blast against the worm within the socialist democracy, the worm of indigenous pedigree.

On the one hand, it might be charged that Mayakovsky's sensitiveness to these elements of Soviet life, incurably anchored in his individualism, never became entirely coordinated with the prevailing gregarious and shibboleth-edged way of life. In this regard, we may recall Lunacharsky's article written following the poet's suicide. In this obituary, Lunacharsky spoke of the two "souls" inside Mayakovsky: one, that of a subtle lyrical writer striving for intimacy; the other, that of a rhetorical collectivist ready to enroll his muse in the proletarian cause. It was as though the poet could never play these two strings in unison, concluded Lunacharsky; too great a distance separated them and the gap was both unbridgeable and tragic.

On the other hand, it might be advanced that the obstacles and pitfalls which faced the victorious Soviet dictatorship and which were daily becoming more evident were especially acutely registered by the seismograph of Mayakovsky's individualism. ("Individualism" is simply a clumsy term we use here to point to this poet's artistic perceptiveness, his open-mindedness and independence of judgment.) As an ardent, tenacious socialist, the "insider" Mayakovsky made an heroic effort to retain access to the reality of the collectivist lodestone.

"Outsiders" and Antiutopias: Zamyatin Having considered Babel and Mayakovsky, I should also think about another work which represents, to some extent, the area I am exploring: Yevgeniy Zamyatin's novel *We*. Zamyatin's case is distinct: he was neither a proponent nor a friend, but, rather, an opponent of socialism. Zamyatin bears witness only to the negative side of the new reality. His skeptical "outsider" stance forces his exclusion from the history of socialist realism. Nonetheless, the cogency of his perceptions requires that we cope with his novel — the more so since, beginning in the thirties, it became impossible for "insider" works on the order of *Red Cavalry* or *The Bathhouse* to appear.

While mentioning chronology, I should stress that all three works came out of the first decade after 1917, when Soviet culture flourished conspicuously and drew the eager interest of the avant-garde of art the world over. Another point to note is that *We* was the earliest of the three works (1923), which suggests that its doubting Thomas author was exceptionally keen in spying the bacilli of what would become a ravaging pathology only later. Rewards only for those who follow rules, glorification of "beneficial" state policy with its pervasive control mechanisms to protect the citizen from the impious thought or deed, a horrid Jacobin passion for the flawless Ordered Society: from these trends was produced the push — fortunately, never carried to the end — towards transforming the socialist society into an anthill. These possibilities were evident even at the start, yet only an estranged and attentive intelligence could then assemble the many hints into the cautionary shape of a relevant antiutopia.

However, having said this it has to be added that *We* is even more pertinent to the future of Europe as a civilization than it is to any given Soviet phenomena. The cutting edge of the Zamyatin novel, as of Orwell's later *1984*, is oriented to the contradiction between the technical rationalization of society and human instincts. Zamyatin, depicting the prejudices of Reason, did not set any national boundaries to the scope of his implications. His route led through a landscape of collectivist gigantism and crushed personal rights in Soviet Russia, but his ultimate nemesis was the homogeneity and anomie of the century. Poland had a like-minded author in Stanislaw Ignacy Witkiewicz; England, in Adlous Huxley, who warned of a "brave new world" of Calibans. Zamyatin spent many years in Western Europe and he had a distinct notion of the suprarational civilization that rose from the carnage of World War I. What he did *not* grasp were certain facts evident to Lenin; in par-ticular, that the socialist-tending Soviet people could not survive against their bour-geois foes without a strong dose of "Americanization." Stranger to the new social system that Zamyatin was, he did not grant to the communist constructive zest its deserved value, and he erroneously identified "revolutionary puritanism" with the terrorist norm itself.

He also proved largely mistaken with regard to the way Soviet Russia would actually turn out to be. Modern equipment and technological knowledge certainly could not eliminate the irrationality of an administration that was to prove wasteful and inefficient. The Stalinist nation-state may indeed remind us of one or another of the twentieth-century antiutopias — but the resemblance to the place described by Zamyatin, where D-503 constructed a vehicle for the cosmos (a prophecy equally applicable to the United States) or to the *1984* of Orwell is only partial. Zamyatin seems to have been guided by the aim of parodying the *proletkult* ideas of Bogdanov and the fantasies of the *Kuznitsa* group. By contrast Orwell directly oriented himself to social reality, which, perhaps not surprisingly, turned out to be more "imaginatively" ghastly than the creations of artistic inventiveness.

Socialist Realism in the 1930s and 1940s I have already explained, I hope satisfactorily, why I make a dividing line at the middle of the 1930s. I should stress that I am not at all of the view that no good Soviet art has been produced since that time. On the contrary, much good art has been produced and it has not been confined only to the sphere of the nonobjective arts, where Soviet talents have been able to express themselves more freely and expansively. In the context of representational art, it is enough to mention the later writings of Sholokhov, and especially the masterpieces of literature, theater, and film that bear witness to the Soviet heroism during the Second World War. No one, except the prejudiced, can deny the bravery of the Soviet people, who without any question saved the whole of Eastern Europe from the subjugation and partial extermination envisioned by the Nazis. Another fact that must be emphasized in this period is the encouragement given by the Soviet power to literature and the other arts among a number of recently illiterate, or nearly illiterate nationalities within the borders of the Soviet Union, peoples which would not otherwise have stood on their cultural feet.

Nevertheless, in the 1930s a changed model of the socialist system emerged and gathered strength. On the whole, artistic production lost great impetus, zest, and unrecapturable values. Criticisms of the emergent model were not possible, even though it was evident that the socialist system had begun to function against its own ideological premises. In place of rendering the anxieties and tensions associated with the gigantic historical confrontation, in place of posing penetrating questions to the entire world and to the communists themselves, Soviet artists now merely reproduced ready-made formulas. The revolutionary enthusiasm of the 1920s had vanished, the charisma of the politics and art also receded, the awareness of an only-too-evident backwardness was officially abandoned, and the naive but glorious faith (closely related to an ascetic, collectivist-minded egalitarian communism) that the world could be made over in a short time was replaced by a slogan about the enemy within. Three propensities of thought (the utopian vision of a disalienated world in the process of coming into being, the spontaneously revolutionary spirit, and the self-disciplined attitude), which were a mutually integrated and a substantial aspect of the Soviet scene from 1917 until the early 1930s, and which we may be positive bulk large in the genuine marxist world view, disappeared. This is the reason for the great disproportion between the first and the second stages in Soviet literature and art. There are plenty of masterpieces in the former; since the middle of the 1930s there have been, alas, only a few.

Russia in the late thirties and early forties offered both an abundant basis and a necessity to treat in fiction the proliferating negative aspect of the emergent socialist potential. However, due to the historical conjuncture, there was little likelihood that a socialist-minded Zamyatin would appear. If nothing else, a nationwide network of informers and security police stood in the way. Then, too, the possible

"insider" satirist or muckraker would surely have conceded priority to the bitter,
heroic struggle with Nazi Germany. A Communist had no choice but to defend
with all of his power the existing Soviet state even with its waywardness and atroci-
ties. The "insiders" elsewhere too—the radical leftists of the world—judged that
they had no right not to protect the aberrant fledgling system, which was being so
relentlessly assaulted. To defend the "besieged fortress" unconditionally was,
seemingly, a way to encourage revolution at home; besides, the foes of socialism
cooked up so many unjust accusations that it was often hard to tell at what point
one should start to lend serious consideration to their possible justness. Anyway,
if one did begin to attempt such finer discriminations would not bourgeois propaganda simply sweep the field, since it always seized on the tiniest Bolshevik mistakes to ridicule the whole idea of Communism? Given the circumstances, the many
inducements to remain silent could not have been surmounted by the "insiders."

Ex-Communists and the Negative Side of Reality: Koestler As the ruthless
censorial activity under the guise of constitutional law continued, the only literature
to tell the negative part of the truth about the Soviet Union was brought out by
ex-communists. Disappointed, frustrated, and haunted by the cruelties of the Great
Purge, these persons now proved to be as inimical to the Soviet Union as previously
they had been friendly. What they reported could not really stand as a truthful
representation of the socialist organization of society, since they offered but a
partial—if crucial—truth, seen through the filter of prison and labor-camp experiences. In this regard, I think of Arthur Koestler's *Darkness at Noon* or the *Memoirs* which document the experience of Alexander Weissberg-Cybulski.

Koestler deserves closer attention. *Darkness at Noon* makes a suitable choice
of subject matter; its hero, Rubashov, and the situation in which he becomes involved embody the fundamental cancerous growth upon the Soviet system. He
is a lifelong communist, an active participant in the struggle, who is imprisoned
by the security police although they are fully aware of his innocence of the imputed
crimes.

Now, unquestionably among the chief characteristic features of the degenera-
tion of the regime were the 1936–37 purges and the subsequent "show trials."
Yet even though his subject matter bears extraordinary promise, Koestler handles
it in a way that is inadequate. Rubashov is presented as one of many necessary
victims steamrollered by the Great Totalitarian Machine. At first glance, the latter
might seem like the incarnation of the Hegelian "cunning of history," which does

not respect the intentions of individuals since only the suprapersonal processes can decide the right or wrong of human deeds. However, if we study the ideological structure of *Darkness at Noon* more closely, we shall see that Rubashov succumbs to the treacherous reasoning of his interrogators, Ivanov and Gletkin, even though he refuses to give credulity to the two intertwined and manifestly false principles that then dominated the official creed of society.

The first of these principles held that communist authorities were certain not to commit any errors owing to the institution that they represented. What this, in fact, meant, was that the tactics and strategies of the day had supplanted the priority of genuinely ideological values. The second principle held that if one's views coincided with those of the enemies of the socialist system on any point whatever, even when those enemies told the truth, then one had automatically betrayed socialism. What this really accomplished was the creation of an atmosphere conducive to the concoction of the fattest lies at Party headquarters, so long as they could be judged advantageous to communism.

Now, Rubashov believed in neither principle, although to the end of his trial he remained committed to communism. Why then did he surrender? He did so because, in place of the two points of propaganda just mentioned, he has agreed to substitute and bow to two points that were, in fact, their philosophical counterparts: first, that the Party is the very embodiment of universal reason, the actual instrument propelling History; second, that History is never the agent of errors, and that the Party can, therefore, never be mistaken. Since Rubashov had already accepted these propositions, he was *internally defeated* from the outset. I do not wish to underrate his remarks on the exhaustion of the old guard (to which he belongs), nor the harsh interrogative methods of Gletkin, nor Rubashov's past (his twisted logic and ethics which—as Koestler stresses—trap him into a full understanding of his oppressors' stance). However, what we see from Rubashov's past record is that his approach to marxist ideology—his critical mind, sense of fallibility, perceptiveness, and curiosity notwithstanding—has been based on blind discipline. His self-defeat thus rests on a genuine meeting of minds with his first Public Investigator (and old comrade), Ivanov. There is nothing out-of-the-way in Rubashov's recurrent thought that he could be in Ivanov's place, and Ivanov in his. Consequently, we are not surprised that he accepts Gletkin's defense of the bastion of revolution at whatever cost, even when the cost is the murder of allies who have developed just a few doubts.

Rubashov's philosophy of history, like that of Ivanov, sees but a single dilemma: the opposition between Christian ethics, which speak of the sanctity of the individual, and collectivist reason, which regards the individual as the remainder of "one million divided by one million" and, hence, escapes from moral scruples and the "metaphysical brothel" of the emotions. The marxism of Rubashov is, thus, entirely fatalistic, a hyperrational experiment for rescuing mankind by enslaving it first.[16] It is in this light that we must understand Rubashov's insistence that he must "own up" to a self-abasing confession of nonexistent crimes before the tribunal, or his struggle with Gletkin (whom he calls a Neanderthal man), which is but a desperate expedient for convincing himself that the juggernaut of history has to bear down on any believer deviating from the Party line of the day.

Koestler seems to take up the stance of the "insider," since he views the events incessantly through the pince-nez of Rubashov, but, in fact, his *porte-parole* is the ex-White Guard officer, the prisoner from cell number 402 who explains that honor lies in decency rather than usefulness. It is from this figure's perspective that we observe the Stalinist massacre. "The red wolves devour one another": this might be the motto of *Darkness at Noon*, and it means that history, once it is judged by socialist principles, has to be approached with Machiavellian methods, with human beings regarded as but expendable sacrifices in the drive towards the great goal. Koestler, of course, questions that goal; and Rubashov perishes with the anguished question of the sense of his death. Nothing remains for the reader at the end but to don a sarcastic smile for the comprehensible but futile self-sacrifice of the chief hero.

Now, it might be argued that my critique is blunted, since Koestler desired precisely to show why the prominent Bolsheviks bent the knee during the purge trials of 1936–37. I do not deny that occurrences such as the capitulation by the fictitious Rubashov did, in fact, happen; and Koestler quite likely achieved his artistic intention. My criticism is in this sense external. *Darkness at Noon* is the dramatic story not so much of a man punished for what he neglected to do (as Rubashov at one point characterizes himself) as that of one who is a self-aware scapegoat. The tragic rendering of the same subject matter (and only this, I think, would prove truly adequate) would be to incorporate a point-by-point refutation of the strictly deterministic and pragmatic marxism of Ivanov and Gletkin. To defend and preserve the bastion of revolution is the communist's duty, but the question of means *becomes* in political praxis the question of ends.

How could the palpably tragic background to Koestler's novel have been realized in it as an authentic parahistorical drama? This could have been done by presenting Rubashov as an insurgent *ideologue*—as one who confessed his oppositional approach, and regretted his previous inactivity—all this as a problem relating to further adhesion to communist ideas. Rubashov need not have been persuaded to confess to crimes; he could have waged irrepressible conflict. The tactics of the moment would collide with the basic foundations of the socialist doctrine.

Perhaps it seems that I am asking a presentation of the time-honored conflict of *ought* and *is*, of *ethics* and *politics*. Yet just this conflict should be superseded in socialist theory and practice. Socialism properly offers no a priori claims of where and how it will emerge and unfold. Only in concrete human praxis is it called forth and defined. From the telling experiences of the existing socialist-based systems we now know the full brunt and truth of the ideas that Lenin, Gramsci, and Lukács set out theoretically much earlier. We realize today that in political life since the thirties we have had to struggle through a tragic rift between the purely pragmatic (instrumental) premises and the profoundly ideological premises of socialism. In the political and theoretical acts of Rosa Luxemburg and Karl Liebknecht we see the proof that *ought* and *is* may make an integral whole.

What we have, in fact, is a clash of two "layers" of reality; for Marxism affirms that politics must be at the same time ethics, and that, deprived of its "oughts," socialist praxis will produce a truncated and distorted democracy governed not by the genuine delegates of the masses but by bureaucrats.

In short, Koestler's novel was couched in a pessimistic attitude, which acceded to the inevitable triumph of the Calibans. We will do well to compare it with a latter book, Arthur London's *The Confession*. It is not the documentary aura that gives to London's work its superiority, for Koestler could easily defend his story line by referring to numerous documents.[17] London obtains the edge by the different pattern he lends events. His protagonist surrenders to the accusations against him only as a form of rite. He still recognizes, as his accusers recognize, that it is a staged phony spectacle from start to finish. The physically coercive torture leads the tale to the plane of ideology, and marxist humanism, while besmirched here, is not entirely trodden into the obscurant mud. Indeed, the very fact of the publication of *The Confession* testified that its marxist ideas are vigorous, and that no loudly trumpeted catch phrases amplified by the holders of official power ("with us or against us") can shut the mouths of committed Communists. However, strictly speaking, London should not be placed among the *litterati;* he is writing as an ex-politician.

Critical Realism: Solzhenitsyn Where shall I find a more definitive instance
of the artistic testimony I seek? My immediate choice could be Alexander Solzhenitsyn, and in particular, the novels *The First Circle* and *Cancer Ward.*[18] No
one, up to the present, has matched his skill in capturing the panorama of the Stalinist period. What many studies have sketched, what Orwell's remarkable parable
Animal Farm presented concisely, is here represented in full circumstantiality. Solzhenitsyn's world, where the "more even" crew have staked out their strongholds,
and where fear, apathy, and conformity are enforced by squads of paid and volun-
teer informers, is not without lighter moments. This is true not only among the
zeks — political prisioners — who have for all intents passed over the threshold of
further risks, but also in the ordinary walks of life where suspicion still reigns. It
is, in fact, Solzhenitsyn's method to deploy those of his figures who are endowed
with a sense of human decency and dignity rather equally between the labor camp
and the workaday world.

Yet it must be added that the novels of Solzhenitsyn are not couched in the socialist world view, whatever their descriptive[19] and analytical merits. They bring
out the horrid truth that was concealed for so many years (and, as of this writing,
is still covered up). Still, it is only a partial truth that they reveal.

Solzhenitsyn does not lay stress on the positive achievements of the Revolution.
He does not make much of what caused (and still causes) many thousands of sincere Soviet citizens to give their energies to communist ideas and goals. For example, Levka Rubin (in *The First Circle*), a man firmly committed to the marxist doctrine,
is provided no moment in which to explore his motives. His conviction can, thus,
have the appearance of complete irrationality, of springing from only his personal
and noble commitment. In *Cancer Ward*, the author's spokesmen, Kostoglotov and
Shubanov, choose the ethical type of socialism that makes a retreat to the ideas
popular in the era of the Second International.

Thus, I cannot agree with Lukács (though I subscribe to most of his superb
analysis) when he concludes that the practice of socialist realism is revived in Solzhenitsyn's works. I want, rather, to distinguish between a critical realism within
the framework of socialism (Solzhenitsyn surely is the paragon of this tendency),
and an integral socialist realism, which still awaits a latter-day revival that will

equal the examples, presented earlier, of Babel and Mayakovsky. From the late thirties to today there gapes an abyss in Soviet literature which separates the artistic image from reality.

Accordingly, I cannot make a smooth amalgam of Solzhenitsyn and even the best instances of studiously optimistic fiction. There are, of course, contradictions between the two extremes which prevent us from doing so. However, even more important is the fact that it is impossible simply to "add" the two "halves" of the truth to one another. They won't total up to a whole. The optimists push heedlessly for the official version of reality, while Solzhenitsyn is quite justly obsessed by the spectre of Stalinism, which, alas, has still not vanished. What is lacking is a *dialectical* comprehension of the very core of the extremes.

Conclusions and Prospects A time has to come when the root questions illuminating the vicissitudes of Soviet-style communism will be asked. The pros and cons will then be explored in their wholeness. A deft understanding will then illuminate this long-sustained and many-faceted drama; and characters and situations will be brought into view which people will admit are worthy of the pen of a Dante.

Who will be the artist capable of meeting the challenge of this subject matter? It seems to me certain that he will possess either intuitive insight into or developed awareness of the modes of alienation evinced in socialism. The basic questions that await the socialist realist are not easy ones of the order of "What is wrong?" or even "What is its cause?" (Orwell's *Animal Farm* gave replies which have not yet been surpassed at this level of perplexity.) Rather, the core of the questions posed till now is to be found in the living, indivisible flesh of the socialist experiments with their successes and defeats. It is impossible to disregard all that has been achieved since 1917. That would be as paranoid as to close one's eyes to the gradual decay of the sociopolitical patterns which, however vital and necessary at one time, have become since the late thirties a rust eating into socialism and severely obscuring its attractiveness.

This observed, it still must be remembered that Russia since 1917 has been the fatherland of socialist revolution, a watershed in the history of mankind. This is a reality that I find absolutely relevant not only to communist artists and intellectuals, but also to all the sincere leftists of the world. That the revolution resulted in bread, clothing, telephones, refrigerators, etc.—a much higher standard of living, obtained in a relatively short space of time, for millions of people—this is disregarded by stubborn opponents, who maintain that all this would have been

achieved even if there had been no Bolshevik takeover (an argument which has
always seemed to me sheer speculation). However, beyond those gains, there has
been widespread education, democratization of culture, and, above all, awareness
that the ordinary people are the legitimate heirs of history.

In light of the Stalinist regime it may seem cruelly jocular to emphasize the latter
issue. It nevertheless has to be raised, for, despite all the distortion, the Soviet system does imbue its people with the sense that full equality is their birthright. In
other lands there is tacit acceptance of inequality based on property, power, etc.
The socialist system is permanently committed to instilling the opposite values;
and the result is that millions of citizens have become highly sensitive to the distinction between "even" and "more even." Also, it cannot be overlooked that up
to the present the existence of the Soviet Union has incited and supported all the
revolutionary movements of the world, and has exerted a necessary pressure on
the capitalist empires to evolve towards milder internal and external policies. Last,
but not least, it should be recalled that the Soviet twenties remain, in the domain
of the history of the arts, a highly intense, vigorous, and stimulating period. The
direct impact of the art of this period on *l'art engagé* elsewhere has not yet entirely
faded. All these unquestionable achievements were, to be sure, interwoven with
some negative aspects and merged into a complex whole. That is why no technique
of mere accounting (debit and credit) can be conclusive here. The dialectics of socialism have to be grasped to the very roots. Only in this way can the accumulated
alienations and also the weed-shoots of newer alienations be shown.

I have spoken of the alienations peculiar to the socialist regime. In this matter
I may refer to Marx, for whom it was clear that no concentrated political power
could in itself embody the socialist ideal, regardless of its legal and institutional
paraphernalia. That ideal is to be accomplished by man's freedom among other
free individuals through a collective effort. Marxism has always been considered
by its best philosophers to be the apt heir to the long humanist tradition. This
means that, far from treating the individual as a manure to be spread according
to law on socialist institutions to make them strong, the highest aim of marxism
has been to enable fulfillment of the individual potential; if it cannot do this it has
failed.

What should be the nature of individual activity in relation to alienation? Optimally, this activity will call into effect a world view oriented towards an ideal; that
is, an attitude which, when absent (or given only rhetorical place, or treated as a
utopian dream), leaves a void, a gap not to be adequately (i.e., humanely) filled

by any legal or institutional forms or guarantees. In this situation, the vocation
of the artist (as of any intellectual) who is committed to Communism must be to
reinstate the world view, that is, to make of it a bread-and-butter sort of awareness and issue, and to impose the problem of this view on the politicians who are
inclined to relinquish it. [20]

Some will doubt that the communist artist could hope to project such a vision,
since he is embroiled with an everlasting censorship. How can he expect to be permitted to act in these circumstances so as to embody this world view in a telling
fashion? The splendidly courageous example of Solzhenitsyn has shown there is,
in fact, space in which it can be done, and socialist realism certainly has opportunities elsewhere in the world. I have focused on the Soviet Union because it is
a very instructive case, and, moreover, none but a Soviet artist could expect to
portray the most *ample* truth of the perplexed fate of socialism in state power. All
the same, socialist artists have appeared worldwide. I could have also discussed
Brecht, O'Casey, Aragon, Neruda, or Fuentes. Moreover, in the so-called Third
World, the issue of socialist realism is not only a present-day problem but probably
one for the coming extended period as well. Indeed, if in history *ex Oriente lux*,
yet in literature it seems difficult to guess from just where might emerge the first
dialectical try at the socialist-oriented synthesis I have described.

It occurs to me, as a final point, that some may reproach me for an emphasis
on literature only. I will plead that in the literary field the problems of socialist
realism have risen to a culmination, and they highlight most poignantly all of the
avenues and byways that I have tried to delineate, however clumsily and briefly,
in this postscript.

Notes

1. See N. Pevsner, *Academies of Art, Past and Present* (Cambridge, England, 1940).
2. Stanislaw Ossowski has discussed this phenomenon in his *Socjologia sztuki* [Sociology of art] (Warsaw, 1936), p. 3 .
3. This idea possesses multiple meanings. Its varied history and its applications to various areas of art demand a special study. See my article "Is It a Question of Facts or Words?" *Studia Filozoficzne*, no. 4/7, 1958, as well as the preceding chapter.
4. S. Ossowski, *U podstaw estetyki* [The foundations of aesthetics] (Warsaw, 1949), p. 114.
5. See R. Ingarden, *Szkice z filozofii literatury* [Essays on the philosophy of literature] (Lodz, 1947), pp. 95–117.
6. The questions of collectivity and employment are also found in nonsocialist literature. However, there the problems have no cardinal meaning for the hero and his attitude. They really begin to count only in a socialist regime; then, the position that one takes vis-à-vis these problems becomes the social and moral criterion by which every individual is judged.
7. See J. S. Smirnov, *Iz istorii stroitielstva sotsialisticheskoi kultury piervyi pieriod sovietskoi vlasti* [On the beginnings of socialist culture in the first stages of Soviet power] (Moscow, 1952); P. I. Liebiediev, *Sovietskoie iskusstvo v pieriod innostronnoi voiennoi intierventsii i grajdanskoi voiny* [Soviet art in the period of the intervention and Civil War] (Moscow, 1949).
8. See A. V. Lunacharsky, *Statii ob iskusstvie* [Essays on art] (Moscow-Leningrad, 1941).
9. M. Gorki, *On Literature* (Warsaw, 1951), pp. 26, 39, 54.
10. A. A. Zhdanov, *Speech on Literature and Art* (Warsaw, 1954), pp. 8, 9. The Gorki and Zhdanov speeches of 1934 may both be found in English in H. G. Scott, ed., *Problems of Soviet Literature* (New York, n.d.).
11. That is to say, show man as he is — Euripides — or as he should be — Sophocles — according to Aristotle's definitions in his *Poetics*.
12. See Stalin's early letters to Bill-Belotserkovsky (February 2, 1929), and to Bezymensky and Gorki (1930).
13. T.-t. Mao, *Duties of the Artist and Writer* (Warsaw, 1956), pp. 28, 32, 35, 42. For an English version see *Mao Tse-tung on Art and Literature* (Peking, 1960).
14. The pretension of politicians to advise and guide artists dates from very far back. Diogenes Laertius tells us in his *Liber de vita et moribus philosophorum* that Solon had already reproached the first Greek tragic author, Thespis, for distorting the historical truth and, therefore, harming society. Plato banned poets from his ideal "republic" in the name of a sovereign ideal because they were capable of distracting citizens from serious matters, inviting them to superficial sensual pleasures. The Church fathers defended artists against the temptation of Satan by applying ecclesiatical and lay powers.
15. It should be noted that the majority of such works treat the theme of the 1905 Revolution, the October Revolution, or the Civil War. Therefore, the stark contrast of the sympathetic and hostile forces was a justifiable artistic strategy. It would be difficult to deny to Eisenstein's *Potemkin* or Pudovkin's *Storm over Asia* the rank of masterpiece. This disposition of fictional forces remained for some time typical in Soviet representational art.
16. See R. Conquest, *The Great Terror: Stalin's Purge of the Thirties* (New York,

1973), the chapter titled "The Problem of Confession." We learn from this erudite and documentary work that a distinction has to be drawn between a confession extracted by unbearable physical torture (he who confesses does not recant because he holds the irrational belief that this tactic may save his life), and a confession of uncommitted crimes which is, nonetheless, made in good faith. If, as we are told, Koestler's novel primarily centers on the Rakovsky and Bukharin cases, the relevance of this distinction is increased. Their seemingly incredible behavior in the dock can only be explained by an obstinate and blind party-mindedness, and by their belief in the mechanistically inevitable processes of history. This is clearly shown in a purported comment of I. Smirnov, an accused "accomplice" of Zinoviev and Kamenev who came to trial in August 1936. Smirnov betrayed a confusion over the matters under examination, and when it came to the execution of himself and those convicted with him, an event that stunned many others, he calmly stated (it is reported): "We deserve this for our unworthy attitude at the trial" (Great Terror, p. 170). Rubashov too "deserves" his death; this is why he is not a genuine opponent of Gletkin.

17. Koestler could, for example, point to the attitudes expressed by Karl Radek, one of the most brilliant of the original Bolsheviks (and a purge-trial victim), in his speech to the 1934 Writers Congress. Unity of purpose called for "subordination of all individual considerations," Radek argued. "When a man thinks that he is only upholding some individual shade of opinion against the Party, a political test will always show that he is upholding interests alien to the proletariat." Radek spoke of writers' work using soldiers' imagery, invoking a

discipline which, so he confessed in the same speech, he had himself learned to accept.

18. I pass over Boris Pasternak's *Dr. Zhivago* owing to that artist's particular approach. I agree with the critics who find nothing antisocialistic in the novel, and who ascribe the ban on it to a post-Stalinist bureaucracy which wanted to see the Revolution only pompously celebrated. Even so, at bottom Pasternak's idea was to see the individual at cross-purposes with history. His novel suggests that nothing else matters save the the individual human condition independently arrived at. Times of social upheaval and breakthrough are hard on this sole self-determination, suggests Pasternak. His work—and I leave apart its artistic merits—cannot be seriously discussed in the framework of socialist realism and its fellow travellers.

19. Many fastidious critics look on Solzhenitsyn's style as a museum-piece dating from the nineteenth century. It is, nonetheless, a deliberate choice, serving to draw together the realities which even the newsreel and television have glimpsed in a selected and arranged context that tends to hide the obsolete and negative side of life. The artistic method of Solzhenitsyn will for this reason be praised in the future by the scholars and readers who, thanks to him, will be able to visualize the mundane facts of the Stalinist epoch: the style of dress, living spaces, habits, etc.

20. I presume that Roger Garaudy had this tenet in mind when he writes (in his *Marxism in the Twentieth Century* [New York, 1970], ch. 5) about artistic creation in terms of "myth." Georg Lukács also discussed this problem. In fact, it recurs throughout his intellectual biography; but, perhaps paradoxically, it comes forward most strongly

in his philosophy rather than in his aesthetics
and literary criticism. In his *Theory of the
Novel* (Berlin, 1920) Lukács explicitly deals
with the problem of "ought" and "is" in its
artistic dimension, but this trend of interpretation vanishes from his later texts on
the arts. (See, on this point, the analysis
by I. Mészáros in G. H. R. Parkinson, ed.,
Georg Lukács [New York, 1970], pp. 34–
85.)

Part III

Genesis and Functioning
of Artistic Values

Art and Society

It is banal and can even be misleading to say that the problem of "art and society" is a basic one for marxist aesthetics. The phrase gives no clue to the traits that demarcate the marxist standpoint from other positions with which it may be confused and, consequently, marxist aesthetic thought has often and erroneously been regarded, at a superficial estimate, as a *sociology* of art, on the whole or primarily (if with distinctive tenets).

The nonmarxist discussions on the matter — which the reader may know are few and rarely well informed or considered — tend to lump the marxist standpoint together with a sociologism emphasizing the economic and political influences on artistic creation and its productions.[1] Undoubtedly, a polemicist can easily adduce evidence which seems to justify the saddling of marxist aesthetic thought with this description. Those who most willingly accept the label, however, must be unaware that nothing was more alien to the structure of inquiry as developed by Marx than a strictly sociological conclusion. To be sure, the methodology of Marx incorporates the tenet of a dependency of art on its material setting and on class conflict. What is ignored by commentators who argue, for instance, from the indubitable sociologism of Plekhanov, seeing it as generally representative of the marxist approach, is that other, well articulated versions of the marxist standpoint exist which have not been prone to simplification and reductivism.[2]

We would expect marxists to provide accounts of their own aesthetic heritage that are more complex and penetrating, but this is not entirely the case. One admirable exception is Mikhail Lifshitz' *The Philosophy of Art of Karl Marx*, which in the 1930s presented the philosophical dimension with much cogency and clarity. Also, the philosophical underpinnings of Georg Lukács' numerous theoretical inquiries into literature have often been cited.

Yet even this latter, seemingly unequivocal case is questioned by the Italian marxist Galvano della Volpe and his followers, who contend that Lukács' philosophical school must be considered a special mode of sociogeneticism. Other episodes in the history of marxist aesthetic thought are much less understood, and this gives rise to unanchored discussion in which sociological and philosophical aspects are jumbled incoherently. At the most fundamental plane, for example, we may be told that marxist aesthetics is guided by a materialism that is both dialectical and historical; yet the injunction is often so nebulously presented that we are given

This essay was originally written for the plenary session of the International Congress of Aesthetics, Uppsala, 1968. It has been published in Italian (1969) and was slightly revised in 1970.

no clue as to which aspects and implications of art phenomena relate to historical and which to dialectical materialism.

These are not negligible distinctions in the marxist perspective, yet the dialectical emphasis of materialism tended to disappear entirely from aesthetic discussions in the era of the Second International. Even today, when we hear commonplace mentions of art's specific cognitive relation to reality, or the dependent relation of art to the material conditions of social life, are we always sure that the coherent interrelations of dialectical and historical materialism are being kept in mind? We could be more certain they were if a clear awareness of past failures to make distinctions were more demonstrably part of these present interpretations. We must not forget that under Plekhanov's influence, aesthetics in the Soviet Union in the 1920s and till the early 1930s was either explicitly or tacitly identified with the sociology of art.[3] This situation did not abate until Lenin's aesthetic views were given prominence, when the issue of specific artistic cognition came to re-place the stress on the social conditioning of art.

Types of Sociologically Oriented Analysis of Art

In what ways, then, is marxist aesthetic thought different from a sociology of art? Or, to put the question in another form: How does marxism approach the issue of "art and society"? What weight does the sociological dimension have among the other methodological features of the marxist approach?

To define an answer, we should start by considering the four principal ways in which sociological orientation to art may be interpreted:

1. Investigation may be directed only to behavioral patterns and institutions connected with works of art. Specific topics may include: the distribution of art to a public; the identities and the interests of the persons in that public; the social background and the occupational prestige of the artists; the attitudes displayed by civic authorities towards both artists and audiences; the influence of the public upon the selection of the subject matter and the communicativeness of art.

In sum, this version of sociological inquiry is curious about the incidences of various kinds of artistic occurrence; the procedures are identical with those which would be employed in a study of divorce, for example, or meat consumption.

2. The inquiry takes on a new aspect if we define the sociology of art as the discipline that provides the means of studying the genesis and the function of art, particularly if we allow this definition to include the responses to a given work of art through several varying periods. In this research procedure, the given work

(usually in its content rather than its form) yields the basic point of reference. However, the focus of attention is not the work of art in itself, but rather the creative
process as it relates to a complex social conditioning, or the process of reception
as manifested by the contemporary and later generations.

   3. The sociological inquiry changes again if we choose to look at the given work
of art as "a document of its time." The artistic content of the work would then be
stressed, although the form as it relates to social reality might also conceivably
be considered. How is a work of art to be sociologically interpreted in the context
of its time? This may be done in the terms of the category of mimesis, or in terms
of the category of expression, or by employing both of the categories.[4] Which
aspects of reality will be matched with which corresponding features of the work
of art? That depends largely on our underlying attitude or philosophy. The aspects
of reality to be dealt with may include: a social milieu (the habits, moods, preferences, and idiosyncrasies of the time and place); the specific moral, religious, aesthetic, and philosophical ideas; the conflicting political attitudes and convictions;
the stage of technology and mastery over nature.

   4. Finally, the sociological orientation to art may be defined as an inquiry into
the isomorphic structures that are socially conditioned; that is, the study of various
semiotic systems in the same time and place context. The stress shifts here to the
work of art considered as semiological data grouped together by certain aesthetic
rules and conventions. Content and form are treated as inseparable as a matter of
principle. At most, the particular work may be treated (à la Saussure) as a *parole*
in relation to the *langue* to which it pertains. The student with sociological interests will especially look into the *langue* aspect, and how it compares to other semiotic systems. Conventionalized modes of behavior or comparative epistemological
models within the period may be considered.

   These are four different versions of the "sociology of art." However, only version (1) can be totally subsumed by that description, in my view. The remaining
three should instead be categorized as *aesthetics responsive to a sociological input*.
Indeed, in any strict sense only version (2) can be discussed as *plainly sociological
aesthetics*. The remaining two versions probe much further and deeper into aesthetic questions, on the manifest assumption that every artistic phenomenon is also
a social phenomenon which is to be explained in the cultural setting of its time.[5]

   These four variants cannot be fully compartmentalized — that is obvious. Their
inquiries overlap. Both (1), the sociology of art, and (2), a sociological aesthetics,
want to know the response patterns of various publics. Moreover, (2) assumes the

existence of peculiarly artistic traits though it does not explore them as do (3) and
(4). The latter in turn are modes of inquiry sustained by the standpoint that they
hold in common with (1) and (2)—namely, that a determinate connection can be
shown between artistic and nonartistic structures.

Yet it is fair to state that the sociology of art, strictly understood, does not take
an interest in artistic values. In contrast, a sociological aesthetics in the rigorous
sense is concerned, at least chiefly, with the genesis and function of artistic values;
and the final two approaches—those belonging to aesthetics proper, as I see it—
apply directly to precisely those values, though the artistic values are interpreted
by different methods. Beyond the dichotomy of approach, both (3) and (4) are
versions that investigate artistic qualities, whether of "form" or of a "content"
that is constituted by the specific cognitive component in a work.

Undoubtedly, versions (2) and (3) have proven notably characteristic of the
marxist standpoint, and version (4) has joined these two in recent years. It should
be evident that any exegesis concerned with just one of the approaches has to
be reductionist; in other words, it will simply fail to encompass the fecundity manifested by the complex history of marxist aesthetics.

Aesthetics, Responsive to a Sociological Input

Version (2) could perhaps be most starkly exemplified in the early Soviet writings
of Joffe, Friche, and Pereverzev, who went to great extremes with the idea of
sociological aesthetics. Following the main methodological doctrines of Plekhanov
and simplifying them, these theorists placed total emphasis on the genetic aspects.
They argued that if we assume the ideological equivalent to be the crucial component of a work of art, then the external factors at work on this component must be
regarded as the main topic for analysis. In this way both the form and content
were reduced to a reflection of certain clear-cut class attitudes. Note, however,
that even what the Soviet Union was to call "vulgar sociologism" in the 1930s[6]
in no way confirms Thomas Munro's assertion that the sociogenetic method is de-
ducible from economic determinism. Indeed, the economic factor was seldom used
as a last resort to clinch an argument. The key point, instead, was considered to be
the class position of the artist. This, in turn, was usually defined by his social extraction, which was said inevitably to define and limit his given artistic world view.
It may, thus, readily be seen how these theorists arrived at their formulas depicting
such ideas as: the strict class subservience of particular styles and forms; the artist
as spokesman for the psychological-ideological strivings of a particular class; and

the existence of a tripartite cycle for art, defined by the development of a given
social class from its rise, through its peak, to its fall.

If in debates Friche was dubbed a "dialectician"[7] as distinct from the "mecha-
nist" Pereverzev, the ascendency of Friche was accorded on ground of his mixture
of genetic analysis and functional analysis as well as the greater sophistication
of his genetic analysis, which not only noted stratification within a class, accompanied by differentiated artistic world views but also admitted an assimilation of
the artistic achievements of a declining class by a rising class at another place
or at another time. In other words, Friche argued that in an altered ideological
context audiences may find in a work a meaning different from that intended by
its author and determined by his age.

This is not the place for a critical analysis of the methodological propositions
of marxist sociological aesthetics (understood in the strict and most stark sense).
This critique has already been made by exponents of the other approaches I have
mentioned, and, undeniably, it has been accurate and effective. I should add that
it would be unfortunate if, in attacking the absolute and oversimplified idea of
the dependence of art on class ideology, we were to cast this kind of relationship under a cloud altogether. If Arnold Hauser's excursion onto this terrain in
The Social History of Art (1953) was bound to draw strong criticism, that was
not so much due to what he said as to what he left out — that is, the omission
of mediating factors such as the individuality of an artist or an artistic tradition.
Be it noted that Hauser's Philosophy of Art History (1958) in effect withdraws his
notions of the primacy of the social or, strictly speaking, the class determinants
expounded in the earlier work.[8]

The sociogeneticists have been engrossed by the external context of the work,
while other authors, such as Lukács or Lucien Goldmann, have proceeded from an
analysis of the substructure specific in the work. Nonetheless, it is not the case
that the former have totally ignored the specific cognitive content of art, or that
the latter have passed lightly over the question of genesis. However, it is evident
that the sociogeneticists' schematic approach has resulted in treating the "slice
of reality" that is transformed in the work of art in a very limited fashion; while
the approach of Lukács and his followers has led to the view that first-rate artists
usually transcend the perspective of a given class ideology.

I might add that this latter approach can be characterized as equivalent to a
return to Marx and Lenin. Marx, in discussing Balzac, and Lenin, in writing of
Tolstoi, subordinated genetic analysis to a cognitive approach; and both sought

the cognitive specificity of the artistic message. Perhaps the reader should also be reminded that Lukács, with his friend Mikhail Lifshitz, was a major figure in the Soviet aesthetics of the mid-1930s; together they did much to revive the broader Marxian (i.e., philosophical) methodology with regard to art as against the dominant sociological (Plekhanovian) principles. Neither then nor at present can this controversy be said to have been ephemeral. The outcome lives on (or does not live) in the quality and character of theory available to guide what has proven to be an undiminishing discussion.

In this regard, it should be remarked that an artistic *Weltanschauung*, "vision of the world," does, indeed, tend to prove ambiguous. If we extrapolate from a given work a certain world view, this does not imply that we shall find its author was or is the standard-bearer of a definite ontological, epistemological, historiosophical or sociopolitical *system* — though in the history of literature and art, such instances have certainly occurred. The derived world view simply provides us with the way the artist has come to define himself in the social world, according to Lukács and his school. The artist's position with regard to the immediate conflicts of his particular age, it is argued, will be immanent in the structure of his work: the choice of heroes, the primacy of certain motifs, the resolution of the plot, etc. Very often, such an artistic point of view restricts itself to the posing of meaningful questions, which are left unanswered. In other words, the relationship between art and society is here worked through primarily in terms of the cognitive dimension of a work, and the genetic aspect is brought out indirectly. Each work of art reflects an entire society with its characteristic political, social, ethical, and ideological attitudes — but only after this society has been passed through a double filter: the first being the individual artist and the second being his social grouping or class (these two perspectives being superimposed). From such treatments of the problem of art and society, one would be logically led to a stress on *realism* as the category that links the content of a work of art with the sum and substance of a specific historical phase, and a stress on *typicality* as the most adequate method to understand this nexus and to transmute it into the intrinsic world of the work, that is, to make from the life of society a literary or pictorial fiction.[9]

Theorists who employ a sociological aesthetics according to version (3) describe the work of art as a distinct structure — a structure situated, however, within the prior and encompassing structure of a social consciousness considered in its entirety and possessed of a dominating world view. They take up an attitude towards inquiry which is as much one of understanding as it is one of explaining. The point to be made here is that, according to this interpretation, the superior structure antedates the artistic structure that is, nonetheless, the chief object of its study, while to extricate the meaning of this object means likewise to open up for one-self—as a kind of feedback— a deeper apprehension of the larger whole that is the social consciousness—which in turn sharpens one's comprehension of art.

The last research approach (4) that I distinguished above is also anchored to assumptions of this order. However, its points of difference are equally marked. Note that with version (4) the structure to which the work of art is referred is not an historical process that is at a certain juncture yet activated with its own dynamics; but, rather, it is an established system of signs. Explanation here consists of a discernment of the relationship between the extant code in force and the sense of the particular work, while understanding involves an apprehension of the actual message as a set of signs characterized by an interaction between the *signifiant* and the *signifié* (sometimes translated into the traditional terminology of the "form" and "content" relationship). Much sharper emphasis is given in this interpretation to the relative autonomy of the communication, and attention is also clearly drawn to its artistic specificity.

The inspiration for this last order of sociological analysis has come from various sources—from Saussure through Jakobson to Lévi-Strauss; and in the marxist tradition probably above all from so-called Russian formalism. In short, the semiological-structuralist strain in modern marxist aesthetics is descended as much from the works of Yuryi Tynyanov and Viktor Zhirmunsky as it is, say, from Lev Vygotsky or M. M. Bakhtin.[10] An analysis of individual mediations is excluded in this interpretation because the inquiry is concerned with signs pertaining to a specified system rather than with expressive symbols. It amounts to a *Kunsttheorie ohne Nahmen* "art theory without names." Moreover, since a strict reciprocal dependence between the wider semiotic universe and the set of specific artistic signs is admitted only within the framework of an established semiotic model of the world, the problem of antecedence—that is, the determination of a work by some anterior factors—is dropped from the field of inquiry (though, be it noted, not in any way invalidated). Since this approach concentrates on the structure of the work itself to the exclusion of any "documentary" or "expressive" function whatsoever, the emphasis will be on the immanent nexus of the elements (what Ingarden has aptly called "subject matter coherence").

For a paradigm of this trend of theoretical investigation, I would cite Bakhtin's book on Rabelais,[11] an explication of his work on the semiotic model of medieval carnival culture. The methodological principles of this approach have been expounded in the Soviet Union by writers grouped at the research center in Tartu.[12] Similar methods have been tried in numerous essays by marxists in Poland (Stefan Zolkiewski, notably), France, and Italy. It should be added that Galvano della Volpe's *Critica del Gusto* (Milan, 1960) undoubtedly pointed toward this trend of inquiry and solution.

The Integrated Marxist Approach

The approaches I have outlined may seem mutually exclusive. A closer analysis, however, reveals that they can be treated as partial yet complementary solutions, which, added up, offer us an integral approach in the sociological dimension; in other words, a comprehensive interpretation of art and society. The starting point of this analysis would be the fourth approach, which considers the artistic communication itself and its semiotic connections. The intermediate link would consist of an inquiry into the symbolic, mimetic, and expressive relationship between the work of art as a whole and the given historical reality. This stage cannot be reduced to a specific system of signs; rather, that system should be seen to dovetail with what is called the "content" and "form" of the artistic structure. That content, in turn, is mediated by both the dominating world view and the individual creative personality. The last stage would consist of an inquiry into the genesis and function of the given work on the given sociocultural terrain. Here I cannot even begin to outline the methods by which the several stages of the study could be verified against one another. Nor can I explore the danger from eclecticism that can loom large with a synthesizing operation of this kind.

What is important, in the present context, is to point out that all three of these versions of a sociologically oriented aesthetics in the special sense I have distinguished, are clearly in the tradition of marxist thought. They are all constituent of that tradition, however one-sidedly they have been accented in the history of the marxist doctrine as a result of specific external influences. If we consider the methodological and aesthetic conceptions of Marx and Engels, we shall see that the problem of, for instance, the class determination of art (in both senses, the genetic and the functional) was among the chief topics to interest them. There is evidence for this in *The German Ideology* and *The Holy Family*, and also in their observations on numerous writers' world views. It is equally easy to demonstrate that the next approach that I singled out is announced with the comments by Marx and Engels on Greek art, Shakespeare, Balzac, and Goethe, and their well-known discussions of realism, for example. Conversely, there are no aesthetic observations that directly point to the last of these approaches. A semiotic interpretation can, however, be extracted from Marx's recommendations of a method to use in studying the origin and evolution of capitalist society, and from Engels' remarks on the method applied in *Capital*.[13] What was the external stimulation in the development of marxist sociological aesthetics? Studying the history of European aesthetics, it becomes obvious that version (2), sociological aesthetics in the strict sense, was advocated by the sociogeneticists and sociofunctionalists of the late nineteenth century; that in the work of Lukács version (3) was vivified and strengthened through the influence of *Lebensphilosophie*; and that the semiotic variant, as I have already noted, took on special importance with the inspiration of the Russian "formal" school and contemporary structuralism.[14]

I have already suggested that the term "sociology of art" should be reserved only for inquiries that treat works of art no differently than any other object. The three types of sociological orientation to which I have given fuller discussion lead me to the question of whether marxist aesthetic thought is totally encompassed within their limits. Were this the case, I could rephrase the statement of the problem set out at the start of this chapter to the following: I cannot accept the interpretation of the marxist aesthetic doctrine in the one-sided terms of either Plekhanov alone or Lukács alone or Bakhtin alone; and, furthermore, it would be wrong to call the marxist position a "sociology of art" inasmuch as I have applied to this term a stricter definition. It is certainly true, however, that due to its key thesis this doctrine belongs to the type of aesthetics that *fully* deserves to be described as sociologically oriented.

I would want additionally to make it very clear that—contrary to the garbled interpretations which still frequently crop up—the marxist doctrine maintains:

1. that art is not dependent on any single factor but on a number of elements idiogenetic as well as allogenetic, in conjuncture, among which the crucial one usually is the contemporary historical situation, which is characterized by conflicts of many kinds that can be linked to the current ideological polarizations;

2. that investigation of these interdependencies will include not only the elements of so-called content but also those of *form* (by no means a phenomenon set

apart from the dynamic artistic processes as a whole—however, the model of such an approach should not be sought in the primitivized sociological strategy of Friche, but rather in Max Raphael's studies);

3. that art not only is influenced by society, but also and conversely that art has an *active* part in molding the social consciousness;

4. that these interrelations between art and society do not arise in some impersonal fashion but are *mediated*, above all by the creator-personality (also by the specific, psychologically and historically determined audience).

Please note that none of the positive statements just made should be thought cancelled if, in conclusion, I suggest that marxist aesthetics does, in fact, go beyond sociological aesthetics (even in this amended version).

If, by a sociological orientation, we mean an investigation of the structure of a work of art in relation to another structure that is richer and fuller (this may be the semiotic model prevailing for a given culture or the dominant world view in the social consciousness of a given period), then it seems we must say that the marxist aesthetic standpoint does transcent these limits. The crux of the matter is that a sociological orientation is necessarily focused on the established pattern of sociocultural interrelations at a given time; even where it picks up on the historical process, this will be structured synchronically. Marx's thought, however, has basic assumptions that lead it towards *historicism* rather than sociologism.

Historicism yields a perspective that (in the Marxian sense) never loses sight of the total historical process—though this process is,admittedly, sure to undergo a certain *découpage* from the point of view of the present. Where this interpretation is employed, art is regarded as more than a set of mimetic and expressive symbols or signs coherent in the here-and-now. Art is also considered an instrument of the social consciousness, that is, it is imbued, as it has been through the centuries, with the dream of liberating the human race from the straitjackets of poverty, chaos, hunger, and injustice, while it presages the end of alienation in all its aspects.

Certainly the disalienation theme is one of the foremost aspects of Marxian philosophy. Persistently asserted as well by the marxist aesthetic doctrine, the disalienation theme makes it impossible to regard marxist aesthetics as only sociologically oriented. In other words, the "art and society" dimension bulks large in marxist analysis, although this analysis is, nonetheless, primarily of a philosophical or, we might say, a historical-philosophical nature. Indeed, only against this background does the sociological perspective gain depth and become meaningful.[15]

For this reason, I would judge that, of the four approaches discussed here, the one that is most nearly identical with marxism, because it is most deeply founded in marxism in its essence, is the one I have exemplified with the works of Lukács. This is not to say that I find acceptable every interpretation advanced by Lukács (I totally disagree with his views, for example, on contemporary avant-garde art). What is important is that Lukács' treatment of the relationship between art and society is the most firmly and organically interwoven with the philosophical basis of Marxian thought: with the prospect of the disalienation of humanity, and with the understanding of artistic creation and the multiplex functioning of art that this prospect gives. I could not, however, disallow the claim that the semiotic approach (which I also included in aesthetics proper) is able to effect a symbiosis with a philosophically interpreted marxist anthropology. Still, everything is yet to be done in this matter, whereas Lukács in *Die Eigenart des Aesthetischen* has already masterfully depicted the origin, development, and outlook for art against the background of a still reigning alienation and socialist anticipation of disalienation.

Notes

1. See T. Munro, *Evolution in the Arts* (Cleveland, 1963), Part I, ch. 7. The author does not attempt to show how the principle of "economic determinism" relates to "the dialectics of class struggle," his second principle. Nor does he fully remain with these principles, since he considers (rightly) in his account of the doctrine, such determinants of art as artistic individuality and social psychology. Looking ahead to the further course of my argument, let me here make the point that Munro treats "the Marxian dialectic" in the manner of Hegel. In consequence, the subject of his analysis in chapter 23—which he regards as being outside marxism—corresponds in fact to the basic assumptions of this doctrine. Another case of this one-sided treatment may be found in Rene Wellek's comments on the views of Marx and Engels on literature in *A History of Modern Criticism*, vol. 3 (New Haven, 1965), pp. 232-239. Though he concedes a coherent "philosophy of history" behind their reflections, he devotes all of his energies to tracking down inconsistencies in their remarks. He concludes that the following methodological strands are wound together: economic determinism; Hegelian dialectics; and realism in the typological version.

2. See, for example, G. Morpurgo-Tagliabue, *L'Esthétique contemporaine* (Milan, 1960), pp. 82–85. See also the essays by Melvin Rader on Marx's aesthetic ideas, notably "Marx's Interpretation of Art and Aesthetic Value," *British Journal of Aesthetics*, VII iii (July 1967), pp. 237–249.

3. Striking examples of shortcomings in marxist histories of the marxist doctrine are provided by the studies by Pavel Trofimov. In *Ocherki istoryi marxistskoy es-tetiki* [Essays in the history of marxist aesthetics] (Moscow, 1963), which covers the period from Marx to Clara Zetkin, Trofimov chronologically discusses the separate ideas of each of the writers in question, while losing sight of the structure of the doctrine; at the same time, without any grounds other than premises that are left unstated, he roundly dismisses many of their opinions as nonmarxist. In *Estetika marxisma-leninisma* (Moscow, 1964), pp. 189–196, 213–271, Trofimov's thoughts on the philosophical basis of the doctrine are sheer assertion. He gives no notion why aesthetics, as the study of "the artistic cognition and transformation of reality," should come under philosophy and not under, say, sociology in the strict sense. Indeed, Trofimov seems quite unaware that there exists a problem of "aesthetics vs. sociology of art."

4. These two categories have often been confused in the marxist heritage. This is true of Lukács no less than of Plekhanov despite their differences of approach. Nor is this confusion restricted to marxists; it is rampant throughout nineteenth- and twentieth-century European aesthetics. For the specific meaning ascribed to "expression" by marxist aesthetics, see the section on "The Expression of Psychosocial Equivalents," in chapter 5.

5. In the abundant literature on the subject, it is commonly held that the sociology of art in the strict sense is *not concerned* with the content of the message constituted by a work of art. Typical representatives of this point of view are: L. Lowenthal, *Literature, Popular Culture, and Society* (Englewood Cliffs, N.J., 1961), and H. Fügen, *Hauptrichtungen der Literatursoziologie* (Bonn, 1965). Nevertheless, we will sometimes find these

writers grouped together with such exponents of this discipline as Hausenstein, Auerbach, Mukerjee, or Hauser—each of whom, according to his lights, concentrates on the work itself as a special kind of historical record. In R. N. Wilson, ed., *The Arts in Society* (Chapel Hill, 1964), Ian Watt interprets *Robinson Crusoe* as the expression of a certain myth, and he rests his case in equal measure on elements within and without the work itself. Albert Memmi, in his essay "Problèmes de la sociologie de la littérature," in G. Gurvitch, ed., *Traité de sociologie*, vol. 2 (Paris 1960), pp. 299–314, adopts an indecisive stance. On the one hand, he wants to examine the work as a social fact. On the other hand, he wants to describe it as a "fait de valeur," impenetrable to the sociological approach—which reduces the sociology of art to a sociology of the artist and the audience.

6. See M. Rosenthal, *Protiv vulgarnoj sociologyi w lityeraturney teorji* [Against vulgar sociology in literary theory] (Moscow, 1936); or his translated article "Vulgar Sociology and Metaphysics," in A. Flores, ed., *Literature and Marxism: A Controversy by Soviet Critics*, Critics Group. no. 9 (New York, 1938), pp. 86–95.

7. See *Marxistskoye iskusstvoznanye i V. M. Friche* [Marxist art criticism and V. M. Friche] (Moscow, 1930).

8. Compare the interesting views on this subject by Frederick Antal, in his essay "Remarks on the Method of Art History," *The Burlington Magazine*, February–March 1949, wherein he also draws attention to findings by nonmarxists, who were inexorably drawn into considering the class equivalents of artistic content. Antal's *Florentine Painting and Its Social Background* (London, 1948) and his later study of Hogarth demonstrated the fruitfulness of such interpretations.

9. I cannot give a history here of the Lukács doctrine. The themes I have noted can be traced, despite shifts in emphasis, from his *Geschichte und Klassenbewusstein* (Berlin, 1923) to *Die Eigenart des Aesthetischen* (Neuwied, 1963). I find especially valuable his discrimination of *falsches Bewusstsein* (explaining the ideological limitations of a work of art) from potential consciousness, on which the broadest, most fruitful artistic world view is grounded. I must also pass over Lucien Goldmann's *Pour une sociologie du roman* (Paris, 1964), which seems a departure from the Lukács interpretation even though it proceeds from the same assumptions; the specification of a homology between economic and artistic structures (e.g., a world reified to an extreme and the oddly parallel "nouveau roman" which lacks a hero) seems to me a solution parallel with the fourth, semiotic version as distinguished here.

10. See L. S. Vygotsky, *The Psychology of Art* (Cambridge, Mass., 1971). This work was written in the 1930s and published posthumously in Russian in 1965. Also see M. M. Bakhtin, *Problems of Dostoevsky's Poetics* (Ann Arbor, 1973), Russian edition published in 1929.

11. M. M. Bakhtin, *Rabelais and His World* (Cambridge, Mass., 1971), Russian edition published in 1965.

12. *Trudy po znakovym systemam* [Studies in semiotic systems], vol. I: J. M. Lotman, *Lekcyi po strukturaloy poetike* [Essays in structural poetics] (Tartu, 1964); and vol. II, a collection of essays (Tartu, 1965). Another two volumes have appeared since I wrote this essay.

13. For a typical example of such a reading

of Marx's ideas see L. Althusser, *Pour Marx*
(Paris, 1966), and *Lire de Capital*, 2 vols.
(Paris, 1966).

14. Though it is a truism, it may be worth
recalling here that the marxist doctrine has
not only assimilated external stimuli, but
has also been assimilated. A revealing example is given by the works of the outstanding art historian Pierre Francastel, who pursues sociological-semiotic studies without
disowning marxist inspirations. See his essay, "Problèmes de la sociologie de l'art,"
in Gurvitch, *Traité de sociologie*, pp. 278–
296. Particular emphasis has been placed
on the influence of marxist thought in stimulating sociologically oriented studies by
Walter Abell in *The Collective Dream in Art*
(Cambridge, Mass., 1957).

15. In view of this doctrine, the important
problem of *work* as the foundation of artistic and aesthetic processes gains its full
meaning only in the anthropological perspective. *Homo aestheticus* as one of the
exemplars of the future humanity for which
work will be a creative activity, a playful
expression of one's personality, is integral
to the marxist concept of disalienation.

Chapter 9

Major and Marginal
Functions of Art
in a Context
of Alienation

A thorough analysis of the functions of art is certainly one of the major desiderata of aesthetic analysis, for neither the structure nor the genesis of art can be adequately discussed without it. However, a conscientious treatment of this subject will quickly lead into the quicksand of the vast realm of anthropology, so that a clear choice of a preliminary and predominant approach will be necessary. The more aware we are of the integration of art and life, the more will such a choice seem necessary. Nor can we hope to impose order on this state of affairs by isolating artistic from nonartistic functions, for, as we shall see, only the stalwart of aestheticism could steel himself to reject preemptorily all nonaesthetic uses of art.

Another obstacle to focusing the object of this chapter suitably consists of the numerous competitive standpoints for defining art's function. Each perspective makes important claims; the sociologist promises no less than the psychologist, the educator has a case every bit as legitimate as the philosopher, and so on.

I must assure my readers that I know the Deweyan conception, and, moreover, that I think very highly of it. The uses of art should undoubtedly be considered in relation to the aesthetic experiences of both the creator and the audience; and the basic element in evaluating art should be the process of intensifying and clarifying everyday experience. Nonetheless, to frame one's approach directly on this premise appears to stress psychology at the expense of artistic structure. Yet I am not at all hostile to the Deweyan position, and, indeed, when I take up the question of the end of alienation (i.e., disalienation), I shall come to a similar conclusion. However, my topographic charts lead me by another way.

My philosophy of art has, in fact, led me to define five functions of art. Now, one might think it the simplest course to assume that one function embraces all of art: the *informative* one. Certainly, no art can act on its appreciators without informing them, at the least, that the arrangement of the words, sounds, colors, and so on, is thus and thus. All the arts, the applied and the fine, the representational and the nonobjective, the esoteric and the diverting, must initially, as a prerequisite to functioning, be communicative. In this sense the fundamental artistic function is semiological. Works of art are signs, and the distinctions to be made among the signs define their functional variations.

I do not know of any argument convincing enough to dislodge the semiological approach, but its universal scope does not assure, to my mind, a further fruitfulness. I especially question how well it illuminates the problem of the *artistic* sign.

This essay was written in 1963 and was published, in Polish, in *Estetyka* (Warsaw), vol. 4, 1964. It was slightly revised and extended in 1968, and first appeared in English in *Arts in Society*.

Let me elaborate somewhat, by commenting on a symptomatic and fascinating book, Nelson Goodman's *The Languages of Art* (Indianapolis, 1968).

Now, since I take a marxist approach to the fundamental aesthetic questions, I would certainly be the last to argue in opposition to the cognitive value of art. No more would I deny the possibility (and fruitful results) of analyzing the status of art in a setting of symbolic systems. Indeed, at least since Cassirer produced his persuasive and comprehensive studies of man as *animal symbolicum*, every humanist has been obliged to recognize this as a matter of fact. If man is a rational and featherless biped, unquestionably this rationality is achieved with a reliance on various symbols. A lot can be learned from Goodman about notational systems (scores, etc.), but not too much—and I apologize to the author for putting this curtly—about the characteristics peculiar to art. One is led to conclude from his tenacious analysis that aesthetic and nonaesthetic phenomena may be discriminated by pointing to the difference between exemplification and denotation, through an explication of the ideas of syntactic density, semantic density, and syntactic repleteness. These terms are really explained from the standpoint of logical analysis; nothing specific is developed as regards the qualities peculiar to aesthetic phenomena. Thus, Goodman's "density" repeatedly relates to ambiguity, imprecision, redundance—in other words, to old-fashioned qualities of art. Regarding representation and particularly expression, his terms stress the infinite potentiality for interpreting art, and here again we are on long-surveyed ground.

What can truly be valuable in the effort to elucidate the nature of the aesthetic by means of the specific kind of symbolization is achieved if we can come a bit closer to the peculiarity of artistic cognition. Just this Goodman does not do: he offers no observations on the patterns of sensory data that we call works of art and no formulation of the problem of the cognitive status of art. If artistic cognition is always a hypothesis that somehow parallels scientific inquiry, should this not be demonstrated? Should not the question of whether cognition is a necessary feature of the aesthetic also be explored?

The very modest results scored by Goodman are, I believe, dictated by his premises. If one sets out with the thought that aesthetic processes are primarily a way of apprehending the world competitive with that of the sciences, and that the matrix of art is a communicative system, then the conclusion one draws will be, at best, that art is symbolic in its own way; what that way is will remain undefined.

Goodman's book is, nonetheless, substantial because it proves that much will be gained by clarifying the problems, by confronting the language of aesthetics with the technical language of analytical philosophy. Yet not much will be accomplished for the aesthetic domain, if all that happens is that the same old thorny questions, however pertinent, are merely translated from the vague and clumsy traditional vocabulary and into a crisper but (alas!) hermetic vocabulary fostered by the logician. This latter mode of discourse is certainly relevant to working through the prickly problems of axiology and, particularly, of aesthetics, which, in no small part owing to the confusions of their focal terminology, have brought about a widespread sense of the dreariness of these disciplines. The warnings uttered by Occam and Francis Bacon cannot be ignored; but, even so, a purification of language has never in itself solved any pivotal philosophical issue.

Therefore, if I may get back to the point at which I mentioned *The Languages of Art*, the bringing of outside viewpoints to the aesthetic perimeters can have a salutary effect, as the observer may thus be able to discern unhackneyed connections in artistic phenomena. Among contemporary observers the semiologists seem among the most welcome, for they help us understand more profoundly the significance of our continual exposure to messages. Semiology is extremely helpful in explaining what it is that art has in common with other categories of culture, but it loses impetus as it approaches the core matters of aesthetic concern. This appears even in the most subtly conducted analysis of the message peculiar to aesthetics (i.e., considered as ambiguous and strongly redundant in its dialectical feedback with the prevailing code).[1] A while back, I declared my nonacceptance of aestheticism; now I must underscore my disagreement with any doctrine seeking to erase totally the demarcation of art from nonart.

The aesthetic experience—and here I refer once more to Dewey, expanding on some of his conclusions and slightly modifying others—preserves our familiarity with the world but is at the same time imprinted with strangeness. Although it does not obliterate our psychic habits, it works against their becoming ingrained. It is contemplative and yet opposed to inertia, to that mode of unapprehending rote response which deadens us to the rhythm of life and to persons and things as they authentically are. The aesthetic response would be impossible if it were not linked to our entrenched schema of familiar perceptions. However, its effect is to freshen, to vivify our encounters with the world. This usually occurs in one of two primary fashions: either by intensifying and—paradoxically—apparently disengaging everyday realities from their habitual contexts, where we know them to the point of inattentiveness and lethargy, to replace their literal communication with a shock value (this we find in the devices of dada, in pop art and happenings,

and, to some extent, in the *Verfremdungseffekt* of Brecht); or by transposing the unknown, the fantastic, the marvelous and unbelievable into the everyday context
so as to evoke, by the clash, the shocking sense that the limits of our reality can
be extended (a device that belongs to the baroque and romantic heritage; the surrealists took it up cleverly and with great sophistication, merging it with the foregoing device).

In sum: the aesthetic experience is one of tension; it is *concordia discors*. Art
creates transgressions against our life attitudes; its means cause us to react in a
special way, very different from the ways of science, philosophy, or engineering,
for example.

Marginal Functions

I am going to distinguish three major functions of art: one is fundamentally aesthetic; the others can perhaps best be termed "para-aesthetic." I propose this hierarchy because what I have just described as art's peculiar idiom is uniquely evocative of the intensity and extent of the audience response to art.

However, two further functions, which cannot be ignored, lie outside of this
central hierarchy. These might be described as marginal functions in a double
sense, for they are *framing* functions which, pivoted at two opposite frontiers between art and nonart, present two polar aesthetic extensions. The first is related to
all art that verges on science or philosophy. Surrealism's place is here, as is exemplified by Breton's well-known remark that art provides the window into the world.
The second framing function pertains to those arts that organize our ordinary,
practical space and time, the paradigm here being architecture or industrial design.
Both of these functions focus our attention once again on communication and information, because the issues that arise in discussing them relate primarily to the
cognitive aspects of art.

It seems impossible to dispute the assertion that the artistic process and the aesthetic experience draw on the knowledge that we possess and that they complexly
transform this knowledge, thus legitimately and irresistibly enriching our understanding of the world. Every artist, including the most mediocre, tells us something
about himself; every looker, listener, or reader, even the dullest, gets something
from an encounter with the arts. In this sense, at least, art is always the vehicle
of a certain amount of knowledge (even a wax-museum figure or an effigy of some
segment of reality can augment what we know about both artistic *objects* and
means, as they lead us to consider their virtuoso technique, or the great power of

their illusion, or the evidence they present of the impossibility of exactly duplicating objects) even if that knowledge is no more than a reconfirmation of attitudes that are already familiar to the audience.

We need not stick with this rather trivial idea of knowledge, however; we may go on to discuss artistic experimenters who put genuinely novel experiences before us. Given this modification, I would extend the assertion to say that attentiveness to the whole range of first-rate, authentic art will rightly instruct us that the *all-sided* cognitive nature of art is an irrefutable fact. This leads me to two contentions:

1. The cognitive nature of art is in modes peculiar to art—which I will later scrutinize as embodied in two myths, primarily in the Promethean, but also, if to lesser degree, in the Philoctetean. The peculiarity of the artistic cognition is significantly reduced, however, in the case of those borderline modes of art to which I ascribe a framing, "communicative" function.

2. Since all art is communicative, it is all somehow of a symbolic character and, therefore, conveys some kind of knowledge (about the work itself, its author, or its time). Nevertheless, I should like to restrict the term "cognition" in this context to those peculiar kinds of artistic symbols which lead us to grasp a world created by the strategy of *as-if*; in other words, fictional artistic symbols. Here, cognition is a term used for a special mode of artistic knowledge founded on mimesis, which evokes in the public the experience of a "suspension of disbelief" in the encounter with a creatively transformed reality.

Thus, as I comprehend the nature of art, it is inaccurate to speak of all artistic productions as cognitive, or as cognition-laden.

Now in turn, "cognitive" and "cognition-laden" are not precisely parallel terms, for there are obviously different kinds and dimensions of knowledge conveyed by art. In the first (cognitive) category I would include art and literature of a representational character, which describe and depict the world (e.g., reportage, pictogrammatic painting, sculpture, and drawing). In the second (cognition-laden) category, I would include art and literature which use the existing artistic vehicles only to set forth scientific (usually psychological and sociological) and philosophical truth (e.g., the essay or diaristic "novel"). The predominant aim of reportage and pictogrammatic art is to inform, to communicate about the likeness of the world here-and-now, while that of philosophical or scientific art is to offer a discussion of reality, with an imagistic vehicle.

This much said, I must argue (see also the argument in chapter 6) that it is the peculiarity of artistic cognition that it both avoids abstract generalization while seeking typification and, above all, that it composes a vision which will, necessarily, entail emotional involvement and an appeal to values. On the one hand, we will agree, reportage and pictograms are intentionally and in practice stripped of a value-oriented approach; their task is not to judge but to state. On the other hand, the philosophical essay, drama, or novel may be value-directed and visionary, but the discourse, being generalized, is only semiartistic, or para-artistic.

By way of comparison, in what I shall later term Promethean and Philoctetean art we find a commingling, an intertwining of the cognition, the moral commitment, and the emotional and imaginary aspects. The whole is pervaded with a valuational gauntlet thrown down to the world and, so far as the work amounts to discourse, the artistic imagery is predominant. Promethean art is more reflective, absorbing philosophical issues into the texture and substance of the peculiar medium, its pattern and means of expression. Philoctetean art turns more towards the active response to the represented set of values, and, if one can subscribe to them, one should live up to the values with deeds. Where the glossaries of film theory speak of an "urge for identification" (a passive, dreamy self-projection), Philoctetean art supposes a dynamic need for continuing artistic vision into the practice of social life.

Nothing would be easier than to attack the foregoing sketch by demonstrating that the differences between a cognition-laden art and a peculiarly ("artistically") cognitive art are indefinite and vague. Moreover, it is undeniable that no depictive (or, more broadly, presentational) art is strictly communicative, since if it manifested only denotation it would be empty of any traits that would make us call it art. How pleasant it would be if we could discriminate in the arts among various types of objects, as, for example, stars or numbers may be precisely and separately located. However, blurred demarcations are a *specialité de la maison* of art. Even so, at the farthest extensions toward the ends of the artistic continuum, we are able to discriminate the symptomatic traits of the symbolic content which is no longer peculiarly artistic. Near to the philosophical pole, for instance, we can locate some characteristic and finely achieved passages of Musil's *The Man Without Qualities*, Borges the teller of stories and Sartre the playwright; and at the pictogrammatic pole we can discern most of the naturalistic painting and sculpture of Soviet Russia.

However, I have not only suggested that a spectrum runs between the extreme instances of "cognitive" and of "cognition-laden" art; I have also said that not all art partakes (in the "fictional world" sense) of cognition. I will add now that neither what I shall later label the Orphic function of art, nor the second framing function, has anything to do with cognition. When the artist sings out of his inner sensibility exclusively, when his work, sensuously and emotionally given, conveys only expressive values, the knowledge to be obtained from it is of a quite specific kind which may be more or less "transparent" with respect to the world around it. Granted that, owing to the makeup of a work of art, the peculiarly artistic cognition cannot be verified like a scientific or philosophical hypothesis, it may still be checked if in an imprecise way; but there is simply no way to verify the expressive values inherent to a sensuously given coherent structure. The reference of such values is simply to the artist, and the key to his expression remains entirely private. We may, of course, hold our focus on the work of art itself, but precisely its structure does not convey any cognition. It provides only knowledge about itself, about its immediacy, and it may secondarily encourage us to guess about its author and its time. My suggestion is that we term such works "self-addressed" and that we recognize that, in contrast to "transparent" or "translucent" works, the self-addressed ones lack the cognitive facets in the strict sense of the term discussed earlier.

The self-addressed works can and should be called messages since they do communicate something by their very substance and structure. Messages, in turn, do imply reference to the extra-aesthetic, psychosocial world, even as mere vestiges or perpetuations of definite artistic conventions (codes) and individual quirks against the paradigmatic background. For this reason I propose to ascribe to them an information function, as distinguished from the specifically cognitive function discussed above.[2]

The same may be urged, even more strongly because it is so much more obvious, in respect to industrial art. Where could its strictly defined cognitive value be? There is none; instead, the work fills a place in the world that we too occupy, and its primary reference is to itself (also, but indirectly, to the artist and to the style of the epoch). The functional (utilitarian) aspects of this kind of art could hardly be treated as "transparent" in the mode discussed above. They can only be — like the qualities of a nonobjective art — "symbols" (tokens) expressive of the individual and collective ideas and moods of a given time.

I must here stress that the works characterized by the first framing function, although they share some noncognitive features with nonobjective art and industrial art, can be said to convey some information "despite" their artistic qualities, whereas such conclusions could not be drawn in cases of the Orphic function.

As concerns the second of the framing functions available to art, it is motivated by an endeavor of art to enter life, to erase the demarcations between the aesthetic and nonaesthetic. The two chief spheres in which this attempt is waged are those of technology and of play. In both cases of this trial marriage, the tendency to aestheticize life is carried to the extent that art ceases to be a special distinct phenomenon. Moreover, all the "sacrosanct" trappings of the artist's profession, his elite, priestly, and hermetic tendencies, are laid aside, so as to divest the aesthetic performance of its aura of exceptionality. Examples include, on the one hand, the Experiments in Art and Technology group (E.A.T) headed by Bell Telephone Laboratories engineer Billy Kluver; and, on the other hand, the makers of happenings and the Living Theatre, by now also accepted around the world and the prime example of our second framing function.

This tendency continues the notion of *zizhnostroyenije*, "organizing life by means of practical arts," which was very popular in the early 1920s among Soviet Russia's proletarian culture *(proletkult)* and futurist proponents. From this perspective, art in the traditional sense is to be rejected, for art should not be the vehicle of cognition, and no comtemplation should attach to the aesthetic experience. Art is to become as active as is labor in the midst of everyday life. The engineer and the ordinary worker will emerge as the genuine artists; they will produce harmonious wholes in harmonious surroundings. The *proletkult* and futurist vanguardists also turned their attenton to pageants and celebrations. They thus anticipated the happenings insofar as recreational activity was concerned and the audience took a part, whether deliberately or willy-nilly, in creating the spectacle. The all-comprehending aesthetic principle was to eliminate the traditional attitude towards art, with its limitations and constrictions, its guild craftsmanship or techne and clear-cut division of assigned roles (creator: work of art: audience). Thus, in the second framing function, the "into life" principle comes to the fore, excluding the cognitive function in the strict sense of the term, and forming the antipode of the informational principle.

Despite its inclinations to aestheticize the surrounding world (a para-Orphic phenomenon), the art I am now discussing is best related to the Philoctetean category described below. Like the Philoctetean it is social-practice-oriented, that is, it means to enter life actively. However, the Philoctetean function remains based on the relatively autonomous structure of the work of art, it is enabled by an aesthetic-cognitive experience suffused with value-commitment. In contrast, the framing function calls out for an immediate response to art directly rooted in life-praxis.

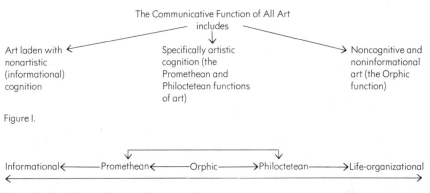

Figure I.

Figure 2.   The Major and Marginal Functions of Art

Figures 1 and 2 present an approximate counterpart of art's fluid continuum and overlapping functions; and figure 2 presents the most elementary, linear differentiation of the functions. The reader will note that I have carried one marginal function to the far extreme of an informational art. This case might form a substitute for reality (a kind of surrogate function) as contrasted with what we find with Promethean or Philoctetean works of art. I should add that precisely the latter works are the most *ideological* (incorporating as they do a function parallel to ancient or medieval mythology), in other words, they are at once a fictional reflection of the social world and its transcendence, a game that is played out over and against the status quo.

Another necessary remark of a synoptic nature pertaining to some extent to all of the above-mentioned functions concerns their *therapeutic* character. I do not mean this in the traditional Aristotelian sense of purging our worst feelings by dramatic catharsis. Nor do I mean the Spencerian sense of giving vent to our collected surplus of emotion, or to the Freudian sense of freeing the libido from repressions and fixation. All of these may occur; but they are secondary aesthetic functions. To speak of therapy in connection with our five functions, the three central ones especially, means basically: that our psychic powers are, through art, unusually concentrated towards waging the human contest in a hard world, and that our understanding is intensified of our own position, of man's victories but first of all of his defeats and discontentments, and of the order but mainly of the disorder in the world, so that we may choose to go by another way, bettering both ourselves (at least in terms of maximal self-awareness) and the state of affairs around us.

Now, it might be objected that philosophy could, and does, offer the same experience. My reply would be that the experience is analogous but not the same,
precisely due to the peculiarity of artistic cognition. Moreover, the therapy which
is characteristic of the best examples of the Orphic function is completely incom-
parable. Indeed, these moments of inner harmony and of full accordance with the
world — which make us prone to utter Goethe's famous phrase, *Verweile doch,
du bist so schön* — are provided only through art. The religious mystical experience,
which may come to mind as the counterpart of this occasion of epiphany, is, however, only an analogy, for the Orphic delight embraces all the faculties of spirit
(perceptive, emotive, imaginative, and conceptual) in a single alloy which relates
us to earthly things.

It is indisputable that the framing functions which I have described as being
marginal in a double sense have been very much in the fore of recent artistic
trends. Striking examples can be seen in pop art, and in the efforts to abandon
fixed artistic structure in favor of more playful, creative, or responsive processes.
I am certainly not biased against the happening and its progeny; I believe this
trend should be explored, not merely because it is thriving now but because it represents an important tendency in contemporary art and civilization which dates at
least from the time of dada. Nevertheless, the predominant activity of art has remained *between* the framing functions. I find it of significance that this distribution
has remained roughly the same up to the present time, although it is also clear
that, with the passage of time, art's basic traits and the responses they evoke have
altered and its content has shifted.

I should not be amazed if John Cage or Allan Kaprow disputed my conclusions
and insisted on putting a systematically aleatory and a ludic (play-rooted) art at
the very center of my scale. They would be joined from another quarter by Billy
Kluver and others who claim the primacy of technology in the civilization of today.
They could point with assertiveness to the extraordinary role occupied by industrial
art (I mean by this term applied art, industrial design, and the aesthetically pro-
gramed production of machines) in the everyday life of the entire world. Still others
who could be marshaled against my arguments would include those writers and
critics who believe that a highly intellectualized prose and reportage, and also the
so-called conceptual art,[3] properly should have the pride of place in both belles
lettres (perhaps including theater and cinema) and the fine arts (painting and sculpture). Possibly the support of Peter Weiss, Jean-Luc Godard, and the *nouveau
roman* group might be gathered too.

It is simply impossible to ignore these counterarguments; the avant-garde of today has definitely eroded the fundamentals of aesthetics which had seemed so firm for many centuries. I shall not urge that the transmitted aesthetics is certain to survive; it may very well be that we will pass through a period of crisis and that at the other side a new continuum of the arts with a considerable shift of emphases will emerge. However, I shall not want to take up the task of sketching that continuum until the 1980s or 1990s if I should live that long. Nor should others want to take it on for the present, for the aesthetic categories transmitted to us — though not so stable as they once were — remain validated by practice, while their most vehement opponents have no choice but to make use of them even in the moment of negating them. It appears that *rebus instantibus* these disparaged categories are cogent, and what we most want is their pliable modification (cf. Chapter 3).

Given the present situation, the best course to follow is to accept the chance of being mistaken and, nonetheless, to try to build bridges between the artistic tradition, with its relevant aesthetic categories, and the "blasphemously" radical avant-garde which, with its "antiart," does tend toward something which ultimately will no longer be described as art (a field of specific phenomena), but rather as a mode of creation latent to all kinds of human activity. Given the incompatible propositions set forth by philosophers and theorizing artists, who match each other in stubbornness, the job of the aesthetician will be to mesh them into a consistent whole — at least for the transitory period of "crisis." If I were to leap to the side of the avant-gardists and to accede to their drastic revisions, the losses entailed by the move would outweigh the benefits gained, since it would then be virtually impossible to avoid confusing the still defensible traditional concept of art with the idea of new phenomena "beyond art." An even greater chaos than at present would reign; as matters stand the pivotal aesthetic terminology is amply chaotic, and I would opt for attempting to vindicate it as against introducing an even greater confusion.

I think I have already made clear that it is my philosophy of art and my devotion to certain values which determines my choice among the alternatives and, consequently, my scheme for presenting the aesthetic functions. No doubt others will want to propose some other choice of fundamental functions.[4] I wish to state in advance my toleration of their views. I want only to emphasize my earlier reservation: No debate on this issue makes sense if it does not draw upon the total resources for aesthetic thought, that is, if it does not relate to the philosophical bases of art criticism.

The Three Principal Functions

The three chief functions of art can, I think, be nicely illustrated with reference to three characters from the Greek myths: Orpheus, Prometheus and Philoctetes.

The myth of Orpheus expresses the restorative, organically living power of music and poetry. Orpheus makes man's feeling whole, imbuing him with an inner balance and a harmony with the surrounding world.

The myth of Prometheus confronts us with the anguished, and yet quickening, arousal of a dormant conscience. Prometheus takes up and typifies the struggle for the destiny of mankind, and although the venture fares tragically, Prometheus persists in striving against the world and against himself —torn asunder yet still seeking to better his lot in the world.

The myth of Philoctetes expresses the idea that life is only supportable in the presence of art, and, moreover, that art can play a significant social role. In art's absence man is bereft of fulfillment and stripped of skills and devices necessary for his victories.

Philoctetes is a seer who has received from Heracles a bow which unerringly finds its target, a bow which will guarantee victory to the Greeks at Troy. On the voyage to Troy, however, Philoctetes is bitten by a serpent; and, as the stench of his wound proves unbearable to his companions, he is put ashore on the isle of Lemnos. Philoctetes lives on the island in total isolation for ten years. The battle for Troy lasts as long, without a clear-cut result, until, at last, the Greeks remember the invincible bow. After Odysseus, who represents practical reason (here, coarse political calculation), has given his consent to the journey, they resolve to hasten to Lemnos. Odysseus stipulates that they bring only the bow; there is no need for Philoctetes; however, Neoptolemus, the young son of Achilles, convinces his fellow seafarers that Philoctetes should be retrieved and brought aboard. The wound then is healed, Philoctetes vanquishes Paris, and thanks to his bow the Greeks carry the fray.

Myths, of course, are subject to varying interpretations, and I do not claim that my interpretations are definitive. They are, however, useful for illustrating my present argument, and that is what is important in this context. Let me repeat for clarity's sake that: first, the Promethean motif is associated with the synthesis of moral, philosophical, cognitive, and specifically artistic values; second, the Philoctetean motif corresponds to the sociopolitical, cognitive, and specifically artistic values; and third, the Orphic motif is based primarily and almost solely on the specifically artistic values, often having, however, an implicit world view which holds that aesthetic harmony is the highest goal of humankind. The two first motifs relate to ideology in the broad sense, but with somewhat different emphasis, the Philoctetean vision having sociopolitical tenets and the Promethean moral and philosophical ones. The Orphic motif can be connected with ideology only in an indirect way; an undivided dedication to purely aesthetic values always implies a certain stance, whether openly asserted or unconscious, towards the conflicting ideologies of the given time and place.

Not only can these three themes stand as emblematic of functions of art; each of them also keeps us in mind of certain constructive aspects of art. If, by contrast, we consider what the inversion of these themes might mean, we shall be reminded of the negative results which can be brought about in the sphere of art.

Let me expand upon this last statement. To settle for an inverted version of the Orphic theme means to grow complacent with what is in many respects aesthetically false. It is to confirm oneself in a debased or an undeveloped aesthetic taste. All ersatz which is advanced as genuine art, if it is accepted as genuine, has to prove damaging. Such ignorance of what is artistically good and base has contributed to the aesthetic illiteracy up to the present, and, to illustrate this, I need only mention the history of the reception of so-called modern art. The contemporary artist is ill understood by many, because his modes of expression are quite simply too difficult due to the public's having been made comfortable with certain stereotypes that have been extrapolated from art and are incessantly advanced as the universally valid models towards which all true art should aspire. Cheap gewgaws come into this category, as does the slavishly academic art that has such a great influence on the reception accorded to avant-garde art. Impressionism, which reoriented the taste of its time, was for a while faced with the real threat of a total boycott. Cubism, fauvism, and surrealism were fought by eternally vigilant "academicians"—and also by some newly spawned fawners on impressionism. The advocates of artistic modes that already are supplanted have two means of frustrating the Orphic impetus. They profusely flood the galleries with epigonal works that are widely proclaimed to be of high standing; and they stubbornly refuse to recognize, usually with every sort of barbed taunt, works that embody the new values. To point out this negative influence is not, however, to deny any other sort of influence to the older artistic trends. Their finest works will remain a healthy element in the best meaning of the word. Everywhere and always, the meretricious compromises the quality of life.

The inversion of the Promethean theme leads, logically enough, to the dulling of conscience. This can occur when reality is appraised as supposedly free of conflicts and contradictions. The extreme inverted-Promethean example is the idyll. Such inversions do not appear only in capitalist conditions, where in some literary works the illusion was and is nourished that this social order functions splendidly and brings to fruition the humanist values; in socialist circumstances the ideal of a conflictless society, coupled with the proposition that what should not be therefore cannot be, has also led to a misappropriation of this function of art.

Yet another possibility of the inversion of this theme lies in the trend towards amoralism. Works of this trend encourage a brutalism that lunges to seize its goal at however high a price; examples include some crime novels and movies as well as the comics of capitalist countries, the United States especially.

The inverted Promethean theme may also channel or displace its primary energies to the Orphic motif. This can occur when sociohistorical conditions are so hostile to the ordinary functioning of the arts that artists can resolve their problems only by resorting to hermetic aesthetic values. In the time of Gautier and of Baudelaire, the defense of Beauty in its purity was still feasible as a mode of expressing protest against the capitalist social order. It was somehow complementary to the way Balzac and Flaubert, from another side, unmasked the rhetoric about the free development of personality. At the time there were few gifted thinkers who had discerned, as had Marx and Engels, the operative laws of the new social system and had located the perspectives (including those for artists) in effect necessitated by the existent social relations. The Paris Commune made it plain, however, that the religion of Beauty "in and of itself," with its devotion to eternal values outside of society was bankrupt. The new social confrontation meant that such an attitude had to be bound up with a flight from artistic responsibility.

It may well happen that the artist is not able to discern the main historical contradictions of his time, but he cannot afford to turn away from those of which he may be conscious if he is to draw as fully as he can upon the functions of his art. From this perspective, Plekhanov was able to justify Pushkin but not Merezhkovsky; he sought to explicate the complex position of the 1840s and 1850s aesthetes but he did not find reasons to exonerate the parnassians.

Rimbaud, Mallarmé, Wilde, and their followers, yielding exclusively to the Orphic theme, were in disaccord with the conscience of their age. Inasmuch as even the best artists at this juncture (e.g., Debussy, Leonid Andreyev, Gordon Craig) preferred the primordial aesthetic values—conveying, to be sure, a symbolic indictment—to the ethical-social values, as their way of rebelling against the capitalist reality, I would sum up the contradiction of Orphic and Promethean themes in such cases as follows: Inversion leads to displacement of the Promethean theme into the Orphic, and, accordingly, the role of the former dwindles to a vanishing point.

This difficulty should attract our thoughtful concern — perhaps now more than ever. The threat of total war, the toppling of the gods, the aggressions in the name of absolutes — in a word, all the phenomena that have perplexed the artistic community — encourage a further flight to ivory towers. At the same time we can also see, particularly in the socialist countries, a steadily greater participation in the life of society by artists and a heightened response by them to these problems of the present. In the capitalist lands and especially the United States, however, artists sense their isolation ever more starkly.

A noteworthy instance of a resort to the para-Orphic attitude combined with a more-or-less philosophical maneuver (the first of the framing functions) is the theory and practice of the so-called *nouveau roman,* whose aim is to show how the methodology of writing a novel can become its very theme. Artistic technique is here pushed to the fore, along with the conception of how persons and things both fill out anonymous social patterns, or of how reality is structured through accidental points of view. Eschewing depiction of how life might go on if persons were to perceive their genuine chances, the *nouveau roman* provides instead a registration of fortuitous structures which are emblematic of chaos as the universal principle. In music, an analogous example is provided by the "aleatory" movement; and in the plastic arts by action painting. The resultant artistic wholes are meaningful — but, paradoxically, this is so because their reference is to man's failure to imbue his deeds and the world with meaning. Although here, too, is entailed a protest of art against the modern phenomenon of reification, nevertheless the Promethean dimension has been reduced almost to naught. What is projected is a tragic consciousness of a devaluated existence. At times, aleatory structure appears not as a metaphysical dimension but as an artistic strategy. The aim of "cutting across the grain" to refresh habits of perception and experience, ends, at best, in achieving the goal of a game or play and the glorification of *homo ludens* — an Orphic rather than a Promethean achievement.

The inversion of the Promethean theme may be compounded by an assertive aesthetic deformation. Similarly, the Orphic theme may be drained of the qualities that make art artistic if it is perverted into a self-congratulatory aestheticism. Now, one case of the deformation of the Promethean theme is sheer moralism — the full subordination of art to criteria of giving to youth the correct experiences. Tolstoi proposed this aim in *What is Art?* (1898), in which he questioned the value of Shakespeare's and Beethoven's works, as well as his own earlier writings, in the name of a true Christianity. Moralism overlooks the fact that art is sustained by its own peculiar values — much as aestheticism tries to get away from the fact that art does comprise manifold categories of value. Hence, the well-publicized quarrel in 1878 between Ruskin the moralist and Whistler the aesthete was entirely insubstantial, since each was one-sided in his viewpoint.

Another suborder of the Promethean theme's deformation is didacticism. Art quickens the conscience with truth; but it does not communicate this truth in the form of a treatise or a lecture. When we meet such interpolations in literature, as in *The Emancipated* by Boleslaw Prus or in Tolstoi's *War and Peace*, we accord them an extra-aesthetic function, considering them appendages of the novel's genuine weave. We react similarly to the allegorical epigraphs on the paintings of the Middle Ages or the Baroque Age. Didacticism here appears in the form of a commentary on the content of the picture. It can also happen that the artist projects a teaching viewpoint within the work of art — as for example when he judges a situation positive or negative, or he scorns or argues on behalf of a character. In children's fables the chief figure is frequently decked out in noble traits so as to reinforce certain ethical precepts. In a letter of 1885 to Minna Kautsky, Engels argued against handling art in this way; but one could find many instances of it. Just go back in literary history — to the writings of George Sand as she sought to pass along the influence of Fourier, or to the Polish authors influenced by Swietochowski, that major ideological exponent of the early phase of positivism.

The typical inversion of the Philoctetean theme may lead to nihilism, the conception that the world is on the way to catastrophe and that there is no worthwhile act for a person to undertake. This point of view was widespread among the turn-of-the-century decadents. Hence, it may readily be seen that, under some historical conditions, inversion of the Philoctetean theme entails its displacement into an Orphic theme.

Admittedly, some persons committed to the struggle for a new society, to proletarian revolution, will not be satisfied with mere criticism of the old system, no matter how incisive. They call for a wholly activist artistic attitude and look on the works of Kakfa, Camus, Faulkner, or T. S. Eliot as taking virtually an escapist position. This is a complex problem. The above-mentioned authors, and numerous others (e.g., Ionesco), do carry out one of art's basic functions. They convey to the sensitive and attentive reader that the contemporary world is antihumanistic. To

ask more than this of them would be to force a view of reality on them which is
not theirs. The problem here is not one that might be solved by simply presenting
to the artist arguments based on historical facts. Rather, it is a reflection of the
many-sidedness of reality, of the fact that its contradictions closely impinge on one
another. Moreover, the artist is not always optimally oriented; he will be affected
by his origins, education, and tastes, the current ideological controversies, the
types of radicals, socialists, or communists he meets, the circumstances of these
encounters, etc. Finally, the work of such artists does, in fact, constitute a call to do
battle. The ways in which it does so are many; they range from Kafka, and Camus,
to Hemingway's *For Whom the Bell Tolls*, to the extreme measure of commitment
lately reached by Sartre.

Hence, the inversion of the Philoctetes theme will result, most pertinently, in a
withdrawal from any criticism of reality. However, the act of refraining from an
activist attitude should be regarded as escapism only in a time of dramatically
heightened struggle. Just such situations have often occurred for Polish literature
owing to the nation's history. For those who know our poetry of the 1840s, the
polemics between Guztaw Ehrenberg and Edmund Wasilewski probe deeply into
this question of escapism. French literature saw comparable times between the
revolutions of 1830 and 1848, during which period nearly all poets and writers
were socially and politically engaged—even those like Baudelaire who would go
over later to *l'art pour l'art*. Those who disregarded the life of their time and an
historical-philosophical perspective met disapproval.

Like the other themes, the Philoctetean theme is subject not only to inversion
but also to deformation that grossly falsifies its significance. One deformation is
the "agitprop"—agitation-and-propaganda—idea of the function of art, which
treats art not as a specially constituted sphere of psychic values, but as a means
(affording a sensory-concrete form) to an end, an ideological persuader. Perhaps
the reader is familiar with the polemical remarks by Heine—he was at that time a
partisan of socialism—against the proletarian poets, particularly Weerth. We must
admit he was not unfair in chiding them if we look closely at the tendentious verse
of that time, which was laden with the sort of propaganda that can put art to death.
Time and again from Weerth to the present the poetry siding with the cause of the
proletariat has skirted or fallen into this deformation. In socialist countries not
many years ago an "agitprop" function of art was officially sanctioned as equivalent to art's great civilizing function—with predictably disastrous results. (This
tendency is still vigorous in China, for example.) Art, however, does not tidily dove-

tail with immediate priorities, which can shift from year to year, month to month, even week to week. Art has always sought to avoid this kind of urgency. When it has acquiesced to pressure, its results have been nil or quickly moribund.

The great Baroque artist Bernini created monumental sculptures assigned to his workshop by the Church, but he instilled these works with enduring values, precisely because he overstepped the official Jesuit ideology and art theory. When Jacques-Louis David responded to the needs of the French Revolution, and when Dickens later satisfied the pressing requirements of liberal bourgeois journalism, they too did not reduce their interests and level their aesthetic taste to those of their institutional employer. It is sometimes asserted that Mayakovsky and Brecht prove that an artistically excellent propaganda art is possible, yet neither one produced propaganda *tout court*. Employing personal and inimitable idioms, each produced images of the individually experienced problems of a modern man —a man for whom the proletarian revolution and socialism provide the center of life, the ABC to which all else relates. They wrote a poetry at once affirmative and difficult. It summons to battle, to the struggle of today; nonetheless, the Promethean element is present.

Another example in the same vein, and perhaps more contemporary to our time, is the poetry of Nicholas Guillen of Cuba. Consider Guillen's "Elegia a Jesús Menéndez," which incarnates the peasant leader as the liberation principle of all the oppressed peoples of Latin America. In this hero is symbolized the earth's plenitude (the sugar-cane) and the revolutionary awakening of those who tend the earth. Where Brecht wrote didactically dialectical parables, Guillen employs a militant and opulent pattern of metaphor. How easy it would be to accuse Guillen of sheer propaganda when he praises the violence inflicted on the oppressors; yet his poetry is so richly imbued with images of love and death, of hunger and poverty, of cruel injustice and the longing for brotherhood, that we could better term it a kind of Promethean scripture for all the suffering peoples of the so-called Third World. The vision of Guillen and that of Pablo Neruda are being continued brilliantly in the best films now being made in Latin America —especially those by Glauber Rocha— which are highly symptomatic of the combination of the Promethean and Philoctetean motifs.

Questions of Alienation and Disalienation

The interrelationships of the different strands of art have been analyzed in the marxist literature in many ways, and from very different points of view. Needless to say, the major problems of art are unsolvable without reference to the question of artistic alienation, which was raised by Marx himself.

In his description of alienation Marx was indebted to Hegel and Feuerbach, but he diagnosed the phenomenon differently. In the *1844 Manuscripts* he showed that the economic foundation of the capitalist social order is the main cause of alienation. Alienation for Marx had three aspects: the alienation of the product; the alienation of the production process; and the alienation of the human species-essence. Its effects are indelible not only on the human condition of the oppressed but also on that of the oppressor; and its results can be felt in many spheres (e.g., the ideological and political). The artist is also profoundly affected in his domain. Marx pointed out how money —the chief nexus of alienation —in capitalist times becomes the measure of value in artistic production, the work being severed from the artist to become a commodity. Moreover, the artistic activity is submitted to scrutiny if not final control; he who can pay art's price will wield an economic, political, and ideological power to elicit and encourage certain subjects and treatments.[5]

Given the facts of alienation, a great many artists will perform negative functions. I grant that the best works in any epoch have combatted conformity of every kind and have thus combatted alienation too. However, this does not mean —in Marx's view —that the artist can actually attain to expressing his full human individuality.

In spite of his enthusiasm for the nineteenth-century novel and particularly for Balzac, Marx returned again and again to Shakespeare and the classics. Like Hegel, Marx saw in the art of antiquity a humankind still harmoniously linked to nature, not yet so alienated that the social bonds have been dissolved. In his remarks on the emergence of the aesthetic sense, Marx focused on the reconciliation of history and culture with nature —in other words, the harnassing of nature to realize a common social product in such a way as also to realize humankind's natural dispositions. Such a man, superseding and achieving himself in his labor, is *homo aestheticus*. Art mobilizes all his psychic powers, liberates his uncharted possibilities, and adapts him to the environment in the dynamic process organized on the creating of objects.

The whole late history of culture entails the removal of art from life, the crystallization of a type of artistic creativity which has turned away from production *sensu stricto*, and the estrangement of the aesthetic attitude (which is said to be incommensurable with all other attitudes, particularly the utilitarian). Art declines to

the standing of a department of human interest. The way it happens is conjunc-
tural: economically, works of art take on commodity traits; politically, there is a
censorship; and ideologically, art becomes more subjective and mystical. The sum
of this is alienation, the loss of any chance for art to achieve a general and har-
monizing effect. It stands, then, a tongue-tied testimony to the condition of society.
The best of this art will probably elevate just one function, accent it, and make it
something absolute; hence, the ideal of the beautiful, or of the artist's awareness
of his responsibility.

Marx indicates that a liberation from this dysfunctionality is only to be had
through the socialist revolution. Friedrich Schiller had dreamt, in *Letters on the
Aesthetic Education of Man*, that the world would be rescued from need and suffering by aesthetic man. Hegel opted to overcome the alienated status of man by
withdrawing from the objectified exteriorized phenomena *(Äusserung)* to the world
of spirit. Hölderlin and Keats wanted to escape to the long gone world of Greece,
since the future held out to art a stark and ineluctable fate. Marx, with his probing
of contemporary society, was to turn Schiller's conception inside out; it was *political* man who was required for the rescue and realization of aesthetic humankind.

Meanwhile, the alienation processes, if deleterious to artistic creation, have secured for art a relative autonomy. They could not have been avoided; and, although
they might have been beaten back (as has been done in the past), art has, through
the interplay, prepared itself for the superseding of alienation. Indeed, the artist
has always been attuned to nature; he has continually drawn fresh sustenance
from it in his fight against the decadence of civilization and culture, which is at the
same time his fight for an authentic humanity. The unambiguous dependency of
the artist on only one class has been rare. His product has also always had a general social significance (this we read also in Marx) which has tended to militate
against a narrow outlook limited by official ideology.

A mutiny is afoot within both the Orphic and the Philoctetean phenomena. Admittedly, the battle done against alienation by the two is not equally divided. In
their midst appears the Promethean insurgence, providing, in general, the high-
point of the resistance of art to alienation. All the same, alienation cannot be completely superseded except with communism, in the Marxian view.

Polemicizing against Stirner in their *German Ideology*, Marx and Engels anticipated an epoch where there would be no isolated, ivory tower geniuses and no

philistines. All men would be artists to some degree. No longer restricted to a single field, they stress, the artist of the future will simultaneously be painter, poet, singer, etc. We read (in *Capital*) that work when not compulsory comes to be free play of the psychic faculties and that the development of every talent will figure as a basic element of the communist system. In this way is the man of the future — among, and together with, his other attainments — the aesthetic man, in Marx's prediction. All of production can become an art; and every art can be made intimate with productivity. The disalienated man will have the capacity to give artistic expression to all phenomena and to all his needs; he will in this way — while augmenting the store of material and psychic resources — not only reach an ethical goal of individual development; he will as well fulfill his species-being, his nature — a stage for which his transposition from the natural world into civilization and culture has already potentially prepared him. His enduring nature, then, among other endowments of *zoon politicon*, is aesthetic.

Marx's prediction undoubtedly has utopian antecedents. The notion of natural concomitants has a basis in Rousseau. It was not, however, the uncivilized man or savage who lent him his most significant model, it was the attainments of Greek man; and in this a direct line starting from Winckelmann leads through Hegel to Marx. Neither is the notion of a society where all men have become artists just an aberration in a genius's thought; it expresses an empirically founded, acute perception of the intolerable antinomy between art and society — along with a genial hunch as to the undoing of the antinomy.

We should be able to understand, then, why marxist aesthetics ascribes an important role to art in transformations of society; and why the notion fostered by Hegel that art is useless and withering away is unacceptable to marxists. The processes of alienation and disalienation involve not only the three major themes but also, undoubtedly, the second framing function. Together with Marx, later marxist aesthetic thought has put emphasis on *zizhnostroyenije*, in contrast to Hegel and his indirect followers who emphasize the spread of *Kunstwissenschaft* (and its counterpart: highly intellectualized art) instead of *Kunst* in the old sense of the term. Indeed, to Marx and also to William Morris whose ideas here are the closest to the Marxian idea, the principle of art is not abandoned but expanded. It does not disappear, but pervades all social consciousness. Where Marx discusses labor in terms of art, he modifies Kant's analysis of *Zweckmässigkeit ohne Zweck* and adapts it for the marriage of art and social life. In Marx's view, accordingly, the aesthetic realm does not lose its relative autonomy in the disalienated future; what is lost is only its splendid isolation. In other words, life will not engulf art but will become its Siamese twin.[6]

Contemporary art and art theory bear convincing testimony that Marx's aesthetic point of view has become central to the whole range of modern aesthetics. Indeed, alienation has become a fashionable term today. Owing to the influence of psychoanalysts and psychosociologists, the idea is applied to every kind of frustration. It seems worthwhile, then, to define the conception more exactly. Moreover, when we speak of alienation today we refer to phenomena which in the time of Marx did not yet exist.

I understand by "alienation" certain processes and their results which occur in a concrete historical situation through the conjunction of economic, sociopolitical, and ideological factors, and which men feel to be independent forces to which they may either submit or oppose themselves, but which they lack the objective and subjective resources to control. The processes of alienation and its results thus curb the freedom of man; they limit the satisfaction of his basic needs both material and spiritual. Artistic-aesthetic alienation is a dimension of an encompassing alienation which can be effected if art has succumbed to myths and mystifications not of its own election, or if it combats these, or if the aesthetic values of the social model are so negligible as to become prized in an exclusive way—resulting in the mythos of the artist closed inside his ivory tower and superior to events, the mythos of the eternal "outsider." Alienation thus understood does not depart from the methodological guidelines of Marx, and is also applicable to our sociohistorical conditions.

Henri Lefebvre, in his *Introduction à la modernité* (Paris, 1962), draws our attention to the new modes of *Entfremdung* affecting art that Marx had no grounds for discussing. These are: scientific and technical alienation (e.g., the discoveries of nuclear physics, cybernetics, etc., and the dangers issuing therefrom) and the political and ideological alienation which has been evoked by and has widely troubled the Stalinist deployment of socialist power. A literary reflection of the former mode is presented in the fate of Möbius, a major character in Dürrenmatt's *The Physicists*. The latter mode is represented in the most convincing fashion in Solzhenitsyn's short stories. On a larger scale and incorporating both modes, Peter Handke's *Kaspar* depicts the counteralienational struggle against speech-torture no less than world-torture (the latter involving deceiving sociopolitical, scientific, and technological myths). These recent phenomena can occur, obviously, only as a consequence of an unresolved antinomy between the artist and society. As to the aleatory aspect of modern creative production, Lefebvre links it to these pervasive discords of our epoch. For the coming period he does not exclude the possibility that a sociopolitical and philosophical resolution might be synthesized. We need not assent to all of Lefebvre's judgments, which tend to be rather rash, to agree with him about the futility of analyzing the function of today's art without reference to the contemporary modes of its alienation. We must also agree when Lefebvre notes that the Dionysian strain prevails in the cultural model of the twentieth century. The Apollonian vision of a Marx is a good deal harder to attain; artists may, indeed, find it unattainable.

I should add that Lefebvre is stimulated not by the visionary but rather by the realistic force of thought in Marx. It is precisely Marx who shows the concrete antagonisms of art and society, one of which is the unprecedented difficulty faced by the artist (whether committed or uncommitted) in his attempt to resolve conflicting aesthetic and sociopolitical claims (i.e., the seeming distinction between the so-called universally human content of art and an ideological outlook embedded therein). Marx attributes to such phenomena a dialectical unity.

Even where the concept of alienation and disalienation does not appear as such in their works, the anlyses of the American scholars (among aestheticians, especially Melvin Rader) lead eventually to this problem. Herbert Read addresses himself directly to it—as in *The Third Realm of Education* (Cambridge, Mass., 1960), where he develops his earlier view that a true education is impossible without an emphasis on art; in other words, that education must be more than just discursive, as it is where only a drilling in facts and moral axioms occurs. Read sees a hope for overcoming the antinomy between pleasure and work in the Marxian alienation theory. Even so, he cannot believe that a society might be organized today in such a way that work is felt to be pleasurable. Read argues that specialization, as its impact grows from year to year, leads irresistibly to ever greater alienation, which he calls a technological alienation. He saw firsthand and was sympathetic to the experiments in aesthetic education in the Chinese People's Republic —but he came, nonetheless, to accept Schiller's thesis that self-integration is to be achieved only outside of work, in the "play and leisure time" of man. I cannot altogether agree for several reasons: First, automation as it ceaselessly advances opens up ever new possibilities, and can evoke a positive attitude toward work, that is, toward work in some degree creative. Second, Marx never claimed that the humanity of the future would be an aesthetic humanity due exclusively to the

character of the work process. Third, in a way Read's vision, although stated very
recently, is more a conjecture of imagination than that of Marx a century ago, for
it leans upon the Kantian and Schillerian idea of three separable aspects of the
world. However, I am not nearly as interested here in differences as in noting that,
in discussing the various artistic functions, Read, too, accords a most prominent
role to the concept of alienation.[7]

This question was linked to the problem of time by Hans Meyerhoff. Man has
grown acutely sensitized to time: the constant need to fragment one's day, the
excess of obligations one has, leads to a loss of the sense of selfhood. The problem
of "alienation through time" recurs in twentieth-century literature from Proust and
Virginia Woolf to the so-called antinovel of Robbe-Grillet and Butor.

Literature and art do indeed lend evidence to the assertion that the concept of
alienation figures as a key to current reality. The life work of Bertolt Brecht is one
sustained unmasking of the capitalist modes of alienation, and Dürrenmatt has
pursued his example. Diverse aspects of the same single phenomenon are illumined
by Kafka and Musil—the alienation of the uninformed or of the aware but still
floundering individual in the power of the state; Thomas Mann in *Doctor Faustus*—
the alienation of modern art; Max Frisch in *Homo Faber*—the technical-rational
alienation which stems from the highly organized nature of life. The alienation
processes in socialism have received an effective portrayal only recently in the
novels of Solzhenitsyn.[8]

I have not been able to discuss the alienation problem fully here, but I could not
pass over it entirely, for the functioning of both modern and earlier art is brought
into focus by the concept as by an optical lens. My marxist interpretation has discerned a fivefold artistic functioning; I can now specify the interconnections and
the hierarchy of the particular themes—or strands—under the conditions of alienation: In comparison with the other themes, the Orphic strand initially plays a lesser
role during the revolutionary period of transition from an alienated past towards
a fully humanized social order. The Philoctetean theme asserts precedence where
the historical processes of alienation are pitted against those of antialienation.
Disalienation processes tend to restore the Orphic strand—together with the tendencies inherent to the "art as life" movement, the second framing function—to
its appropriate operation; in the aftermath of the socialist revolution and the creation of the socialist state an aesthetic education *sensu stricto* will acquire increasing
importance, helping to prepare the aesthetic humankind of the future.

We are witness to artistic processes which to some degree would seem to con-

firm the Marxian hypotheses about the future of art and its integration with life.
Applied art has come to occupy a central place in the art of the twentieth century;
indeed, it now appears to have prefigured the style of the epoch. By organizing
the space of the locales in which we live, work, shop, and take walks, art enters
directly into life. A task force of persons specifically concerned with *l'art implique* —
to borrow a term from Etienne Souriau — are employed in the machine-dependent
industry of today, bringing it closer to the handcraft industries of the past. They
lend the personal touch to items which always had been treated as technical, impersonal products. We may glimpse in this a disalienating development. It is, however, limited and only fragmentary. First, although an enlargement of the field for
aesthetic perception is gained, the (Marxian) question of *homo faber* as *homo
ludens* is wholly begged — with no likelihood of its being dealt with in this mode.
Second, the "do-it-yourself" (in French, *bricolage*) tendency does not necessarily
imply that a competence in work technology can be turned into artistic activity.
Third, the authentic liberation of a human being only occurs when his entire psychic
energy is activated in expression of the most completely human sense of his existence, and when his principal aspirations (the Promethean theme) are thus fully
embodied; that is, when he is able to be the actor of history and not its slave, to
finish with all kinds of tyranny and authoritarianism, to live in a society which is
free of hunger, poverty, violence, and repression.

All of these qualifications, however, do not diminish the significance of "the
aestheticization of everyday life." They only serve to explain why the second framing function is marginal and not central in coming to terms with the domain of art
and with art's intrinsic and extrinsic potentialities.

Somewhat similarly, we can see a limited disalienation in the continuous life
spectacles organized by television — that is, a lessening of the demarcations between the life model and the art model. In improvisatory jazz, moreover, the mode
of experience to be had by a listener is such as to induce us to reconsider the effect
of art. There is the story of King Saul who sent his retinue to Nayoth to clap David
into custody. But the prophets at Nayoth frustrated the aims of these emissaries,
by artfully beguiling them: "and when they saw the company of prophets prophe-
sying, and Samuel standing as head over them, the spirit of God came upon the
messengers of Saul, and they also prophesied" (I Samuel 19:20). I attended a performance of the Dizzy Gillespie Band in San Francisco; and as I sat among the
rhythmically swaying, enraptured throng of listeners, in a near-dark hall lit by a
few dull-red electric candles in the corners, it struck me that I was participating in a

modern ceremony. The rhythm and the never-to-be-duplicated expression of the
jazz ensemble induce a state in the listener such as to tear down the boundaries
separating the ego from its environment, if full attention is diverted to the body.
This effect is reminiscent à *rebours* of the syncretic birth of poetry, song, and dance
in collaborative labor—described by Karl Bücher in the eighth chapter of his book
Arbeit und Rhythmus (1896). In two ways the concert affected me: as a structure
of sounds (the Orphic dimension) and as a sensory-rhythmical climate the perva-
siveness of which was intensified by the milieu. I quite early yielded myself to the
performance and experienced a pleasing aesthetic emotion such as I had never
previously known in this way. The Orphic theme was illustrated here in a special
mode: I, and the other members of the audience, submitted to the identical aesthetic spell. The second framing function was here, of course, equally obvious, but
I must emphasize that this modern ritual was imbued by the aesthetic exigencies:
Art was not rendered obsolete but extended. This distinctive, unique experience
became merged with life-experience, and I was ready at a single word from Dizzy
Gillespie and his group to respond with my own act; I was ready to go out into the
streets rendering changes on his tune. I was virtually a jam session participant myself, prepared to take initiative or to be propelled along willy-nilly.

Without question we likewise observe a fusion of the Orphic, the "art-as-life"
trend with the Philoctetean strand in the particular case of communal celebrations and demonstrations. There may be Orphic presentations included (music,
dance, plastic arts), but just let the participant or spectator get caught up, and he
will develop a practical-ceremonial attitude. If the situation or times move into a
dramatic sequence, the Promethean strand often emerges as well. Let me give just
one offhand but most revealing example. American friends have informed me that
in the spring of 1965 Alan Ginsberg wrote a poem which was a kind of proposal
for the Vietnam Day Committee's demonstration in San Francisco. This poem—a re-
buttal to the brutal actions of the Oakland police against the earliest demonstrators
—celebrated love and peaceful activity, and was adopted as the scenario for the
protest, which was "staged" on San Francisco's streets.[9]

Again, I should stress that this mode of disalienation—much like applied art
or, more specifically, industrial art—affords a somewhat increased freedom to the
aesthetic sense, indeed extending its domination over the technical world; but,
just as certainly, it does not in itself solve the major human problems. Moreover,
there is the danger that such freedom will prove illusory and fleeting if the problems coped with by the Promethean outlook in art remain essentially unchanged.

How practicable then is the Marxian vision of an aesthetic humankind? Of
course, history alone will deliver the final verdict. The prediction is based on the
idea of a humankind delivered from misery and necessity. Marxism, and the theories closest to it, again and again refer to this vision. Accordingly Christopher
Caudwell wrote, in *Illusion and Reality* (1938): "Art is a mode of freedom. . . .
Communist poetry will be complete, because it will be man conscious of his own
necessity as well as that of outer reality. . . . Art is one of the conditions of man's
realization of himself, and in its turn is one of the realities of man." Ernst Fischer's
The Necessity of Art (1959) holds that, in the future, art will enlarge its function
of developing the personality, in contribution to the process whereby the individual
develops identity with nature and with his fellow man. Art, says Ernst Fischer, is
to become a genial faculty of the society as a whole.

The passages just cited do have a note of the prophetic to them, as their authors
certainly were aware. If we adopt instead of a visionary a scientific view of social
development, it is feasible, in line with Comte's rule — *savoir pour prévoir* — to set
down a few predictions, yet no genius has ever forecast the concrete processes of
the historical development to come. From certain indications it does appear — as
I have said — that elements of the Marxian vision are starting to be realized. In
countries of very different ideological stamp, similar trends can be observed —
whether they are the conscious aim of politicians, or are present, for all that, in
the arts and the theories of art.

This is not to say that there are no grounds for skepticism. As I said in discussing
Herbert Read, the question seems to be whether the individual's entire psychic
potential can be brought all together to accomplishment. The epoch of an ever
burgeoning specialization appears not to favor realization of the ideal of the aesthetic man in this respect. Those who support the idea (Read is among them) will
reply that even if the production process does not lead towards this goal, the ex-
pansion of leisure time yet enables, increasingly, the emergence of aesthetic sensibility and an emotional life. A return to Hegel — to his thesis about the termination
of art, and its replacement by philosophy — is now being made by some thinkers.
These theoreticians draw a smidgeon of evidence from the intellectualizing tendencies of the arts, for example the antinovel, antifilm, antipainting. But alongside
the highly intellectualized work, so nearly related to the essay and manifesto, the
twentieth century can lay claim to direct and spontaneous creations, which theorists who wish to prognosticate the end of art have overlooked.

There remains the possibility that, rather than becoming identified with life, art will (unavoidably) retain its independence in a century of increasing specialization. Or again—even if disalienation does prove practicable, in other words, if the aesthetic values can be realized in a particular social model and at least some modes of production come to be identical with artistic creativity—even so a great deal of artistic creation, though fundamentally always operational (i.e., due to techne, arrangement, etc.), will remain apart from the strictly productive domains. Precisely beyond this juncture where art and production do not coincide, the situation may become exceptional, that is, a situation of alienation; for the evolution of art does not lead to the overcoming of all internal and external antinomies. These cannot but remain, although they will present themselves in a changed context and one unknown to us.

If art is to be shucked off, then the Orphic theme is anachronistic and major changes are required in the other strands. However, if art is to be amalgamated to everyday life, then the Orphic strand will either wither away and be replaced by what I have called the second framing function (the *zizhnostroyenije* tendency), or it will absorb and supersede that tendency. My other two major functions might then be pushed to the margins of artistic life, or gradually wane. Should art retain its independence, then all the themes will persist; however, new tensions and conflicts will emerge to replace the tensions of today among these themes.

If we reject the updated Hegelian theory of the end of art, we must then choose the more plausible of the two remaining possibilities. It is not the business of a scholar, whose job is to analyze the facts available to him and to generalize cautiously from them, to make predictions about the far future. What he should do— working with the questions supplied by a philosophy of art—is to try to explain the dominance of certain art functions.

This has been the aim of my essay, and, for this reason, I cannot go the full way with Herbert Marcuse in his fascinating *Essay on Liberation* (1969; especially chapter 2). Certainly, I am not opposed to the utopian approach, in the sense that it is thinking based on the contemporary dynamic reality and it entails negation of the actual state of affairs and reflection on the development of tangible potentialities; and I wholly agree with Marcuse in locating an antialienational trend in the contemporary avant-garde. However, I find that his understanding of "the aesthetic" pushes to the extreme just one of the aspects inherent to Marxian theory.

Marcuse focuses on the idea of what Marx termed the "rich man" in full and integrated possession of his psychic faculties and functions. Marcuse bolsters this notion with Freudian and surrealist concepts; and he concludes that the era of the

New Sensibility, which we should eventually achieve, will be founded on Aesthetic Forms as equivalent to the Reality Principle. He accordingly envisages the man of the future as essentially *homo aestheticus*. This seems to me a rather speculative interpretation, especially if due weight is given to the growth of specialization, which even the proposed nonrepressive society of tomorrow will not be able to discard. Given his overly hopeful premise, Marcuse is led unquestionably in the direction of projecting the dissolution of all art forms and the transformation of art into the "mode of life." I do not see this happening—any more than I see likelihood in the opposed prophecies, which speak of impending restoration of the centrality of the representational arts.

I will readily grant that the value and function of art undergo essential changes (see chapter 2). If the aesthetic is destined to become a *gesellschaftliche Produktivkraft*, however, then Marcuse must be prepared to make all the arguments that are called forth by the notion of the end of art; yet that assertion is undoubtedly too sweeping. My own approach avoids dangers of this order by sticking to short-term utopian reflections regarding the present and future. Art, due to its "second reality" (confronting the primary realities of society and nature) and relative autonomy, seems able to go on delivering cathartic effects, which, of course, need not yield purely illusory gratifications in relation to life's hardships and frustrations. As Ernst Fischer rightly argues, the contemporary art endowed with human ethos has some leverage to enhance and remodel life values.

Conceding all the complicated moot points in the discussion, I am inclined to conclude that the major functions in the priority discerned here will persist as the long contest of alienation and disalienation proceeds: First, in the preparation of a disalienated world, the Philoctetean motif is basic, and it may remain vital in new circumstances that must be unknown to us. Second, the Promethean theme is surely pivotal to the challenge hurled against an alienated world, and it cannot grow obsolete as long as human history unflaggingly continues to pursue the "ought" in contrast to the "is". Third, if the disalienation processes are nourished increasingly and organically on the aesthetic values (as these are understood against a background of the human heritage), the Orphic function will survive—not only by its immersion and dispersion in "art-as-life" activity, but still more through the example it sets to such phenomena by its integral structures. In this way, it will contribute maximally to the achievement of a fuller humanization of social life.

Having cited the ideal of "fuller humanization," I wish to append a few succinct words on the goals and pattern by which human desire and will can be oriented to the fulfillment of this ambition. In my view, those means ought to be pursued which are pervaded by the optimum attainable degree of *justice* and *freedom*, and which should, then, provide both a springboard and a field of play for *creativity* and *harmony*. These four goals, which are treated as end-values, will only be tangible to us when patterned (embodied) as means. We shall then find that we can pursue these means/ends only in the rhythms of their recurrent mutual oppositions, which do, nonetheless, achieve concordances.

Notes

1. See U. Eco, "Messagio estetico come l'idioletto," in *La struttura assente: Introduzione alla ricerca semiologica* (Milan, 1968).

2. Nelson Goodman places overriding emphasis on the problem of the purpose and function of art, and we explicitly diverge regarding this matter. I am, however, astonished to read on p. 248 of *The Languages of Art* that the emotions function cognitively to discern what properties a work possesses and expresses. So far as I can see, Goodman is saying more than just that we respond emotionally to expressive qualities: he is using "cognition" not in the metaphorical, Pickwickian sense, but rather in a sense that implies epistemological inquiry. Thus, taking this statement in its literal locution, I find that it espouses the rather odd phenomenology of Max Scheler, who argued for emotions as the faculties of spirit that were truly capable of intuitively comprehending values.

Another way to tackle this issue, and a more promising one in my view, is that of Georg Lukács in *Die Eigenart des Aesthetischen*. Lukács adopts the Diltheyan hermeneutics, according to which expression in art can be interpreted as a *psychosocial* phenomenon. (For a further discussion of expression and its meanings, see chapter 5.)

3. I am fully aware that the proponents of conceptual art turn away all attempts to establish durable definitions, since they hold that the artists must permanently unsettle the status of art. If you read the manifestos of, for instance, Joseph Kosuth or Alain Kirili, however, no doubt can remain that they chiefly mean to exchange artistic creation for a "methodology of art." They want to alter the bias in favor of formal excellence, expression, representation, and communication, so as to secure the uttermost implications of Duchamp's strategy (the art-world as the permanently self-problematizing challenge) and of Ad Reinhardt's minimal art. In my schematization of art's tendencies, this "art-follows-philosophy" view which, as the authors intend, becomes paralogical and paramathematical, and is akin to synoptic charts, scientific programs, and physicists' diagrams, is art immensely intellectualized. Its counterparts should be sought in the *nouveau roman* and in French structuralist semiology (the *Tel Quel* grouping). Although the movement was originally American, it is most valuable to trace it in its world-girdling contemporary European variants. (Cf. the "Art conceptuel" issue of the French-Swiss quarterly *VH101*, 1970 no. 3.)

4. See, for example, the scheme set forth in F. C. Sparshott, *The Structure of Aesthetics* (Toronto, 1963), ch. 8, and also the two subsequent chapters, which concern art in relation to the individual as well as the society.

5. I must here omit discussion of precapitalist alienation. However, a thorough study of Marx's thought (see, for example, the illuminating discussion in I. Mészàros, *Marx's Theory of Alienation* [1970]) may well conclude that the three aspects of alienation have been functional from the origin of our civilization. It should be added that prior to capitalism the predominant aspects were political and ideological (chiefly religious). A keen insight into the precapitalist situation of the artist may be obtained from R. and M. Wittkower, *Born Under Saturn* (New York, 1963).

6. Incidentally, in this context of historical

development the affinities between Marx's
and Dewey's aesthetics could be rewardingly
explored. I leave the question in abeyance,
however, as there is no brief, compact way
for me to formulate the affinities.

7. The importance ascribed by Read to this
crucial issue of modern artistic life emerges
even more clearly from his last published
volume, *Art and Alienation* (London, 1967).
Another interesting example of the importance of this theme is R. McMullen's *Art,
Affluence and Alienation* (London, 1968),
especially its introduction and a concluding
chapter on the open-ended future.

8. An illuminating treatment of the issues
of this subject matter is provided by Georg
Lukács in his two recently translated essays
on *Solzhenitsyn* (Cambridge, Mass., 1971).
However, I must add that I disagree with
Lukács' assessment of Solzhenitsyn as a
"socialist realist." He is, rather, a critical
realist in an era of bureaucratically maimed
socialism. In this sense, we still await an
"insider's critique," that is, one from the
viewpoint of a communist-oriented artist.
(For a further discussion of Solzhenitsyn and
socialist realism, see chapter 7.)

9. This corresponds to ideas advanced in
Lee Baxandall's stimulating 1969 essay on
the dramaturgy of radical confrontation,
reprinted in the anthology which he has
edited, *Radical Perspectives in the Arts*
(Baltimore, 1972).

Chapter 10   Quotation in Art

In what context does the use of quotation arise? On the whole, it is where respect exists for a knowledge of precedents or sources. Quotes are a proof if not a badge of learning. We expect to find them in the scholar's dissertation, a legal brief or decision, an essay which popularizes science, a treatise on philosophy. Due to this same connection of quotations to past precedents and previous knowledge, we are often disgruntled to find them in a journalist's impression, a love letter, when chatting with an acquaintance, or in a reader's letter of opinion to a newspaper, where the freshness of response is to be highly prized. At such times, the citing of precedents may come across as pedantic or otherwise out of place. I believe that the possible use of quotations in art objects is likewise limited, but this is a proposition to be tested, not merely asserted, and I should like to analyze the elements that constitute the quotation and its significance in a particular context.

Tracing the usage of the term "quotation" will lead us first to the early courts of law, where witnesses were summoned before a magistrate and required to swear to the accuracy of their statements. The law courts have always placed emphasis on the *authoritative* character of a quotation that is accepted into evidence. Right here, we should stop and take note of the dual nature of the phenomenon. On the one hand, the *new* context, which may be an institution such as a law court, tends to assert the authoritative status of a quotation. On the other hand, the quotation emerges from a particular setting or context which usually to some extent lets us test the fidelity, or truth, of its attribution within the newer context.

If we trace the use of quotation through the emergence of civilization, we see that for very long the institutional assertion of its status has been paramount, not only in the law courts but also in the military, where, for example, "citation" has meant an order or decision conveyed to the troops or the public. Quotation of necessity became a central practice of the ecclesiastical authorities, since the Church pointed for its transcendent authority to the Bible and the various commentaries thereon. With the Renaissance, the content of quotation shifted, and the activity of quoting became a prerogative of the layman; but there was still little emphasis on original contexts. At this time the classical authors of antiquity were reintroduced to shore up one or another traditional authority that had come under suspicion. As the nuclei of authority had multiplied, the same quotation might now be employed from several standpoints for competing aims. Gradually, by the sixteenth and seventeenth centuries, and as often as not to validate a personal claim

This essay was written in 1965 and originally published in Polish in *Nurt* (Poznan).

to a disputed quotation from a favorite author, the original context was gaining
more attention.

The seventeenth and eighteenth centuries marked the turning point, and in the
next century it became common for a writer to consult original contexts rather than
rely on textual authority as such. Out of the European framework an *historicist*
mode of thought had emerged. I mean by historicism a pervasive inquiry into the
past, accomplished by various intellectual disciplines at different levels of abstraction, with the respect for the past dictated by a concern for the present and future.
This kind of scholarship then developed its own institutional features, more or less
assuring that quotation would not be able to lapse into ahistoricity once more. I
do not mean to imply, of course, that quotation has now become the exclusive
prerogative of science, historicist scholarship, and humanist essays. The use of this
device still flourishes in the law courts, where it is invoked by the defense no less
than the prosecutor, as well as in many other kinds of public situations.

I can give no more than this brief account of quotational praxis, for I am concerned here not with the history of quotation, but with its theory. My goal is to
provide a definition that will accommodate the conventional ideas of yesterday and
today, and also the formulations set forth by various dictionaries or encyclopedias.

Towards a Definition of Quotational Praxis

Let me start with the assertion that *quotation is the integral reproduction of a
written or spoken text of a certain length, or of a certain set of images, sounds,
or movements, or of a combination of such materials, in a way which allows what
is reproduced to provide a coherent part of a new whole and yet remain readily
detachable from the new whole.* Here is a definition which deliberately is left
"open" so as not to exclude the possibility of quotation from such nondiscursive
"languages" as are used in music or painting (a possibility which needs further
examination).

The decisive traits of a quotation are its literalness and its discrete character in
the context where it is inserted. By "literalness" I mean accuracy or fidelity. By
"discrete character" I mean the setting off of the quote by quotation marks, either
actually or implicitly. A semantic element, the quotation is meant to achieve a particular function in a new, "higher semantic structure" which is operatively extraneous to it. The quotation is a subentity which the new, larger whole cannot completely absorb. The quotation is not so much distinct as it is distinguishable, not
so much separate as it is separable. Examining the quotation, we can surmise the

relation between the original from which it derives and the work that has borrowed
it, and I want to propose a typology of quotations based on the functions the quotations perform while out on loan to the higher semantic structures.

   To derive this typology, I must first review the situations which give rise to a
literal incorporation of an original referent. These can superficially be summed up
in the phrase "a maintenance of cultural continuity." It is clear from our historical
overview how strictly connected quotation is with a sense of tradition. The constancy of its occurrence confirms an irrepressible need and desire to keep in touch
with the prior attainments and values of the species. Glancing at the introductions
to The Oxford Dictionary of Quotations, 3rd ed. (1956) or the Encyclopédie des
citations (Paris, 1959), we are not astonished to read the editors' assertions that
the works are compiled to meet the requirements of persons with an appreciation
of the history of the human spirit. I should also note that the questions posed over
and over by history, and not simply the answers supplied, make important claims
on our attention. However, whether we go to the tradition for its evidence with
regard to problems or its assertion of solutions, we can see that in our age of revolutions the consultation of the past has taken on renewed urgency; the availability
of historicism has by no means made history out-of-date.

   In other words, quotation does not simply equate with antiquarianism, although
it is often enough used to dredge up the past uncritically and keep it comfortably
and nostalgically at hand. The vitality of quotational praxis is, however, seen more
in the confrontation with, than in the literal preservation of the perennial issues
and the attempts at solutions. This occurs whenever a new tradition crystallizes
to replace those which had previously exercised hegemony. Such abrupt trans-
valuations of value, such sharp breaks with what had recently seemed the best
available tradition, seem implacably to erupt as part of evolutionary cultural development. Thus, quotation can give accent to the dilemma of every age, to the eternal
tensions between innovation and a preservation of the past.

   How is this tension manifest? Texts from the displaced tradition may be cited
in scientific or philosophical inquiries with the aim of systematically refuting or
qualifying their claims; or, the writers in the new tradition may scan sympathet-
ically their own "classic" forebears with the goal of sanctioning a particular future
line of interpretation. From this latter operation (which is itself interpretive) a re-
patterning of the still emergent "living" body of texts, questions, and propositions
appears. I must also here mention the malicious use of quotations from either the
"dead" traditions or from competing tendencies within one's own tradition; how-

ever, where the goal of disparagement replaces analytical intent, the quotational praxis is transformed into worse than antiquarian musing: it becomes a blow against a meaningful past.

The creation of a positive connection with the past is certainly not the job of quotation alone. This point may seem obvious; yet we should take care to see how the study of quotation leads us by an immediate route into the heart of the dialectical problems of cultural processes. We have in the quotation not only an (interchangeable) semantic element, but also a *semiotic* element. The semiotic material is inherently part of both *synchronic* and *diachronic* structures. When the diachronic structure is recalled in thought, a past which can be almost infinitely repatterned is available. Quotation, however, has the trait of presenting this semiotic material in a synchronic present-day structure which lends to it a certain context, which we may analyze for the relationship which is thus created between the quote-inclusive structure and those who respond to it. In this way the *actual* functional *application* of quotation is connected with the functional *relationship* to the past.

In what follows, I shall primarily consider the synchronic, contemporary use of quotes. Accordingly, I may seem to elaborate the functions without concern for the original context of what is quoted, and with the assumption that the semiotic elements are ahistorical constants. This is, of course, not the case, and we need not overlook, either, that the contemporary use of the quoted semiotic element may dovetail with the original, diachronic integrity of meaning. In any case, the past will become wholly unintelligible if we do not regard it ultimately as a sociocultural process productive of synchronic elements to which we can, attendant upon specifiable difficulties, relate.

A Typology of Quotational Functions

I have noted that the earliest major function of quotation, which obviously continues to this day, is the assertion of legitimate authority. In this sense of a solicitation of trust and deference, quotation often serves as a means both to avoid and to forestall independent thought. The quoter does not have to discover his own opinion; nor need he provide reasons to back up his use of quotation. This function plays a chief role in periods when one philosophical system is clearly dominant, particularly if powerful institutions lend it official support.

A few examples will help to make this point clear: medieval Church officers cited either the Bible or their predecessors in office in order to acquire the authority of that institutional and ideological tradition; the early Renaissance humanists who

retrieved the thought of Plato and Aristotle held the views of those philosophers
to be self-evident; the writers who remained in favor through the Soviet "cult of
personality" became adept at employing quotations from Stalin, together with a
wholly conventionalized commentary, as a quasi-philosophy. Quotation can thus
feed, and feed on, an unquestioned authority, although it will display the intellectual torpor of the writer and reader alike. The ritual, the canon, are paramount;
and any challenge to the ascendant tradition is considered at least as a social
malfunction, and probably as a heresy or sin. The selection and manner of presentation of the quotes betrays this function — an interesting geneticofunctional aspect
that will be explored later — but it is evident that one's favored notion of authority
will curtail the field from which the quotations may be taken, and the possibilities
of applying them will be determined mostly by current social imperatives, as interpreted by the legates of the authority.

From these remarks, it might seem that quotation which simply promulgates a
legitimate authority must be an anachronistic and pernicious phenomenon. However, this device is, in fact, appropriate to some kinds of discourse, particularly
where the context is acknowledged as doctrinal or institutional: a sermon or an
ethical homily; a legal brief, where a similar case was decided in another court
with an inescapable application; or a presentation of a philosophical, sociopolitical, or other system with a long-preserved structure (i.e., a doctrine whose scope,
thematic hierarchy, and interpretation have been effectively settled). These are
cases where it would be quite illogical to anticipate any other sort of quotation but
quotation from authority; the cause of discourse within the perimeters is best served
by argument from the agreed-upon postulates.

Nonetheless, we are all well aware that the authority of such quotation has
been undermined by the scientific and technological advances of our century. The
trusting attitude survives chiefly in cases where the whole sociocultural situation
fosters a respect for tradition as the guide to both conduct and thought. Fascinating, in our day and age, is the idea of studying the function of quotation in an
Asian or African culture where nationalism has stirred both a socialist consciousness and religious fanaticism. We might find a combination of, say, a "personality
cult" socialism and ritualistic Islam. The character of these two authority-systems
would, on the whole, be opposed to one another; it seems unlikely that the absolute
role of either one could be maintained, no matter how the quotes might be deftly
chosen and interwoven.

A second function of quoting is to provide erudition. This function appears to be in the strictest accord with my definition. Here, someone makes extracts from a particular context so as to communicate its salient aspects. The knowledge-spreading quote may appear in the body of a new structure or in a note or addendum. If in the body, the idea generally is to let the original statement "speak for itself"; the quote is regarded as firm ground on which to erect the new structure of interpretation. If in a note, the implication is that more may be achieved by reformulating the views from the past while maintaining the coherence of the new statement. The goal of erudition is to quote aptly and concisely. Aptness (or relevance) is a scholarly standard, while conciseness, is as much an aesthetic as a scholarly standard.

In part, the aptness of a quotation is dependent on the context in which it appears. Unless one is simply piecing together "a presentation" of the original author's views, one will choose quotes with an eye to the expositional requirements of the argument underway.

This brings me to a third function which is, however, closely related to the function of providing erudition. Again, a certain number of faithfully presented, apt, and concise quotations are used; but, whereas quotations may well be sufficient in themselves for pulling together a topic in an erudite monograph, the writer here is concerned chiefly with presenting an original argument, and introduces the quotations as a restrained, tactical element in a much larger, comprehensive strategy. This strategy might use quotations as bridges between positions, as springboards to speculation, or as evidence in deciding whether or not to proceed in freshly formulating a commonplace question or in rejecting an apparently settled answer. Although not everyone might agree that the praxis here is categorically different, I shall demarcate more or less dense quotation with an erudite function from erudite quotation inside a comprehensive strategy of original argument. Accordingly, to the authoritative and erudite functions of quotation I add this function which stimulates and amplifies an exposition.

Reasonably, we expect to find that the functions may overlap or even coincide. Where the erudite and stimulative-amplificatory functions are mingled, we get a result worthy of separate mention. Here, quotations are intended at once to *present* a tradition and to *interpret* it. A Polish anthology of *Existential Philosophy* (1965), for example, excerpted its represented figures extensively, and in a way which insisted on serious differences with them; the specific published texts provided both a useful "defense" and a presentation of the ideology. Within the anthology, a similar effect was evident in the personal readings of Kierkegaard given by such leading existentialists as Shestov, Sartre, and Camus, each of which tended to reinforce the author's own view (which, in fact, had sprung from idiosyncratic antecedents). Another instance of this dual functionality of quotation, for another tradition, is Adam Schaff's *Marxism and the Individual* (1965) wherein the author simultaneously expounds Marx and directs our attention to selected themes.

Indeed, it is evident that, at various stages of the development of marxist doctrine, different aspects of the basic writings have gained attention. This fluctuation of preferences affects every body of classic texts. Succeeding periods revaluate the heritage. The legacy is restructured, priorities are reshuffled, and a somewhat altered general sense of the classical tradition emerges. This treatment gives the quotations or readings a double significance inasmuch as the heritage is both preserved and breached: which is only to say, finally, that aspects of a tradition that have been neglected or forgotten may be recovered. Strict exegesis is always claimed although, in fact, the interpretive activity is inherent. An actualization of the old texts thus corroborates the vigor of the theory while modifying its original total meaning.

The place of quotation in this ongoing process of revaluation will always be equivocal. On the one hand, it brings forth the received philosophical heritage. On the other hand and especially, the quotation functions in a new totality which is bound to modify what is preserved. In aesthetics, a case of dual functionality is seen in the way both "formalists" and "nonformalists" often appeal to the same quote in their protracted quarrel; they will both take any text employing the terms "form" and "content" and try to explicate the priorities and the interrelations in their own terms, but, as time goes on, each side will increasingly use the consulted text chiefly to stimulate the efficacy of its own interpretations and to amplify their centrality, while the old, classical text, however reinvigorated, will inevitably slip away from the center of the discussion. Another instance of this process is the growing "structuralization" of Marx's aesthetic thought. The customary texts from Marx and Engels are cited, while interpretation turns increasingly towards the specific structure of the work of art as the key problem of art. This modification may be seen in Lukács' *Die Eigenart des Aesthetischen* (1963), in the writings of Ernst Fischer, and in my own work. When such modifications are adequately conducted, the pertinent quotations from Marx will be treated as decisive in the problems of the interpretation. Arbitrariness and fudging may creep into interpretation—but they need not, and should not.

To restructure a theoretical heritage, one must not only be concerned with current needs and trends in the theoretical domain; one must also establish a firm grip on the dynamic potential of the tradition, whether this is one side of it or the whole of it. The implicit assumptions and aims of the founder of the tradition — where determinable — should explicitly be considered. In brief, one should not treat material from the founder's basement or lumber-room or attic as though it belonged in the parlor. There is no scientific rationale for inflating or skewing the significance of a theoretical heritage.

Can strictly scientific inquiry benefit from the dual functionality of quotation? It can indeed, and, although there is less precedent for the stimulative-amplificatory interpretation of such texts, it should clearly be seen that interpretation cannot be entirely dispensed with. Consider David Bohm's *Causality and Chance in Modern Physics* (London, 1957), wherein the author attaches his individual interpretation to the findings of the Copenhagan school, which he juxtaposes with the Laplace theory. Bohm includes no quotations in the body of his text. Either they appear in footnotes, or else Bohm simply paraphrases the views of the scientists involved. A similar interpretive account of modern scientific theory is Hermann Weyl's *Symmetry* (Princeton, 1952); Weyl, however, does not dispense with main-text quotations.

Another function of quotation is to act as an ornament. This application is particularly common in public speaking or in the occasional essay. Quoting decoratively differs markedly from quoting with an erudite aim. One does the latter to render the original author's communication faithfully, prior to endorsing and developing it further or perhaps rebutting it; one does the former as a mere intellectual conceit, often with no pretense of concise application or coherence. In ornamental contexts, the handling of quotes is similar to their handling in an interpretive context, but scientific criteria of selection and usage are out of place here. The quotation may be taken wholly out of context, or it may be in context but entirely marginal to the quoted writer's basic view.

In considering this function we are brought up abruptly against the *semiotic* side of quotation and its dualistic semantic character: it performs literally with respect to its parent structure and subserviently with respect to its host context, in greater or lesser degree. The literal quality and all that that semantically implies is evident in all of the functions I have considered. The reception within the host structure, however, varies with the function. Erudition handles quotes in a detached way; ornamentation seems wholly to absorb the quotation into the new setting. Authoritative quoting sets its material out in an unchallengeable fashion;

but the stimulative-amplificatory approach seems to want to spur new intellectual constructions by its presentations.

In ornamentation, the favored form of quotation is the epigram, and its handling is symptomatic. Whereas in the case of authoritative quotation the authority is the decisive element, here the accuracy and the attribution of the quote are almost unimportant; what will matter for the listener or reader are certain associations evoked by the passage. Thus, the epigram may be set apart typographically, but for all practical purposes it might be original to the host text, since it expresses not the thought of the quoted writer but an idea that will be expounded in the host text. Quotation might be termed "aesthetic" where it is ornamental in function, for the writer is so intent on the effect of his product that he dissolves or blurs the demarcation between his original work and his borrowings. Here, too, however, we must not neglect the dualistic functioning where it occurs; for instance, some masterly philosophical, scholarly, and "aesthetic" essays will not overlook the stimulative-amplificatory function.

Undoubtedly, I have not exhausted the possible functions of quotation. I would contend, however, that the four functions I have taken up are the chief ones, and I shall now proceed towards some conclusions in the matter of quotation in works of art.

The Possible Modes of Quotation in Art

What would be the equivalent in a work of art of quotation with an authoritative function? Some might be inclined to locate it in *any* element or motif which constantly recurs. However, this would be a mistaken conclusion; any faint resemblances between the two phenomena are canceled by the fundamental differences. Some persistent motifs are canonical traits peculiar to and ubiquitous in a given culture or period (Lévi-Strauss links the persistent motif with static civilizations); while the general question of recurrent motifs can best be considered in the perspective of Jungian archetypes or E. R. Curtius' notion of *topoi*. Although there are important differences between archetypes and *topoi*, they are similar to the extent that both afford compositional or conceptual patterns which cannot on any account be regarded as extraneous or interpolated into the given artistic structure; and, stereotypical though it may be, the motif, much like the archetype or *topos*, comprises, in whole or in part, the skeletal matter of a work of art and not a "foreign element." Our task in this regard is simply to see to what extent the stereotype incorporates some individual modification or is a straight replica.

Jung maintained that archetypes result from congenital psychological dispositions evinced in the history of culture and invariable through the differing historical
contexts. Jung's theory of the "collective unconscious" (a notion which, by the way,
seems unverifiable) led him to regard creative energy as the basic manifestation
of the libido (a category here defined differently and more broadly than in the work
of Freud); the artist-seer brings to light the collective unconscious where the artist-
psychologist will only obscure its basic features. Maud Bodkin's classic study
Archetypal Patterns in Poetry (1934) argues that the visionary will distill the underlying archetypes in the greatest works of art: resurrection ("The Ancient Mariner"),
the opposition of heaven and hell (*Paradise Lost*, "Kubla Khan"), the great mother
(from Homer, Dante, and Goethe to D. H. Lawrence), saint and satan (Shakespeare
and Shelley to T. S. Eliot), and the like.

This interpretive approach is not confined to literary works. Erich Neumann's
Kunst und schöpferisches Unbewusstes (1954) looks at da Vinci and Chagall in
this way, analyzing how each painter employs the archetype of the great mother;
Herbert Read in "The Dynamics of Art" (*Eranos Jahrbuch*, 1952) finds this same
symbolism in the sculpture of Henry Moore, and he also finds the archetype of a
childlike freshness and spontaneity in Picasso's *Minotauromachia*.

Just from these few examples it must be evident that archetype and quotation
are dissimilar. The only point they have in common is the persistence with which
a given passage may recur. The archetype is, however, conceived as more a biologically than a culturally rooted phenomenon, while quotation is purely cultural.
The archetype permeates the whole of a signifying structure and cannot be detached from it; the nature of a quotation is that it is separable. While the quotation may turn up in many different works, it is always as a loan, defined by its ex-
traneity; the archetype is instead antinomical, an utterly private experience of the
creator employing it, although, at the same time, it partakes of the universal.

Topoi are conceived of as cultural phenomena, but this distinction from the
archetype does not overcome the predominant dissimilarity of the *topos* and the
quotation. Curtius regarded *topoi* as being beyond the merely recurrent rhetorical
figurations that could ultimately be regarded as a kind of paraquotation. Rather,
the *topoi* are certain modalities of mind and expression that are embodied in a
particular constructive pattern. For example, in his analysis of *European Literature
and the Latin Middle Ages* (1948), Curtius showed how the themes of *sapientia*
and *fortitudo* in the construction of the hero were at first opposed, and were only
later merged. No more than an archetype is the *topos* a quotation, for it is the con-

trolling principle of any artistic or nonartistic structure in which it appears. It cannot be extraneous. The *topos* carries echoes of other manifestations of that constructive bent which it shares (and here is where it recalls quotation), but always in modified form. Two examples of the transmutations of *topoi*—*furor divinus* and *altera theologia*—are explored by Otto Pögeller in "Theory of Poetry and Investigation of the *Topos*," *Jahrbuch für Aesthetik und allgemeine Kunstwissenschaft,* 1960. The *topos* then is operative within the limits of certain cultural ambits, which are demarcated by adjacent and analogous signifying structures. Curtius speaks of *Sinneinheit;* this spiritual kinship is said to promote the same or similar artistic models. Undoubtedly, the *topos* thus understood makes one think of Erwin Panofsky's patterns of iconography or iconology or simply of conventions in art, continuously passed down and transmuted. Quotation can have a part in such signifying cultural wholes, but its part is of a distinct order: its participation is conditional and can be withdrawn, most often without major harm.

Of particular interest to my discussion is the mutability of *topoi* without the loss of their conceptual identity. In view of this process I can, for instance, consider how motifs are taken over from the past and incorporated into new wholes. (This way of considering motifs shows them being handled in a way parallel to quotation.) Yet what is meant by the mutability of the *topoi*? In what manner is a concrete motif borrowed and assimilated? Briefly, in a new historical and cultural context the *topos* (the "motif") produces a changed artistic structure, that is, it does not slip into a new whole, but, rather, creates that whole. It is not the woven but the weaver.

At once we see how this process of the *topos*/motif differs from that of quotation. However, perhaps I wrongly use the case of the authoritative quotation, when I might better compare the historical continuity of the *topos* with the stimulative-amplificatory function of quotation? This shift may seem reasonable, but the analogy still isn't convincing. Quotation in all its functions remains a literal reproduction, a separable microworld in the new context, whatever ramifications are attached to it. The ornamental quotation might seem an exception, placed as the epigraph to an essay expounding at length on its theme, for instance; but even here its literalness and autarchic fragmentary quality preclude us from treating the quote as we would a *topos*. The latter, after all, is the backbone of a new whole; the former, as epigraph, scarcely offers more than the label of a *topos*.

Since I dismiss the possibility of parallelism between quotation and archetype, and also between quotation and *topos*, should I conclude that quotation has no

place in art? Surely not, and the evidence proves otherwise. I now turn to a discussion of the varieties known to appear in works of art.

Some works contain a kind of fugitive and nonprepossessing motif which makes
us doubt whether it rates mention as a quotation. Probably it does not — for these
glimmers of a microcoherence are so fully absorbed by the new whole that they
have to be pried out; whereas, in contrast, a quotation draws attention at first
glance. I shall return to this case later.

I should ask whether quotation ever appears in literature not merely in its ornamental or its stimulative functions, but also in its erudite function. This is a question
to which I should like to give extended attention. Its importance comes from the
fact that precisely the extreme instances cogently demonstrate the presence or
absence of the erudite quotation in works of art.

Consider *The Waste Land:* literary allusions play a crucial role, and Eliot even
gives notes to indicate their sources. More than being quotations in a strict sense
these are basically paraquotations, they are nonemphasized phrases which are
struts or spurs to the poet's own ideas and imagery. Their presence — veiled
though it is — is palpable in the style and the symbolism of the poem. The only
conventional, literal quotations are demarcated with the standard inverted com-
mas; these demand of the reader a considerable literary background, for Eliot
draws in bits of Shakespeare, Marvell, Baudelaire, Dante, Milton, Verlaine, the
Bible, and Saint Augustine.

The Waste Land uses quotation in every function I have delineated. Additionally, it should not be forgotten that the poem was written fundamentally as the
expression of an artistic philosophy, and Eliot explicitly refers readers in his notes
to the two learned works inspiring it, namely, Jesse L. Weston's *From Ritual to
Romance* and James Frazer's *Golden Bough.* The intention of the poet is here exceptionally binding on us, for it is so strongly impressed on the structure as to guide
the reception of the poem unequivocally. Quotations are used profusely because
Eliot regarded himself as both artist-scholar and artist-prophet and he wanted
the reader to accept this self-estimate. (We need not be concerned with the self-
irony he later displayed in his commentary to the *Waste Land* in *The Frontiers of
Criticism* [1957].) The prophetic tinge was catastrophic at the time the poem was
written, while the erudite bent was the natural extension of his philosophical and
linguistic investigations.

Eliot's aesthetic aimed at making poetry more vernacular, while he also wanted
to eliminate the difference between "verse" and the philosophical essay. This pur-

pose was reflected in his theory of "objective correlatives" (equivalents found in diction and imagery for emotional tensions). Eliot provides an instance where personal motivations — but also the cultural and historical situation (this was the time of dada, which denied both the old definitions of art and art in general) — led as a meaningful poetic device, to the embrace of both the simply erudite quotation, and the erudite-stimulative quotation.

Should Eliot be regarded as an exception? In my view, yes, he should be seen as rather exceptional; but this does not mean that quotations don't turn up elsewhere. A somewhat parallel Polish case is the collection of satirical poems by Tadeusz Boy-Zeleński called *Bon Mots* (1905–30). One, "Expiration," has an epigraph taken from *Ecclesiastes* which is also paraphrased in the poem itself. Another, "I Think No One Will Contradict Me," incorporates *Lasciate ogni speranza* the well-known tagline from Dante. While in both cases the quotation's function is primarily ornamental, in the former poem there is a stimulative plus-factor, from which the epigraph in no way detracts, while in the latter the tagline performs an amplificatory function for the main theme of the poem. The role of the quotes is, however, marginal in Boy. In other works he employed quotes or paraphrases so as to attack the conservative catch phrases endemic in the fields of politics, manners, and literature. These he parodied — not by deformation but by ironic commentary.

In prose the varieties of quotation appear in analogous contexts. Its erudite function is discovered where the writer has philosophical or learned intentions. Thus, in the novel *Insatiety* (1929) by the Polish philosopher and dramatist Stanislaw Ignacy Witkiewicz, we see quotations from Husserl, Beethoven, Tadeusz, Miciński, Ernst, Mach, and others. Some of these, characteristically, are provided in the apparatus which the author supplied for his own text. Beyond these, it is easy to find in the "metaphysical" conversations among his heroes Genezyp and Tengier, Prince Bazyly and Benz, paraphrases of the author's own views, elsewhere set out in his theoretical writings. The quotes in Witkiewicz are usually extremely truncated and sometimes not literal. Thus, at times their function is but quasi-erudite, despite the aim of the author (or of his characters) for a literal confrontation of quotes, a battle of ideologies presented *modo philosophico*.

We find in Aldous Huxley's *Point Counter Point* quotations from Claude Bernard and Shakespeare, Walt Whitman and Adam Smith, Baudelaire and zoology textbooks. This is but part of the erudition deployed through the novel, often in paraphrase or paraquotation. Each of the fictional characters represents a specific philosophy, and critics have been at pains to locate the real-life originals on whom they are modeled. *Point Counter Point* is an intellectual novel peopled by intellectuals; it expounds a pluralist philosophy of many equivalent, compatible truths. It is feasible to regard the quotations here as imploded elements of the created whole; nonetheless, they preserve their discrete aspect. Their function is in some contexts (as in the statements of Philip Quarles) erudite; and in others stimulative-amplificatory. Quotation is here as refractive as in an essay or a scholarly but interpretive exegesis. The fact that it lends itself to two semantic structures — its own original, and the host one — affords an especially fascinating character in this case.

These quotations have a dual character for yet another reason. They represent the attitude of the author but at the same time pertain to the character uttering them. As attributes of the characters, they weave into the structure of *Point Counter Point*, augmenting and sharpening its system of meanings. Simultaneously, they exude the climate of the novel (only the character Rampion resists; all the other characters are so laden with culture that they are unable or unwilling to forego the compulsion of tradition and intellect), and they fortify our feeling that Huxley is an erudite author interested mainly in people's minds. This impression is even more strongly made by the later novel *Eyeless in Gaza* wherein Anthony Beavis' diary is replete with quotations of an encyclopedic range.

I think I may make the fairly safe generalization from the four preceding examples that quotation most frequently appears in literary works when the writer has philosophical or learned ambitions and seeks — either in fiction alone, or in conjunction with discursive undertakings — to put across an intellectual perspective. Another motive for quotation's appearance may be parody — that is, the wish to discredit an idea or cliché — or an aesthetic effect, paradoxically furthered in the form of an apparently erudite ornament. In such cases quotation serves a function as either a trigger for some association, or a startlingly incongruous interpolation whether of (foreign) language or of style. Either mode is quite uncommon in literature, where it must be reckoned a peripheral phenomenon. As prose and poetry come closer to the essay (i.e., as they grow more intellectual) the more do we find erudite quotations used also in the aesthetic quasi-erudite function.

We thus see that literature — the art closest to science and philosophy — affords relatively small opportunity to quotation; how much latitude can it then have in the other arts? We may quickly decide that its place is even more negligible, for even the most consummate and well-rounded experts will have to rack their brains to find quotation in painting, theater, or film as it appears in writing. If the quotes must be painfully sought for, then they are rare. Yet rarity is not of itself proof of insignificance. On the contrary, where the infrequent phenomenon occurs we may be obliged to give it special importance. However, in the arts this is not the case; quotation not only is rare, it is also—the crucial point— of little significance from the artistic standpoint. Its cultural import may, however, in this field too loom large.

A few examples may bring these general observations down to earth. As for theater, we need not seek the quotation in the actual text of the play, where it would be simply a variant of the literary quote. A genuinely theatrical quotation would inhere in a certain stage effect. Inasmuch as the knowledge of theatrical "scores" remains embryonic it is difficult to say whether a given production borrows from another and interpolates the citation into the new whole on the basis of at least relative discreteness. There is a certain improbability in the thought that it would be done in this way. Yet we do know that Piscator, for one, made use of such effects as captions or film sequences anticipating the action onstage. I believe this can be treated as paraquotation with a stimulative-amplificatory function. I use the term "paraquotation" because Piscator meant these interpolations to be among the meaningful elements of the pattern of his staging.

An analogous use of paraquotations can be found in Robert Aldrich's film *What Ever Happened to Baby Jane?* (1962) where excerpts from old Bette Davis and Joan Crawford movies provide an organic element of the artistic structure, yet may be isolated from this whole as literal copies taken from an earlier work. A different view should be taken of the use of newsreel clips in a film like Orson Welles' *Citizen Kane* (1941), where they may be regarded as straight quotation. In contrast, the singing of a popular song in a film—such as "Red Poppies of Monte Cassino" in Andrzej Wajda's *Ashes and Diamonds* (1958)— does not qualify as quotation in any way. Film, where it hopes to achieve maximum authenticity, must take its material from life. "Quotation" for cinema means operatively to photograph real people, real buildings, a real singer in a particular cafe where the camera is introduced, etc. "Red Poppies" is an element of the immediate situation, not a small work embedded in a larger one. (In contrast, Piscator's interpolations of film into stage productions are a relatively autonomous operation.) The song in Wajda's film carries the expressive values of the particular scene. There are also examples of pseudoquotations in film. In Jacques Doniol-Valcroze's *Denunciation* (1962) the hero, a film-studio executive, watches a movie which is reminiscent of the work of Robbe-Grillet. It is not, however, a genuine excerpt, although the pseudoquotation plays a key role in the script of the film.

How about the so-called fine arts? It is easiest to locate a quotation in a cartoon, poster, or book illustration where a verbal text taken over from an original can serve as a focus. The more imaginative artists who look for loans have, however, dispensed with the mere borrowing of crutches. Easy to discern, too, is the quote in the medieval tapestry, print, or mural, with its appended text—but here the quotation is often scriptural, and this element of religious authority contrasts with the usually stimulative caste of the quotation in modern graphic arts.

A remarkable case of paraquotation is the reproduction of a Japanese print in Manet's famous portrait of Emile Zola of 1867. Zola, depicted in his study, was championing the artists who had been refused by the then-official academic art. Zola had first assumed this role a year earlier by disputing with Courbet and Proudhon and defending the view that art depended primarily on the temperament or the originality of the artist. *Japonaiserie* was not only in vogue, it was a model invoked by these "refused" artists as exemplary for their argument; moreover, it provided an essential component of modern, sophisticated interior decoration. Zola stumped for *Japonaiserie* as fervently as had Baudelaire and the Goncourts before him. Thus, Manet was using a quotation-symbol. It had a dual function, stimulative-amplificatory and ornamental. Analogous examples are Van Gogh's *Father Tanguy* (1887) and Gauguin's *Still Life with Japanese Print* (1889).

I do not feel, though, that the *papiers collés* of Braque or Picasso can be treated as paraquotations. Nor can the "shocking" juxtapositions of bits and pieces of material in the dadaist works, or the photographic collages inspired by dada, be so treated. The point of the *papiers collés* and especially the collages of Max Ernst was precisely that they had to pierce the established reality with an imaginative new synthesis. The creative moment was the whole point. Synthetic cubists fastened onto everyday objects in order to destroy their literalness and their legibility. The same can be said of the dadaists. Duchamp's ready-mades didn't quote; they provocatively evoked ordinary rather than aesthetic responses. Man Ray, Heartfield, and Hausmann brought together fragments of reality not as meaningful structures but as examples of an overarching chaos, demonstrating that all principles—artistic and otherwise—were moribund. The quotation as a discrete signifying entity here had no function whatsoever.

In music, examples of quotation can doubtlessly be found. But, if I may rely on expert opinion, it seems that such examples are rather exceptional. Instances in the stimulative-amplificatory category are Karlheinz Stockhausen's *Hymnen*, which

cites fragments of national anthems, or Charles Ives's compositions, which incorporate numerous snatches from the popular music of the day in a wondrous interplay of public and individual sensibility. Rarity seems, however, the rule, especially
since we must disqualify such contenders for the description as fantasies or sets
of variations on a given theme or, indeed, parodies of a theme, since what occurs
in these cases is a treatment or transmutation of previous musical data (elements
or combinations of elements, in other words, substructures), so that the relationship
between the new work and the old work is best comprehended through the notion
of the *topos*.

Architecture seems to be the art least amenable to quotation. It would be difficult to regard as quotation the mere inclusion of a fragment of old city walls or of
an ancient edifice in a new construction — for after all, if quotation were to be defined as simply placing anything older in a newer setting, the idea would be so gro-
tesquely expanded as to lose all point. Nor should we expect to see quotation in
the particular details of architecture; if these do provide elements or patterns reminiscent of older buildings, we shall find that we must regard them as conventional
devices on the order of *topoi* or of motifs peculiar to a given ethnic-cultural provenance, or else as negligible features transformed in the context of the new whole.
Only in special — and, no doubt, extravagant — cases do we find genuine interpolations or insertions in modern architecture. For example, many modern Roman
villas along the Appian Way contain quotations in the form of the scraps of col-
umns, capitals, or bas-reliefs cemented into the front of the house. A less effulgent
but equally pertinent example is a Renaissance house in Arles which has Roman
foundations and a Romanesque sculpture above the doorway. A similar example
can be seen in Poland in the Goluchowski Castle.

Conclusions
I have not argued here that quotation has never been formidable in art and never
will be. I say only that:
1. strictly defined, it occurs much more frequently in literature than in the other arts;
2. in literature it can be found performing the various functions I have listed, and
   its likelihood is the greater the more a literary work borders on scholarship,
   philosophy, or journalism;
3. in the other arts it chiefly performs a stimulative-amplificatory or an ornamental
   function, which is why it so easily goes over into a paraquotation;

4. architecture has provided almost no cases of quotation; and

5. its fittest function in the realm of art is correlated to the fullest absorption of
   an interpolated substructure into the total structure of a work.

Quotation in this sense, far from clearly contrasting with the whole, contributes
to cohering it. Its own integral sense becomes as if metaphorized, or it comes to
form one of the coordinates of a multivalent semantic structure. Here I must again
stress what was said in point (3) above, that in such contexts the status of quotation per se is highly uncertain. Accordingly, a final proposition may be advanced,
that

6. in both literature and art, the significance of quotation does not appear to be
   great.

   I readily concede that these contentions, and particularly the last, require more
confirmation — although my view seems to be bolstered by the results and the pet
uncompleted project of the literary and cultural critic Walter Benjamin. An unceasing collector of quotes, Benjamin dreamt of making a book that would have
nothing but quotations, and would yet, due to an interpretative patterning of the
sections and the whole, be an original study. This montage composition (its inspiration was dada-surrealist) would surely have bled the old literal integrity and have
overwhelmed the discreteness with transfusions of a posteriori meaning. If this
is the transformation that citations encounter in high-calibre criticism, what must
happen in art?

   I do not argue that the constituent traits of art exclude the functional role of
quotation. However, I am suggesting that the function of art — apart from the definition of art in 1900, 1920, or today — pursues an individualizing and integrative
creational trajectory; the artist generally wishes to transmit the cultural tradition
germane to himself and in his own way. The traits of quotations seem at odds
with the artistic process in this view. The artist modifies as he borrows, he is intent on *not* duplicating what has been, he will submerge his erudition (if he has
any) in his new material and new ideas and sensibility. Even if the modification
does not come off, the artist is still not quoting. He is either drawing on archetypes or is imprisoned in a canon. He is at worst an imitator — but even this is not
tantamount to a preference for quotations. Rather, the entire imitated work might
be termed a plagiarism, an entirely different mode of loan-object.

   In sum, art may have recourse to quotation for individual or historicocultural
reasons which are exceptional. It is employed by the scholar-artist or the artist

with a thesis, for whom art is one among other media for the expression of philosophical messages. Quotations accumulate in art when the boundaries between it and other forms of social consciousness become vague. This may happen in an era of sociopolitical revolution or of domination by an institution such as the Church, in a time of convulsive aesthetic crisis.

Yet we may not say that the lengthening, darkening shadow of a cherished tradition is what necessarily perpetuates quotations in art, for even in this case art resists the imposition of quotations—partly just because philosophy, scholarship, and all traditional institutions and their attendant ideologies submit to art's incursions.

Ideologies necessarily invoke their legitimacy with quotations; they incessantly flaunt their past. Without this an ideology would seem insubstantial. Science and philosophy refer to earlier achievements because their current achievements owe very much to previous breakthroughs, and these disciplines are understood at every turn through their continuity, even where some new concept revolutionizes thinking. In such matters, quotation is indispensable. It is a working tool in the cultural stock, which anchors time present to time past. Art, however, is different. The participation in past achievements, the place in a continuity, are not different— but the artist does not play up these points, and he is, in fact, reluctant to own up to them. Instead, he invariably tries to break with the received ideas, to overcome them freshly with what appears like their modification or rejection. The artist submits *his own* vision, one not previously extant. He dissociates himself from quotation since any *individual whole* has to be a unique, never-before type production.

Of course, I speak of an optimal situation, pushing my points to the extreme. Nonetheless, the tendency I have emphasized seems entirely tangible in any period of art and in any artistic trend. We may consider the most difficult test for my premise—namely, the avant-garde movement of today, which deliberately abandons the specificity of forms, of individual expression, and even the personal craft touch of carrying through an artistic vocation. In their place, anonymity and serially produced multiples are provocatively substituted. Even so—here, where impersonal technology and the mass media are exalted shibboleths—the *artist's own idea* (his invention) remains the most precious factor. Superficially, the artist may agree to a nameless and unrecognizable status, undifferentiated from others. Yet beneath the skin he strives to be remembered for his unique contribution. It is a striking antinomy; and it obviously bears on the assumption I have presented about the quotation-resistant character of artistic activity. Even in the case of pop art, where the logos and visuals of everyday marketplace transactions are "quoted," what we get is quite other than a quotation. Indeed the interest lies in a pervasive game with such objects, to the point that they are deprived of their colloquial meaning. The same may be said of the materials gathered by happeners or conceptualists. These are by no means "quoted"; either they simply *are*, as part of an arranged environment; or their significance and status is definitely modified in the transfiguring context.

Possibly I have stretched too far the contrast between the function of quotation and what I see as the function of art. Yet, even if the sharp antithesis I have drawn is tenable, it in no way denigrates the quotation as a cultural phenomenon; nor does it diminish the place and importance of quotation in art. Quotation pertains to that broad area of social consciousness where originality counts for less than does continuity, where vision is less important than knowledge, where a spontaneous sense of the moment is subordinated to a sense of participation in an ancient and continuing culture. There can be no doubt that humanity moves forward with a continual glance backward over its shoulder, akin to Narcissus admiring himself in the spring; and no less stimulus is drawn from the past than from the present or from the aspired-for prospect of the future. At the interior of this sustained dialogue with the past, quotation — mostly outside of art, but within it too — exerts an undoubted vitality and importance, and sometimes it grows to be almost sacred. It imparts knowledge and insists on knowledge; it encourages a play of the mind; it may be allusive and symbolic; and it provides the means to a wide-ranging associativeness, like a riddle or conundrum. Lastly, it is not an inherently complacent or a meanly conventional resort, for it relays information not otherwise available and it helps us to understand, if we wish to, these texts that we retain from the past.

In conclusion, let me apologize to the reader. I have been obstinate. I wanted to write an article about quotation which would entirely lack quotes — and I have succeeded. It may be that the price of my persistence has been to hamper somewhat the building of the argument; if so, in this cost lies some token of the value of quotation.

Postscript

When I wrote this essay I was unacquainted with Hermann Meyer's *The Poetics of Quotation in the European Novel* (Princeton, 1968; German original published in

Chapter 11   Art and Obscenity

How shall I plan a strategy which will allow me to estimate the common ground — if any — connecting art and obscenity? It would be all too easy to stray into a vast labyrinth of bordering issues which distract more than they enlighten this problem. Furthermore, the question may be raised from several standpoints: from a purely analytical perspective; a purely practical perspective (perhaps with moral, religious, or political ends in mind); or a mixture of the analytical and practical perspectives with the aim of promulgating theory so as to accomplish some strategic objectives. My own aim is strictly that of analysis. Yet this decision alone still leaves the approach unclarified, for the analysis of art and obscenity is open to a range of systematic interpretations — those of sociology (or, more broadly, culturology), psychology, ethics, aesthetics, or a more comprehensive viewpoint not so much scientific (in a strict sense) as philosophical.

Explicitly, then, my frame of reference is aesthetic thought, and I am particularly interested in the problem of art and obscenity from the aspect of artistic structure. This clarified, I can specify the questions to be explored:

1. Can art *be* called "pornographic"? In other words, does common ground exist between "aesthetic" phenomena and those cultural attractions widely described as "dirty"?
2. Suppose we find that aesthetic phenomena and "filth" never coincide. Can obscenity still find a niche in art? If so, precisely what role does it occupy in the artistic structure?

These questions are framed with a concern for the structural analysis of the phenomenon of "pornographic art." I must, nonetheless, first direct a glance towards the genesis and function of the views regarding this "filth" — views which often err through terming something aesthetic which is only obscene, or else through treating as merely obscene something which makes genuine aesthetic claims on our judgment. To avoid such errors, I will start by clarifying the two terms of the title. I should note first that "obscenity" and "pornography" are here used synonymously and interchangeably. It is true that "obscenity" is often understood in a broader sense which includes acts that do not directly arouse sexual desires (e.g., defecation) and also many words which do not have purely sexual connotations, but I shall omit this distinction here. Let us simply agree that pornography fits the definition of obscenity; and everything obscene that shall concern us here will have a pornographic character.

The first version of this essay was written in 1962; an English translation was published in the *Journal of Aesthetics and Art Criticism*, Winter 1967.

Tentative Definitions of Art and Obscenity

The problems involved in the definition of art have already been discussed in Part 1; let me summarize the principles derived there. In my view we should reject the two extreme points of view that have persistently recurred in aesthetic thought: first, the absolutism which holds that art is a suprahistorical phenomenon which fulfills certain a priori conditions; and second, the relativism which argues that the list of the qualities that define art is truly limitless and, in fact, must be so, given the variety of views on the scope and character of art expressed by different individuals and groups in the course of its ever changing history. My position avoids both these poles by seeking certain constants which emerge from the natural dispositions of the human species and from the accumulated social and cultural experience of the species.

Artistic values have been distilled in a gradual historical process of detachment from a matrix of magical and religious phenomena, informational or purely recreational pursuits, and technical-productive aims. Eventually these values become distinct and relatively independent, coherent structures supplied either with purely sensory elements or with mimetic or functional features. These more or less complex structures display additional specific values, which are denoted by the term "expression." In brief, the fundamental value of art and thus its chief constituent element is what we might tentatively call, in this context, its expression-imbued structure. Artistic values are, nonetheless, of several kinds: the purely formal; the mimetic (in representational art); the functional (in applied art); the specifically and primarily expressive. The art object always presents a "rival" world in comparison with ordinary objects which are wholly of this world; and yet the work of art is likewise always a physical or at least cultural artifact and, often, a commodity in the everyday world.

For the purposes of this chapter the mimetic values are crucial. A distributive but integral component of the fundamental artistic structure, these values enable the embodiment in representation of moral, religious, political, philosophical, or other ideas of the experiential reality. (The mimetic embodiment is, of course, modified by form and the specific formal and expressive patterning of elements.) Frequently, such embodied ideas are the salient feature of an artistic structure; therefore, we cannot exclude the (often agitated) reactions of the public to these idea-aspects. Besides, every work of art is a sociocultural as well as an aesthetic phenomenon. Yet, finally, it would be mistaken to rule on what is or is not art according to the character of the ideas that are implied by the work's mimetic values. Just as questionable is ranking of works according to the merits of their moral, political, or religious ideas.

The position towards which I have developed might be termed structuralist-historical; my view is that in the course of the historical processes of culture a class of relatively autonomous objects has emerged and been established, which we term artistic and whose fundamental values are of course aesthetic. [1]

If the idea of art causes major definitional difficulties, the idea of obscenity causes even more formidable trouble. We often hear the statement, "I can recognize something dirty when I see it," and when international conventions gathered at Paris (May 4, 1910) and Geneva (December 31, 1924) to discuss pornography, the conferees thought the same. Yet no one has yet offered any clear definition, which would let us, say, distinguish pornography from all art.

I should like to look more closely at conventional notions of pornography, tentatively defining "obscenity" as the representation or suggestion in words or images, with the aid of objects, themes, motifs, or situations, of all those elements which pertain to the sexual life. (This definition is deliberately cast in such general terms as to embrace every kind of sociocultural stereotype.) But what do I mean by "the sexual life"? Nudity? Intercourse? Perversion? Don't the limits of obscenity run differently in different cultural formations? These are good questions, but before I tackle them let me try to concretize my working definition of obscenity. On the basis of judicial rulings and notorious acts of censorship, it appears that the key test is whether a deliberate appeal to the prurient sexual imagination can be found (by authorities, it should be noted) in the work. On this ground Henry Miller's *Sexus* was seized in Norway in 1958–59; while *Lady Chatterley's Lover* and *Ulysses* were banned for years on the charge that Lawrence and Joyce were soliciting readers to follow their characters' examples and to act lasciviously. [2]

Another charge that recurs in court cases is that pornography publicizes what is properly the *private* side of sex. Coitus, homosexuality, and masturbation are private; but kissing, teenage flirting, and caresses between husband and wife are properly public when tactfully portrayed. This leads to the argument that the pornographer treats sexual phenomena crassly and explicitly: explicitly due to naturalistic description, and crassly because sex is deliberately raised to a status equal to, if not exclusive of, all the other relationships among men and women.

Accepting these refinements, I shall mean by "obscenity" not merely the suggestion or representation of erotic themes or situations but a specific kind of treatment: their exploitation for the purpose of arousing the reader's or spectator's sexual

instincts with the aid of symbols, objects, or scenes of a highly intimate character
presented in a vulgar and unrestrained way. This definition improves on the earlier
one because it is more substantial; yet it, too, raises doubts. One is immediately
put in the position of relativizing such terms as "arousing the sexual instincts,"
"intimate," "vulgar," "unrestrained." One is thus thrust into the domain of psychology and of social anthropology; and examples could easily be produced to show
that the effectiveness of a given sexual stimulus is relative to one's background,
nationality, class, etc. (e.g., what is private to the English is often public to the
French; what is vulgar to the European is often accepted and tender to the Trobri-
and Islanders; what is grossly unrestrained in middle- or upper-class company is
natural among the working class).

Therefore the statement, "such-and-such a work is obscene," must always be
subjected to specific historical and psychological analysis. Otherwise we shall not
be able to appreciate why, for example, Judge Lockwood sentenced Oscar Wilde
to two years in gaol for an offense which the Greeks in the time of Plato and Al-
cibiades viewed as an acceptable practice, or why at the close of the nineteenth
century the German parliament banned the Venus de Milo, although the sixteenth
through eighteenth centuries had revered it as a matchless monument to feminine
beauty.

Obscenity is — in a word — always dependent on idiosyncratic moral taboos;
and since human sexuality is irrepressible, highly diversified, and volatile, the system of taboos is continually shifting. Nevertheless, the act of transgression at any
moment is labeled pornographic.

This is, however, just one way of looking at this question; we might also look at
obscenity as it relates to the codes of an increasingly striated society where the
rights of the individual are held up as inviolate. From the former perspective, we
watch a pitched conflict between nature and culture, an incongruity dating from
early human civilization. (The constrictions of nature are most effectively discussed
in the vocabulary of Freud.) From the latter standpoint, we watch the emergence
of a humanity less and less involved with religion and more and more opposed to
laws restricting the gratification of a multivalent individual need (especially to be
noted in the lands with democratic tradition in Europe and North America). Here,
the problem of obscenity is not at all limited or isolated; it is inseparable from a
vast, far-reaching process, which dialectically sees on the one side a permanent
tendency to impose controls on the variety of sexual options, and on the other side
an unceasing impulse to profane the taboos "obscenely."

The present trend is undoubtedly to more civil liberty, with the result that what once were *obscoena* have become socially acceptable erotic themes. We observe all over the world a convergence of the political and ethical struggles, under a banner which includes the demand of absolute sexual freedom. The social majority is still backing a condemnation of so-called smutty writing, dirty pictures, filthy behavior, etc. The laws have to take account of both extremities and, in their oscillations, the dialectical process is played out.

In 1967, the Danes took the innovative step of decriminalizing obscene materials both verbal and pictorial, an act which has spurred parallel efforts in other countries, usually under the auspices of committees of experts. Especially instructive is the *Report of the American Commission on Obscenity and Pornography*, commissioned by President Nixon. This Commission had a multifaceted character, exemplified by a minority report confirming a still active religious view that the corrupt character of pornography is obvious and eternal. What stands out, despite the selectiveness of the Commission data, is that in a single society at a single moment, attitudes may vary widely. True, some visibly (and tacitly) common beliefs emerge; yet there is no consensus as to the effects of exposure to explicit sexual materials, nor is there even agreement as to the meaning of obscenity.

The section written by the Legal Panel emphasizes this. It impugns all of the federal, state, and local legal standards, accusing them of subjectiveness and arbitrariness. At issue is the so-called Roth Test and the notion that materials should be prosecuted only if they meet three criteria:
1. the dominant appeal is to prurient interests;
2. current community standards regard the material as patently offensive;
3. the material lacks redeeming social value.
Commenting on these criteria of obscenity, the Legal Panel said that studies made at the order of the Commission had discovered no general agreement as to the threshold of sexual prurience, nor could a clear correlative be discerned between arousal and offensiveness. Indeed, many respondents to the inquiry found positive social value in arousing materials.

The chief attack of the Commissioners on existing law centered on the definition of "community standards." As I have indicated, I am prompt to note a considerable relativity in sexual proclivities; and yet it would be a mistake to ignore that a given society at a given time does possess some kind of ultimate common understanding as to how difficult matters of sex should be resolved. This is *not* to assert any assumption of harm in explicit sexual materials—and I should add that I agree with the Legal Panel in favoring repeal of restrictive legislation in regard to the sale, exhibition, and distribution of "obscene" materials. Pornography flourishes only where there are deeply established disintegrative trends in society; and it makes no sense to apply superficial checks when an incisive analysis of the etiology of the phenomenon is appropriate.

Anyway, although my aim here is different, it seems possible to define obscenity tentatively according to the legal tests just described. The ultimate criterion of obscenity would thus be a lack of redeeming values. Surely it is clear that obscenity can be (and often is) of social value, but the predominance or monopoly of obscenity does often tend to blur or efface other values which may be judged desirable. It is my aim to exclude the test of "offensiveness to the community" for my present purposes, and to propose as the test of obscenity the dominant (or exclusive) attraction of prurient interest due to a weakness (or absence) of other, redeeming values.

I might still at this point be criticized for the ambiguity of the concept of prurient interest. Some recipients will be sexually aroused by a given content; some will be bored; some will be informed or entertained. I do not dispute the range of responses; but I emphasize that the object of prurience behind the responses will remain constant. Also, the capacity for sexual excitation should be judged at the recipient's first encounter with the object, since a factor of satiation may set in. If my definition of the obscene is in this way somewhat slack, the fault would seem to have no remedy. Yet I hope it is sufficiently sharp to allow the reader to anticipate that I found *Oh, Calcutta!* obscene. I agree with Lord Longford in comparing it with the pornographic shows of Soho, but I disagree with his wish to have it suppressed. The reader should also see why I judge Sjöman's *I Am Curious (Yellow)* heavily obscene but also imbued with some redeeming values. A predominant or exclusive prurient interest is not proven by the sexual content in itself; rather, this can be determined only by the sexual content in conjunction with the mode of its presentation within a whole (i.e., in its context).[3]

I shall put off for the moment a discussion of the alleged harm done by pornography and the arguments for censorship.

Obscenity Which Clashes with Art, and Erotic Art

A work of art cannot be, in my opinion, an obscene object; and, in fact, the phenomena are mutually exclusive. This judgment is founded on a consideration of the three basic contexts of aesthetic investigation: the genetic, the structural, and the functional; in other words, the standpoints of the work's structure, of its creator, and of its audience. Let me add that a test of pornographic content cannot be made with reference solely to the stated intention of the artist or the stated reaction of the public. This is secondary evidence; the primary criterion must be found in the art object itself. Nonetheless, the secondary evidence is needed because identification of a work as pornographic can never be accomplished by structural analysis alone. A syndrome of elements provides that evidence. The artist's intention, or the audience's reaction, or both, will provide the control-check that substantiates the accuracy of a structural interpretation.

In the method here proposed for defining the pornographic quotient of a work, then, the structure is taken as an independent variable, and the intention of the artist and the phenomena of the reception are taken as dependent variables. Due to interaction among the independent variable and the dependent variables we obtain alternative pornographic estimates; and works classified in this category can be ranked as to whether the interpretations of them as pornographic are more or less strong. I must also add that this definitional operation has to be related to the particular historical period in which the work was produced. Any subsequent patterns of its reception must be referred back to the original circumstances, that is, to the work's genetic context.

We can see in this framework of investigation the antithetical relation of art and pornography. Genetically, the aim of the artist is not primarily to arouse sexual excitation. Structurally, the sexual elements of a work of art can never be the exclusive or predominant ones, or even as prominent as the aesthetic values. Functionally, it is in the nature of aesthetic experience to eliminate a practical, operational attitude such as would obtain if the work involved us in a real situation. Perhaps it might be countered that in a primitive work, and not only there, the sexual elements overwhelm or at least eclipse all others; that sexual motifs have been aggressively embodied in artistic structures through the centuries, never becoming subordinate; that any interpretation of works of art which sees only aesthetic values is skewed, and that those who make such interpretations are the slaves of aestheticism. I shall try to answer these points, and, in so doing, build my own position.

It cannot be denied that in primitive art, Indian art, and some periods of European art (e.g., the fourth-century Sicyonian school, French rococo painting, or the work of Félicien Rops) priority is given to sexual appeal. Yet it would be wrong to interpret this indiscriminately, in every case, as an effort to cause sexual excitation.

For instance, Bronislaw Malinowski emphasized the magical-religious aspect of the sexual games and themes in the Trobriand folklore which he presented in his *Sex Life of the Savages in North-Western Melanesia*. These elements cemented cultural bonds, fortified social approval for the acknowledged ideal of beauty in both sexes, and ritually affirmed the primacy of life over death, of procreation over barrenness. Similarly, in Indian, African, Mexican, or Brazilian art the sexual motifs are interwoven with the religious. We can speak here of a specialized order of mimetic content; special because of the ideal and emotional associations of those who, in experiencing a certain mode of religious perception, organically perceive inseparable sexual motifs.[4]

The case is different with the work of a rococo painter such as François Boucher or a modern like Rops, but here too a distinction must be brought out. Among Boucher's audience, a deliberate stimulation of sexual imagination seems to have accorded with the psychosocial climate; additionally, and this seems to me the crucial point, Boucher simply used nudity as an accepted, fashionable subject for his artistic purposes. Here, we see again that it is not only the structure of a work but also its framework, its sociohistorical context, which determines its character and its status as art or obscenity. (We can make a comparison with the conduct and acting style of the Italians, which to the non-Italian seem so flamboyant but which in national context are quite natural.) The work of Félicien Rops is another matter entirely. His intent of conveying sexual thrills is only too transparent. His case, however, goes beyond the scope of the question now being considered, being a borderline case needing separate study.

The case of Rops takes me to the second (the structural) framework with which I shall have to deal in showing that sexuality can never be the predominant feature of an artistic work. If counterexamples are produced, I shall then have to decide whether they are nonetheless marginally artistic and to what degree. (The next section will explore this question further.)

I now turn to the third (the functional) framework, which involves the public's reception of the possibly obscene work of art. I have already shown that the charge of aestheticism sometimes lodged against scholars who claim never to find sexuality outweighing artistic traits in any example of art is false since the artistic traits subsume both the mimetic values and the moral, political, religious, and philosophical ideas therein imbued. Obviously our response to Rembrandt's *Return of the Prodigal Son* differs from our response to Mondrian's *Boogie Woogie;* and our response to the Sienese Madonnas differs from that to Renoir's nudes. We read

Rabelais' *Gargantua et Pantagruel* or Brantôme's *Dames galantes* differently from
the novels of Richardson or Dickens; and the plays of Wycherley have a different
effect on us than do the plays of Goethe or Hugo. None of this, however, alters
the fact that in each instance we are reacting to artistic *mimesis*, that is, to a specific quasi-world represented in the art object within the limits of its structure. Just
as soon as the ideas plucked from the mimetic tapestry loom larger in our response
than does the structure of the work taken as a whole, we pass to the sphere of
nonaesthetic experiences, of which sex is one.

The distinction that concerns me here was grasped by Freud, though he had
little reason to wish to restrict the field of effectiveness of the libido. In writing
about the relationship between art and sex, he notably classifies aesthetic experiences under the heading *Vorlust*. According to his theory, poetry, like children's
games and daydreaming, satisfies our deepest sexual desires, but the poet not only
condenses his material and hides his real longings behind symbols, but also to
some extent neutralizes these drives of the libido by arranging the psychic contents
associated with them into artistic form. This operation releases in us not only enjoyment of a cathartic type but also and above all pleasures of a strictly aesthetic
character.[5]

Accordingly, I regard as misleading the interpretation given by Eduard Fuchs
in his remarkable and still interesting work *Geschichte der erotischen Kunst* (1912).
Leaving aside the fact that, while orienting himself expressly to the methodological
position of historical materialism, he stated—without noticing the inherent contradiction—that the *sexual* impulse was the regular, fundamental drive of art, I should
like to note Fuchs's contention that the basic law of art (its *Lebensgesetz*) is its use
of sexual motifs and his argument that the stronger the erotic effect of a work the
more artistic it is. Yet even Fuchs speaks of a degradation of art at least since the
rococo period due to a decadent attitude towards sex. Several times he emphasizes
that the predominant trait of all art is a "healthy sensualism," and he does argue
that this sexual motif (*das Stoffliche*, the subject matter) should be subsumed artistically to the extent that its mere or forthright sensuality—*das gemein Sinnliche*—
is eliminated (*aufgelöst und völlig überwunden*).

The weakness of Fuchs's case lies in his failure to explain the implications of this
"healthy eroticism" and to draw the necessary conclusions from his sensible realization of a formal artistic predominance in the presentation of sexual elements.
(It is impossible, for instance, to react primarily with sexual attention—although
this is the response postulated by Fuchs—to works in which the erotic has been in

a sense neutralized by the artist.) As a result we can learn a great deal from Fuchs's book about the recurrent obsession with sex evinced in works of art; but the best use is not made of this evidence.

Fuchs fails to see that the art objects he cites can be ranged along a continuum: from the blatantly pornographic (the priapic statues of Pompeii and the Naples museum, the frescoes in the Casa Vetii, the sixteenth-century painting by Van Orley of Neptune having intercourse with a nymph) through works like Poussin's *Satyr Discovers Venus Sleeping* or Rembrandt's etching *The French Bed*, to works in which the sexual is only a means towards quite different artistic objectives. Among the latter works are Fouquet's noted portrait of Agnes Sorel, the mistress of Charles VII, shown with a breast exposed, as the Madonna; Rubens' portrait of his wife Helene Fourment in the nude; the antipapist Dutch etchings which decry the lascivious conduct of monks and nuns (among these *Monk with Girl among the Reeds*, a little-known copper engraving by Rembrandt); or the English cartoons of Gillray, Rowlandson, and Cruikshank, where great play is made with sexual elements for the purpose of sociopolitical caricature.

If this argument has been persuasive, then we should put behind us all counterarguments and affirm that art and obscenity are mutually exclusive. Some examples will highlight the conflict between the aesthetic standpoint that seeks to do justice to a work, and the nonaesthetic attitude that trims and reduces a work to the needs and the prejudices of a perceiver. I shall begin with what is perhaps the most obvious problem, the portrayal of the nude in the European tradition.

In Greek art the portrayal of Venus nude was the natural representational decision. However, the point is not simply that Greek custom approved the public display of nudity, since it might then be responded that what may have suited the Greeks cannot, after centuries of Christian (or rather Puritan) civilization, strike us as other than indecent. Rather, the point here is that the Venus Anadyomene and the Venus de Milo were above all else ideal expressions of feminine beauty cast in harmonious forms. Anyone who studies purely from the sexual point of view the sleeping figure of the Hermaphrodite in the Rome National Museum — engrossed by the erect phallus, and lost to the expression and formal rhythms of the sculpture — is quite simply aesthetically blind, and nothing can be done for him until he is taught to see.

Rubens bared the bosom of his Queen when she encountered the King in his Maria de Medici cycle; but the entire body had already been presented naked from the time of Masaccio, Botticelli, and Van Eyck. It is true that the Adam and Eve in the Ghent Altarpiece modestly conceal their pudenda and that Botticelli's Venus is more a poetic symbol than a flesh-and-blood woman, but even before Rubens the great Venetians (Titian, Giorgione, Tintoretto) had painted a pagan and sensuous beauty in their women's bodies, while in the same century Rembrandt did not hesitate to show ugliness in the nude.

In none of these cases, however, was the artist seeking simply to arouse the sexual imagination. The further history of European painting only confirms this view. Ingres' *Turkish Bath* caused as great a scandal in its time as did Manet's *Luncheon on the Grass*, and yet neither used its sexual motif as more than an inducement to achieve an elaborated aesthetic aim. Artists of the early modern period (e.g., Toulouse-Lautrec, Marquet, or Friesz) accented an everydayness in their choice of model and situation, and we can detect in their work an attitude of unconcealed earthiness and also a sexual tantalization. Nonetheless, these artists too have achieved primarily a painterly set of values. This approach has been a staple since Renoir's and Cézanne's depictions of *Bathers* and Dégas' *Woman at Her Dressing Table*. Each avant-garde grouping has modified the programmatic intent of their eroticism and in this regard we may note a swing away from the overt portrayal and towards the nonfigurative (Delaunay's *Three Graces*), the decorative (Miro's *Nude Before Her Mirror*), or the surreal (Coutaud's *Erotic Magic*).[6] It is true that such works (or at least the more representational among them) have suffered frequent attack for undermining and debauching wholesome social values. Can this be a correct accusation from any aspect? I shall put off answering this charge until I have set out the arguing points and the values of those who regard the nude in art as a seducer of the young.

Literature offers a more munificent source of cases for an understanding of the difference between a legitimate response to art and a distorted one. From the troubles met by Flaubert's *Madame Bovary*, Baudelaire's *Flowers of Evil*, or Zola's *Earth* we may judge the frequent gap between the work, which indeed makes not the slightest appeal to the prurient imagination, and a type of reader who reacts to it according to nonaesthetic criteria stemming from a particular set of taboos. I shall confine myself here, however, to a few notorious and controversial examples from the twentieth century.

In *Lady Chatterley's Lover* D. H. Lawrence asserted the right to full personal happiness that was denied by middle-class prudery. The same right had been defended by Freud, whose individual therapy was meant to relieve neuroses traceable to sexual disturbances and repression. Although Lawrence made something of a

religion of sex, his attack on the moral chains and cobwebs of his day was salutary.

The case of Henry Miller is more troublesome. *Tropic of Cancer* must be seen,
however, as an act of protest, not one of simple temptation; in fact, a protest by
an artist against the whole of capitalist civilization. Early in his book Miller speaks
of the need to shock readers, to provide a blood transfusion, and states that this
infusion could only be drawn from his own direct primitive experience of life, in
which sex holds a central place. Through his hero Miller confesses: "I am spiritually
dead. Physically I am alive. Morally I am free. The world which I have departed is
a menagerie. . . . If I am a hyena I am a lean and hungry one. I go forth to fatten
myself."[7] This hero feels utterly isolated; Paris is for him an escape from humanity,
and he is an outsider in a city which is "a blind alley at the end of which is a scaf-
fold."[8] Hating the world he has fled, this hero wants something more tenable, a
foothold with more substance ("I belong to the earth"). He proselytizes, and his
message is that sexual passion alone can revitalize existence; it can recapture the
elemental desires and the natural drives.[9]

It is of course possible to read *Tropic of Cancer* as pornography, but this is to
read it against the grain. Miller's is a philosophical novel, distilling much of the
rebellious mood of the artists of the 1930s. It breathes the same air as the work of
Joyce and Kafka. All three authors raised intransigent protests against the realities
of their times, although each of them pursued a different artistic solution. We may
glimpse a world kindred to Miller's in the oppressive and harshly tense paintings
of Soutine. His world too implies the still widespread notion of instinctuality as the
sole alternative to the false ideas and misleading phrases carried in the head.

Notwithstanding its tone of nihilism, then, *Tropic of Cancer* is the counterthrust
of a deeply lacerated person. To paraphrase Marx's *1844 Manuscripts*, we might
say that Henry Miller's aim was to return man to himself, to his intrinsic potential;
he sought a release from capitalist alienation, but, not entirely grasping the processes by which he was held, he found no recourse but the most ancient coursing of
the blood and semen. This is not a titillating book. Its premise is appalling. It incites
us to adopt a purgative attitude. The Dionysian element is its hope.

A somewhat different case is presented by Vladimir Nabokov's *Lolita*. Nabokov
shows us his hero Humbert as a man who is sick but who deserves our sympathy
since his intentions are worthy. Humbert's passion and love for the teenage girl
Lolita are shown as genuine. He may censure himself (chapters 31, 32, and 36),
but this self-accusation is offset by the portrayal of Lolita as a precocious tease

and voluptuary. We may speak of Nabokov as a humanist author in the *nil humanum* dimension. People are taken by various infatuations, and see them through in diverse ways; Humbert is different from Othello or Werther but certainly no worse. *Lolita* does not protest against an entire civilization, nor does it present a compact personal philosophy as does *Tropic of Cancer*. Yet there surely is an outcry against a repressive moral code which abominates certain sexual irregularities and which labels their inclusion in a work of art as obscene, ignoring the fact that Freud held such inclinations to be as admissible as the normal patterns in a civilization which requires neurosis-formation to survive. Persons who pick up *Lolita* to "read it for the dirty parts" are very much deceived. This is a serious and a difficult work; its author has distanced and controlled his theme and written with profound compassion for a tortured, complex hero. Nabokov says in his Postscript to *Lolita* written in 1956: "For me a work of fiction exists only insofar as it affords me what I shall bluntly call aesthetic bliss."[10] In this same essay, he says of pornography: "Obscenity must be mated with banality because every kind of aesthetic enjoyment has to be entirely replaced by simple sexual stimulation. . . . Thus, in pornographic novels, action has to be limited to the copulation of clichés. Style, structure, imagery should never distract the reader from his tepid lust. The novel must consist of an alternation of sexual scenes."[11]

Film presents an even richer vein for our inquiry. We can rather easily distinguish Literature (books of high artistic intent) from merely commercial literature, but this line tends to blur in cinema. Film is primarily a mass medium, an entertainment for the multitudes. To the extent that within this context it strives also to function as a "high art," its loyalties generally are torn. Malraux said that the East has opium and the West has women; Lo Duca used the aphorism as the epigraph for his three-volume *L'Erotisme au cinéma* (Paris, 1960), adding that eroticism is so characteristic of contemporary European culture that a highly realistic, "documentary" art form such as cinema could scarcely avoid the subject. Yet if we think of some films with a pronounced sexual emphasis — Autant-Lara's *Le Diable au corps*, Malle's *Les Amants*, Vadim's *Et Dieu créa la femme*, Clouzot's *La Verité*, Fellini's *La Dolce Vita*, Antonioni's *L'Avventura* — we shall conclude that in none of these movies was the portrayal of sex an end in itself; none of these directors was out merely to titillate the public. Fellini stares at orgy scenes with the cold eye of a moralist. Antonioni demonstrates the vacuity of the hero through his nonstop pursuit of kicks; the figure is an emotional cripple in a devastated world where friendship is an impossibility. Autant-Lara and Malle extol the passions which lend richness and poetry to the whole of life. Vadim sings *das ewig Weibliche*. His direction of Bardot makes her a reborn Aphrodite with the profligate abandon and innocent charm of nature herself. Clouzot is interested in a tragic pursuit of love in a world without bearings which can offer no more than temporary unions.

Let us take another film which, when it appeared, was the center of a storm of controversy throughout the European press. Ingmar Bergman's *The Silence* was denounced by some as filth, period. Scorecards of the offensive sequences were offered: copulation, masturbation, etc. Undoubtedly some persons *were* drawn to this film from prurient motives, as some had been to *The Tropic of Cancer* or *Lolita*, but this does not alter the fact that the erotic episodes in this film are all essential to the central motif of desolation. The two heroines live in a world so alienated that all communication, even with those nearest them, is severed. Sex seems a kind of lifeline, which may allow them to make contact with others if only for a moment's gratification. When others fail them even in this, they turn in on their own bodies. Even this ruse fails, for their world is, in fact, empty. In their alienation, symbolized by the labyrinthine corridors of the hotel, the socially ostracized dwarfs, and the parallel figures of the boy and old man both hungering for affection, the women want to break out. The dying aunt writes a note to the boy which is Bergman's *porte-parole*. Whether its philosophy is convincing is beside the point. What matters for our inquiry is that this film, far from being titillating, is shatteringly true to the experience of our time and handles its medium and subject with consummate artistry.

Possibly it will be responded that Bergman deliberately sets out to shock. Perhaps so, but this would in no way diminish the complexity or seriousness of his work; nor would it prove anything lubricious in his motives. The worst we might say of *The Silence* is that Bergman did not scruple to show a woman in so intimate an act as masturbation. However, this in its context betokens an intellectual and moral courage rather than an intention to seduce and deprave. It seems fair to suggest that if *nil humanum alienum est* then no subject in the world can be off-limits to the genuine artist. Let me repeat once again: not content, but the presentation is the test of the obscenity of a work; although, of course, content and presentation will be mutually composed of erotic elements and will, undoubtedly, also generate sexual elements in our aesthetic response.

We must, in other words, distinguish between eroticism and obscenity. This is a conclusion strongly supported in a work I find excellent, Eberhard and Phyllis Kronhausen's *Pornography and the Law* (1959). I agree with their distinction that ob-

scenity can be ascribed to a work only when the reader or viewer is unremittingly
bombarded by sexual stimuli, and the work is, in fact, used only or primarily as an
aphrodisiac. In contrast, an erotic literature or art incorporates sexuality and its
ramifications in a rich life-framework.

This greater life-tissue is not all that serves to complicate and deepen the response to the sexual element and transfigure the potential obscenity into *eroticum*,
a category which is among the most fundamental of art. As already suggested, the
cultural context is inescapable. What might to a raw observer seem pornographic,
often reveals after some study its deep roots in the erotic ambience of a time and
place. Much of the ancient art of Asia astonishes and unsettles the European by
the immediacy with which it treats various sexual motifs. It may be hard not to
believe these works were not created primarily to arouse lust, and yet this suspicion
is wholly unfounded. Our ignorance of the symbolic framework is what disables
us from accurately reading the temple sculptures of Konarak, say, or the sixteenth-
century Chinese novel *The Golden Lotus*. This tale of destructiveness emanating
from sex has direct links with the philosophy of yin and yang which describes the
achievement of perfect harmony through the balancing of opposites. The sexual
yoga *(maithuna)* so commonly depicted in Far Eastern sculptures is founded, as all
scholars emphasize, on tantric buddhism. Here is symbolically embodied the unity
of spirit and nature, of so-called male and female cosmic sexuality. By no means
is orgy the point of the display.

A further factor (to which I shall return) transforming obscenity into *ars erotica*
is just the refinement of artistry. Historians often point to certain Chinese scrolls
of the nineteenth century or Japanese scrolls of earlier date as instances of pornography, due to the detailed presentations of love-making both heterosexual and
homosexual. However, so masterful is the execution, so imbued with charm or
vigor of line and with beauty of composition, that it is impossible not to be ravished
by the artistic form of these works. In these cases, the knowledge of cultural symbols is not important; the immediately apprehended iconic dimension neutralizes,
as it were, the forthrightly sexual stimuli.

I experienced a similar aesthetic response to a performance of *Mutations* by the
Netherlands Dance Theatre (at the Brooklyn Academy of Music, March 1972). The
dancers' full nudity, developed as a main theme of the piece, eventually becomes
almost imperceptible as such. This dance work is a paean to the human liberation
of spirit and body; it is also a virtuoso artistic composition. For these reasons *Mutations* scarcely offers occasion for sexual arousal. I am not even certain that in

this performance the nudity retains an *erotic* appeal. If it does then this role is im-measurably reduced from the place it holds in the Chinese or Japanese scrolls. My distinction between obscenity and eroticism is pivotal in any case, since erotic art does not eliminate the evocation of sexual imagination, but neither does it fail to situate that appeal in a context of other values.

In contrast, when one encounters a work such as *The Perfumed Garden*, which is an oft-reprinted, thinly fictionalized guide to the varieties of sexual organs and positions, this developed and ingenious erotic appeal is scarcely found. It is worth noting that sheik Abu an-Nafzawi, the author of this fifteenth-century brochure, undoubtedly had sexual instruction and excitation as his sole aim. Where we do find the extreme case of man subdued to his sexuality, depicted in what can be qualified nonetheless as erotic art, we must also find, at a minimum, some kind of manifest or latent reflections concerning this peculiar subordination.

This is a view shared by the liberal judges who have taken their stand resisting the persistent efforts to ban works which deal with themes regarded as taboo in some sectors of society. Let us consider two cases summarized in Alec Craig's book. A true breakthrough for libertarian law was the decision by Justices Woolsey and Hand to clear *Ulysses* in 1933, a decision upheld in the U.S. Court of Appeals. Points 3 and 4 of the original opinion clearly imply that the author's intent is to be deduced from the structure of the work itself. Arguing that literature is to enjoy the same immunity as works of science, Judge Hand states: "The question in each case is whether a publication *taken as a whole* has a libidinous effect. . . . In apply-ing this test, relevancy of the objectionable parts to the theme, the established reputation of the work in the estimation of approved critics, if the book is modern, and the verdict of the past, if it is ancient, are persuasive pieces of evidence, for works of art are not likely to sustain a high position with no better warrant for their existence than their obscene content."[12]

A second case led to Judge Bryan's decision which revoked the confiscation of *Lady Chatterley's Lover* by the U.S. Postmaster General. This opinion repeats the argument that the author's intent must be judged by the structural content of the work. Conceding that an author might write an obscene book despite his best in-tentions, Judge Bryan added that the evidence of literary and intellectual merit is sufficient for deciding whether a work is pornographic; and, on this showing, Law-rence's book was artistically outstanding.

The Kronhausens are also persuasive on the legal tests. They object to the use of such arbitrary labels as "lewd," "lascivious," "predominantly appealing to prurient interests," and the like, and they trace such campaigns to individuals or groups suffering from sexual frustrations. The Kronhausens' conclusion is that a penal code on obscenity derived from "community standards" is untenable, since such standards may easily be impugned. Therefore, the only objective criterion must be the structure of the controversial work, and, within this structure, the content.

These legal decisions, the opinions of juridical authorities, and the writings of such experts as the Kronhausens, which all argue that the intentions actually expressed rather than those imputed by hostile parties to a work are what must be judged—on such grounds, I gather confidence in my own argument that the artistic object and the obscene object are basically incompatible.[13] I want now to add just a few expansions, so as to be able to answer the second of my opening questions: Having concluded that art and obscenity are basically incompatible, can obscene elements still find a place in the artistic structure—and if so, then how?

How Naked Sex Achieves a Presence in Art

The time has come to stress that, in arguing the disparity between art and obscenity, I have invoked something of an ideal model. In actual practice what we often find is a jumbling of the artistic and obscene; they coexist side by side within the same overall structure, which may then be described as artistic or as obscene in varying degrees. We must, then, admit the tangibleness of the lewd in works of art. Its place depends on the kind of work and the particular proportion of artistic to "dirty" aspects and functions.

My analysis has till now emphasized that the erotic features of a work of art are so interwoven in the aesthetic values that they cannot exert a separate and relatively independent role. Yet there have been and there are today art objects which include certain obscene portions, sometimes extended into obscene sequences, which have a measure of autonomy. These passages are either so obtrusive that they burst out of the overall fabric, or they are interpolations or even imposed elements unconnected with the substance of the work. We can find a fair sprinkling of such episodes in Pietro Aretino, and some purple passages in Henry Miller more than stake their claim in this department. More restricted but equally striking fragments of this kind turn up in Rabelais, in Casanova's *Memoirs*, in Diderot's *Jacques le fataliste,* in Faulkner's *Sanctuary,* and in *Lolita.* They are notably absent, on the other hand, from Laclos' *Liaisons dangereuses,* as we can see by considering Letters 79 and 85, which detail the Chevalier Prévan's adventures, and in which the prevailing tone is one of intellectual naughtiness and of delight in the art of cynical seduction. The latter moods have nourished a major strain in French literature, and one which should not be confused with pornography, even though the tone evokes a sexual atmosphere.

In all the works just cited, the obscene portions do connect with the artistic design. The same cannot be said of Sjöman's film *491*, for example. Here there are two scenes (homosexual intercourse and bestialism) that cannot be justified by reference to the needs of plot or drama. Though set in a tale of juvenile delinquency and reeducation, the episodes are sure (again, due to their mode of presentation rather than their substance) to stimulate a response that is more sexual than aesthetic. Even more can this be said of the same director's *I Am Curious (Yellow)* for the directly obscene passages are here more extensive. The fellatio and cunnilingus exchanges between Lena and Borjé, or the sequence in which the couple copulate in a tree crotch, seem wholly centered on the sexual motifs, although elsewhere in the film the nudity and sexual games do appear as an organic part of their mutual infatuation.

Two recent American movies produced by Andy Warhol and directed by Paul Morrissey, *Flesh* and *Trash*, are of a similar character. They project the current climate of sexual anarchism against its social background; they bring in homosexuality, which has been one of the primary issues in the quest for liberation, and they focus on the naked body in numerous intimate positions and situations. All of this is fine from the aesthetic viewpoint. What is dubious are the many segments of both films which exhibit the penis as a patently self-contained effect. These close-ups do not arouse sexual excitement, but are, rather, somewhat repugnant and in the end boring. The crux of the matter, nonetheless, is that they concentrate the viewer's attention solely on the sexual exhibition. I do not question, however, that Morrissey's films do fall on the side of cinema art; they need only be compared with such hard-core products as *The Stewardesses*, *Mona*, or *Hollywood Blue* to see where episodic obscenity and the unrelieved article differ.

I now want to return to Félicien Rops. His work seems often to lie on the very midpoint of the fragile line between art which contains elements of pornography and pornography which is lacking in art. Not all Rops' works qualify but his most popular output achieves this consummate balance. It seems a little fulsome to compare his gifts with the Pyramid of Cheops, as Baudelaire did in a sonnet of 1865, and Rops himself surely exaggerated when he claimed the discovery of "une formule nouvelle." Yet the artistic merit of his drawings and etchings is indisputable. We cannot deny him, either, a philosophy of life, idiosyncratic though it was; his mentors were Baudelaire, Poe, and Huysmans, and he shared their dandyism and misogyny, their contempt for the bourgeoisie and their hatred of the mob. Rops's sexual obsessions were chiefly Satanic—as, for example, in his *Pornocracie* (symbol of the blind lusts which drive men to destruction) or *Le vol et la prostitution dominent le monde* or the visions of men and women ravaged by syphilis and drink.[14]

All this notwithstanding, the bulk of Rops's output is plainly lewd. Women are seen from the rear, their legs apart and bent forwards; invariably they sport Folies-Bergère-type black stockings and gloves which emphasize the stark nudity of their breasts, thighs, and bellies; usually there are men shown present at these repellently gross displays of "pulchritude," and the women themselves are made to narcissistically fondle or eye their sexual parts. The aesthetic response is not encouraged, while a sexual one is, in *Le miroir de la coquetterie, Seule, le Maillot, Nubilité, Impudeur, Suffisance*—to sample at random a few of Rops's works.

Granted, these water colors, prints, and drawings do partake of the savour of the entire period: of Toulouse-Lautrec, Strindberg, or Stanislaw Przybyszewski. Women were indeed treated as the envoys of the devil and—since *am Anfang war des Geschlecht*—eroticism was both demonized and dwelt upon in a crude naturalistic mode. Thus, it might be said that obscenity fitted in with the artistic vision of the time, but even so no one portrayed it so broadly, aggressively, and abundantly as Rops. Yet the pictures I have cited seem less artistic than Rops's other works. The sexual motifs appear overemphasized; the means of expression are subordinated to the exposition of sexuality. Again the mode of presentation is more relevant than the subject matter. Huysmans was right when he said Rops elevated a fascination with the demi-monde of whores into the apocalypse of prostitution. This aspect helps raise much of his work into the category of genuine art, but the examples cited transform the apocalypse into the dalliance of prostitution. Thus, the approach to the selfsame sexual subject matter is decisive even in a single artist's oeuvre.

The whore has been a theme of the drama and literature from the start of the nineteenth century and remains prominent as the twenty-first century approaches. She looms attractively and frighteningly among the dispossessed and the rebels of capitalist society. From Fleur de Marie in Sue's *Mystères de Paris* to Shen Te in Brecht's *The Good Woman of Setzuan* to the whores in such films as *Nights of Cabiria, Never on Sunday,* or *Klute,* the prostitute has been shown as among a select company of the pure in heart. Again, it is the artist's interpretation of the theme which decides, not the theme as such.

The balance between obscene and aesthetic values breaks down when the latter are unremarkable or meager. In such cases even themes of no compelling power will take control and exert an atmosphere more sexual than artistic. A film like *Gilda* is an example. Indeed, the film industry has made a specialty of this kind of pap since it does have a built-in appeal for the less discriminating portion of the public. A slick mock-up of art offers a transparent window through which the calculated snatches of sex are shown. It was in such films that Marilyn Monroe and Brigitte Bardot launched their careers and were duly snubbed by exacting cinema critics. Given more substantial filmscripts, these actresses were able to reveal their latent dramatic talents; others, however, have never been given the chance to become more than "sex symbols."[15] Their counterparts in painting and sculpture are such works as the Venus Callipygos (Museo Nationale, Naples), the Renaissance woodcut *Eroticum* by Peter Flötner (Friedrich-Museum, Berlin), or the anonymous Dutch work *Monk and Nun* (c. 1600, Haarlem Museum) in which the monk lustfully hovers over a nun while fondling her bared breast.

Another category of works that feigns artistry is the one that blends sex with sadism. These works elicit a response to sexual violence by any available means, no matter how crude. The grouping is obviously the product of a neurosis- and perversion-ridden civilization.

Also weak on art and direct in solicitation is the ubiquitous use of women's bodies and female charm to promote and advertise in every medium, and I should also include here the pseudoartistic striptease, such as Paris and London's Soho district have long purveyed. The best of these shows — interspersed with witty banter, graced with attractive performers and apt music and lighting — have certain attributes of art, but chiefly the goal is to put the audience into a sexual trance, and even the more pretentious elements will be used in such a way as to aid the sexual effect. We find sexual dances among the primitive peoples of Brazil, Africa, and India which employ the same elements as the striptease of Europe. Yet here, though the act of sex is mimed, it is done either as a ritual in which the entire tribe participates and in which the erotic and religious elements are merged into an inseparable whole, or as a rudimentary mode of theater in which socially important phenomena are enacted. The striptease reduces the mime to the aphrodisiacal function. With cold calculation it is either a preparation or a surrogate for *ars amatoria*.

Certainly, sex with a mere nod to artistic effect goes far back. I mentioned the statues of Pompeii, with their erections and displays of sexual technique. In the first volume of Eduard Fuchs's book, many works are reproduced which have as their main goal the parasexual stimulation of the viewer. In the Middle Ages this trait even stands out from the architecture as an obscene joke. Textbook examples of sex-with-airs are provided by some of Hans Beham's engravings in the Renaissance, and especially by the numerous rococo etchings in the salacious *style galant*. Some English caricatures of the late eighteenth century qualify too. Fuchs reproduces a lampoon of flagellations which appeals to the most coarse associations: a man with trousers lowered straddles a woman while another woman with breasts bared flogs him; the whole scene is lit by a phallus-shaped candle.

I think I have sufficiently answered my second question. The obscene definitely finds a place in art objects, although variously, in dependency on the vividness and assertiveness of the lewd passages and the degree of pallidness of the artistic values. We can therefore scale articles of culture along a continuum: at one end are those where the artistic tissue virtually absorbs the obscene without a residue, while at the other end are those where pornography nods little or not at all to art. I discern four basic creative methods by which even a potent obscene aspect may be, so to speak, neutralized. These are:

1. The sexual elements can be handled *metaphysically*. Sex is here regarded as the Absolute in life, or it is tied in with some Absolute. We see this in D. H. Lawrence and, in Polish literature, in Stanislaw Przybyszewski and S. I. Witkiewicz.

2. The sexual can be *poeticized*, invested with a suffused but charged emotion. The scenes of love-making in *Les Amants* by Malle or *La Verité* by Clouzot are of this kind.

3. The sexual can be *intellectualized*. This occurs chiefly where characters are made to describe and reflect upon their own behavior; Aldous Huxley was a master of this approach.

4. The most frequent method is *aestheticization*. Here, the valuational qualities associated with the sexual, such as sound, shape, movement, or color, have their sexual connotations artistically extended.

Now, there remain other ways than these to offset the plain lewdness of sexuality, but this listing will serve to demonstrate my view of the disparity between the artistic and the obscene. Yet I must emphasize again that in the pornographically weighted end of the spectrum, certain sequences may be experienced as obscene even though that was never the artist's intention. This effect is due to an imbalance in the artistic structure which permits the aesthetic values to be overwhelmed, either by vigorous sexual matter or by an inadequacy of the aesthetic aspect which lets even weak sexual material predominate.

I have not so far mentioned any nonrepresentational artists or groups. In architecture and music, the evidence for an obscenity measurement is scant; which is not to say, of course, that eroticism may not be strongly suggested by, for example, one of Scriabin's ecstatic compositions or an erect victory monument. The applied arts (Greek vases, for instance) carry mimetic features, which in turn may have sexual elements; a free-standing representational sculpture (the thirty phalluses and twenty vaginas of Dinapur) might be regarded as a kind of architectural complex; music tied in with a libretto (Shostakovich's *Lady Macbeth of the Mzensk District*) or dance (Strauss's *Salome*) may well generate more literal associations. Nonetheless, these are all special and qualified cases. If primitive architecture and sculpture tend to be interpreted by some as libidinal,[16] it is often overlooked that architecture has depended on the given need and the available materials and technology, while sculpture had a magical-religious character.

Music is a nonobjective art which is so multivalent that its mere texture—separate from literalizations—is incapable of being pinned down as being sexual. However, when Luigi Nono's *Red Coat* was choreographed for a Warsaw performance in October 1962, the passages played with the scenes of Don Perlimplino's impotence and Belisa's wedding night acquired sexual impact—a classic instance of episodic obscenity. Conversely, the sexual thrust in Stravinsky's *Rite of Spring* is so subsumed in the musical conception that the artistic values control the whole.

Thus, I will stand by my contention that the representational arts, with their referents in reality (objects and situations), are the most open to the interpolation of obscene parts and passages.[17] However, let me also repeat that where we are not familiar with the historical background of a work (as in the case of a work with magical-religious symbolism), we often too hastily assert the presence of obscenity where that intention did not, in fact, motivate the creator and where its traces are not finally verifiable in the art object. I would say that this is the case with uninformed opinion concerning the Pompeii frescos.[18] In contrast, where we lack the connotational "key," we may overlook the blatant presence, if camouflaged and symbolic, of obscene elements even in more nonrepresentational forms. I cannot, however, carry this line of thought too far here, as it would involve me in the general problems of the interpretation of content and meaning.

Encourage Eroticism, For It Is Disalienating

The conclusions to which my theoretical approach has led me might be questioned on two counts.

The reader will be aware that many persons concerned with obscenity do not and will not accept the key distinction which I draw between eroticism and obscenity. For them, the mere presence of a sexual element is tantamount to pornography. These writers speak of "pornographic art," whereas my premises allow me to speak only of a certain art of pornography—and note that there is a paradox in this phrase since the person who crafts pornography knows that his market demands that the presentation of the sex episodes be artless, that is, that the medium be transparent. The more successful the rendering of the pornographic material, the greater is the absence of art in any strict sense of the term. These potential objectors, on the contrary, assume a category of obscene art just as there is a category of religious or of poetic art.

Another possible objection would reject my basic conception of art. Many writers consider art to be a system of signs expressive of individual or group behavior and seeking to evoke similar behavioral responses in the audience. The specificity of art's means is thus treated as a secondary matter, a presumably flexible feature which alters in light of what A or B (individuals or groups) think art is. This approach enfeebles or eliminates the relatively autonomous status of art, although it does comprehend both art and pronography as aspects (sometimes partially interwoven) of a given system of signs in a given sociocultural context. Of course, these two objections may be united to impugn in one package my conceptions of both art and pornography.

Obviously, it is unlikely that I will convince my opponents, unless I can first persuade them of my fundamental tenets and the evidence supporting them; yet even if I should gain consent for my notion of the relationship between art and obscenity, there will remain another problem. It could justifiably be asked whether I was not motivated to demarcate pornography from art because I find the former pernicious. When I wrote the first version of this essay in 1962, I was convinced that all pornography should be eradicated by all the means available. In the ensuing years I have changed my mind, in part because of the highly persuasive Kronhausen book, which was issued in 1964. The argument of Phyllis and Eberhard Kronhausen is that even hard-core pornography may sometimes be the agent of purgative cathexy. This finding is reinforced by the extensive studies of the above-cited *Report of the American Commission on Obscenity and Pornography*. So far there is no irrefragable proof that pornography induces criminal behavior, initiates delinquency, encourages deviance, etc. Doubt has even been cast on the farflung belief that pornography undermines moral standards and produces callous attitudes towards the opposite sex.

If expert research and analysis thus eroded my conviction of the obnoxiousness of obscenity, my change of mind was speeded by the Danish experiment which, as is widely known, so satiated the public with a flood of lewd articles that their attraction was quickly lost for most people. Accepting, then, that pornography need not be pernicious always, for everyone, everywhere, and accepting also the estimate of the American commission that some control on availability with respect to juveniles is inevitable, I want now to repeat what I said in 1962: There should be no censorship exercised towards a genuine erotic art for it is (in one aspect) a principal means to win people away from a hard-core or a soft-core pornography. The more subtle the censorship and the more understanding the law in this matter, the greater will be the chance of encouraging and facilitating an artistically admirable body of work dealing with sexual themes.

The true problem lies in the pornographic tyranny, hard or soft, within the mass media. I continue to believe that a pornography that goes hand in glove with a cult of brutality and violence, and a pornographic commercialism that exploits the most base needs of man, can be dangerous. That is to say, it impoverishes the human being, generating a repetitious compulsion similar to drugs or gambling, and distracting him from more beneficial entertainment and more humanized values.[19] For this reason I believe we are justified in confronting pornography with all possible weapons and not just with an erotic art alternative. I do not, however, believe that the "possible" weapons should include legislation or legal decisions banning pornography outright. The urgent, underlying task is not to come up with the correct way of writing a law; that will not eliminate the problem. What is wanted is the means to alter existing societies so as to provide free and healthy opportunities for all kinds of sexual enjoyment.

Whether pornography will prove to be as obdurate and ineradicable as man's own existence is a matter I would not presume to answer. What can be debated is the fantastic boom in pornography, which seems to be a manifestation of an ill-functioning civilization. The anthropological-philosophical and sociological points of view can be of the greatest relevance to the search for an explanation of why contemporary culture verges on pathology — that is, why it calls forth pornography, which, instead of healing the frustrations of social life, exacerbates the horrible sexual taboos and entrenches the immaturity of so many persons.

The human body is our earliest and basic experience. We might well follow here the phenomenological analysis given by Jean-Paul Sartre in his *Being and Nothingness* (Part III), without adopting all of his existential premises. Sartre holds that three dimensions of our attitude towards the body have to be distinguished. First and primordial, the body is simply the medium through and in which we enforce our being and by which we respond through pain, pleasure, and other affects. Second, we are aware of the body as an object; a reflexive intentionality is focused on employing it in all feasible ways and also on being recognized in this dimension by other human agents. Third, the body is seen by *l'autrui*; it is treated as an object by another's intention to grasp us only in the dimension of physical entity. Sartre explains the phenomenon of prudery in relation to this third dimension.

To this point I am assisted by Sartre with much benefit for my topic. Pornography is only to be elucidated, however, by combining the existentialist with the socio-historical interpretation. The usefulness of *Being and Nothingness*, which sees the body as a contingent, potentially reified being *(facticité)*, must be augmented and superseded for, while alienation may be founded in man's ontological status, it is above all culturally engendered, determined, and finally limited. I earlier noted that the nature/culture conflict is essential to our understanding of the continuous tussle between pornographic impulses and tendencies and the moral code of a time. Pornography is not so much the product of a man's practice of sex as it is of his thinking about sex; and I do not think it is a difficult task to respond as to why pornography has remained fascinating and exciting since the dawn of human civilization. What is truly hard—and would require a chapter in itself—is an elucidation of why pornography has grown problematic (more or less the Heidegger issue of *Fragwürdigkeit*) in man's mind at this time.

In this matter, I can here only delineate a possible line of inquiry. First of all, once the fixed order of values ("the great chain of being") established by a scripture or gospel of one kind or another had been undermined, there was no holding back the sexual question from emerging.

Second, the progressive autonomization of the individual (a concomitant of the democratizing processes) had to raise the question of priorities: Shall the gratification of private needs be deferred wholly and indefinitely in the face of legal (moral) fiats? Or shall the latter be subordinated to the former? In our tradition, Sade was the first to assert this question in an aggressive fashion and to make of sexual blasphemy a new cult.

Third, this emerging individual, proud of his expanded and hallowed rights, was, nonetheless, increasingly oppressed by the alienational situation which had grown since the end of the eighteenth century. One way for "the discontents of civilization" to make their protest was through a revitalization of sexual conduct. The Freudian and the post-Freudian revolution will bear witness to the theoretical implications of this tendency. In the writings of Wilhelm Reich and Herbert Marcuse with regard to the possibility of liberation through the release of libidinal energy directed towards the achievement of harmonious interaction with others, lies the most conspicuous proof of a nascent sexual eschatology.

The spectacular outburst of pornography is a phenomenon of the post-World War II era. No one can ignore the fact that it has accompanied an era of harrowing civilizational transition (towards the second industrial revolution), of continual anxiety over the very survival of humanity, of persistent rebellion against all forms of empire owing to the bureaucratic, anonymous, and antihuman character of their administration. The battle for an open, multifarious pornography is, accordingly, one of the pointed protests against an overpowering and increasingly unbearable alienation. It is, however, an abortive challenge, which turns the rebellion into another servitude. Some radicals will object at this point, arguing that the defense of an unrestricted pornography parallels the fight for the rights of women and homosexuals, which is in turn part of the larger struggle of the political left. To this I must reply that to frame the struggle in these terms is a mystification. It is sheer self-deception to believe (as many do) that one of the routes to achieving real freedom is the pornographic highway. For not the first nor the last time, the alienational processes have been countered with an alternative mode of alienation. The pro-obscenity radicals "out-Herod Herod" when they hold that *Playboy* magazine and its like help to spread the evangel of a liberated mankind. Let me take up two examples to clarify the matter: striptease and nudism.

The striptease and topless fad, like all kinds of voyeur spectacle, derive from the entrenched antinomy of culture and nature. Leszek Kolakowski has dealt with this tension in an exhaustive way.[20] However, it should be added that with striptease, as with all pornography, the chief oppositions occur *within* culture itself. Striptease debases intimacy, it makes sex dirty by reifying it utterly. Second, striptease is an excrescence of male domination; it flaunts the power of men to treat women as commodities to be bought and sold upon prior inspection. Third, striptease is an ersatz myth, fulfilling the lowest needs by reversing them to the status of the highest attainable value. It has been observed by Roland Barthes that the striptease *de-sexualizes* women.[21] Possibly this is true for the stratum of curious intellectuals whose sophistication quickly turns the show into a boring ordeal. I surely belong in this category; and yet during the course of numerous stripteases I have noticed how many men stare fixedly at the performing women; they relish the performances — it is standard business practice — so as to select a stripteaser for fornication after-wards. Thus, the striptease manifestly proves that open pornography only deepens and confirms the state of alienation; it reasserts the frustrations and neuroses, it divides man into a chaste soul and a dirty body, and makes of the latter a thing, a sheer commodity.

Nudism on the other hand seems to offer some relief from alienation. Nudism is derived from a desperate effort to return to nature, to shed the taboos of civiliza-tion, to divest oneself of the shame of being made an object in another's eyes. The last of these points is especially significant, for the users of pornography believe mistakenly that they get rid of sexual shame when they turn themselves and their models into objects in a paid charade. This mystification proves how greatly we all are enslaved and how easily we are entrapped into glorifying open pornography as a suitable liberating instrument. In any case, authentic nudists understand (not without a certain dramatic *hubris*) that they cease to be objectified bodies looked at as though before an auction. Nudity in time (how long depends on both the individual and the environment) becomes as natural as it once was at the dawning of civilization. However, even nudism where it has at the last superseded the dra-matic *hubris*, culminates in what seems no more than a great illusion, if we reflect on its possibilities as an implement for restoring a sexual existence which has gone out of joint. Why? First, the nudist "colonies" are small and dispersed enclaves. Second, considerations of climate, ugly bodies, and so on, would inhibit any general development of nudism. Third, it is evident that nudist beaches are visited by many persons who are looking for something other than a Rousseauian, animalized cul-ture wherein one tries to recoup the primal dimension of living in and through one's body in Sartre's sense.

Let me add that such an "animalized" state of mind seems to be an impossibil-ity. Man's sexuality is distinguished by the presence of the two other dimensions pointed out by Sartre. In other words, the reflexive awareness of employing our bodies and the sense of being looked at are ineradicable. The basic goal to be aimed for, then, is to disalienate the sexual culture without reducing it to the level of nature, which just introduces another version of alienated sexuality. I am leaving aside the question of whether nudism manages to avoid the animalization of sexual *attitude*. What matters for my present purpose is the utopian projection of the nudist program, even should nudism be able to intensify the consciousness of being free in glancing at an alien body and in being glanced at.

Due to such considerations, I have urged that pornography must be resisted. It must be resisted for the very reasons espoused by those radicals who argue that the gates must be opened to pornography. Nor am I spinning a sophistry. We cannot cure our ill-functioning culture by seeking symptomatic relief while not going after the causes. The disalienation of the existing societies — the complete, harmonious fulfillment of all the riches of the various natural needs of the human species (the sexual impulses included) — is not a goal to be reached through the gates of pornography.

Let me again stress that I am *not* in favor of a conclusive ban on obscene materials. If there is worth in what I earlier argued, then sanctions against pornography can only bring unintended consequences. Those punished for spreading *obscoena* will be persons who have but haplessly preserved the corruption of the predominant culture.[22] The only effective way to eradicate or minimalize the range and influence of pornography is to alter the underlying social systems, their basic fabric, their value hierarchies.

Those who would abolish obscenity should, moreover, make it part of their strategy to protect all genuine erotic art. If art can have a cathartic (therapeutic) function then it lies in this direction. Moreover, there should be an extension of the idea of the erotic domain. At one time notable for scandalous (and today innocent) works like Bellocq's photographs of New Orleans whores, today it should admit, for example, Jack Smith's film *Flaming Creatures* or Warhol's and Morrissey's *Trash* and *Flesh*. The latter works are controversial, but they certainly do not exhibit sex for its own sake. They have referents in actual life problems, in the neurotic complexes and the desires of young people who exist on the margin of society and in contempt of its laws, beliefs, and habits. Thus, even though Morrissey's frames emphasize male and female nudity, and especially the genital presence, the films basically promote a most serious attitude towards the possible disalienation of society. Likewise — although I cannot share his eschatological program — I must agree with Marcuse when he says that Marx's idea of *homo aestheticus* (or, to put it more adequately, the communist person) includes also the anticipation of liberating and fully humanizing the sexual drives.

Notes

1. The view presented here seems consistent with the methodological precepts of Karl Marx, and also his remarks on aesthetic axiology (few and unsystematized though these are). This line of argument has rarely been advanced within the marxist tradition since the ideas of Plekhanov dominated the field; although recently, similar interpretations of artistic values have been presented by other marxists; see G. Lukács, *Die Eigenart des Aesthetischen* (Neuweid, 1963), L. Goldmann, *Recherches dialectiques* (Paris, 1959) and E. Fischer, *Von der Notwendigkeit der Kunst* (Dresden, 1959).

2. See A. Craig's instructive book, *The Banned Books of England and Other Countries* (London, 1962).

3. My position differs from the well-known one set forth by D. H. Lawrence in "Pornography and Obscenity" (in Lawrence, *Sex, Literature and Censorship*, edited by H. T. Moore [New York, 1968], pp. 64–81). He treated pornography as the mob's vulgar degradation of sex, the way the masses insult what they do not comprehend. I would hesitate to declare that all "obscenity" vilifies and caricatures sex, in part because I do not share Lawrence's intense sexual mysticism, which he advanced with greater explicitness and fervor in "A propos of *Lady Chatterley's Lover*" (1929). Here, Lawrence describes the sexual (blood) nexus as being threefold: involving the love partner, the species as a whole, and the vital universe. A kindred erotic religion has been advocated by Timothy Leary, in particular in a *Playboy* interview of 1966, reprinted in his *Politics of Ecstasy* (New York, 1968). Yet the approaches of Lawrence and Leary are most helpful for discriminating the sexual (erotic) and the obscene, a fruitful distinction in the study

of the relationship between art and obscenity.

4. See T. Hakenssen, "Sex in Primitive Art and Dance," and A. Ellis, "Art and Sex," in *The Encyclopedia of Sexual Behaviour* (New York, 1961), pp. 154–179.

5. See Freud's essays "The Poet and Daydreaming" (1908) and "The Uncanny" (1919), in B. Nelson, ed., *On Creativity and the Unconscious* (New York, 1958), pp. 53–54, 155–161. In texts on Leonardo da Vinci and on wit, his only other writings concerned with aesthetics, Freud developed this view and used it to show that psychoanalytic methods of study stop on the threshold of art. Of the followers of Freud that I have read, the subject is best and most profoundly analyzed by Ernst Kris. Following Freud closely, I feel, Kris suggests that dreams actually employ some formal devices not unlike art to "mask" the dream material. See E. Kris, *Psychoanalytic Explorations in Art* (London, 1953), pp. 13–63.

6. See V. George, *Corps et visages feminins* (Paris, 1955).

7. H. Miller, *Tropic of Cancer* (New York, 1961), p. 90.

8. Ibid., p. 164.

9. Ibid., pp. 229–233. Compare also his *The World of Sex* (New York, 1965), esp. pp. 16–27. I omit here a question taken up by Kate Millett in her *Sexual Politics* (New York, 1969, Part III) — Miller's attitude towards women. I agree with Millett's persuasive analysis, which stresses the adolescent narcissism and the smoking-car fantasies in most of Miller's work. However, she also helps confirm the aspect of Miller most pertinent to this analysis, namely, his cathartic *self-revelations*, his truthfulness and artistic greatness in laying bare the sexual neuroses of our time and in unmasking their deeper sources in the pathology of the civilization. The same claim might be made for D. H. Lawrence, whose sexual rebellion should be judged against a background of a still Victorian England. Incidentally, I should like to emphasize the paradox that all these literary rebels on whom the feminist Millett passes a severe verdict were preparing the ground for today's women's liberation movement. The sexual liberties they helped to gain were among the factors which enabled the shaping of the question of sexual equality.

10. V. Nabokov, *Lolita* (New York, 1959), p. 286.

11. Ibid., p. 284.

12. Craig, *Banned Books*, pp. 145–146; my italics.

13. Craig, in *Banned Books*, p. 214, rejects, as I do, the view that authentic literature can be pornographic. The position is also set forth in D. Loth, *The Erotic in Literature* (London, 1962). However, neither writer offers a theoretical underpinning to support this belief. Where they argue (quite reasonably) that the author's intent is insufficient grounds for judging whether a book is obscene, they ignore (1) that the intention can often be surmised from the structure of the work; and (2) that the intention may be articulated outside of the work per se (as in the case of Thomas Mann's commentary on his novel *Doctor Faustus*) and this at least provides important interpretive material. It will be seen that my position here departs from "The Intentional Fallacy," the well-known essay by M. C. Beardsley and W. K. Wimsatt, Jr. (Cf. Wimsatt, *The Verbal Icon* [New York, 1958], pp. 3–18.)

14. These are the primary grounds on which all the major writers who treat Rops have defended him against charges of decadence

and pornography. See E. Ramiro, *Félicien Rops* (Paris, 1905); C. Lemonnier, *Félicien Rops, l'homme et l'artiste* (Paris, 1908); G. Kahn, *F. Rops, in L'Art et le beau*, numéro special (*Librairie artistique et littéraire*, 1965), pp. 5–59; R. Klein, *F. Rops*, ibid., vol. III, numéro special, pp. 5–63. Each of the authors does concede that the obscene is the dominant trait of his work.

15. See A. Kyrou, *Amour—erotisme et cinéma* (Paris, 1957). Kyrou holds that since World War II cinema has become dominated by the ideal of a woman impersonally and mechanically providing sex, just as love has come to be handled in the same terms as other consumer products. This sharply critical observation also comes through in the film by Carlo Lizzani, *La Vita agra* (1964).

16. See the Freudian interpretation in E. von Sydow, *Primitive Kunst und Psychoanalyse* (Leipzig-Wein-Zürich, 1927).

17. Which of the representational arts— if it introduces obscene portions—is most open to the charge of being pornography plain and simple? I suspect the parasexual responses are most likely to be stirred by theater, mime, and dance, owing to the immediate physical presence of performers. The matter is complicated because in films and literature the absence of physical contact makes identification with a character or situation easier.

18. See the analysis of the Dionysian friezes in the Villa dei Mysteri in A. Maiuri, *Pompei* (Rome, 1938, 1952) and K. Schefold, *Pompejanische Malerei* (Bâle, 1952).

19. The dialectically ambivalent character of the process of reception is emphasized in the "identification/projection" formula presented by Edgar Morin in *L'Esprit du temps* (Paris, 1962). Morin concentrates on the cinema as a case of mass media and on

violence as a chief attraction. The audience
(primarily adolescents — but many adults
too) rids itself of accumulated repressed
materials, at the same time identifying with
the heroes in suggested situations. The analysis applies equally to the reception of
verbally or iconically communicated pornography. If sexual fare were regularly
sought out for amusement, it is likely that
obscene material would predominate. Would
not the attitude-reinforcement stemming
from the identification/projection of the
fantasy indulgence overbalance any purgative benefit?

20. See L. Kolakowski, "Epistemology of the
Striptease," *Tri-Quarterly*, Fall 1971; in Polish in *Twórczość*, April 1966.

21. See R. Barthes, *Mythologies* (Paris,
1957), pp. 165–168.

22. See J. Frank, "Obscenity and the Law,"
in M. Levich, ed., *Aesthetics and the Philosophy of Criticism* (New York, 1963), pp.
418–440.

Index